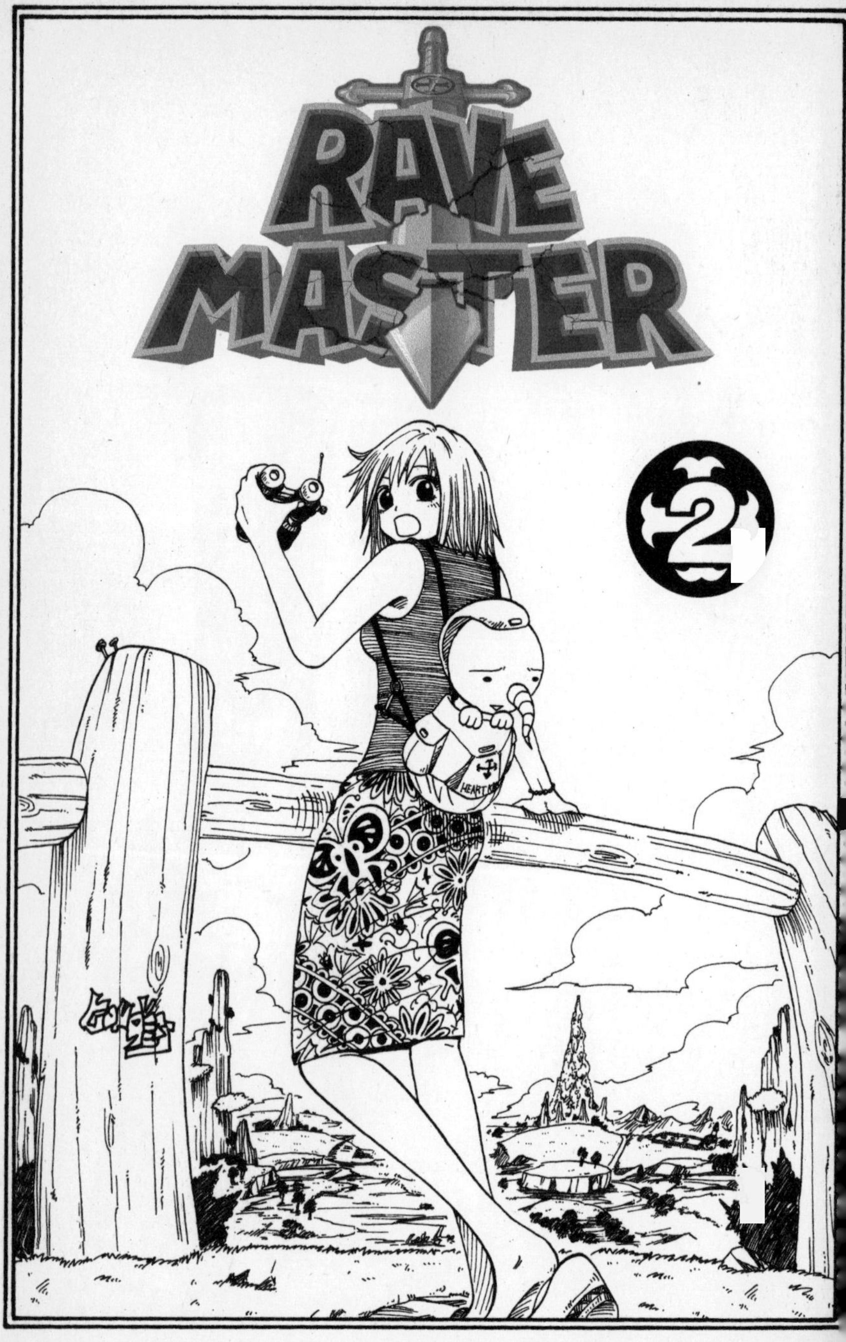
RAVE
MASTER
2

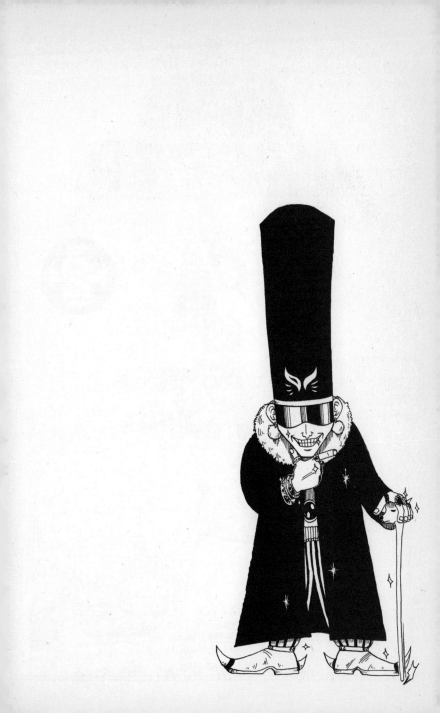

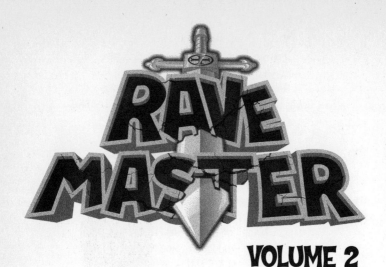

VOLUME 2

Story and Art by
HIRO MASHIMA

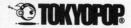

Los Angeles · Tokyo · London · Hamburg

Translator - Amy Forsyth
English Adaption - James Lucas Jones
Copy Editors - Carol Fox, Jennifer Wagner
Retouch and Lettering - Krystal Dawson
Cover Colors - Pauline Sim & Raymond Makowski
Cover Layout - Raymond Makowski

Senior Editor - Jake Forbes
Digital Imaging Manager - Chris Buford
Pre-Press Manager - Antonio DePietro
Production Managers - Jennifer Miller, Mutsumi Miyazaki
Art Director - Matt Alford
Managing Editor - Jill Freshney
VP of Production - Ron Klamert
President & C.O.O. - John Parker
Publisher & C.E.O. - Stuart Levy

E-mail: info@TOKYOPOP.com
Come visit us online at www.TOKYOPOP.com

A ☺TOKYOPOP Manga

TOKYOPOP Inc.
5900 Wilshire Blvd. Suite 2000
Los Angeles, CA 90036

ISBN: 1-59182-065-0

First TOKYOPOP® printing: April 2003

13 12 11 10 9 8 7 6 5 4

Printed in the USA

T 252254

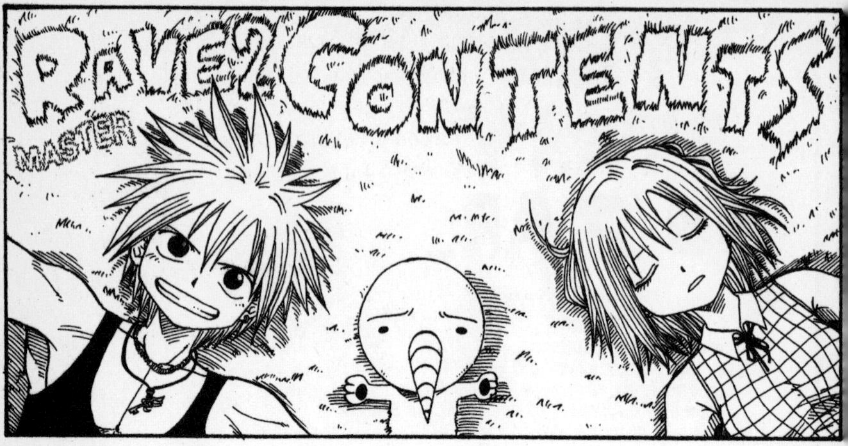
RAVE 2 CONTENTS
MASTER

THE STORY SO FAR...

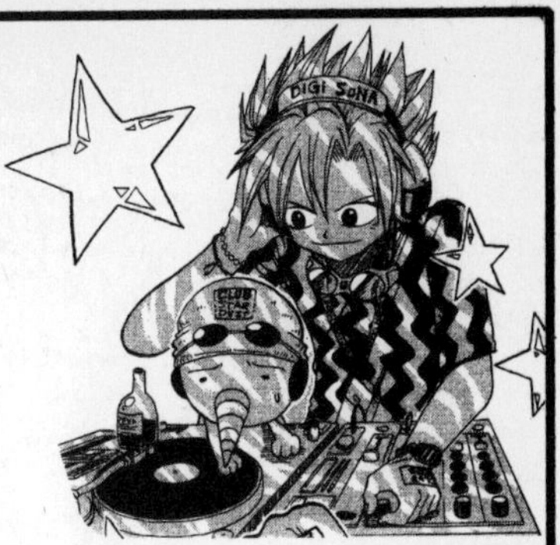
DIGI SONA

*YO, PLUE, LET'S **KICK IT!***
RAVE RAVE MASTER, RAVE RAVE MASTER...

ALL RIGHT, ***STOP!*** I'LL RECAP, SO ***LISTEN.***
HARU'S BACK WITH A BRAND NEW MISSION.
HE USED TO RELAX BOTH DAILY AND NIGHTLY ,
BUT NOW HE'S ON A QUEST TO SET THE WORLD RIGHTLY.
WILL HE FIND THE WAY? ***YO*** -- I HOPE SO.
HE'S JUST A KID -- BUT HE'LL GROW.
HIS HOME, GARAGE ISLAND, WAS ***ROCKED*** BY SOME VANDALS--
THOSE DEMON CARD ***PUNKS*** BURNED IT DOWN LIKE A CANDLE.

CHANCE BROUGHT PLUE TO THAT LAND--
A CONE-NOSED DOG THAT LENDS A HELPING HAND.
HARU FISHED HIM OUT OF THE SEA LIKE A FLOUNDER.
HE USED TO FOLLOW SHIBA, A CRAZY OLD BOUNDER.
SHIBA USED TO BE THE ***RAVE MASTER***.
BUT NOW HE CAN'T USE RAVE TO STOP THE DISASTER.
THERE'S A NEW HEIR TO RAVE WHO WILL SOLVE IT!
BREAK DOWN, HARU GLORY, WHILE THIS DJ REVOLVES IT.

RAVE RAVE MASTER, RAVE RAVE MASTER
RAVE RAVE MASTER, RAVE RAVE MASTER

BUT JUST WHEN HIS QUEST GETS ***JUMPIN'***,
THIS BADDIE NAMED SHUDA COMES ***THUMPIN'***!
ARMED WITH DARK BRING, THIS MAGICAL STONE,
HE COOKS OUR BOY HARU DOWN TO THE BONE.
BUT HARU HAS SKILZ THAT START A COMMOTION.
HIS TEN POWERS SWORD TURNS INTO ***EXPLOSION***.
WITH HIS NEW POWERS HE STOPPED THE DOPE FIENDS
BUT NOW HIS SWORD'S JACKED (IF YOU KNOW WHAT I MEAN)
TO GET THE THING ***FIXED*** HARU LEAVES FOR HIP HOP TOWN.
SO READ WHAT HE FINDS AS THIS RECORD GOES ROUND.

RAVE RAVE MASTER, RAVE RAVE MASTER
RAVE RAVE MASTER, RAVE RAVE MASTER

YO MAN, LET'S GET OUT OF HERE.

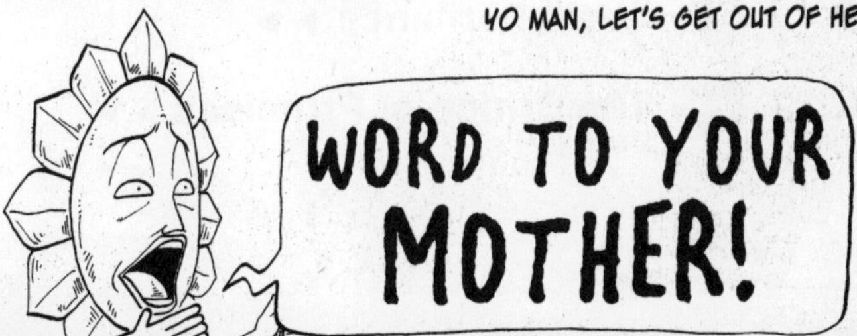
WORD TO YOUR MOTHER!

RAVE MASTER

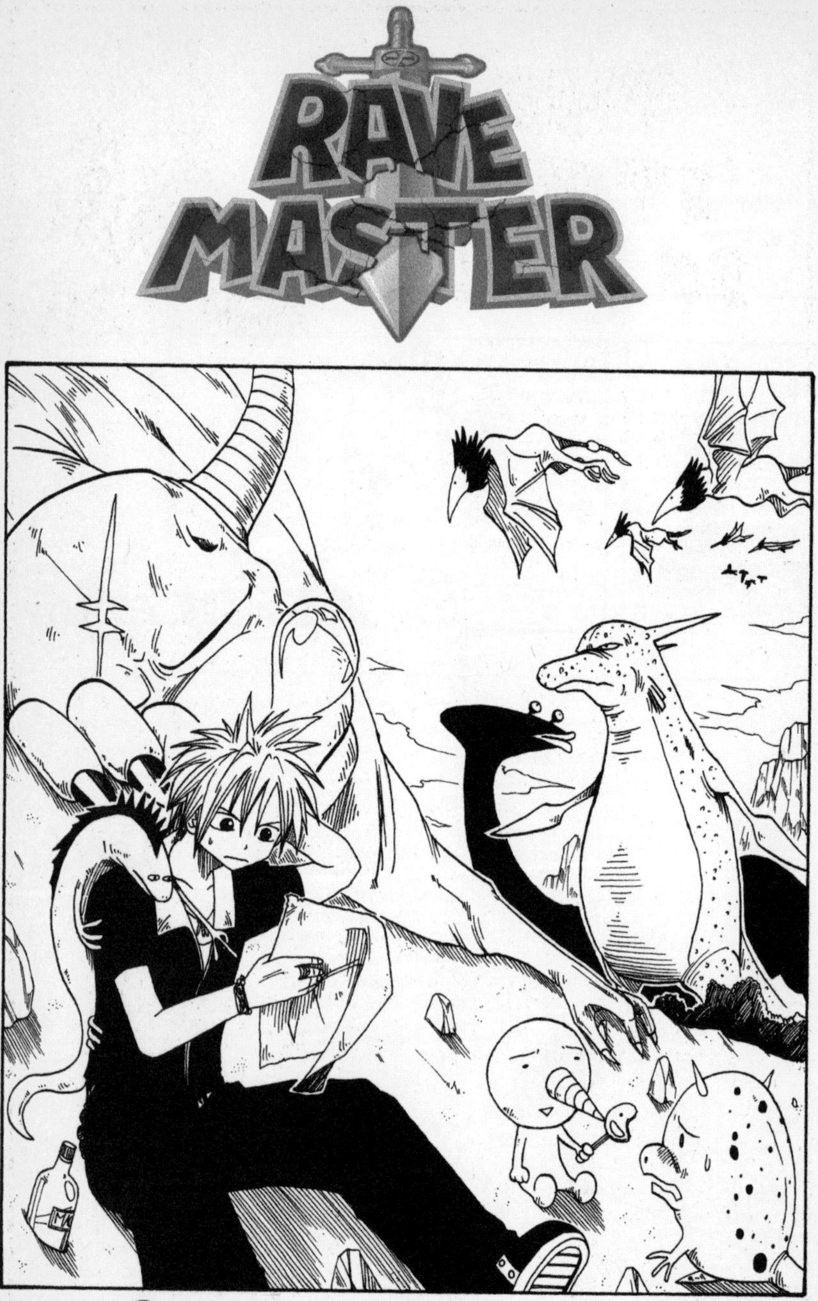

RAVE 5 ✚ TRAVEL TROUBLE?!

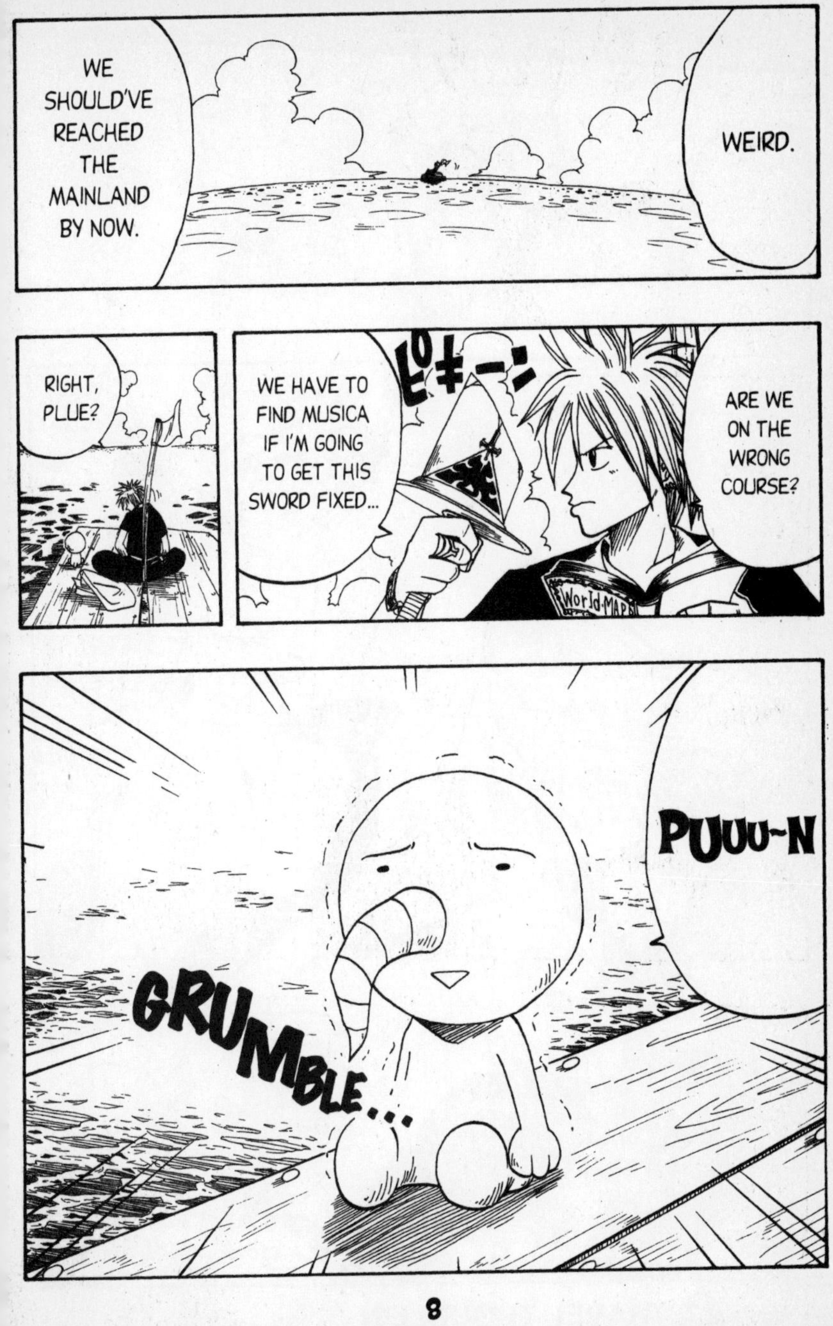
WEIRD.
WE SHOULD'VE REACHED THE MAINLAND BY NOW.
ARE WE ON THE WRONG COURSE?
ピキーン
WE HAVE TO FIND MUSICA IF I'M GOING TO GET THIS SWORD FIXED...
World MAP
RIGHT, PLUE?
PUUU~N
GRUMBLE...

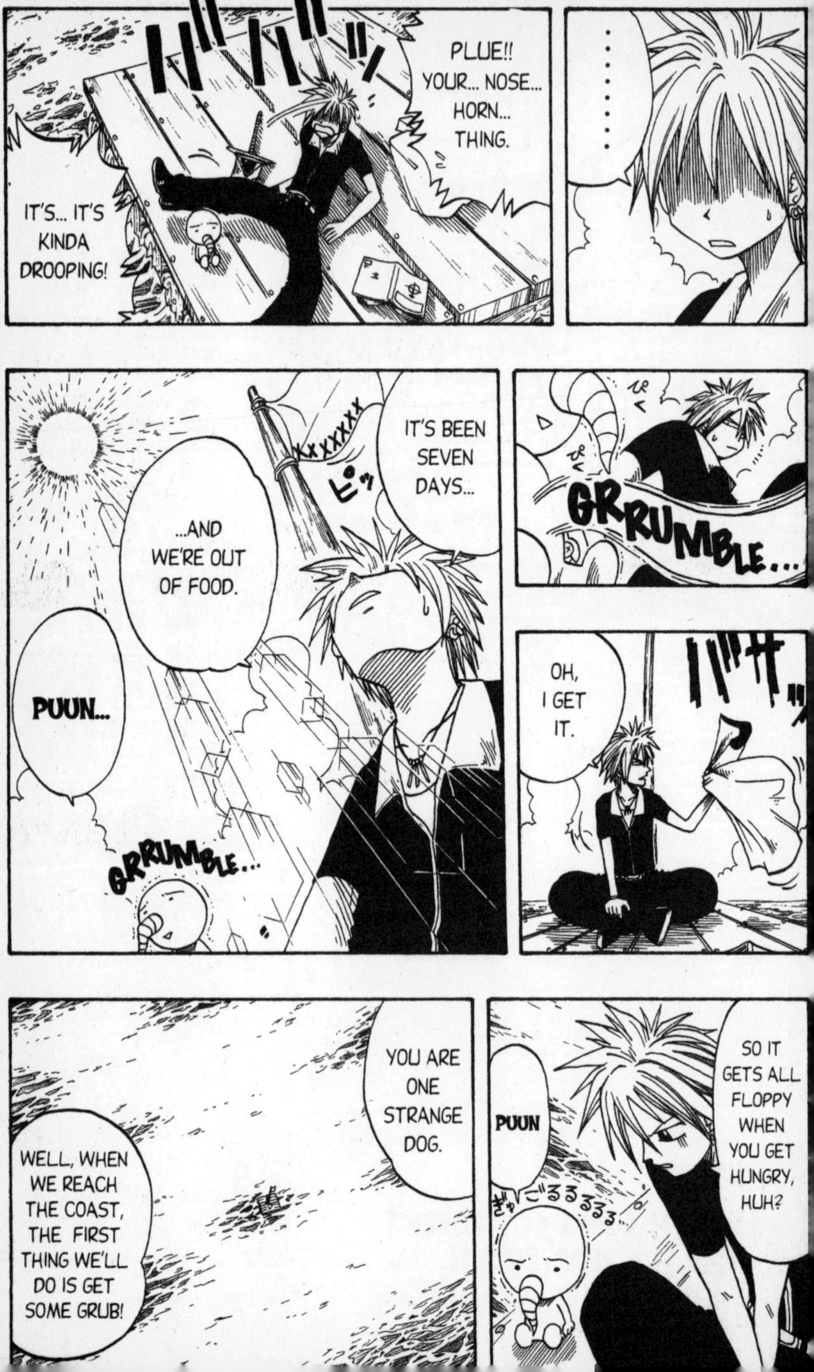

......
PLUE!! YOUR... NOSE... HORN... THING.
IT'S... IT'S KINDA DROOPING!
GRRUMBLE...
OH, I GET IT.
IT'S BEEN SEVEN DAYS...
...AND WE'RE OUT OF FOOD.
PUUN...
GRRUMBLE...
SO IT GETS ALL FLOPPY WHEN YOU GET HUNGRY, HUH?
PUUN
YOU ARE ONE STRANGE DOG.
WELL, WHEN WE REACH THE COAST, THE FIRST THING WE'LL DO IS GET SOME GRUB!

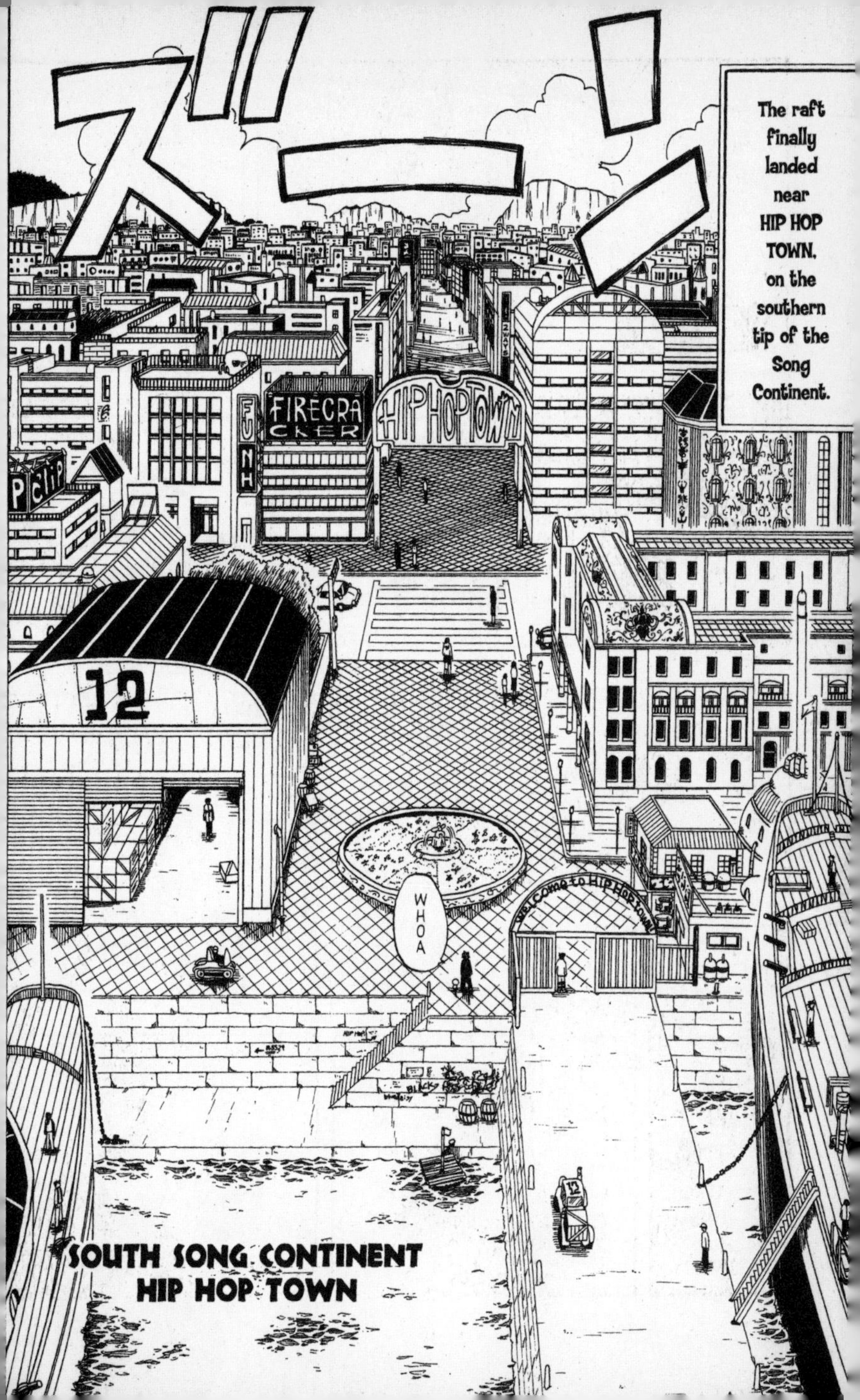
The raft finally landed near HIP HOP TOWN, on the southern tip of the Song Continent.
ズーン
HIPHOPTOWN
FIRECRACKER
Welcome to Hip Hop Town
WHOA
SOUTH SONG CONTINENT
HIP HOP TOWN

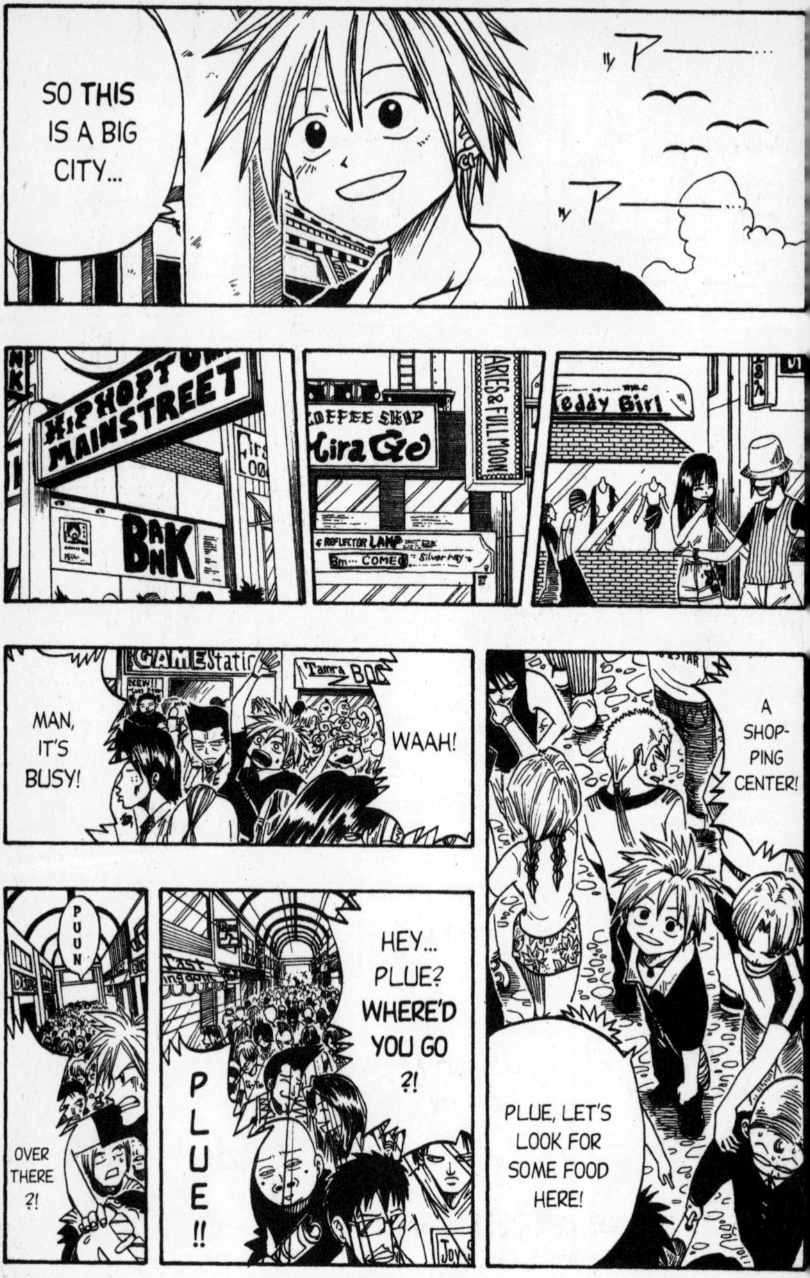
SO THIS IS A BIG CITY...
ア——……
ア——……
Teddy Girl
ARIES & FULLMOON
COFFEE SHOP
Mira Geo
REFLECTOR LAMP
Silver ray
HIPHOPTOWN
MAINSTREET
BANK
A SHOPPING CENTER!
PLUE, LET'S LOOK FOR SOME FOOD HERE!
GAME Static
Tamra
WAAH!
MAN, IT'S BUSY!
HEY... PLUE? WHERE'D YOU GO?!
PLUE!!
PUUN
OVER THERE?!

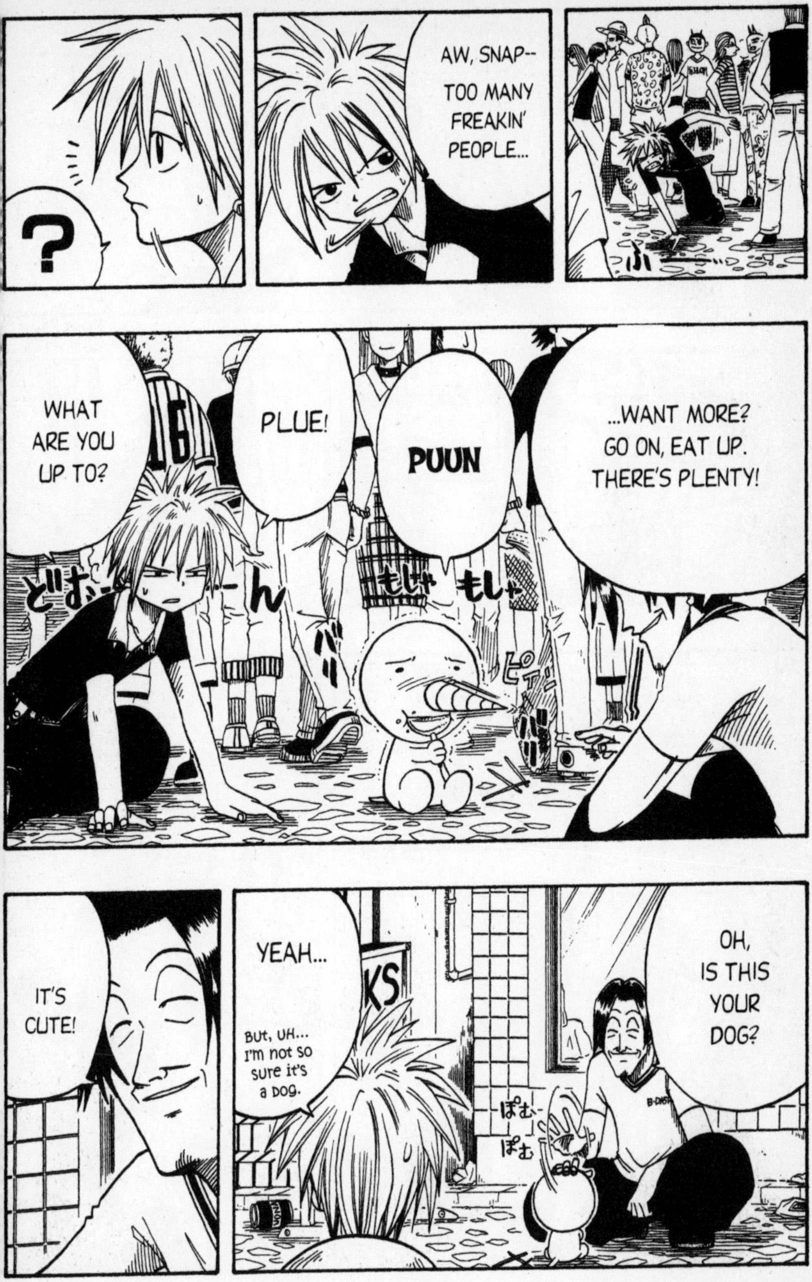
ふ
AW, SNAP-- TOO MANY FREAKIN' PEOPLE...
?
...WANT MORE? GO ON, EAT UP. THERE'S PLENTY!
PUUN
もしゃ もしゃ
PLUE!
WHAT ARE YOU UP TO?
OH, IS THIS YOUR DOG?
ぽむ ぽむ
YEAH...
But, uh... I'm not so sure it's a dog.
IT'S CUTE!

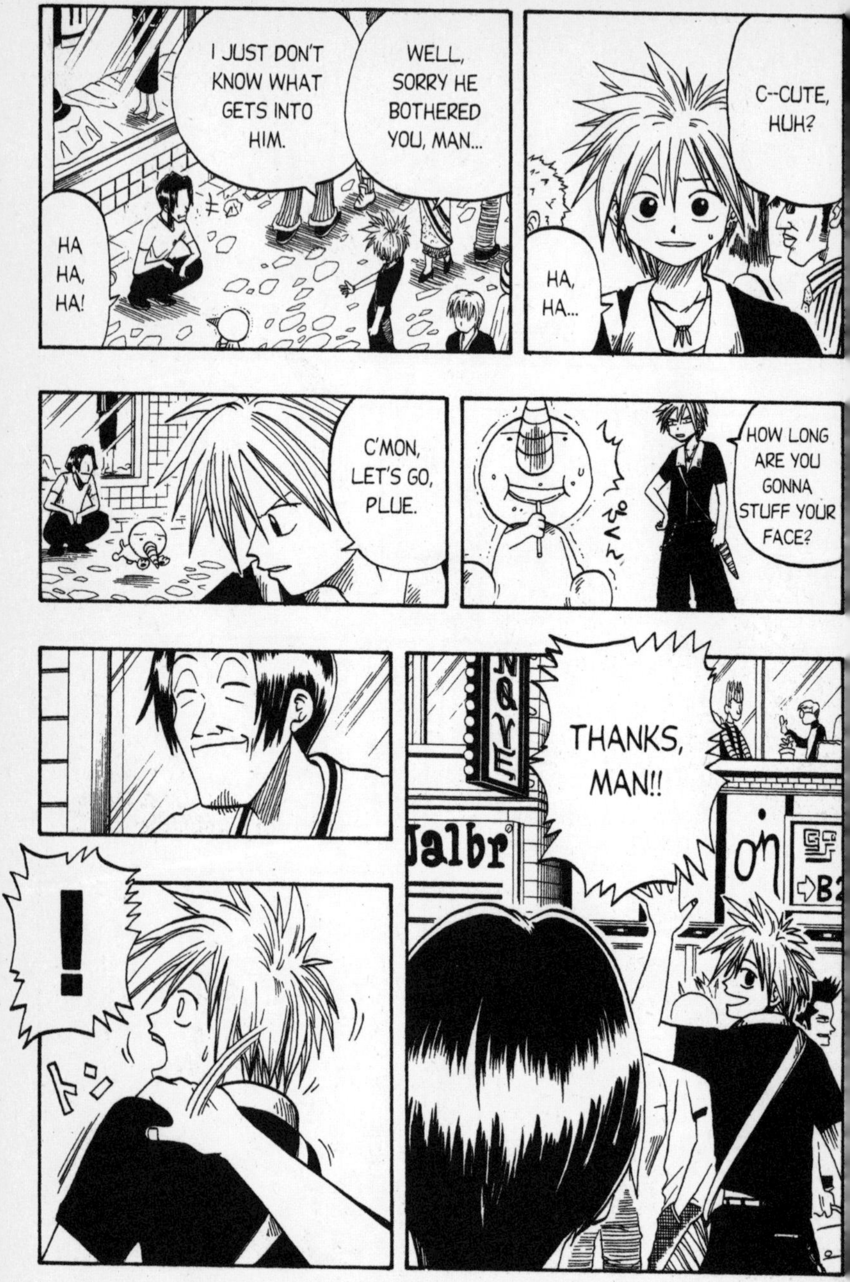
C--CUTE, HUH?
HA, HA...
WELL, SORRY HE BOTHERED YOU, MAN...
I JUST DON'T KNOW WHAT GETS INTO HIM.
HA HA, HA!
HOW LONG ARE YOU GONNA STUFF YOUR FACE?
ぴくん
C'MON, LET'S GO, PLUE.
THANKS, MAN!!
!
トン

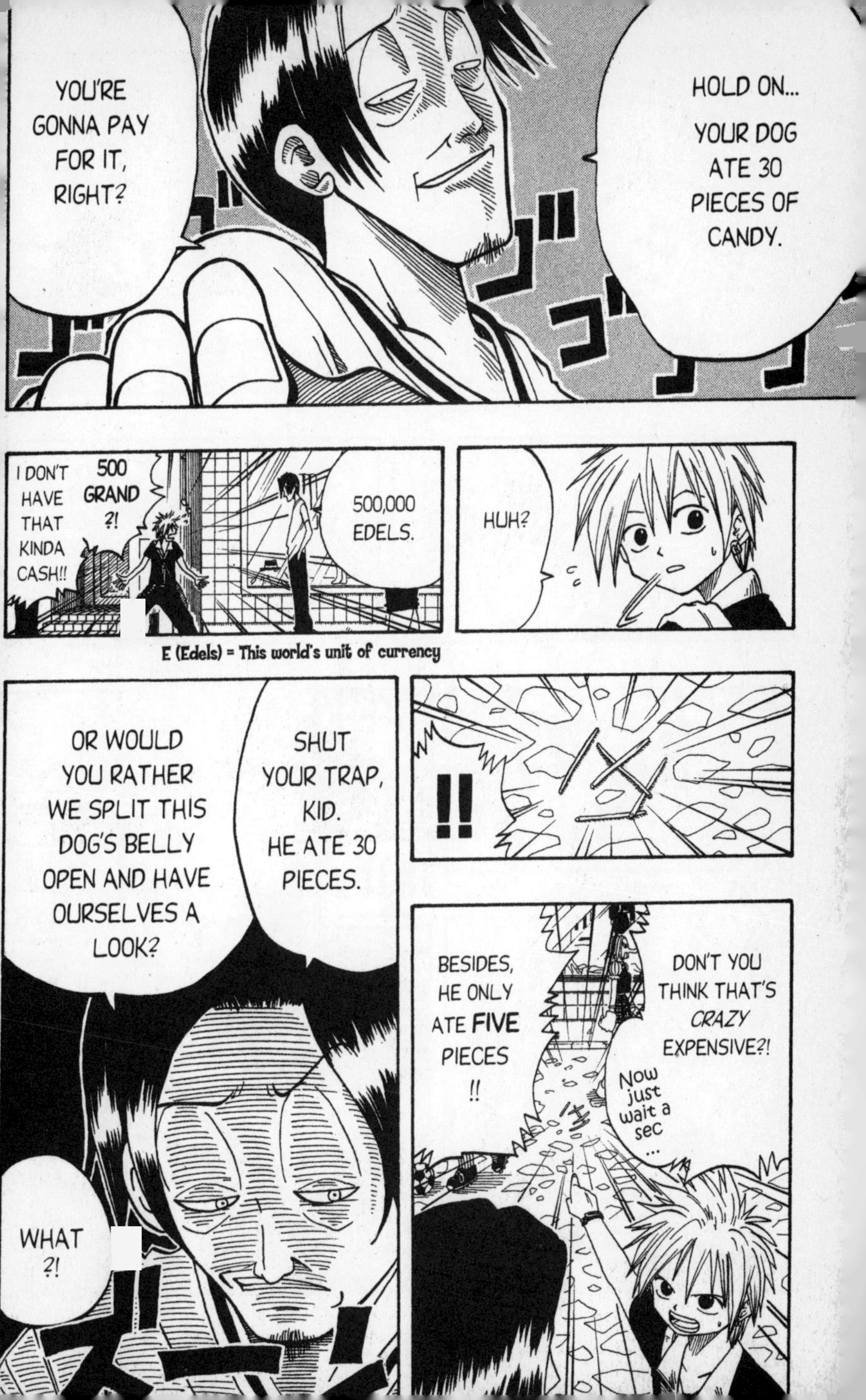
HOLD ON... YOUR DOG ATE 30 PIECES OF CANDY.
YOU'RE GONNA PAY FOR IT, RIGHT?
HUH?
500,000 EDELS.
500 GRAND?!
I DON'T HAVE THAT KINDA CASH!!
E (Edels) = This world's unit of currency
!!
DON'T YOU THINK THAT'S *CRAZY* EXPENSIVE?!
BESIDES, HE ONLY ATE **FIVE** PIECES!!
Now just wait a sec...
SHUT YOUR TRAP, KID. HE ATE 30 PIECES.
OR WOULD YOU RATHER WE SPLIT THIS DOG'S BELLY OPEN AND HAVE OURSELVES A LOOK?
WHAT?!

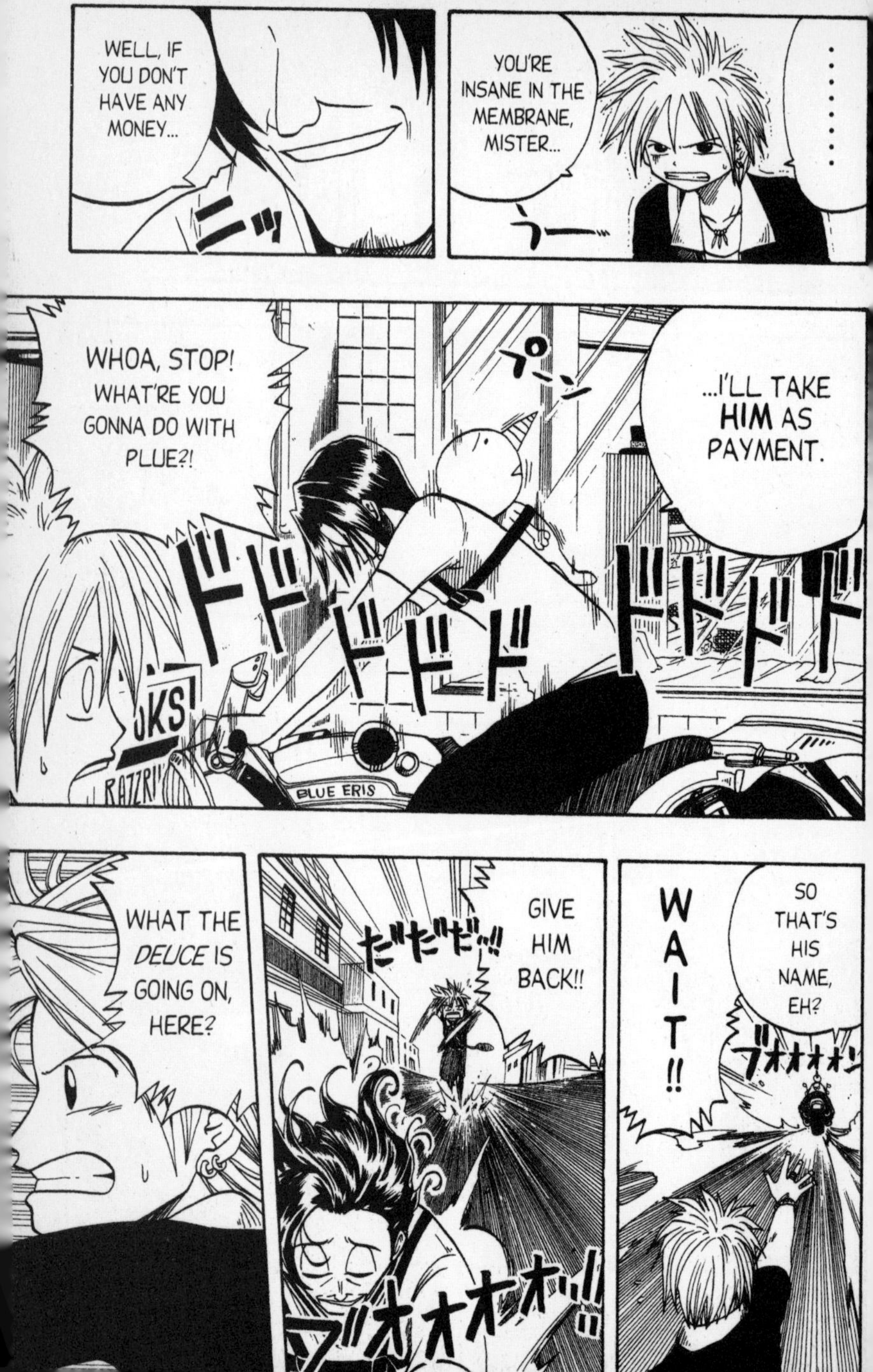

......
YOU'RE INSANE IN THE MEMBRANE, MISTER...
うー…
WELL, IF YOU DON'T HAVE ANY MONEY...
ニッ
...I'LL TAKE HIM AS PAYMENT.
WHOA, STOP! WHAT'RE YOU GONNA DO WITH PLUE?!
BLUE ERIS
SO THAT'S HIS NAME, EH?
WAIT!!
GIVE HIM BACK!!
WHAT THE *DEUCE* IS GOING ON, HERE?

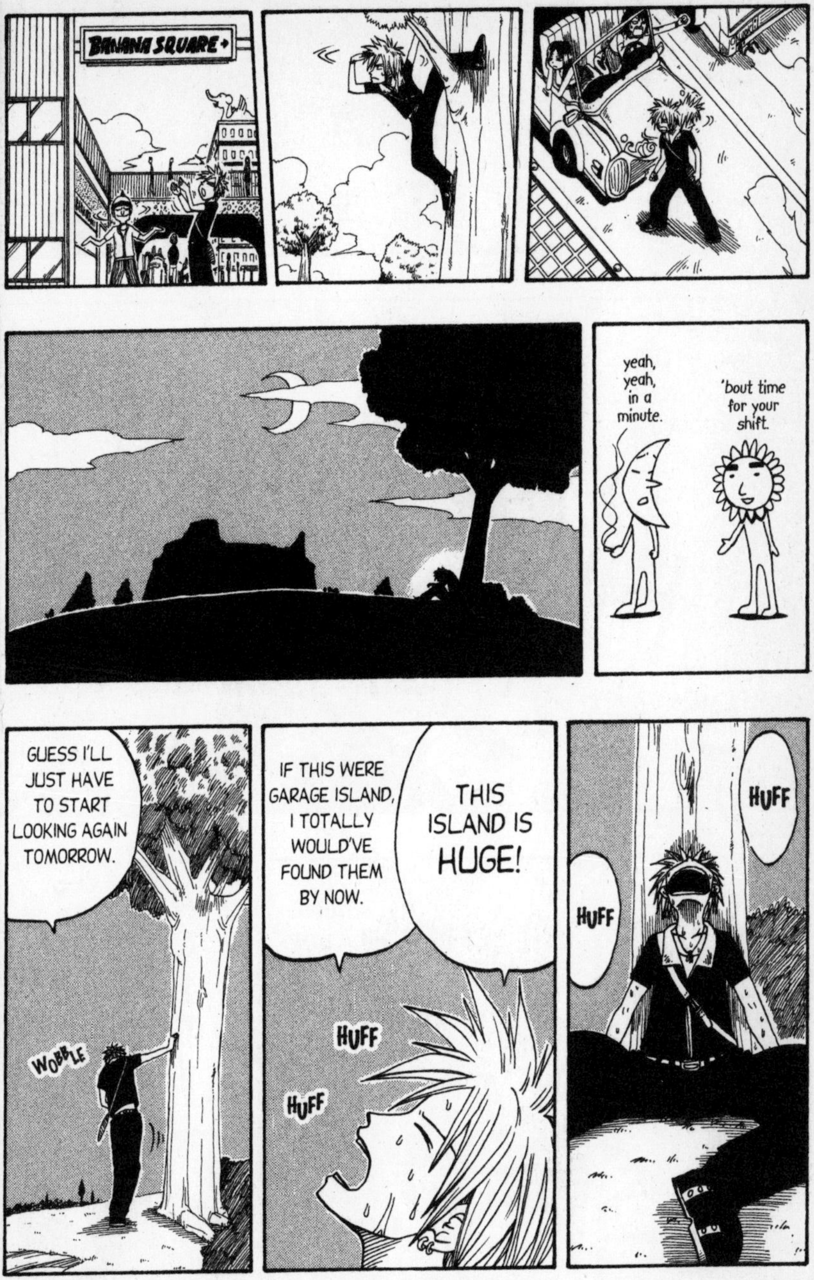
BANANA SQUARE
'bout time for your shift.
yeah, yeah, in a minute.
HUFF
HUFF
THIS ISLAND IS HUGE!
IF THIS WERE GARAGE ISLAND, I TOTALLY WOULD'VE FOUND THEM BY NOW.
HUFF
HUFF
GUESS I'LL JUST HAVE TO START LOOKING AGAIN TOMORROW.
WOBBLE

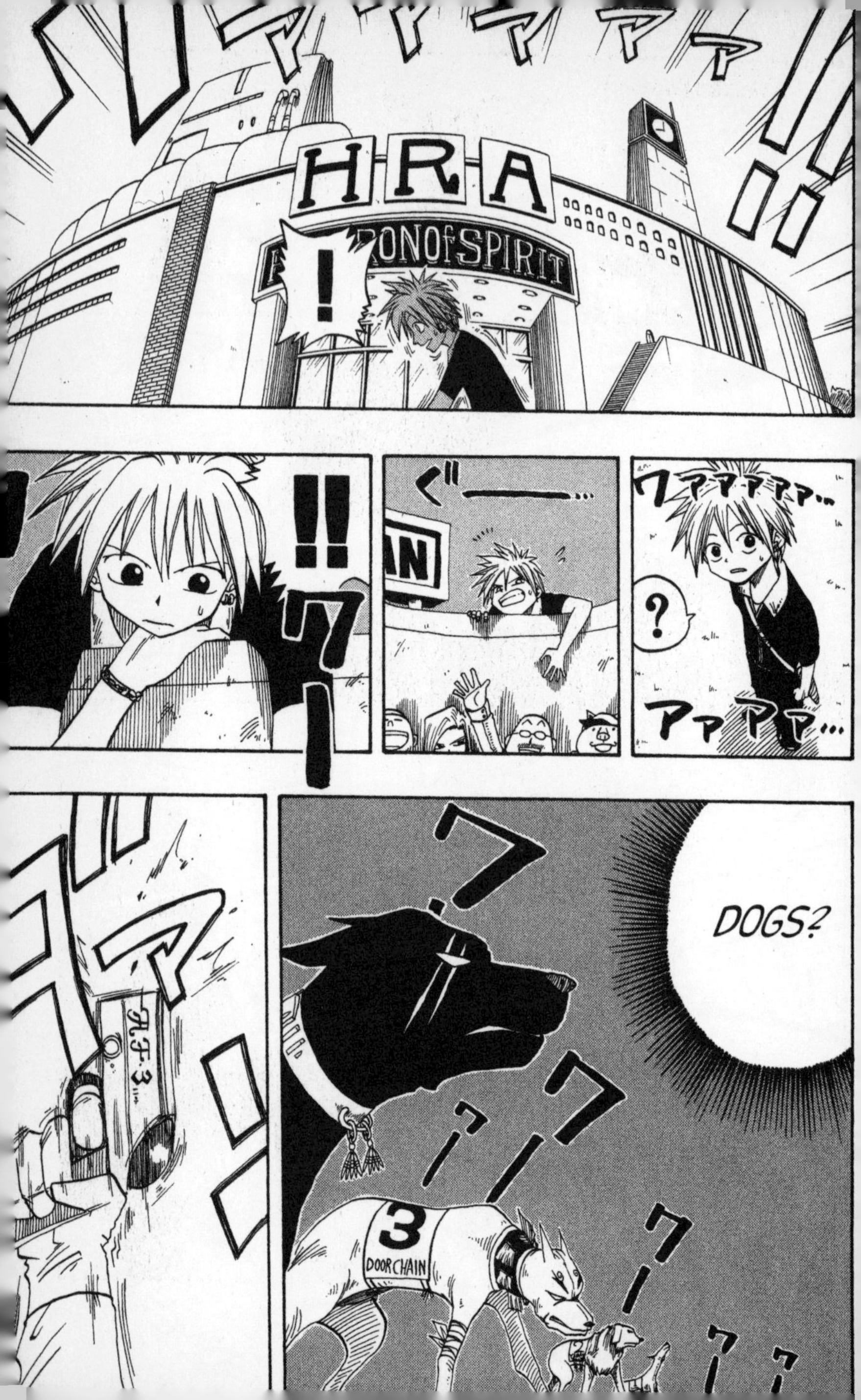
ワアアアアア!!
HRA
RONofSPIRIT
!
ワアアアアアア…
?
アアアアア…
ぐ――…
AN
!!
DOGS?
3
DOORCHAIN

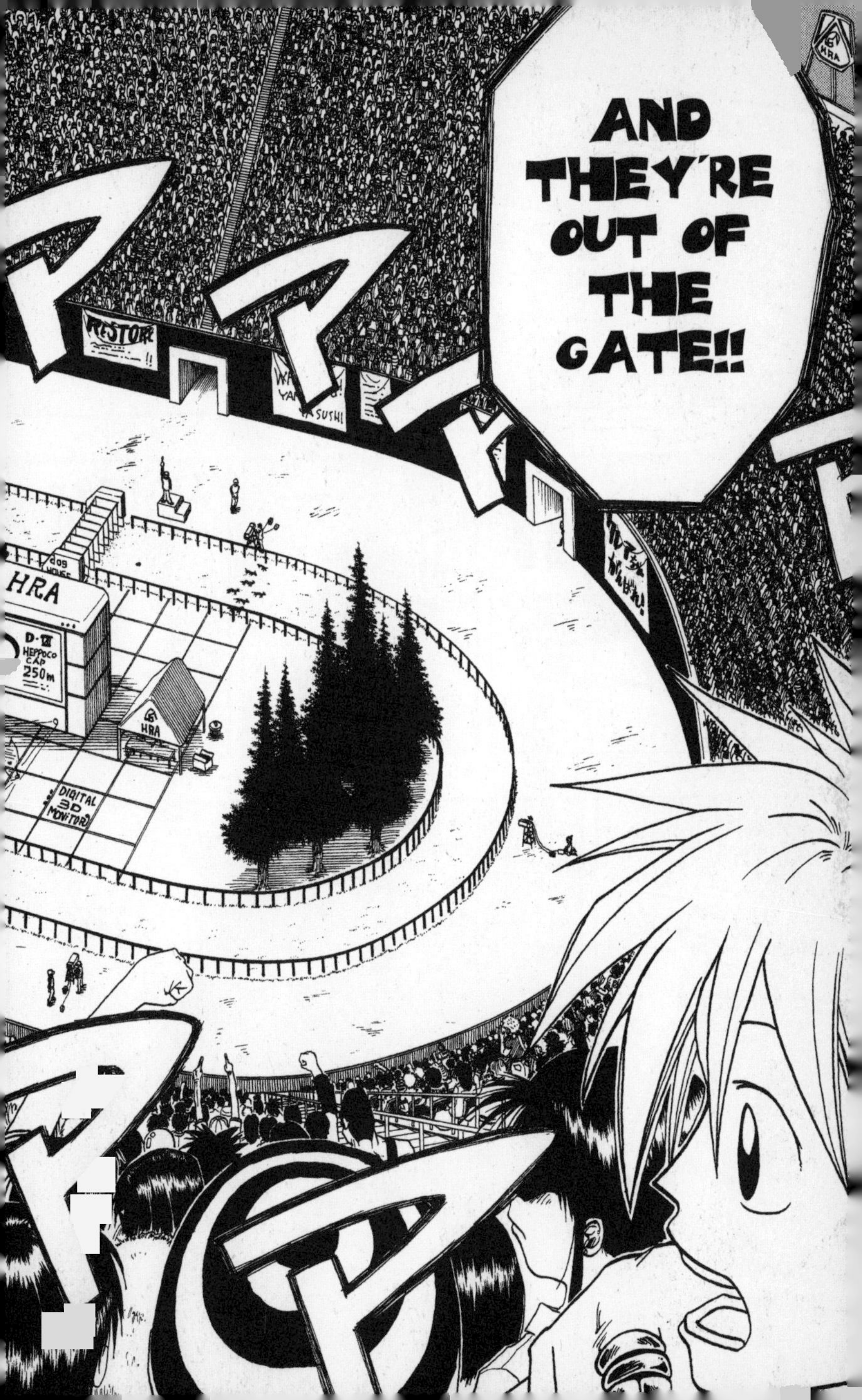
AND THEY'RE OUT OF THE GATE!!
HRA
dog HOUSE
HEPPOCO CAP 250m
HRA
DIGITAL 3D MONITOR

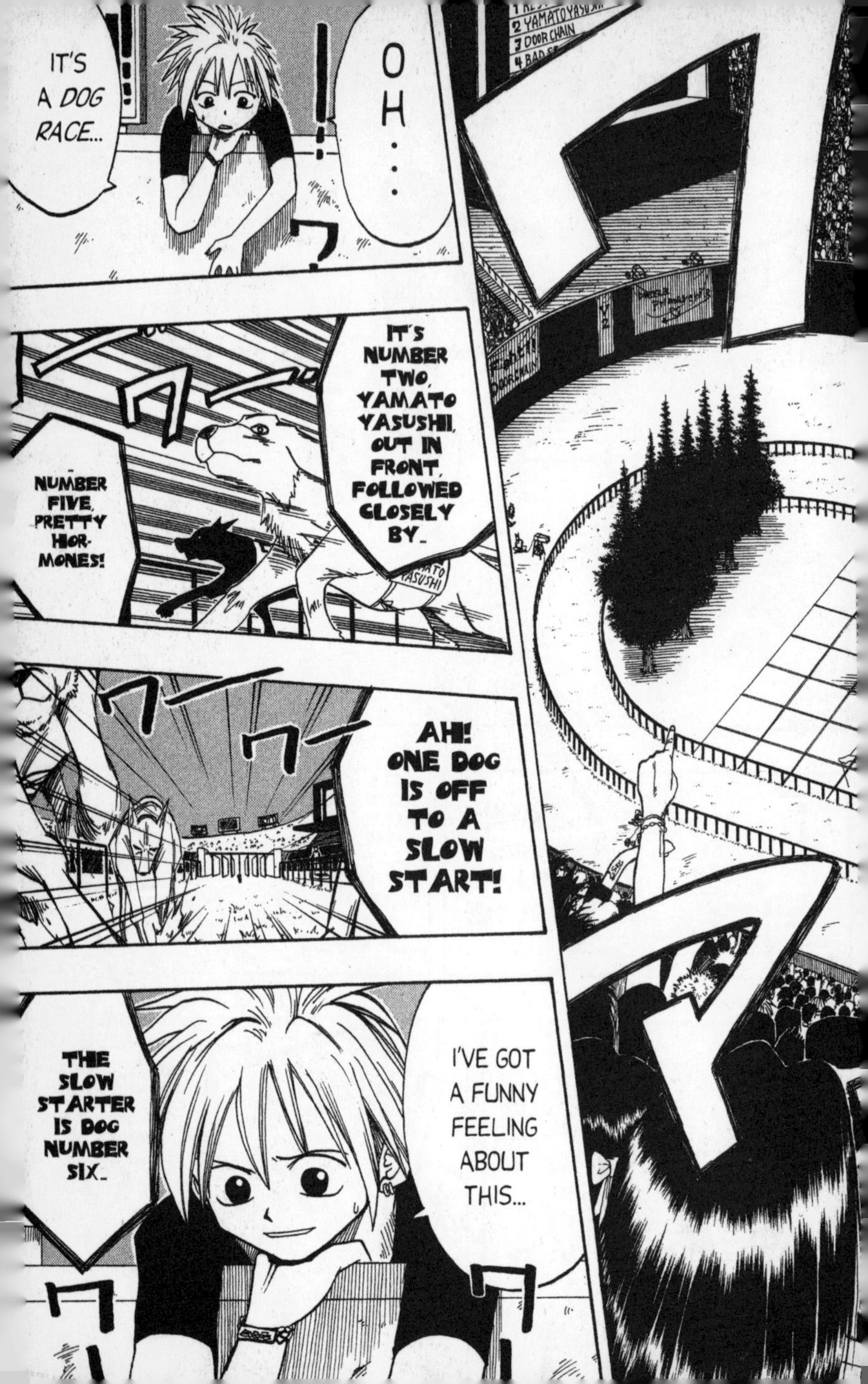
2 YAMATO YASUSHI
3 DOOR CHAIN
OH...!!
IT'S A DOG RACE...
IT'S NUMBER TWO, YAMATO YASUSHI, OUT IN FRONT, FOLLOWED CLOSELY BY...
...NUMBER FIVE, PRETTY HORMONES!
YAMATO YASUSHI
AH! ONE DOG IS OFF TO A SLOW START!
I'VE GOT A FUNNY FEELING ABOUT THIS...
THE SLOW STARTER IS DOG NUMBER SIX...

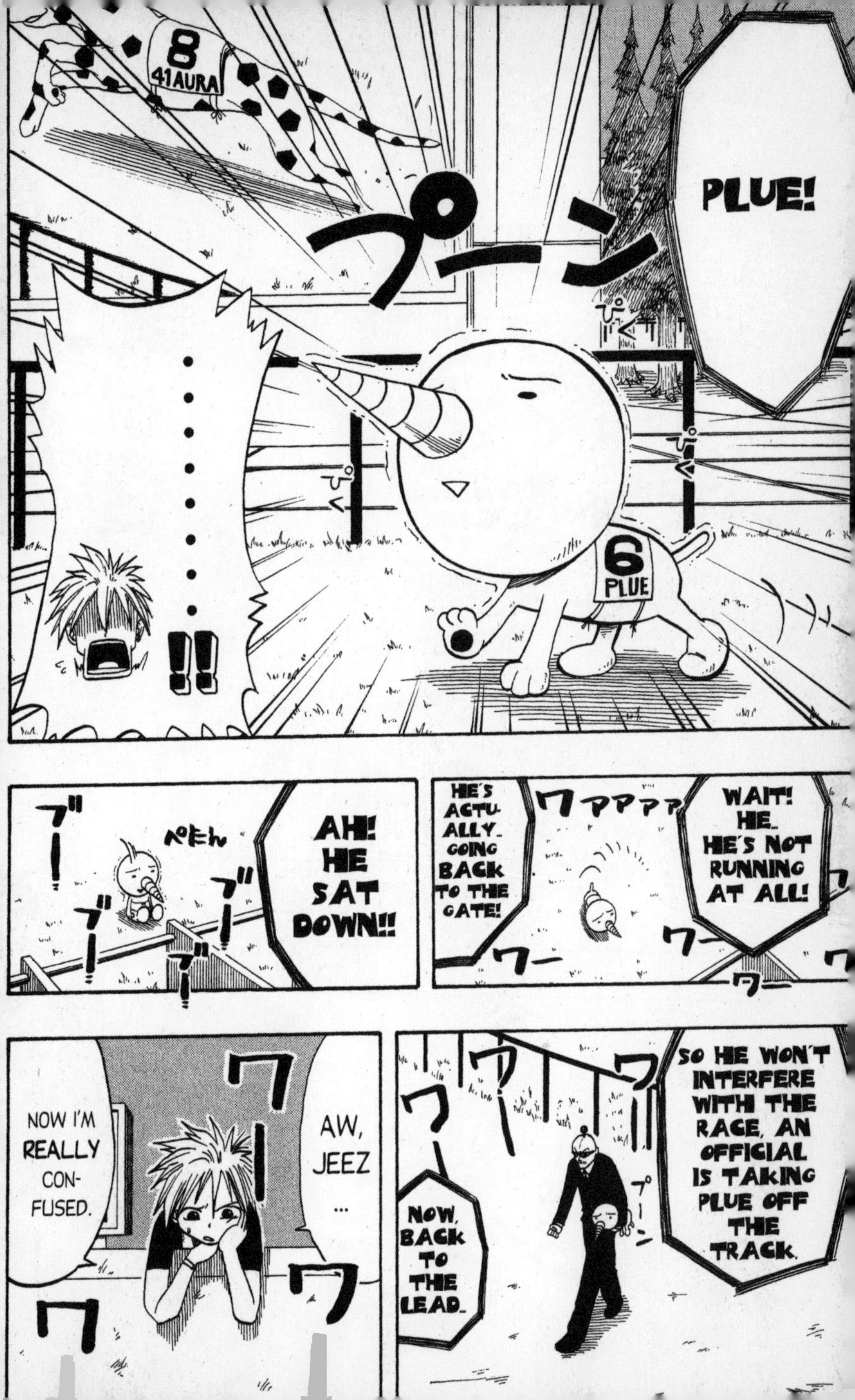

PLUE!
プーン
ぴく
8
41 AURA
6
PLUE
.........!!
WAIT! HE... HE'S NOT RUNNING AT ALL!
HE'S ACTUALLY GOING BACK TO THE GATE!
ワァァァァ
AH! HE SAT DOWN!!
ぺたん
SO HE WON'T INTERFERE WITH THE RACE, AN OFFICIAL IS TAKING PLUE OFF THE TRACK.
NOW, BACK TO THE LEAD...
AW, JEEZ...
NOW I'M REALLY CONFUSED.

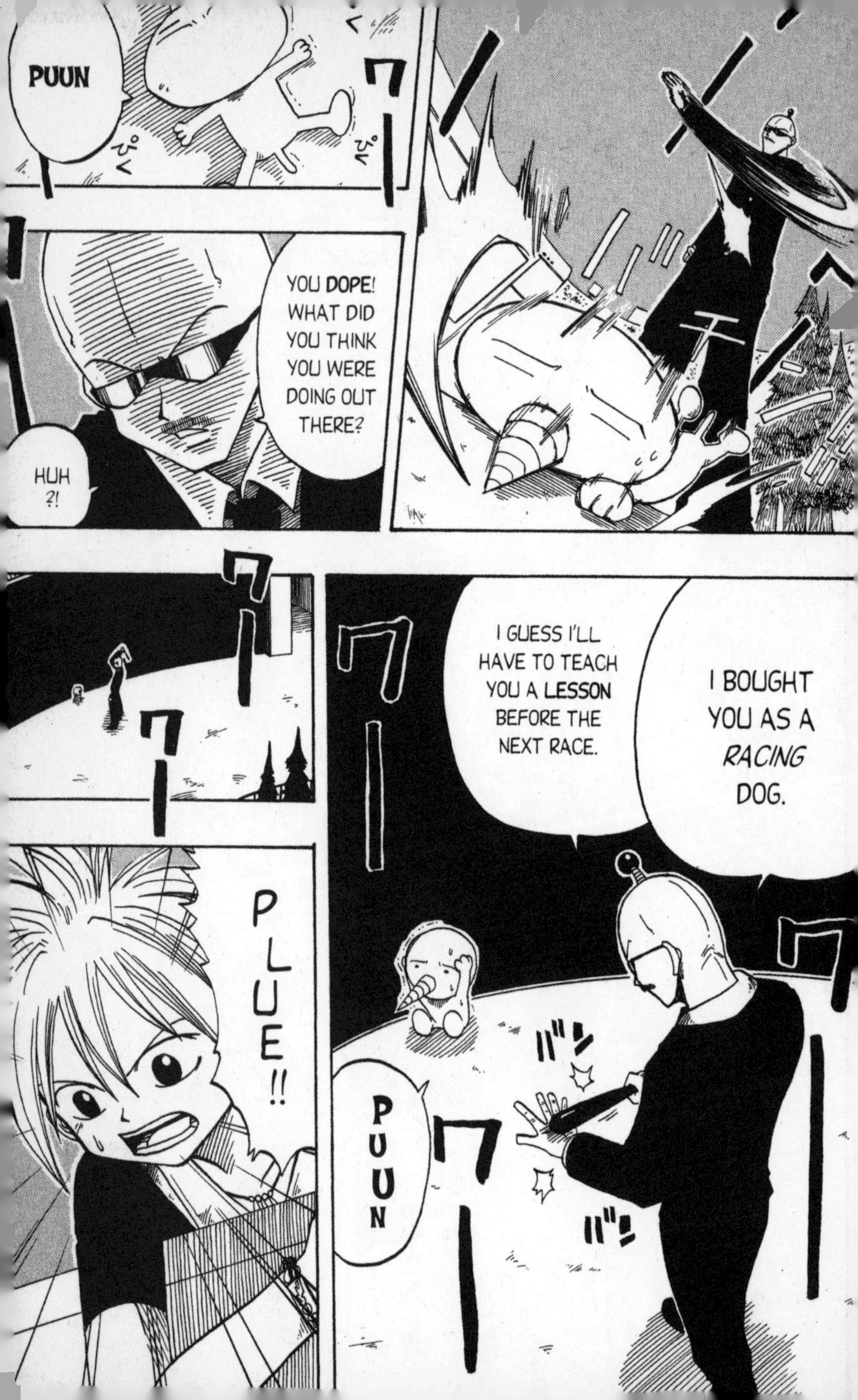
PUUN
ぴく
ぴく
YOU **DOPE**! WHAT DID YOU THINK YOU WERE DOING OUT THERE?
HUH ?!
I BOUGHT YOU AS A *RACING* DOG.
I GUESS I'LL HAVE TO TEACH YOU A **LESSON** BEFORE THE NEXT RACE.
PUUN
PLUE!!

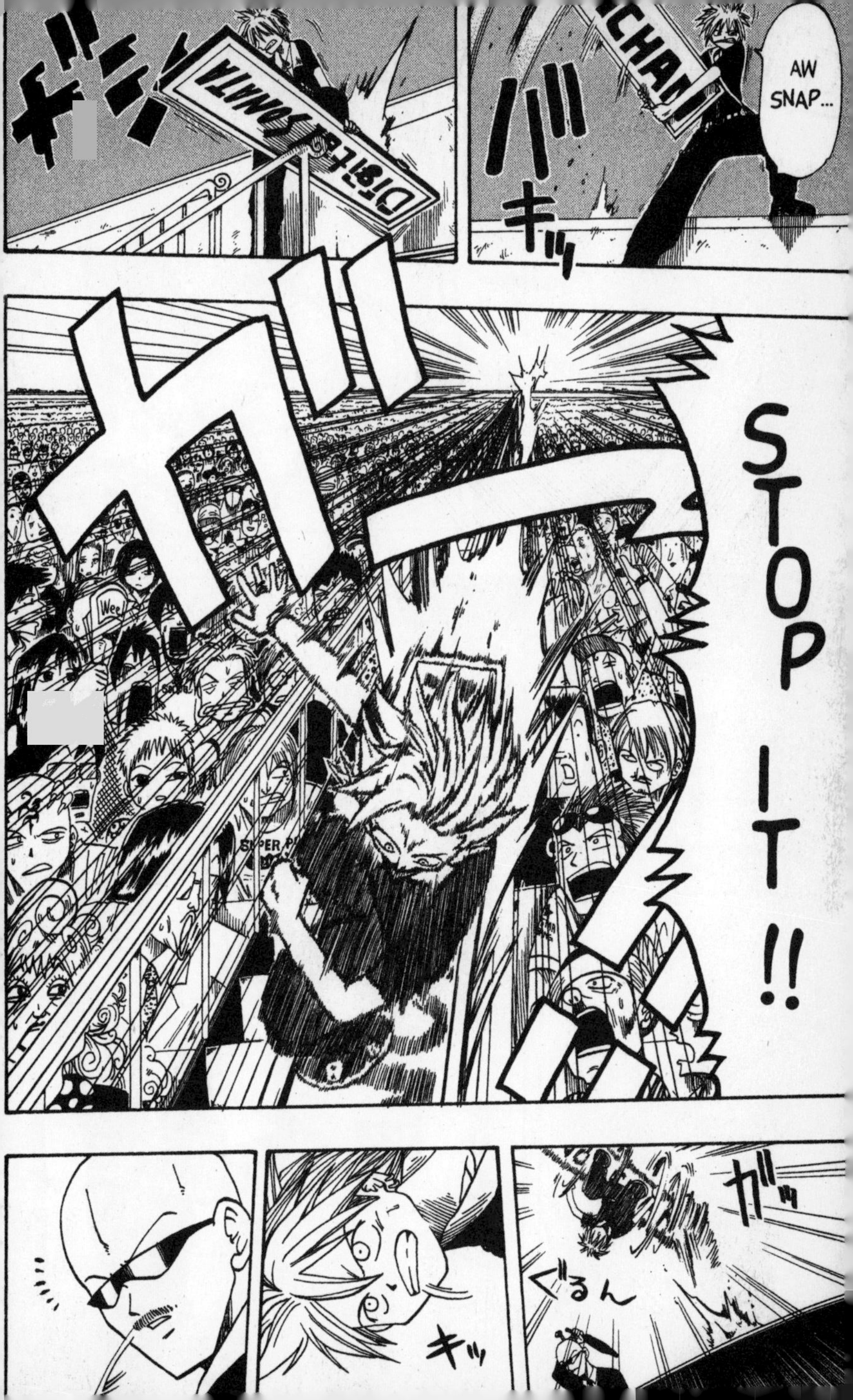
AW SNAP...
STOP IT!!
ガッ
ぐるん

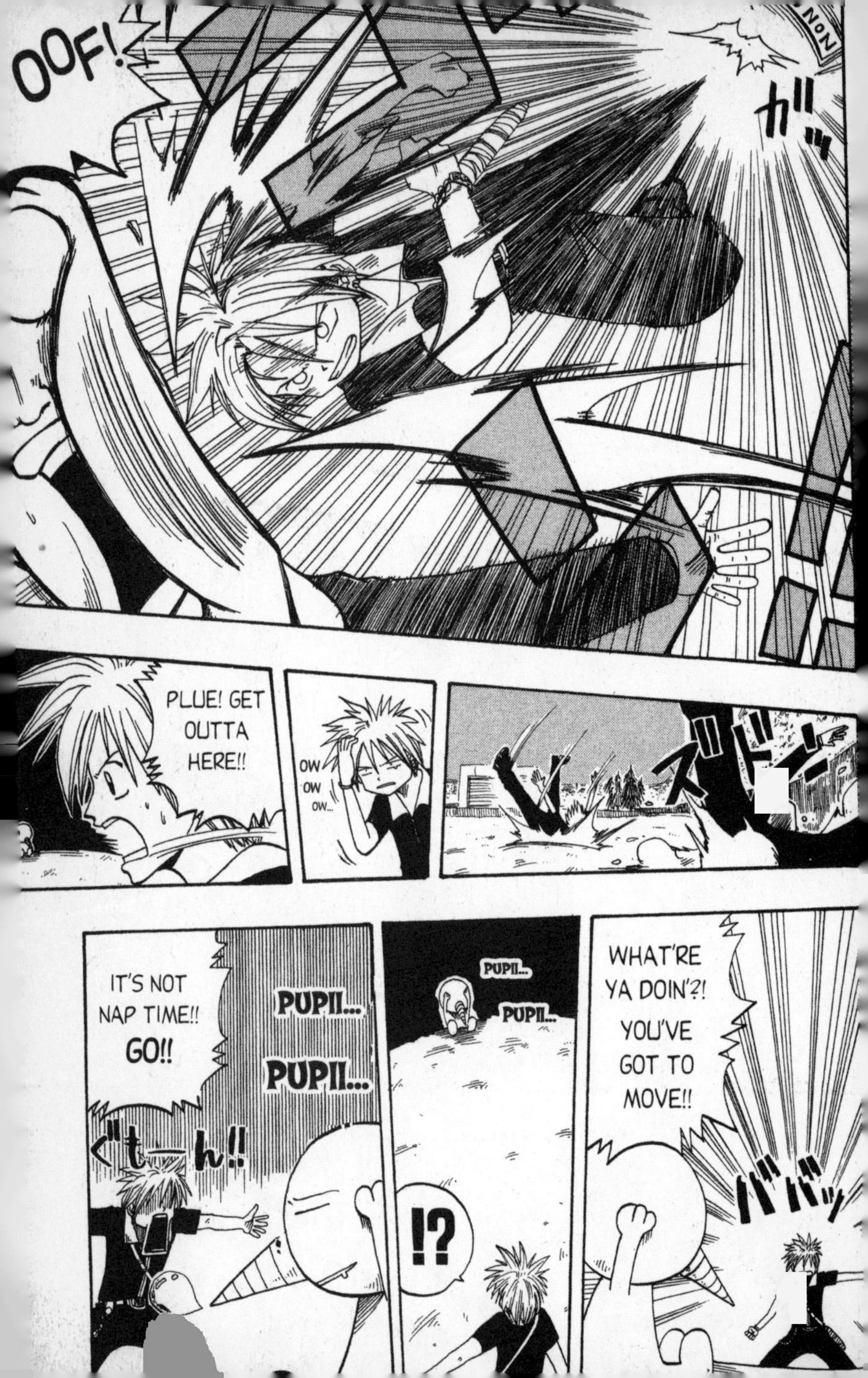
OOF!
ガッ
ズドン
OW OW OW...
PLUE! GET OUTTA HERE!!
WHAT'RE YA DOIN'?!
YOU'VE GOT TO MOVE!!
ババッ
PUPII...
PUPII...
!?
PUPII...
PUPII...
IT'S NOT NAP TIME!! GO!!
ぐでーん!!

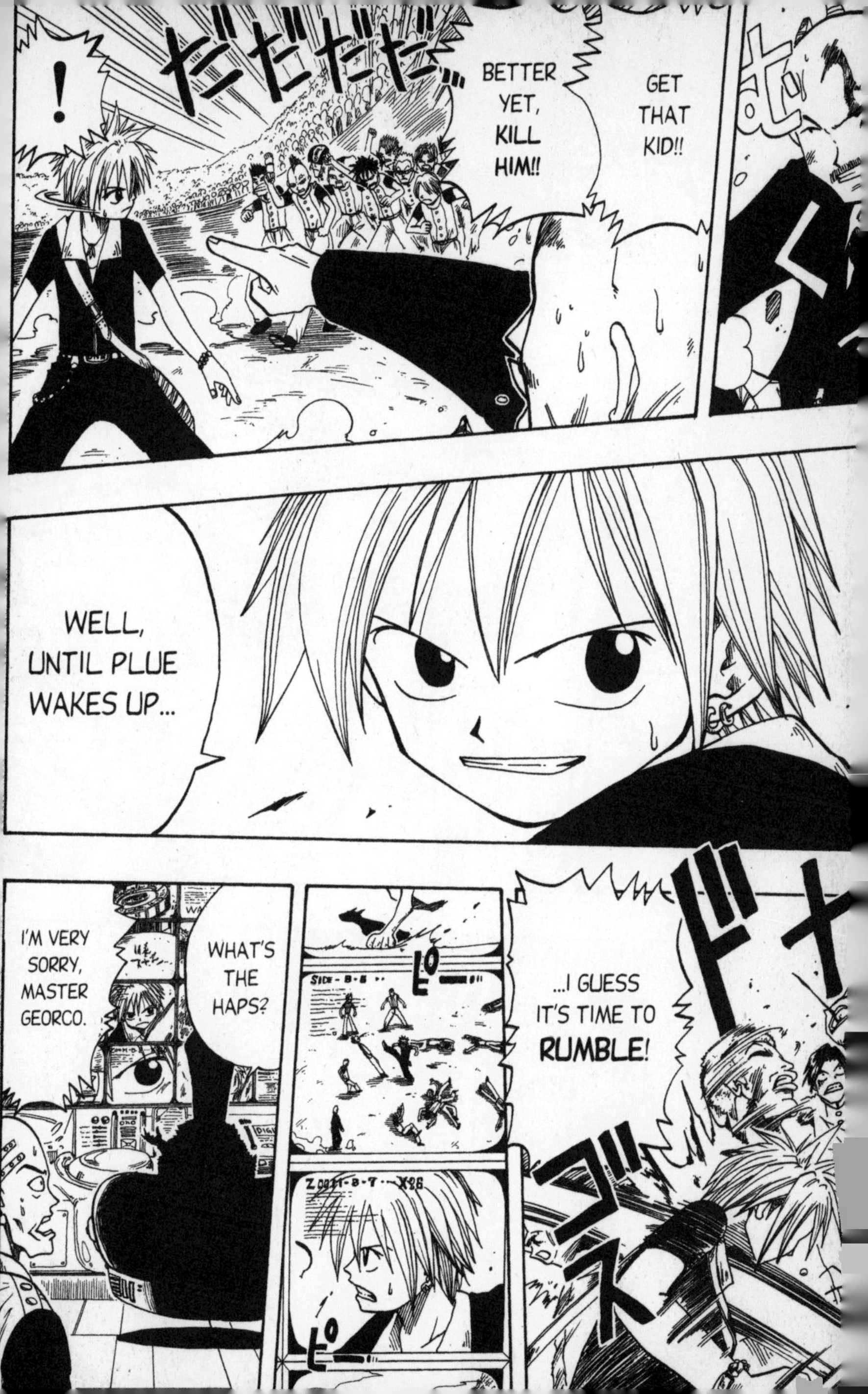
GET THAT KID!!
BETTER YET, KILL HIM!!
!
WELL, UNTIL PLUE WAKES UP...
...I GUESS IT'S TIME TO RUMBLE!
WHAT'S THE HAPS?
I'M VERY SORRY, MASTER GEORCO.

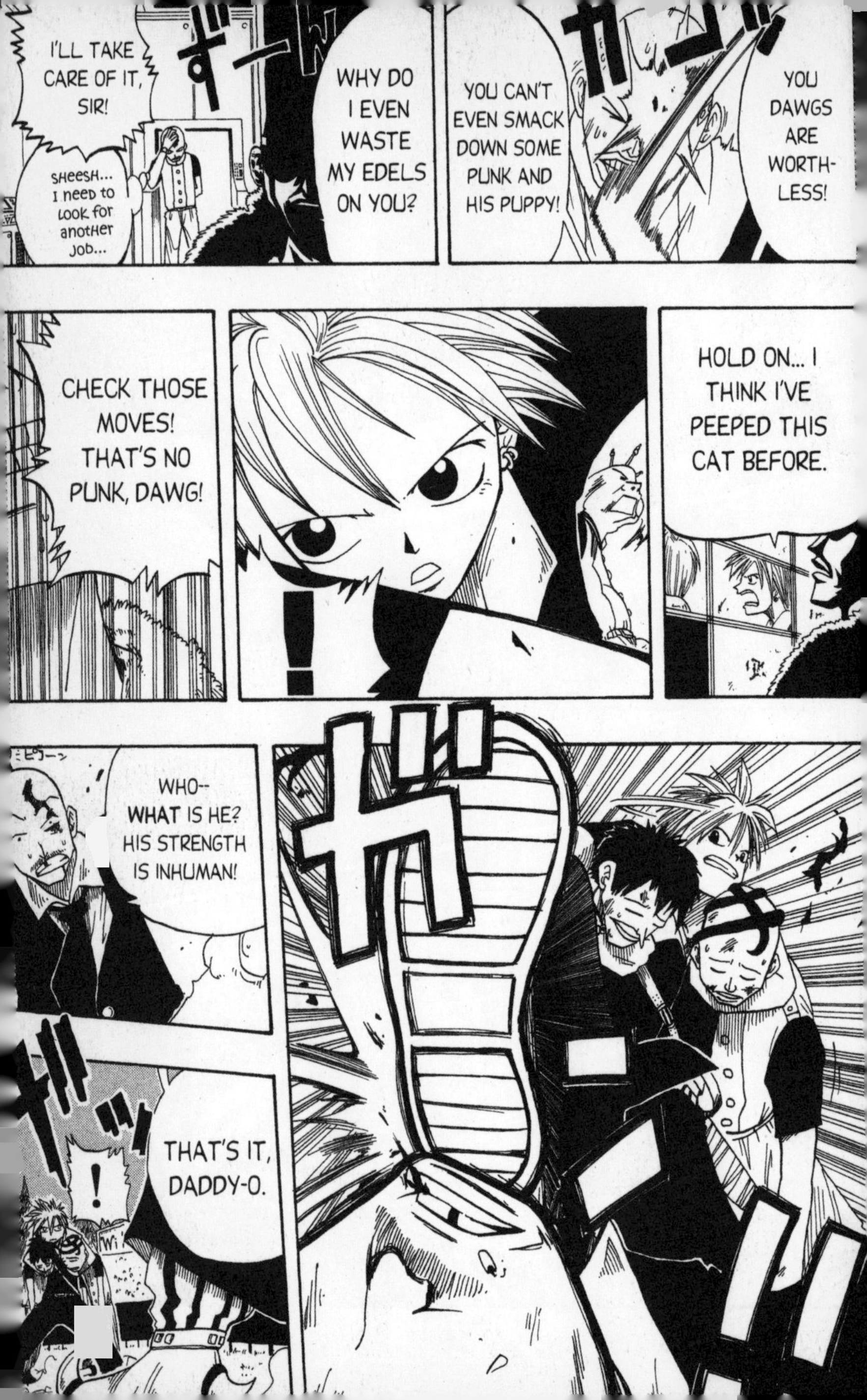
YOU DAWGS ARE WORTHLESS!
YOU CAN'T EVEN SMACK DOWN SOME PUNK AND HIS PUPPY!
WHY DO I EVEN WASTE MY EDELS ON YOU?
I'LL TAKE CARE OF IT, SIR!
SHEESH... I NEED TO LOOK FOR ANOTHER JOB...
HOLD ON... I THINK I'VE PEEPED THIS CAT BEFORE.
!
CHECK THOSE MOVES! THAT'S NO PUNK, DAWG!
WHO-- WHAT IS HE? HIS STRENGTH IS INHUMAN!
!
THAT'S IT, DADDY-O.

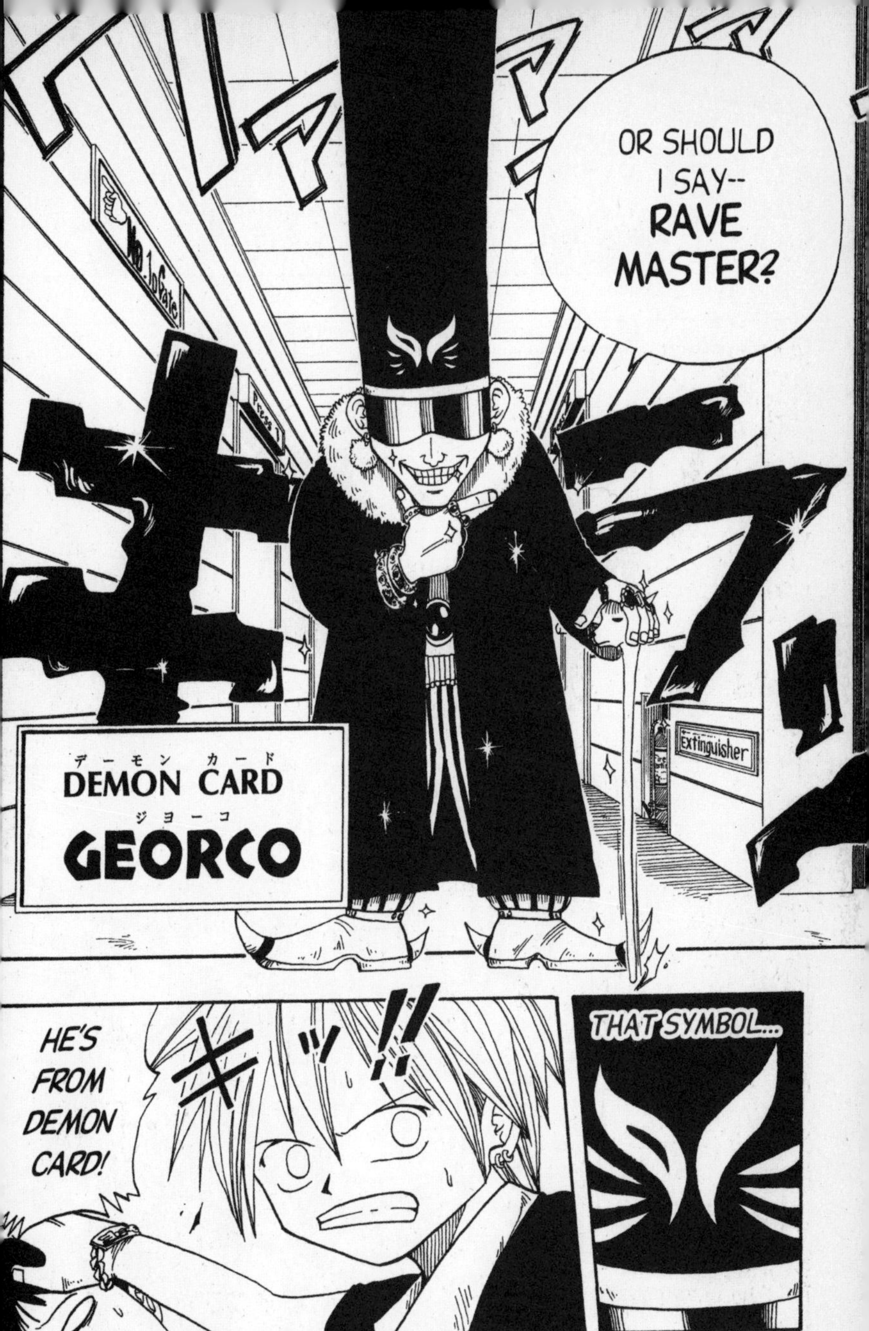
OR SHOULD I SAY-- RAVE MASTER?
デーモン カード
DEMON CARD
ジョーコ
GEORCO
extinguisher
THAT SYMBOL...
HE'S FROM DEMON CARD!

RAVE MASTER

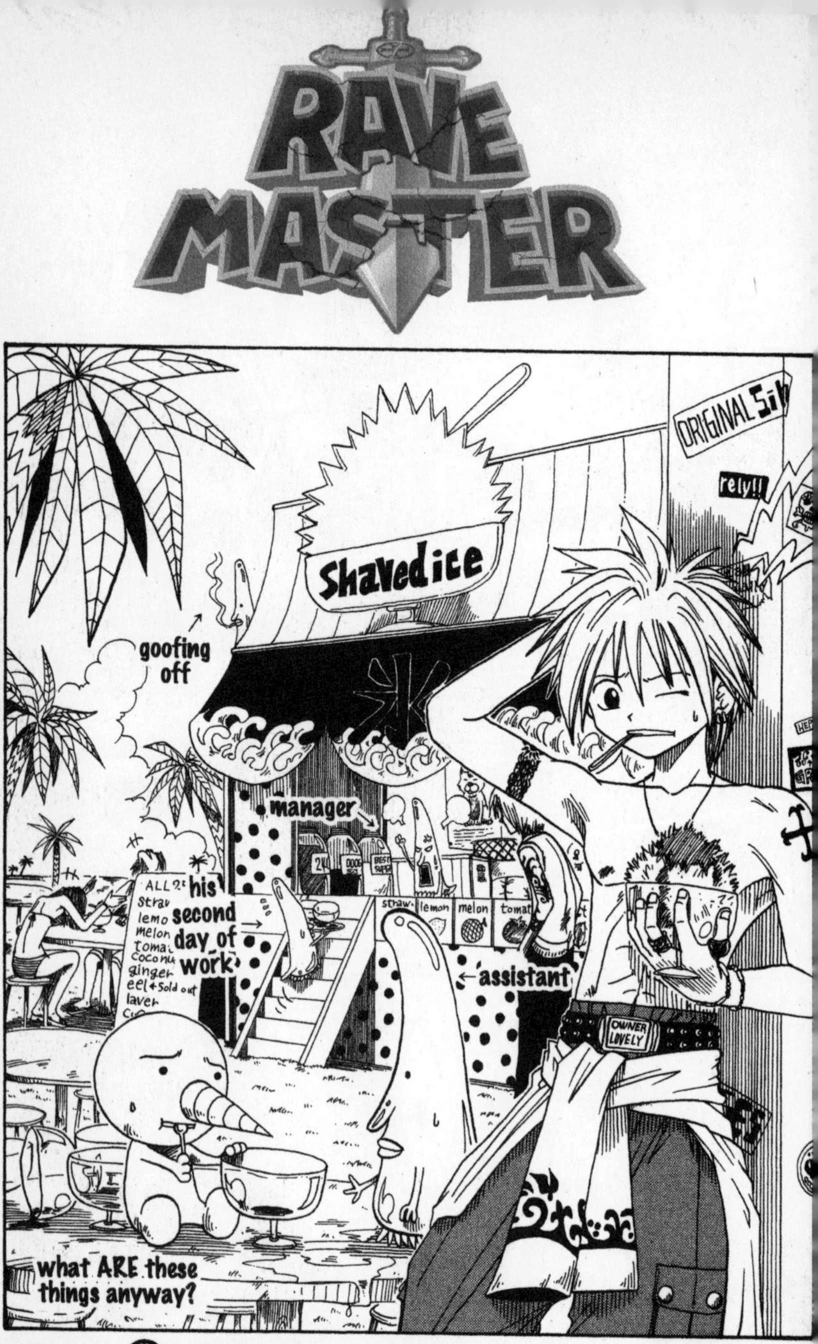
rely!!
Shaved ice
goofing off
manager
assistant
his second day of work
OWNER LOVELY
what ARE these things anyway?

RAVE 6 ✚ DEAD OR ALIVE

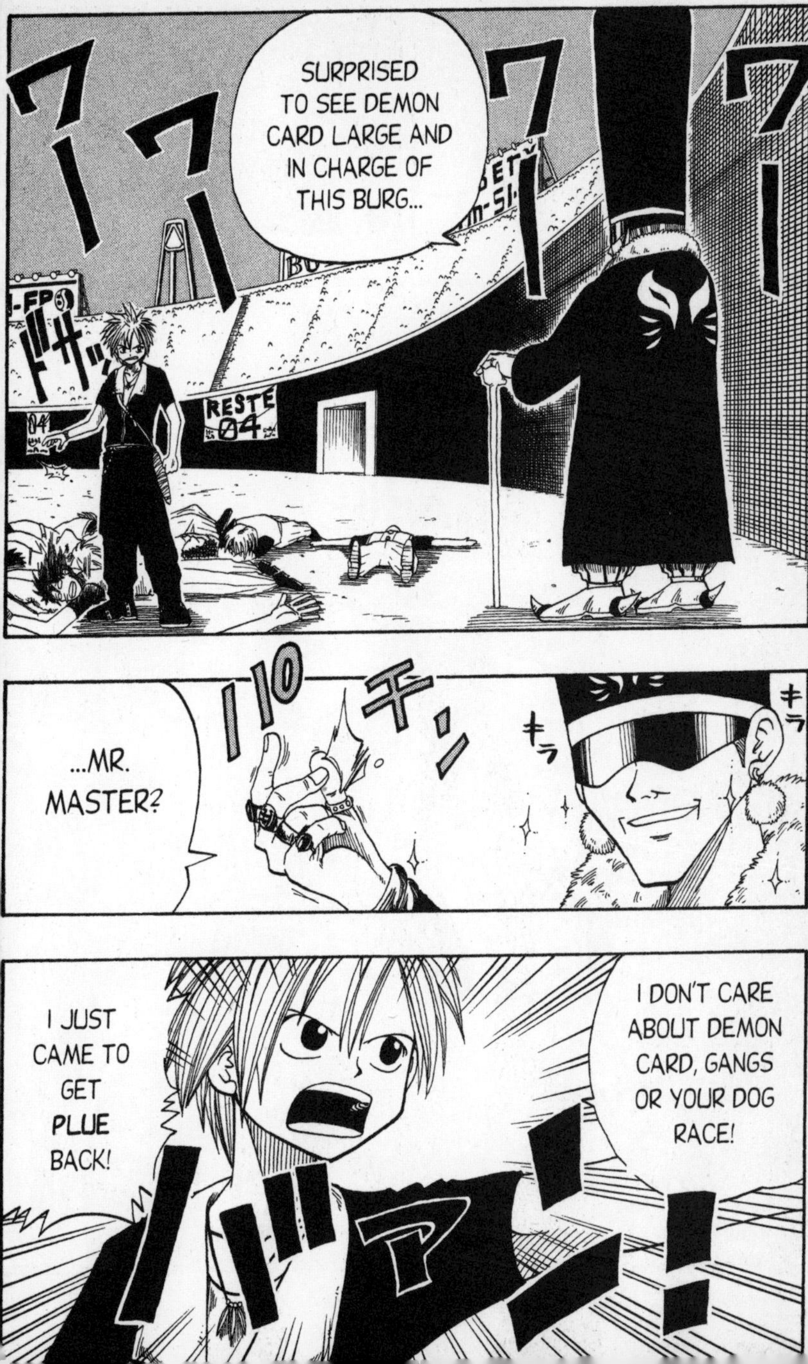
SURPRISED TO SEE DEMON CARD LARGE AND IN CHARGE OF THIS BURG...
RESTE 04
...MR. MASTER?
I DON'T CARE ABOUT DEMON CARD, GANGS OR YOUR DOG RACE!
I JUST CAME TO GET **PLUE** BACK!

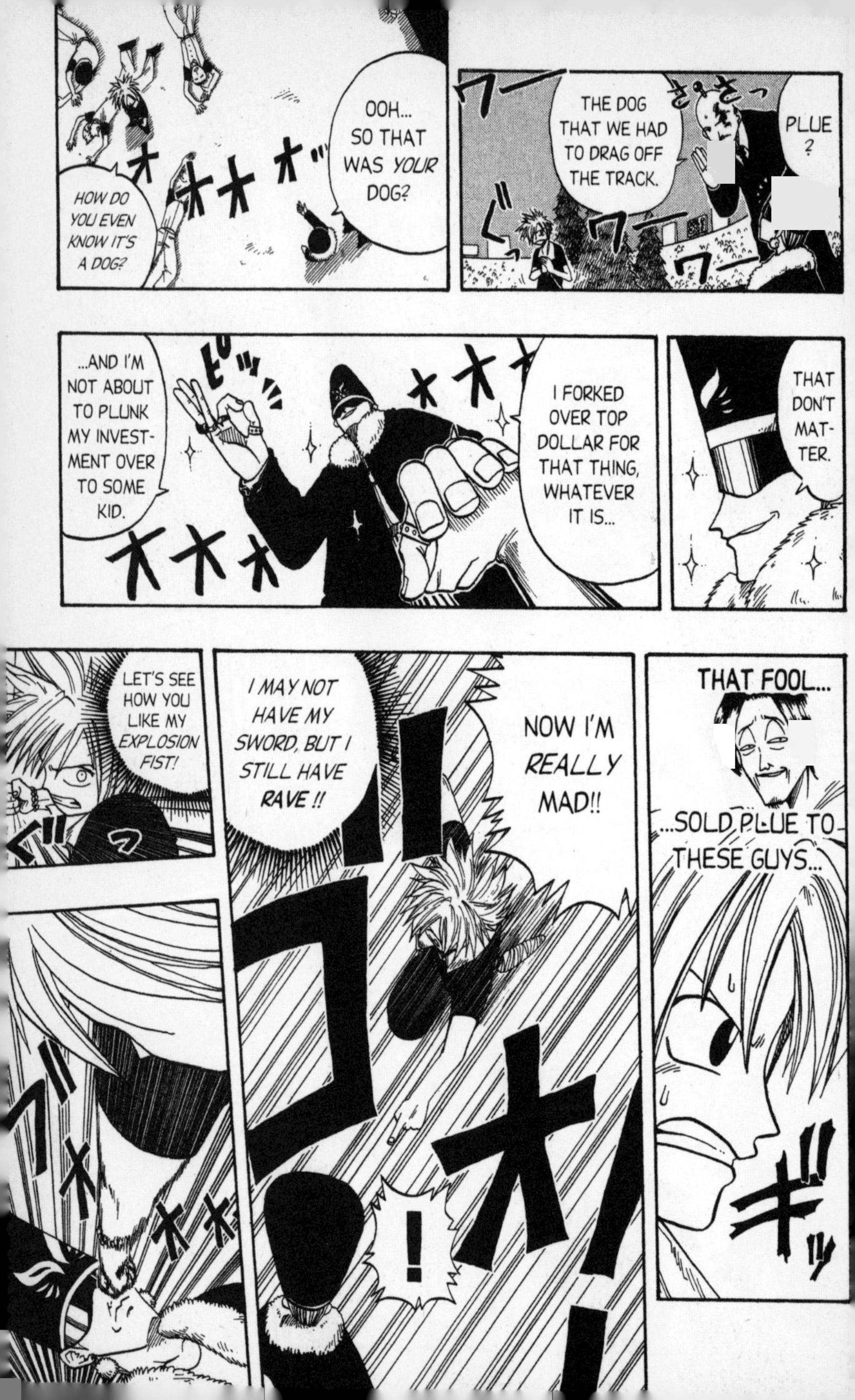
PLUE?
THE DOG THAT WE HAD TO DRAG OFF THE TRACK.
OOH... SO THAT WAS YOUR DOG?
HOW DO YOU EVEN KNOW IT'S A DOG?
THAT DON'T MATTER.
I FORKED OVER TOP DOLLAR FOR THAT THING, WHATEVER IT IS...
...AND I'M NOT ABOUT TO PLUNK MY INVESTMENT OVER TO SOME KID.
THAT FOOL...
...SOLD PLUE TO THESE GUYS...
NOW I'M REALLY MAD!!
I MAY NOT HAVE MY SWORD, BUT I STILL HAVE RAVE!!
LET'S SEE HOW YOU LIKE MY EXPLOSION FIST!
!

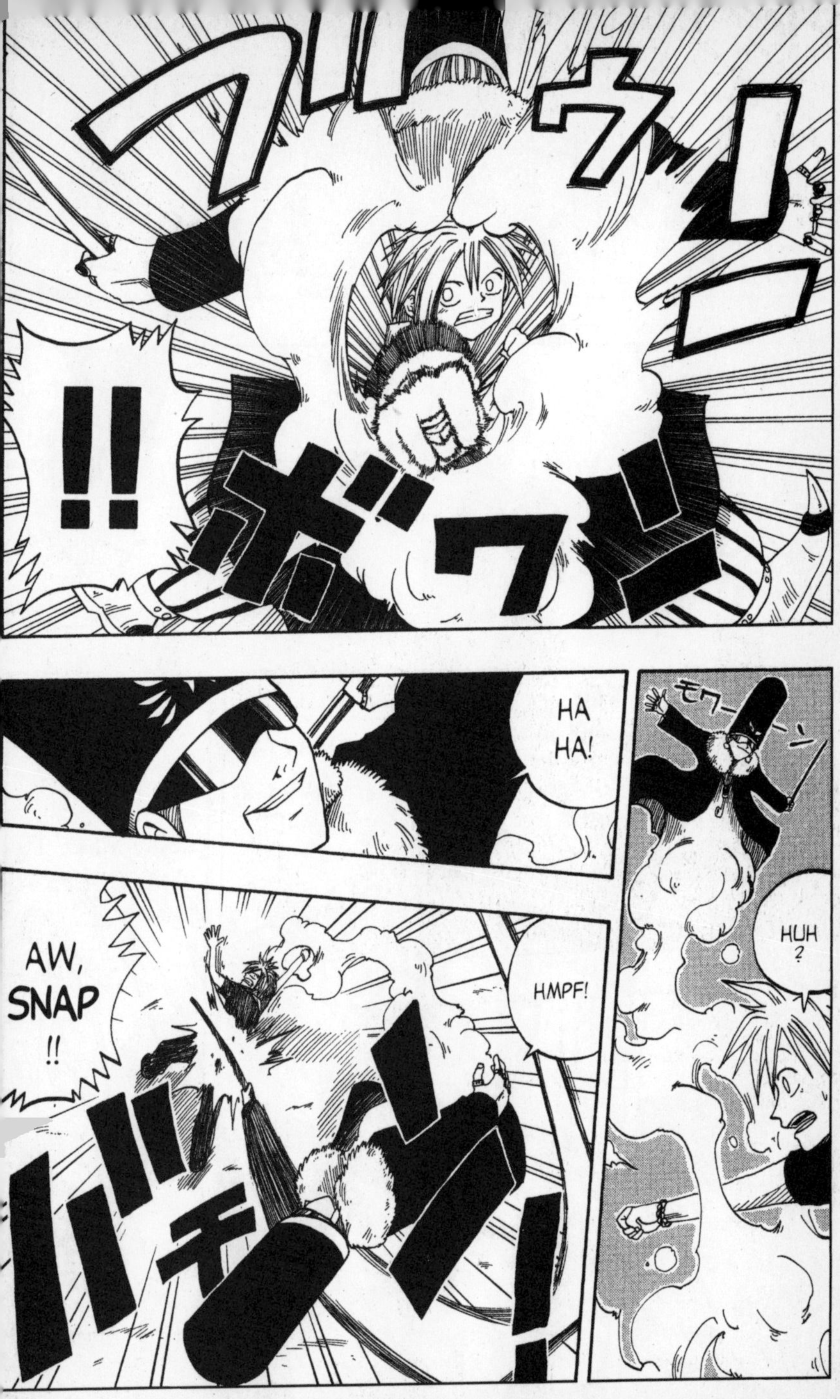

ブウーン
!!
ボワン
モワーン
HA HA!
HUH ?
HMPF!
AW, SNAP !!
バチーン!

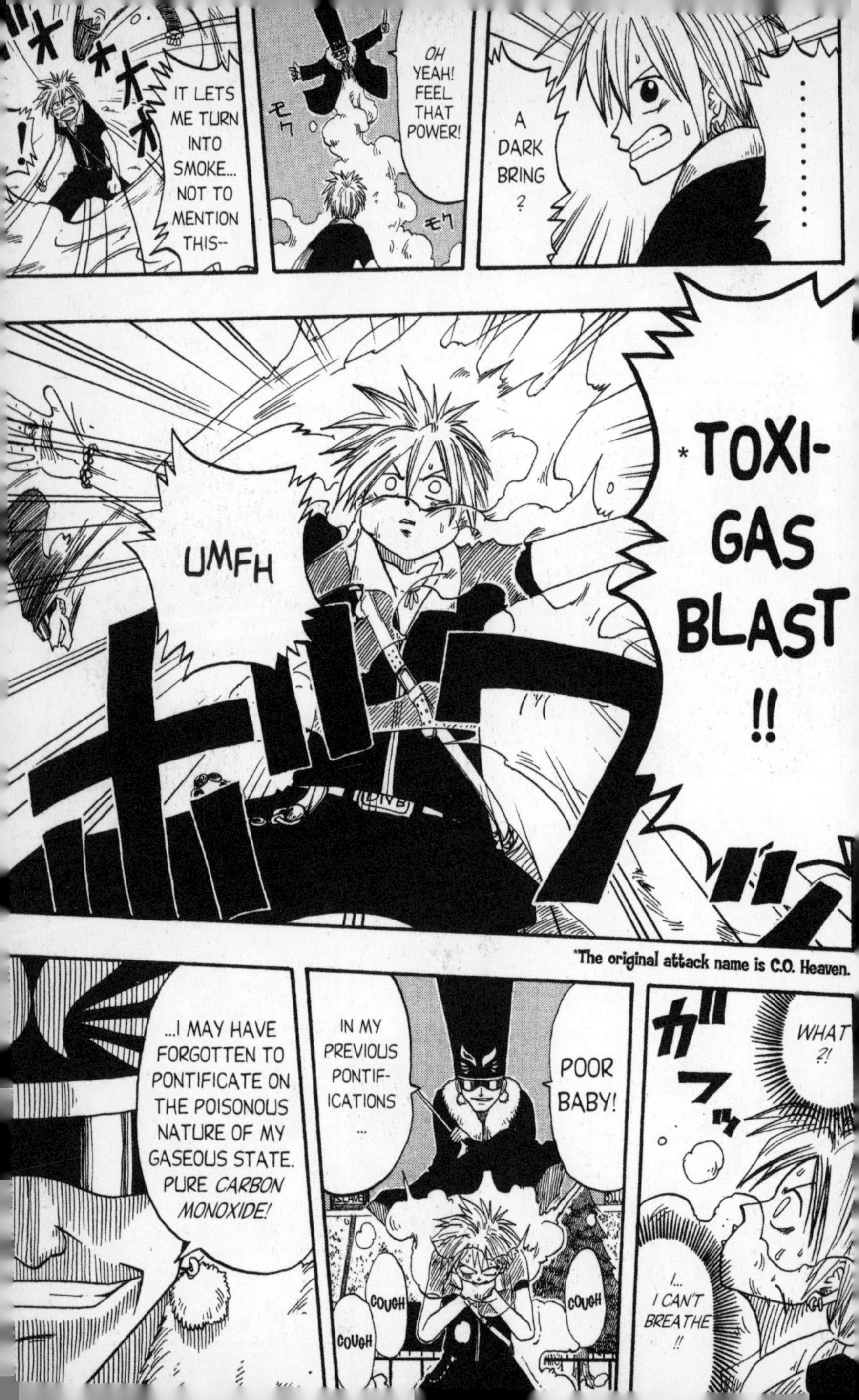
A DARK BRING ?
OH YEAH! FEEL THAT POWER!
IT LETS ME TURN INTO SMOKE... NOT TO MENTION THIS--
*TOXI-GAS BLAST!!
UMFH
WHAT?!
I... I CAN'T BREATHE!!
POOR BABY!
IN MY PREVIOUS PONTIFICATIONS...
COUGH
COUGH
COUGH
...I MAY HAVE FORGOTTEN TO PONTIFICATE ON THE POISONOUS NATURE OF MY GASEOUS STATE. PURE *CARBON MONOXIDE!*

*The original attack name is C.O. Heaven.

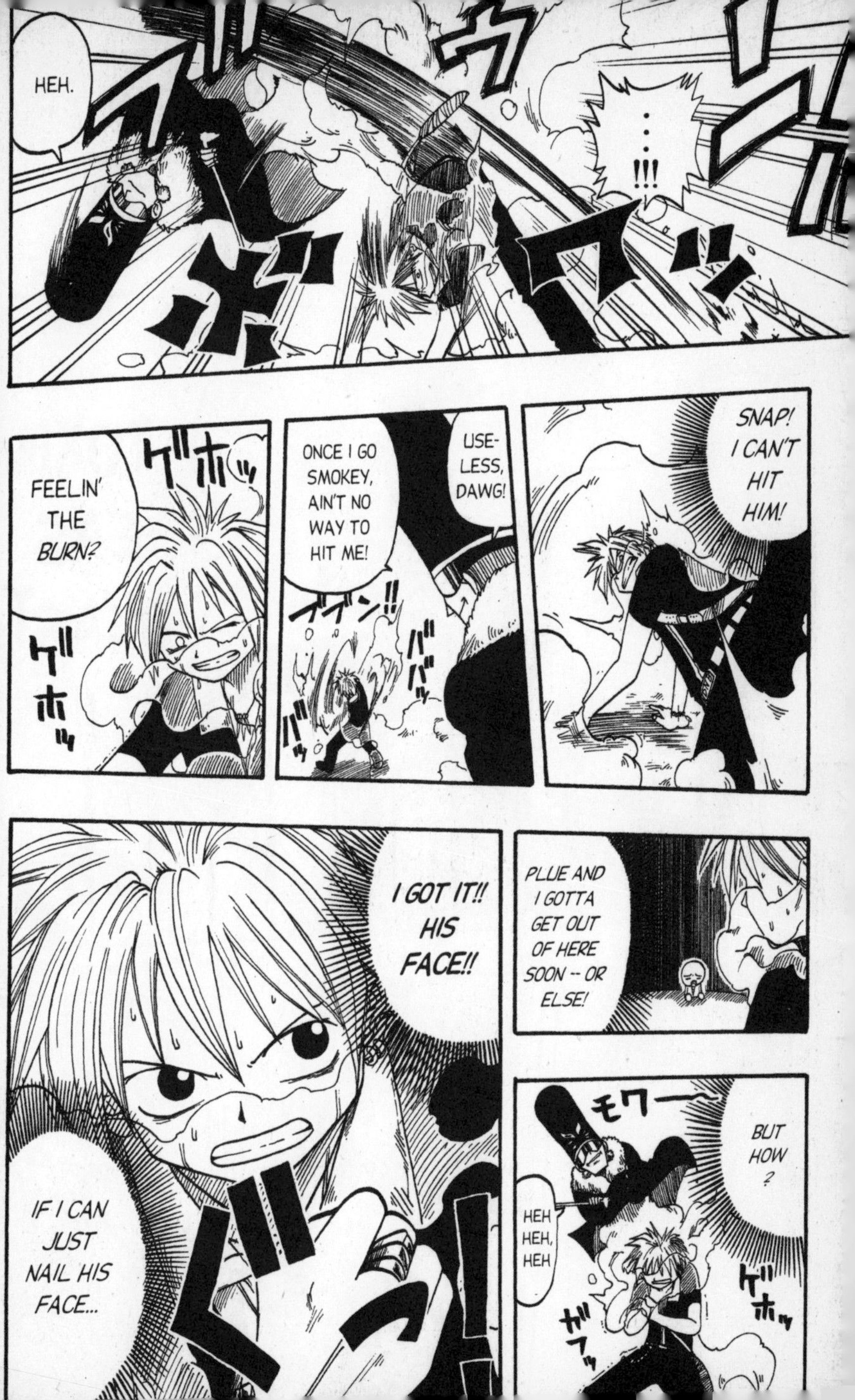
...!!!
HEH.
SNAP! I CAN'T HIT HIM!
USE-LESS, DAWG!
ONCE I GO SMOKEY, AIN'T NO WAY TO HIT ME!
FEELIN' THE BURN?
ゲホッ
ゲホッ
PLUE AND I GOTTA GET OUT OF HERE SOON -- OR ELSE!
BUT HOW?
モワー
HEH HEH, HEH
ゲホッ
ガフッ
I GOT IT!! HIS FACE!!
IF I CAN JUST NAIL HIS FACE...

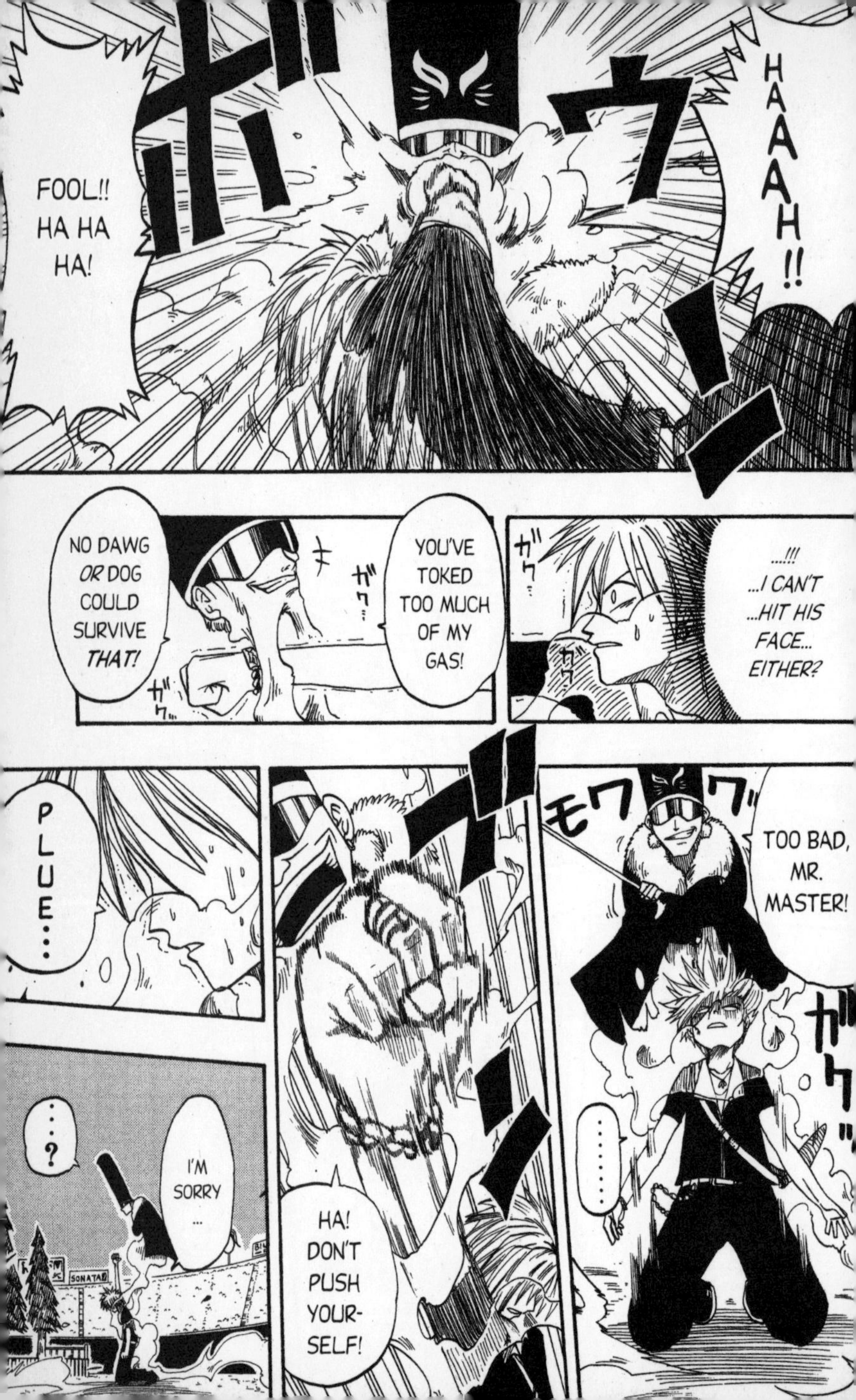
HAAAAH!!
FOOL!! HA HA HA!
...!!! ...I CAN'T ...HIT HIS FACE... EITHER?
YOU'VE TOKED TOO MUCH OF MY GAS!
NO DAWG *OR* DOG COULD SURVIVE *THAT!*
TOO BAD, MR. MASTER!
......
HA! DON'T PUSH YOURSELF!
PLUE...
I'M SORRY ...
...?
SONATA

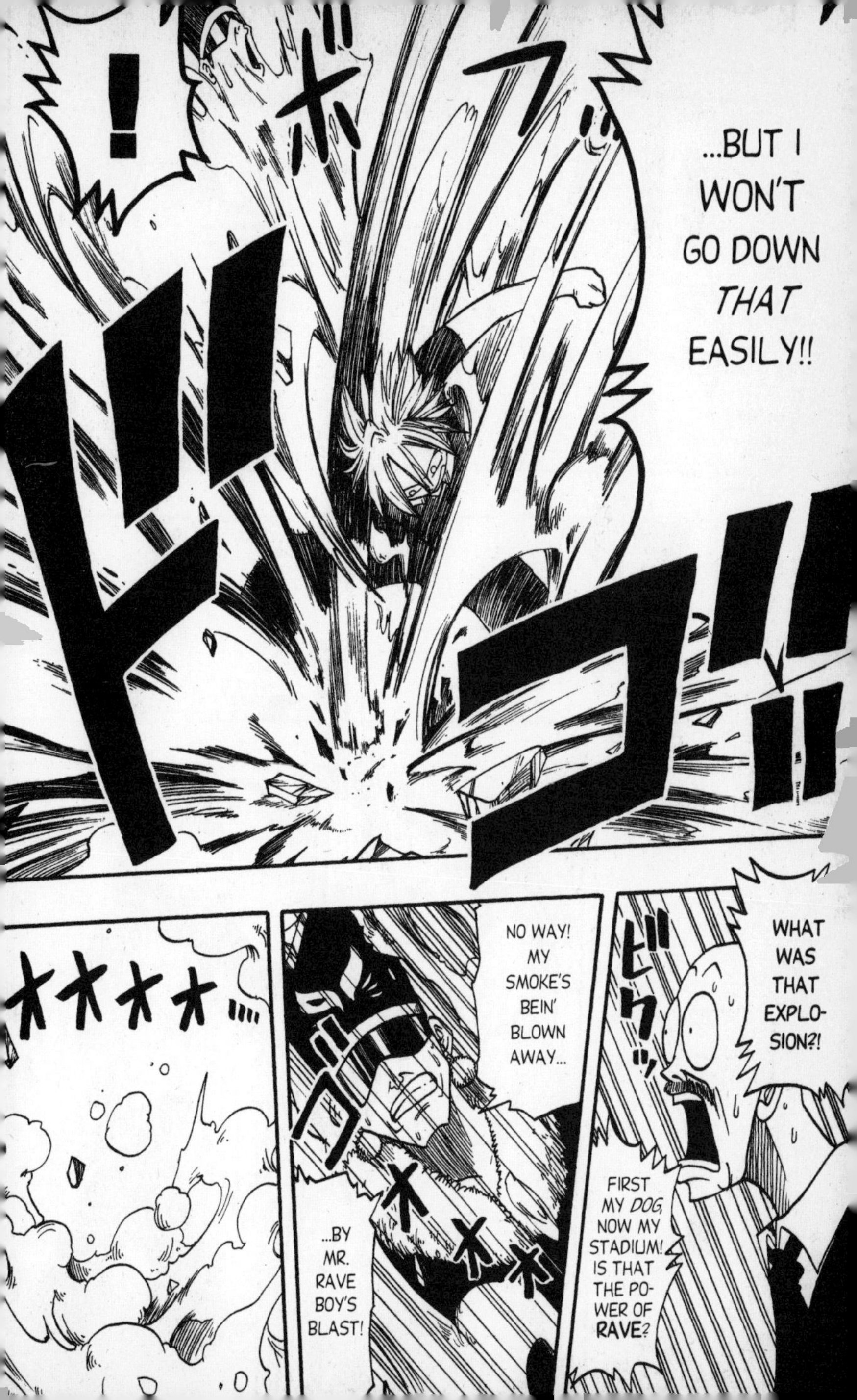
...BUT I WON'T GO DOWN *THAT* EASILY!!
WHAT WAS THAT EXPLOSION?!
FIRST MY *DOG*, NOW MY STADIUM! IS THAT THE POWER OF **RAVE**?
NO WAY! MY SMOKE'S BEIN' BLOWN AWAY...
...BY MR. RAVE BOY'S BLAST!

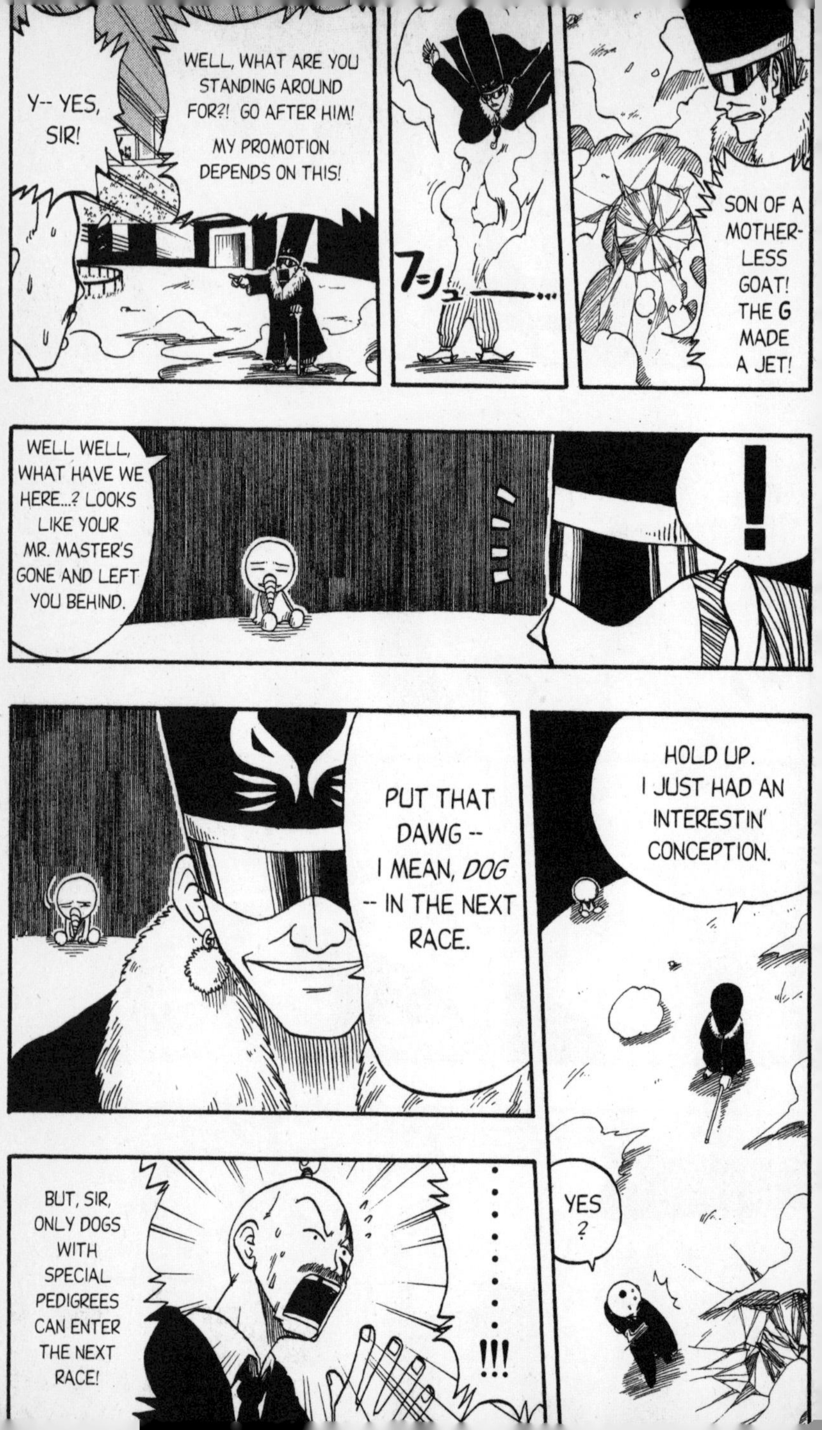

SON OF A MOTHER-LESS GOAT! THE G MADE A JET!
フシュー……
WELL, WHAT ARE YOU STANDING AROUND FOR?! GO AFTER HIM!
MY PROMOTION DEPENDS ON THIS!
Y-- YES, SIR!
!
WELL WELL, WHAT HAVE WE HERE...? LOOKS LIKE YOUR MR. MASTER'S GONE AND LEFT YOU BEHIND.
HOLD UP. I JUST HAD AN INTERESTIN' CONCEPTION.
YES?
PUT THAT DAWG -- I MEAN, *DOG* -- IN THE NEXT RACE.
........!!!
BUT, SIR, ONLY DOGS WITH SPECIAL PEDIGREES CAN ENTER THE NEXT RACE!

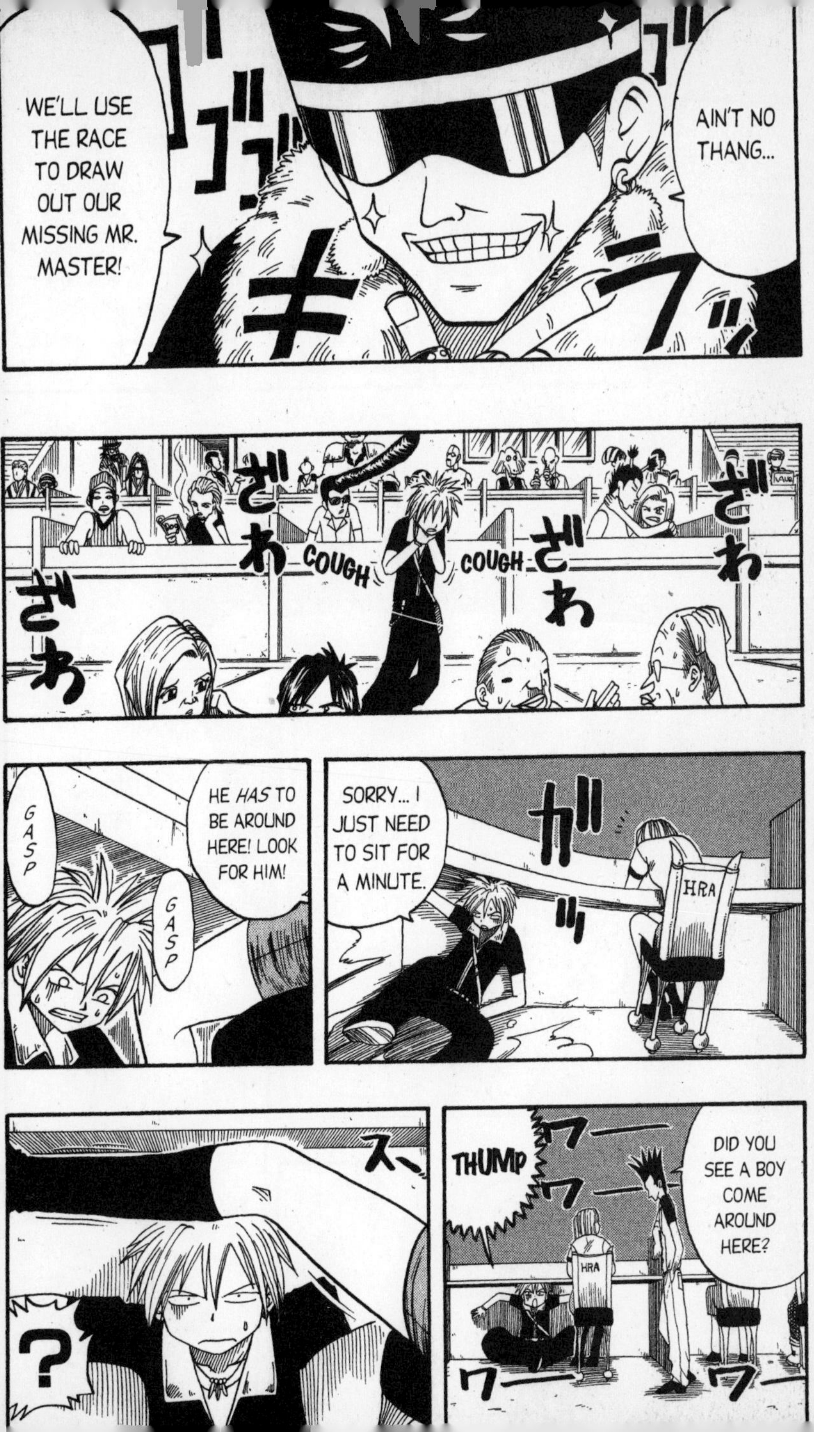
AIN'T NO THANG...
WE'LL USE THE RACE TO DRAW OUT OUR MISSING MR. MASTER!
COUGH
COUGH
SORRY... I JUST NEED TO SIT FOR A MINUTE.
HRA
HE HAS TO BE AROUND HERE! LOOK FOR HIM!
GASP
GASP
DID YOU SEE A BOY COME AROUND HERE?
THUMP
HRA
?

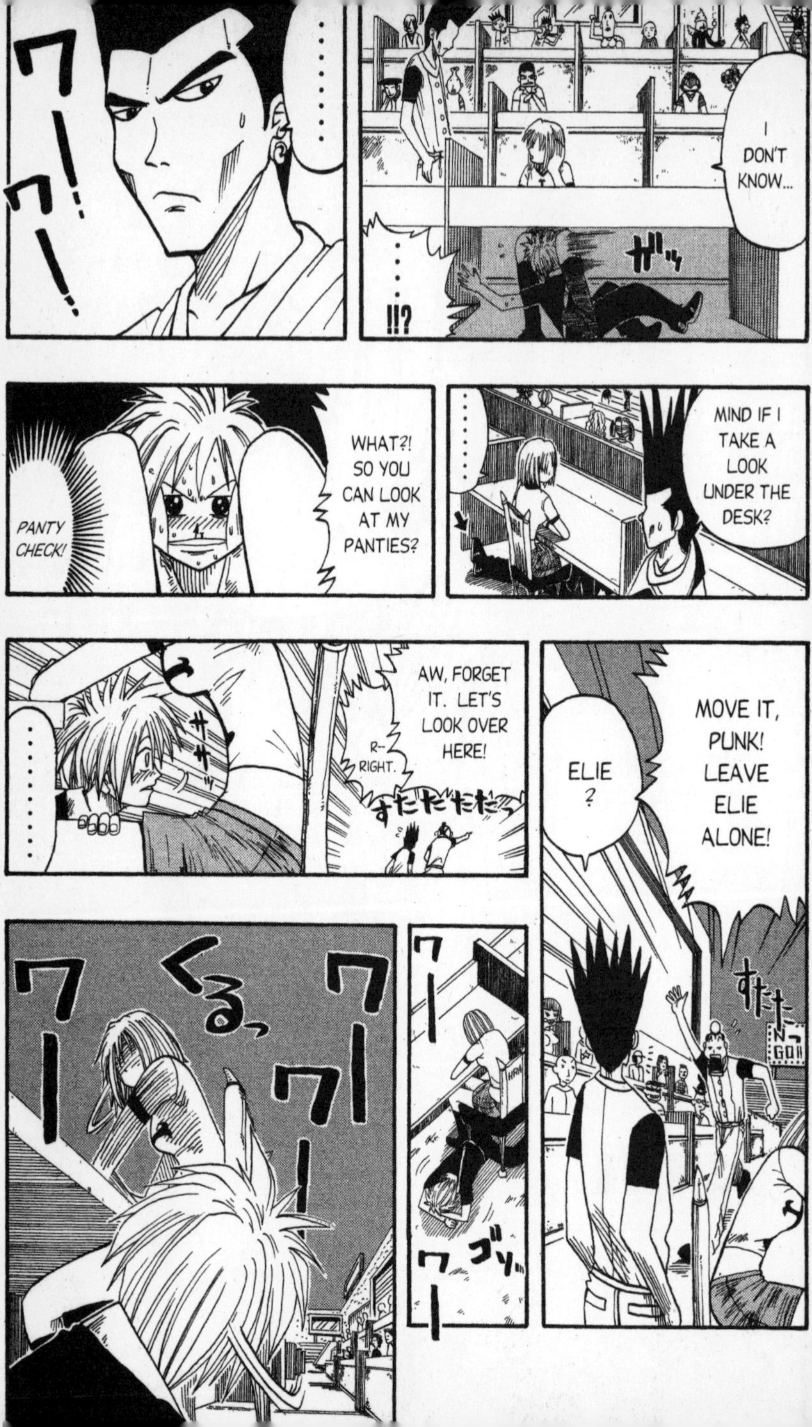
I DON'T KNOW...
ザッ
...
!!?
...
ワーー!!
ワーー!!
MIND IF I TAKE A LOOK UNDER THE DESK?
...
WHAT?! SO YOU CAN LOOK AT MY PANTIES?
PANTY CHECK!
MOVE IT, PUNK! LEAVE ELIE ALONE!
ELIE?
すたた
AW, FORGET IT. LET'S LOOK OVER HERE!
R--RIGHT.
すたたたたっ
ササッ
....
ワー
ゴツ
ワー
くるっ
ワー
ワー
ワー
ワー

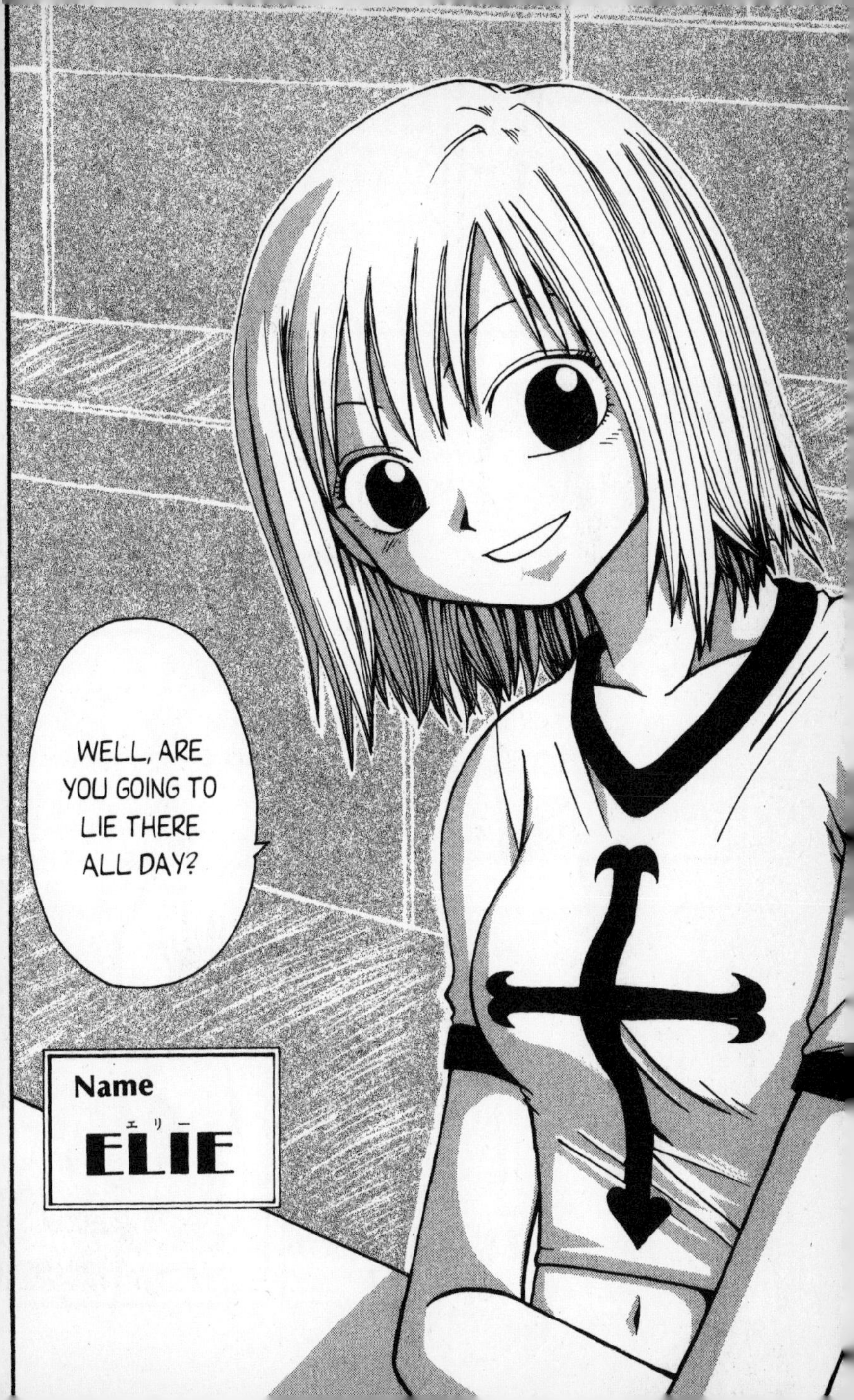
WELL, ARE YOU GOING TO LIE THERE ALL DAY?
Name
エリー
ELIE

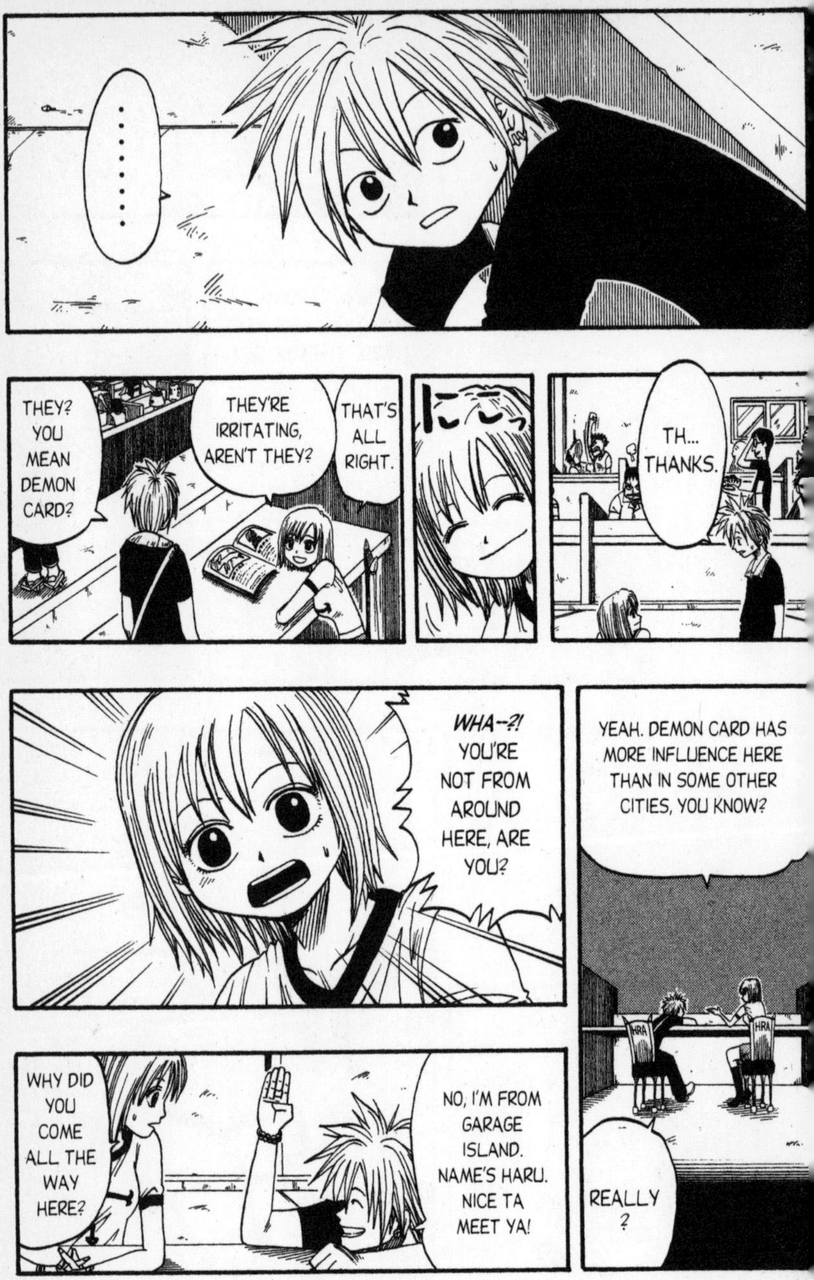
......
TH... THANKS.
にこっ
THAT'S ALL RIGHT.
THEY'RE IRRITATING, AREN'T THEY?
THEY? YOU MEAN DEMON CARD?
YEAH. DEMON CARD HAS MORE INFLUENCE HERE THAN IN SOME OTHER CITIES, YOU KNOW?
REALLY?
WHA--?! YOU'RE NOT FROM AROUND HERE, ARE YOU?
NO, I'M FROM GARAGE ISLAND. NAME'S HARU. NICE TA MEET YA!
WHY DID YOU COME ALL THE WAY HERE?

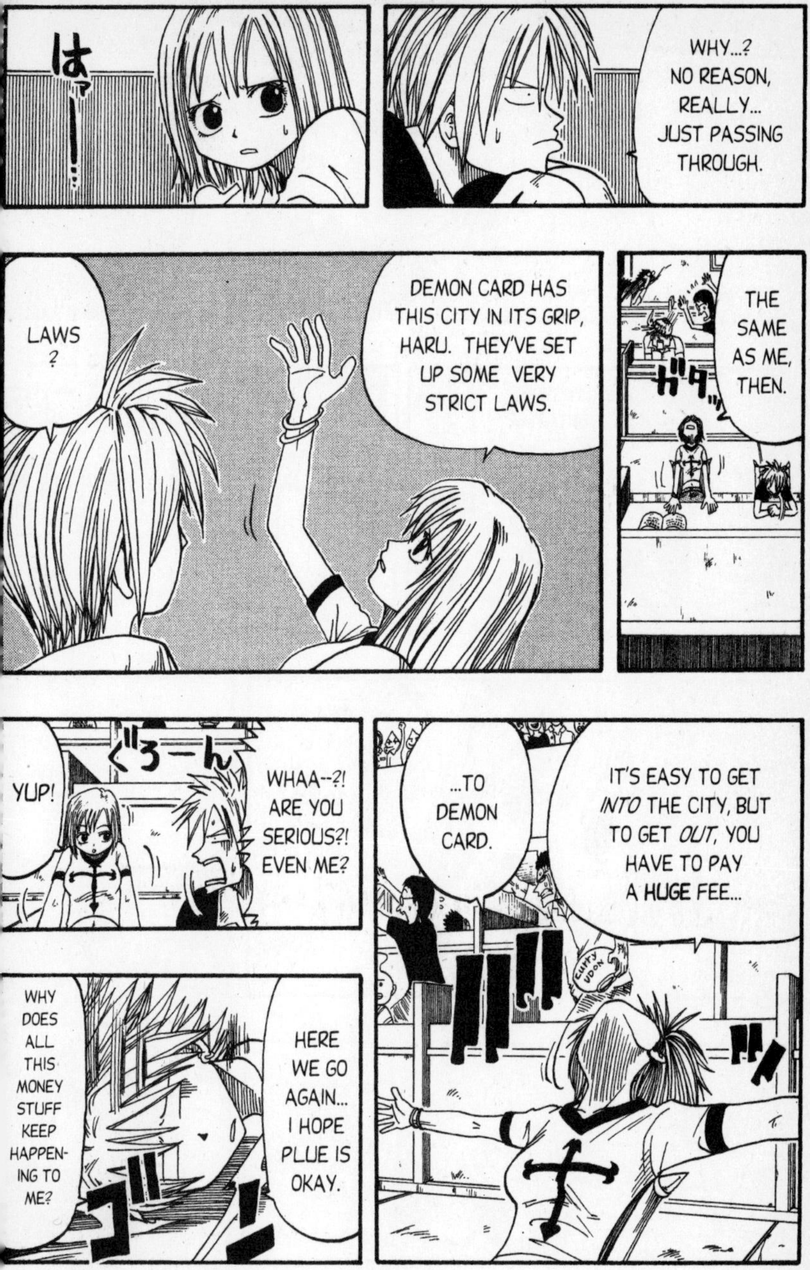
WHY...? NO REASON, REALLY... JUST PASSING THROUGH.
はァー…!!
THE SAME AS ME, THEN.
ガタッ
DEMON CARD HAS THIS CITY IN ITS GRIP, HARU. THEY'VE SET UP SOME VERY STRICT LAWS.
LAWS?
IT'S EASY TO GET *INTO* THE CITY, BUT TO GET *OUT*, YOU HAVE TO PAY A **HUGE** FEE...
...TO DEMON CARD.
WHAA--?! ARE YOU SERIOUS?! EVEN ME?
YUP!
HERE WE GO AGAIN... I HOPE PLUE IS OKAY.
WHY DOES ALL THIS MONEY STUFF KEEP HAPPENING TO ME?

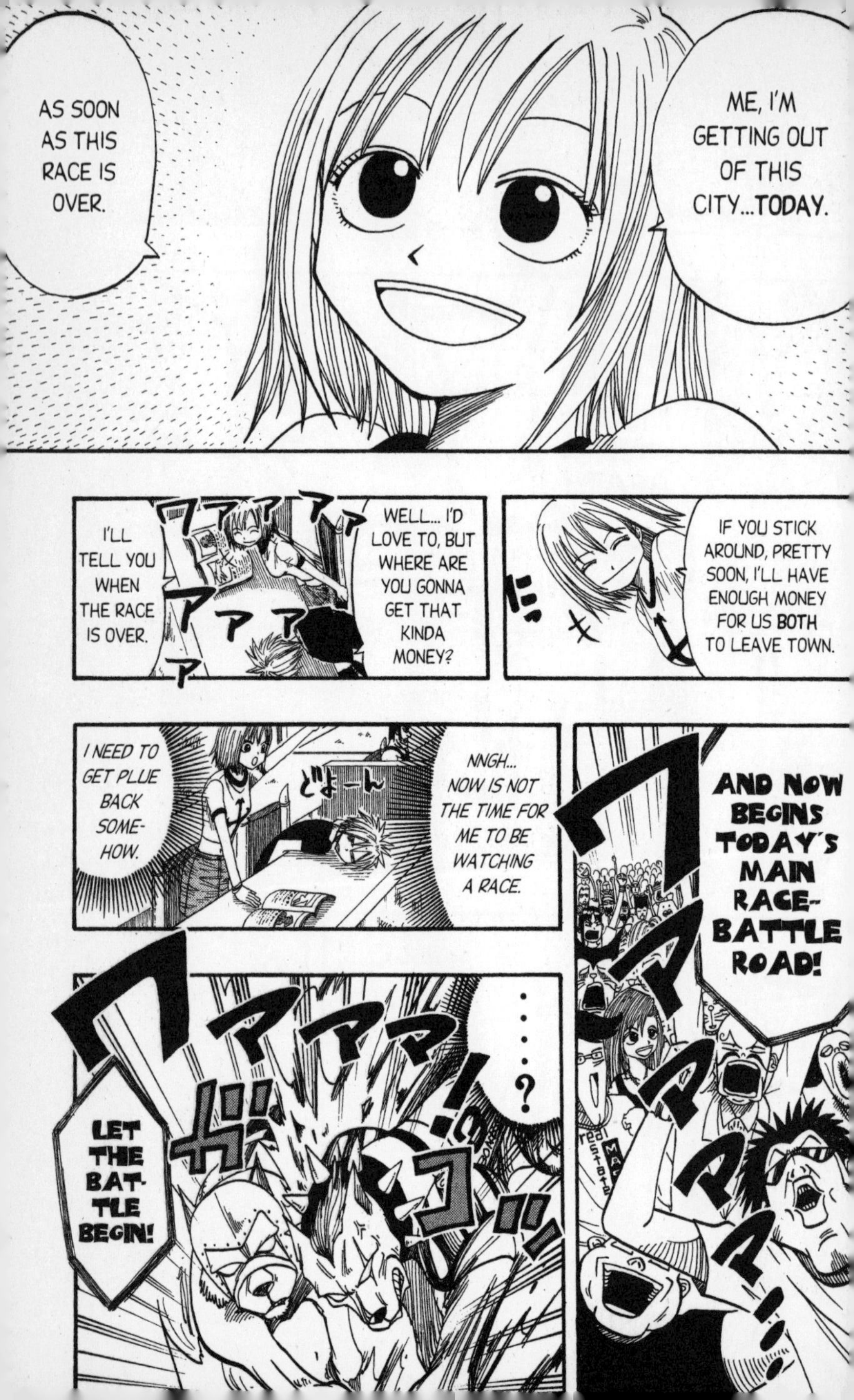
ME, I'M GETTING OUT OF THIS CITY...TODAY.
AS SOON AS THIS RACE IS OVER.
IF YOU STICK AROUND, PRETTY SOON, I'LL HAVE ENOUGH MONEY FOR US BOTH TO LEAVE TOWN.
WELL... I'D LOVE TO, BUT WHERE ARE YOU GONNA GET THAT KINDA MONEY?
I'LL TELL YOU WHEN THE RACE IS OVER.
AND NOW BEGINS TODAY'S MAIN RACE-BATTLE ROAD!
NNGH... NOW IS NOT THE TIME FOR ME TO BE WATCHING A RACE.
どよーん
I NEED TO GET PLUE BACK SOME-HOW.
...?
LET THE BAT-TLE BEGIN!

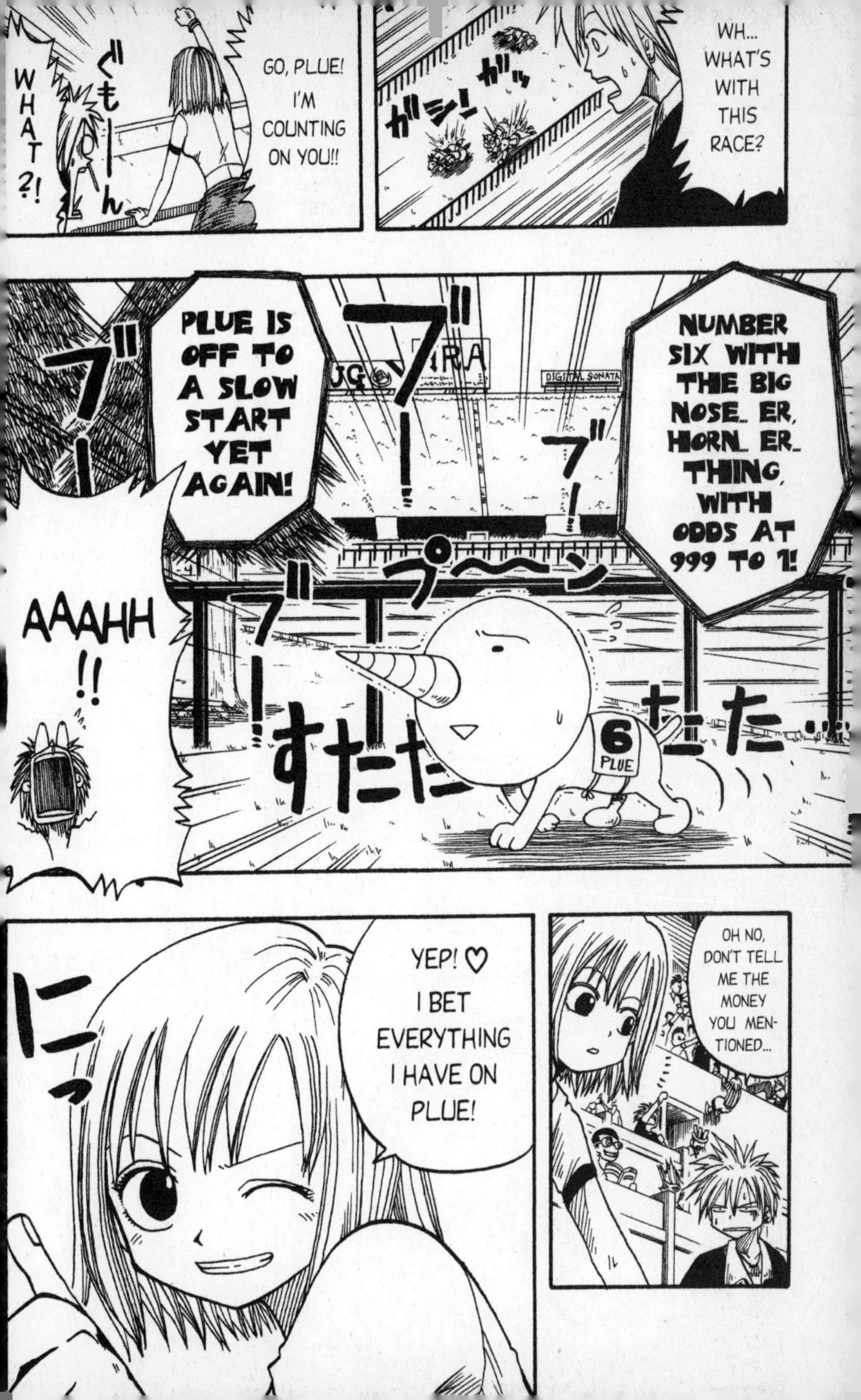
WH... WHAT'S WITH THIS RACE?
ガシ!
ガッ
GO, PLUE! I'M COUNTING ON YOU!!
WHAT?!
ぐもーん
NUMBER SIX WITH THE BIG NOSE... ER, HORN... ER... THING, WITH ODDS AT 999 TO 1!
ブー!
プ〜ン
PLUE IS OFF TO A SLOW START YET AGAIN!
ブー!
ブー!
すたた
たた...
AAAHH!!
OH NO, DON'T TELL ME THE MONEY YOU MENTIONED...
YEP! ♡ I BET EVERYTHING I HAVE ON PLUE!
にっ

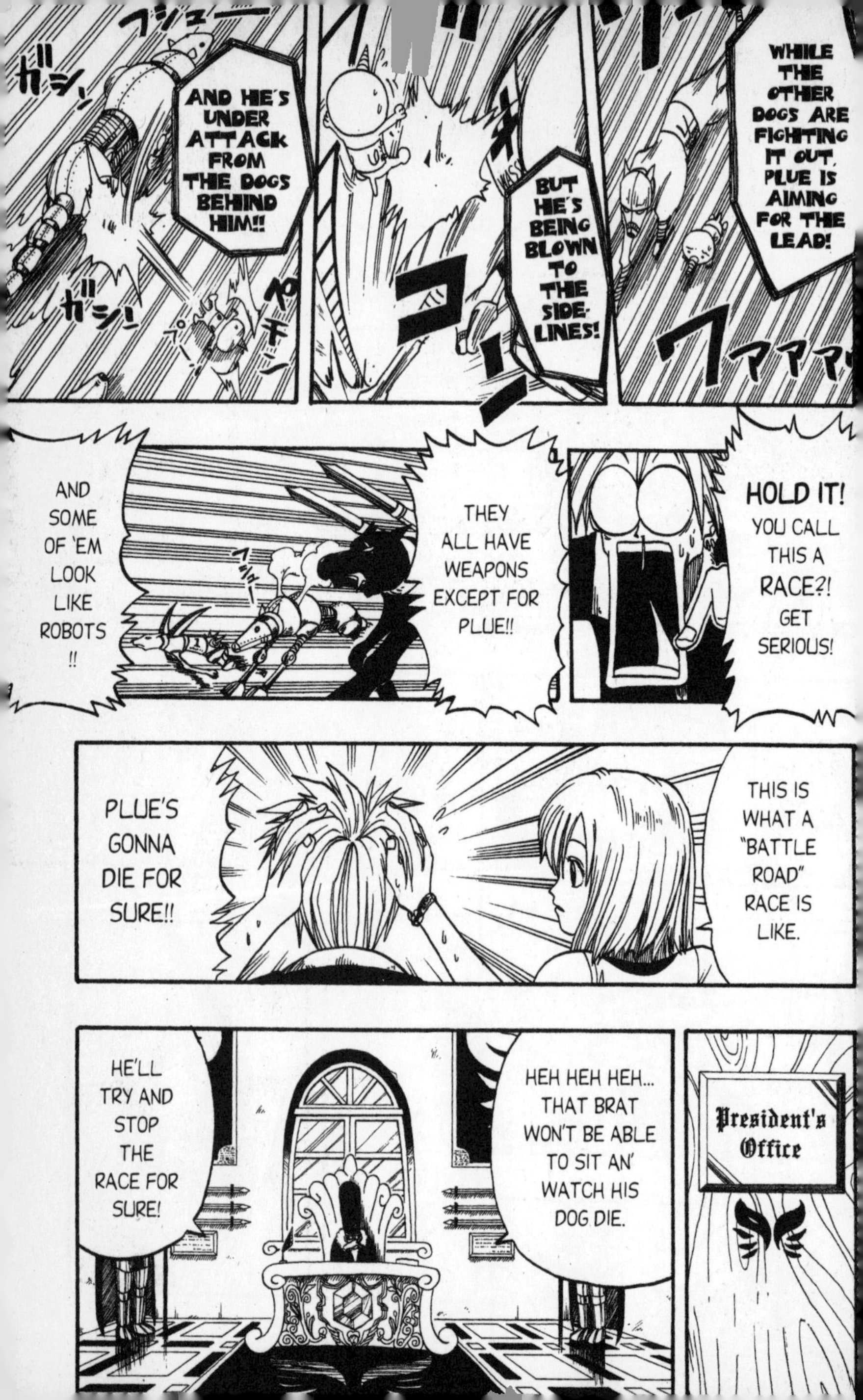
WHILE THE OTHER DOGS ARE FIGHTING IT OUT, PLUE IS AIMING FOR THE LEAD!
BUT HE'S BEING BLOWN TO THE SIDELINES!
AND HE'S UNDER ATTACK FROM THE DOGS BEHIND HIM!!
HOLD IT! YOU CALL THIS A RACE?! GET SERIOUS!
THEY ALL HAVE WEAPONS EXCEPT FOR PLUE!!
AND SOME OF 'EM LOOK LIKE ROBOTS!!
THIS IS WHAT A "BATTLE ROAD" RACE IS LIKE.
PLUE'S GONNA DIE FOR SURE!!
President's Office
HEH HEH HEH... THAT BRAT WON'T BE ABLE TO SIT AN' WATCH HIS DOG DIE.
HE'LL TRY AND STOP THE RACE FOR SURE!

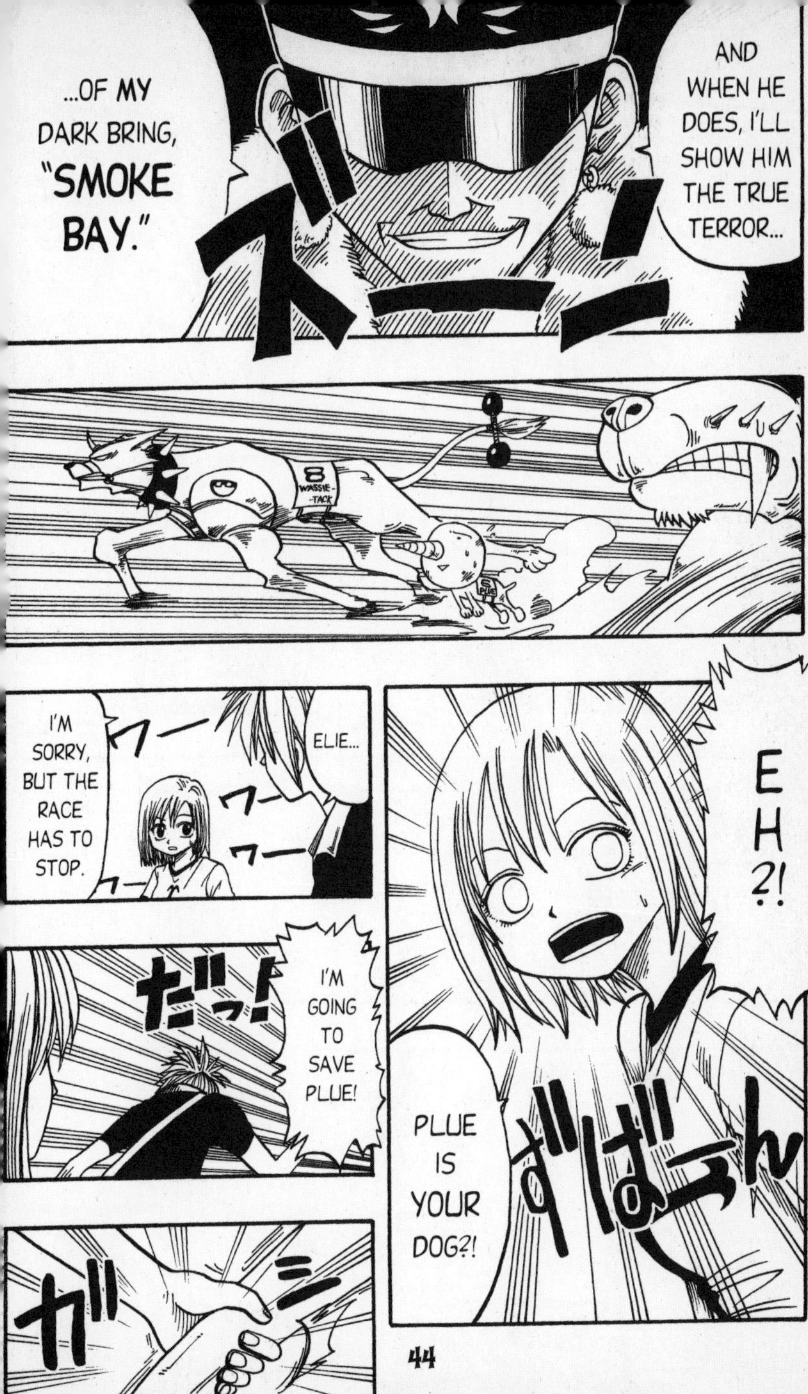
AND WHEN HE DOES, I'LL SHOW HIM THE TRUE TERROR...
...OF MY DARK BRING, "SMOKE BAY."
8 WASSIE-TACK
EH?!
PLUE IS YOUR DOG?!
ELIE...
I'M SORRY, BUT THE RACE HAS TO STOP.
I'M GOING TO SAVE PLUE!

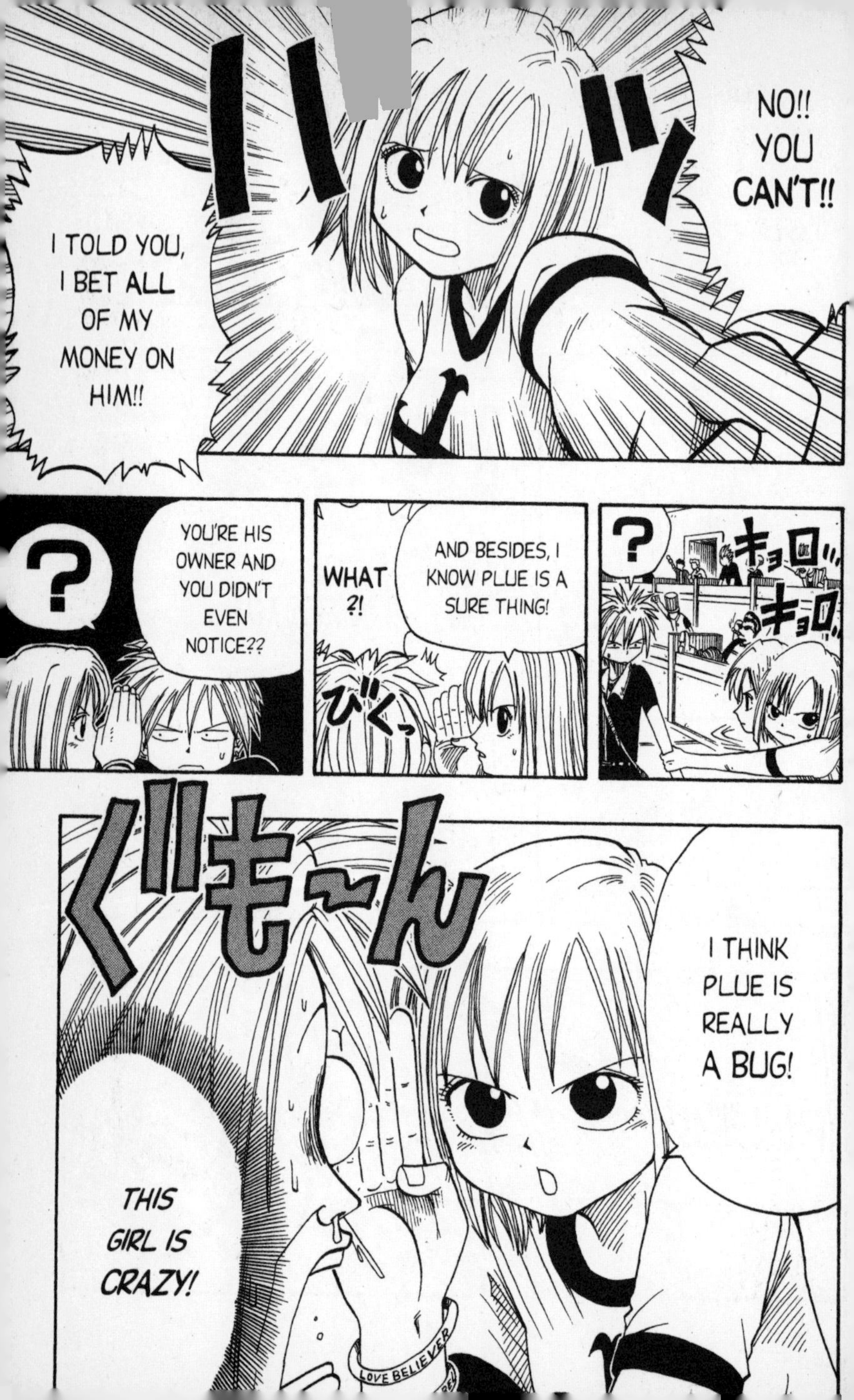
NO!! YOU CAN'T!!
I TOLD YOU, I BET ALL OF MY MONEY ON HIM!!
?
キョロ
キョロ
AND BESIDES, I KNOW PLUE IS A SURE THING!
WHAT?!
びくっ
?
YOU'RE HIS OWNER AND YOU DIDN'T EVEN NOTICE??
ぐも～ん
I THINK PLUE IS REALLY A BUG!
THIS GIRL IS CRAZY!
LOVE BELIEVER

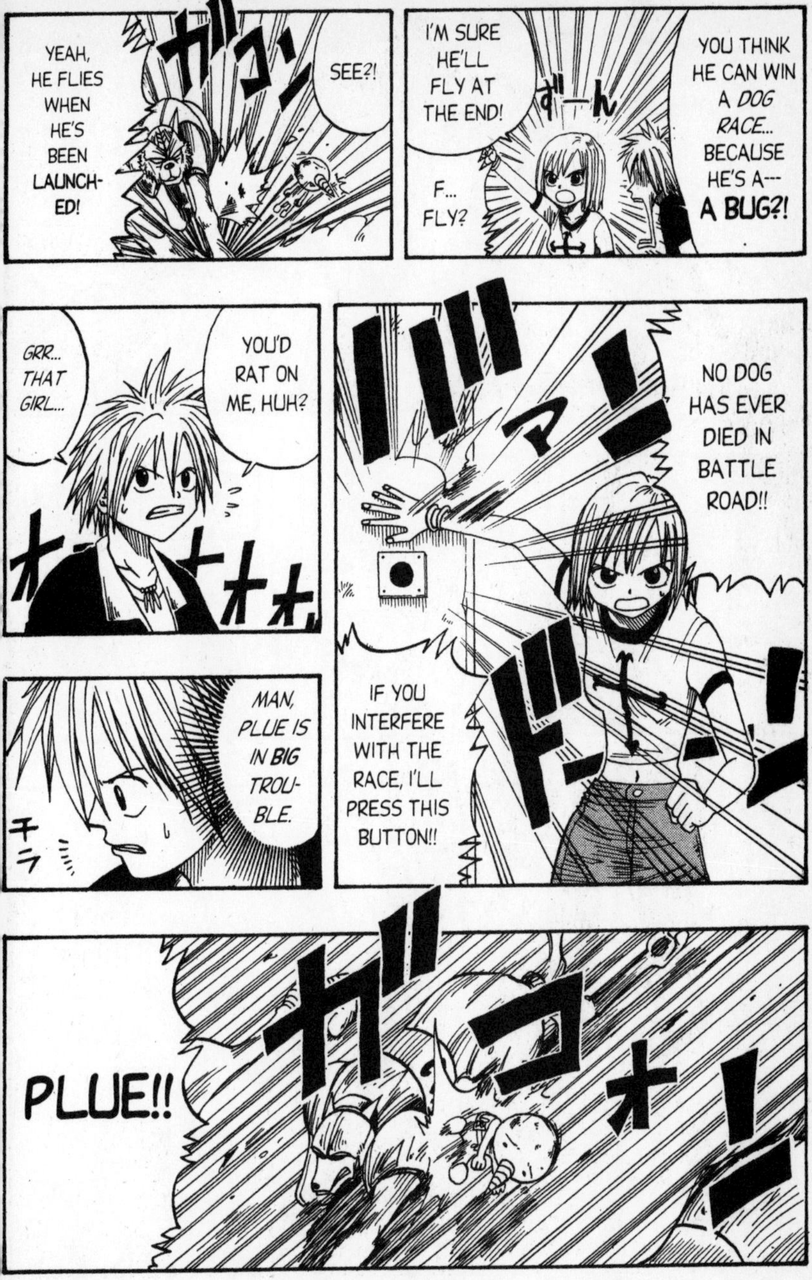
YOU THINK HE CAN WIN A *DOG RACE*... BECAUSE HE'S A--- **A BUG?!**
I'M SURE HE'LL FLY AT THE END!
F... FLY?
SEE?!
YEAH, HE FLIES WHEN HE'S BEEN LAUNCH-ED!
NO DOG HAS EVER DIED IN BATTLE ROAD!!
IF YOU INTERFERE WITH THE RACE, I'LL PRESS THIS BUTTON!!
YOU'D RAT ON ME, HUH?
GRR... THAT GIRL...
*MAN, PLUE IS IN **BIG** TROUBLE.*
PLUE!!

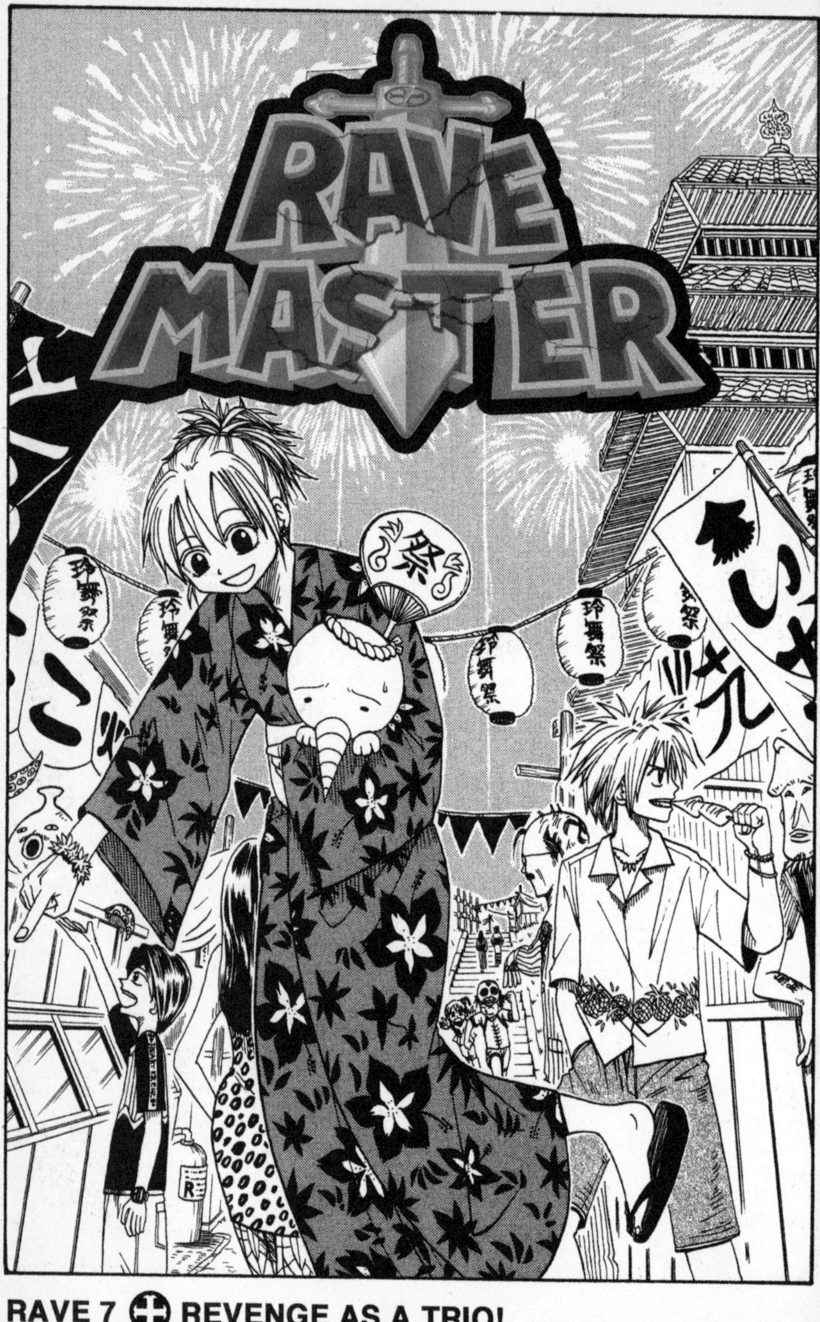
RAVE MASTER
祭
玲舞祭

RAVE 7 ✠ REVENGE AS A TRIO!

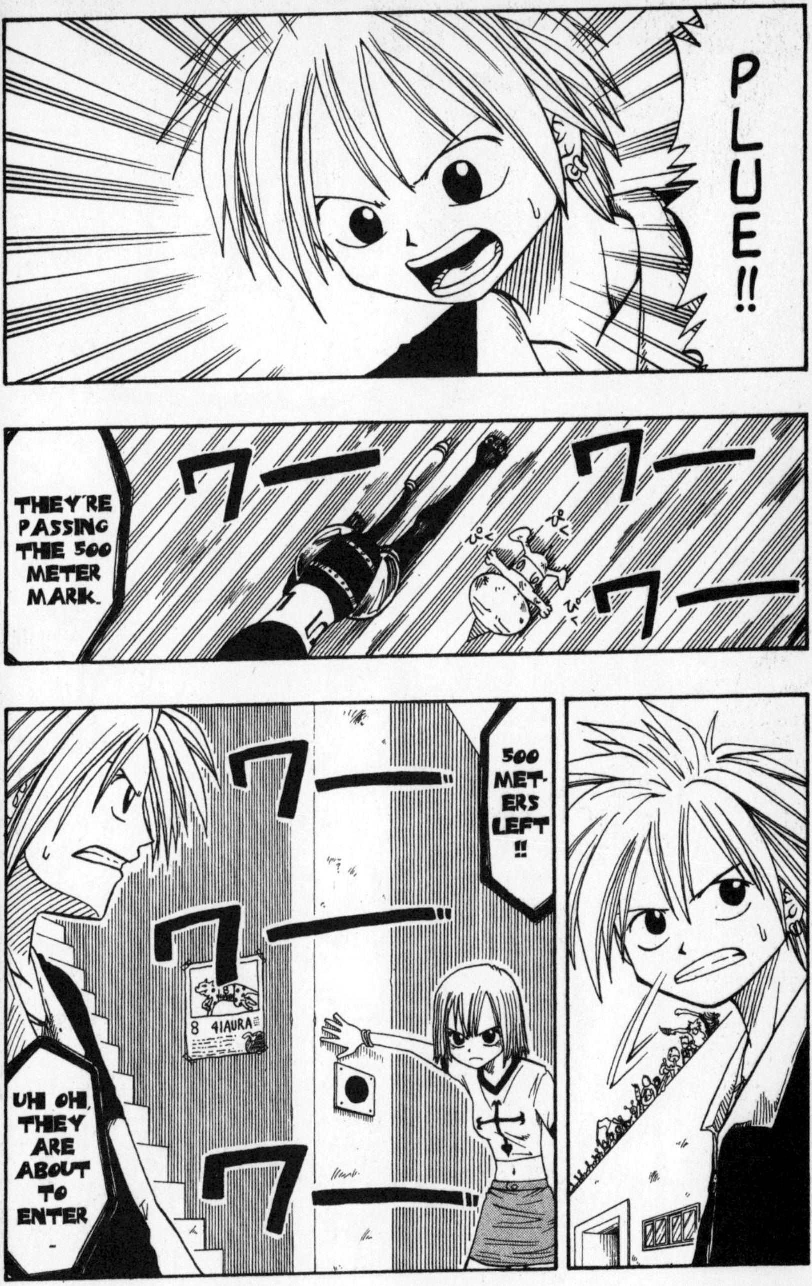
PLUE!!
ワー
ワー
ワー
THEY'RE PASSING THE 500 METER MARK...
500 METERS LEFT!!
ワー
ワー
ワー
UH OH, THEY ARE ABOUT TO ENTER...

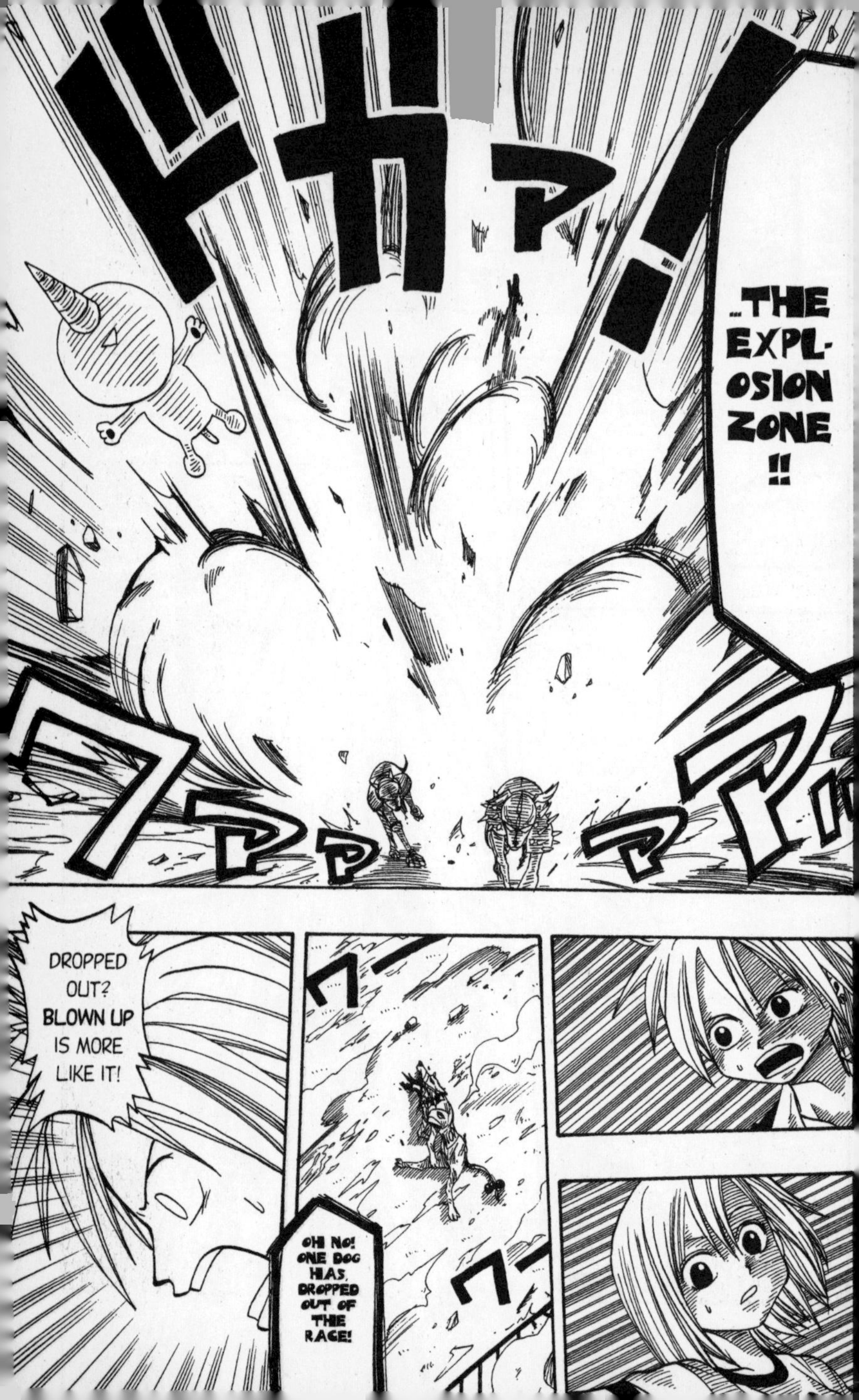
..THE EXPL-OSION ZONE!!
OH NO! ONE DOG HAS, DROPPED OUT OF THE RACE!
DROPPED OUT? BLOWN UP IS MORE LIKE IT!

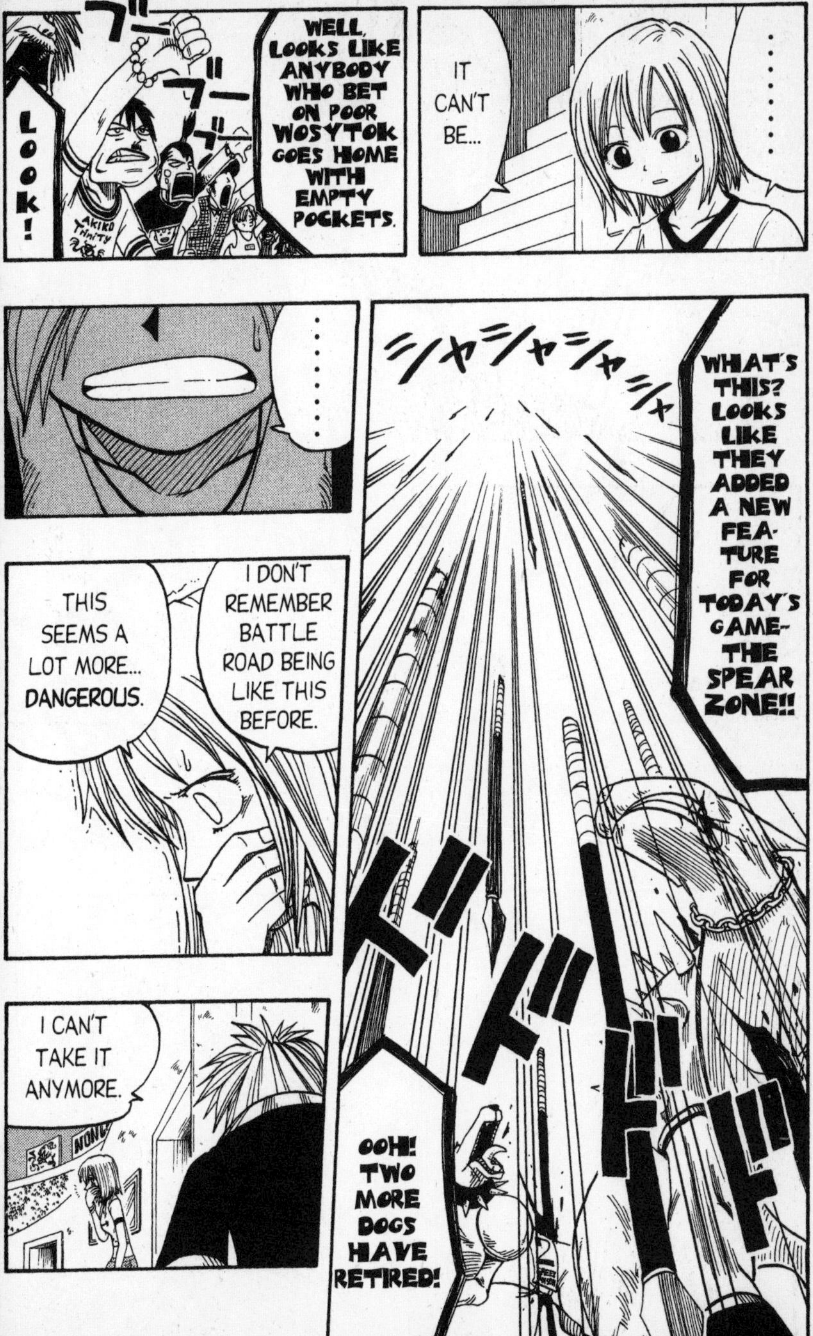
......
IT CAN'T BE...
WELL, LOOKS LIKE ANYBODY WHO BET ON POOR WOSYTOK GOES HOME WITH EMPTY POCKETS.
ブーブーブー
LOOK!
WHAT'S THIS? LOOKS LIKE THEY ADDED A NEW FEA- TURE FOR TODAY'S GAME- THE SPEAR ZONE!!
シャシャシャシャ
ドドドド
OOH! TWO MORE DOGS HAVE RETIRED!
......
I DON'T REMEMBER BATTLE ROAD BEING LIKE THIS BEFORE.
THIS SEEMS A LOT MORE... DANGEROUS.
I CAN'T TAKE IT ANYMORE.

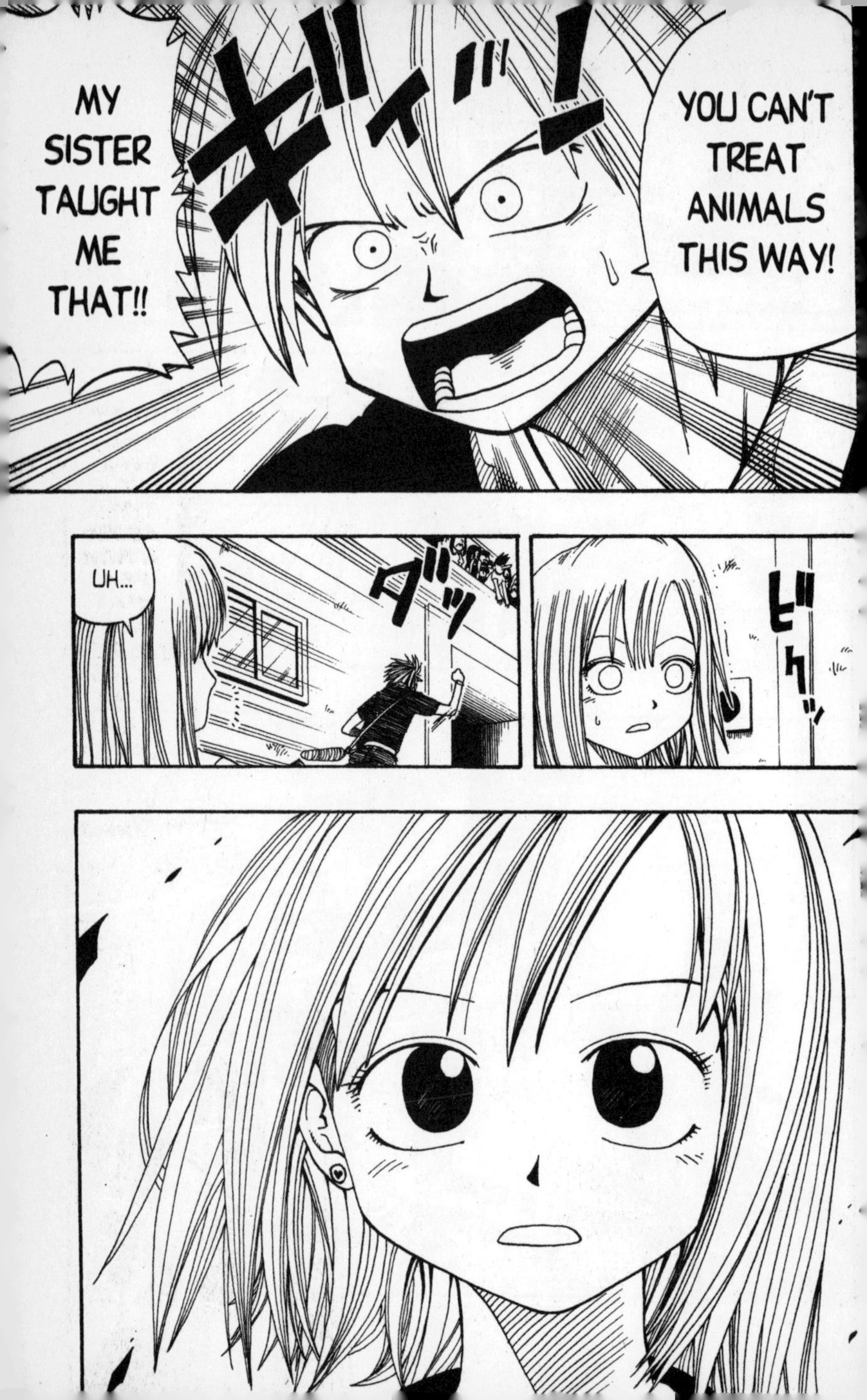
YOU CAN'T TREAT ANIMALS THIS WAY!
MY SISTER TAUGHT ME THAT!!
UH...

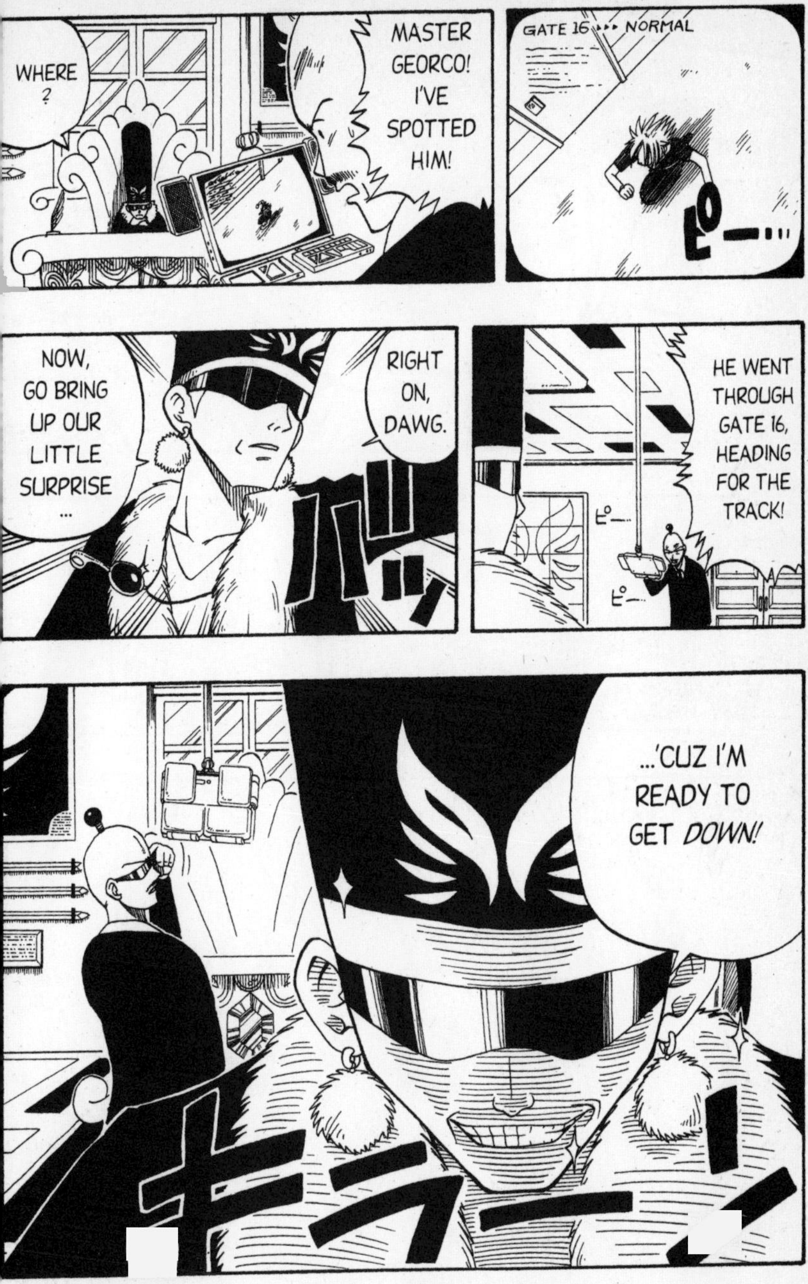
GATE 16 ▸▸▸ NORMAL
MASTER GEORCO! I'VE SPOTTED HIM!
WHERE ?
HE WENT THROUGH GATE 16, HEADING FOR THE TRACK!
RIGHT ON, DAWG.
NOW, GO BRING UP OUR LITTLE SURPRISE ...
...'CUZ I'M READY TO GET *DOWN!*

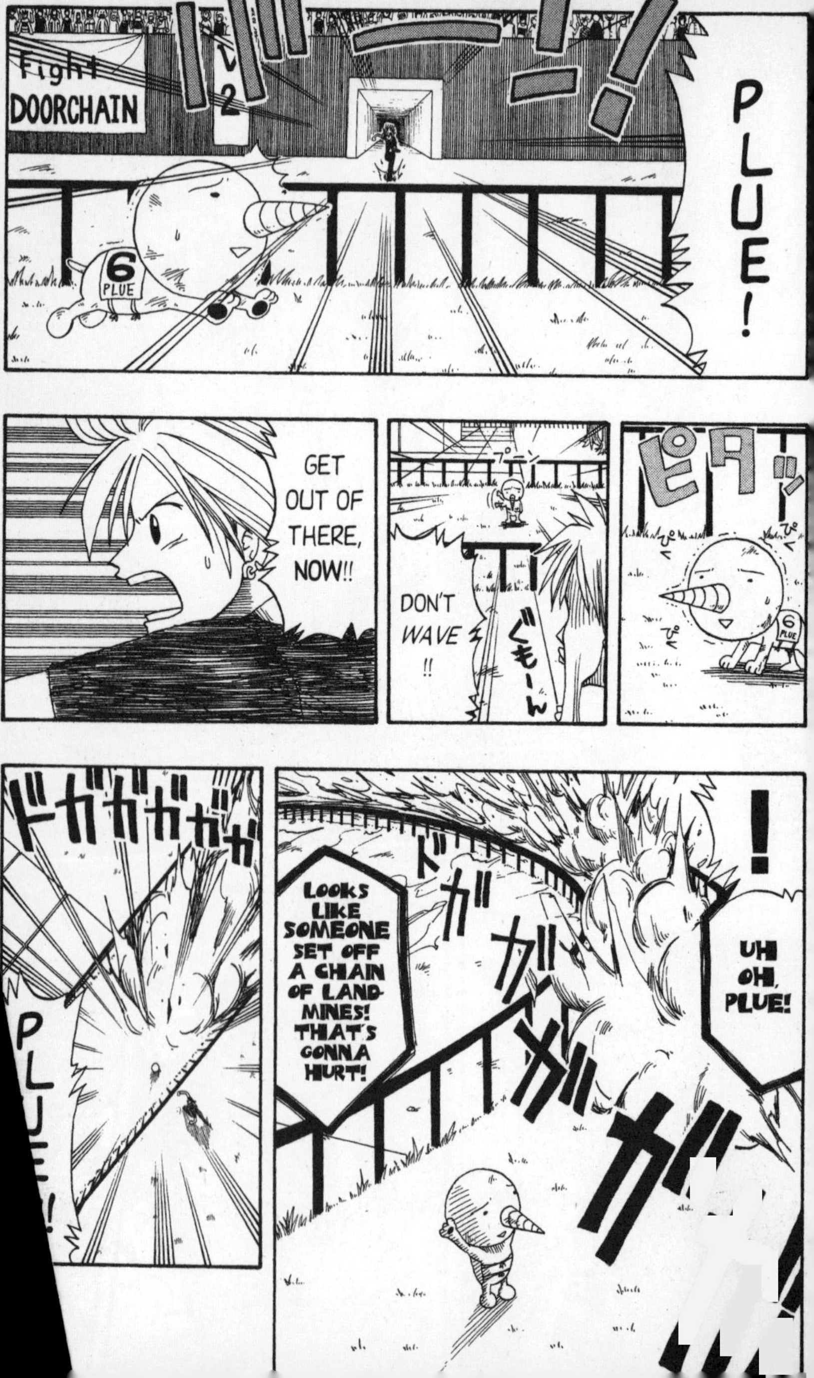
Fight
DOORCHAIN
V2
PLUE!
DON'T WAVE!!
GET OUT OF THERE, NOW!!
!
UH OH, PLUE!
LOOKS LIKE SOMEONE SET OFF A CHAIN OF LAND-MINES! THAT'S GONNA HURT!
PLUE!

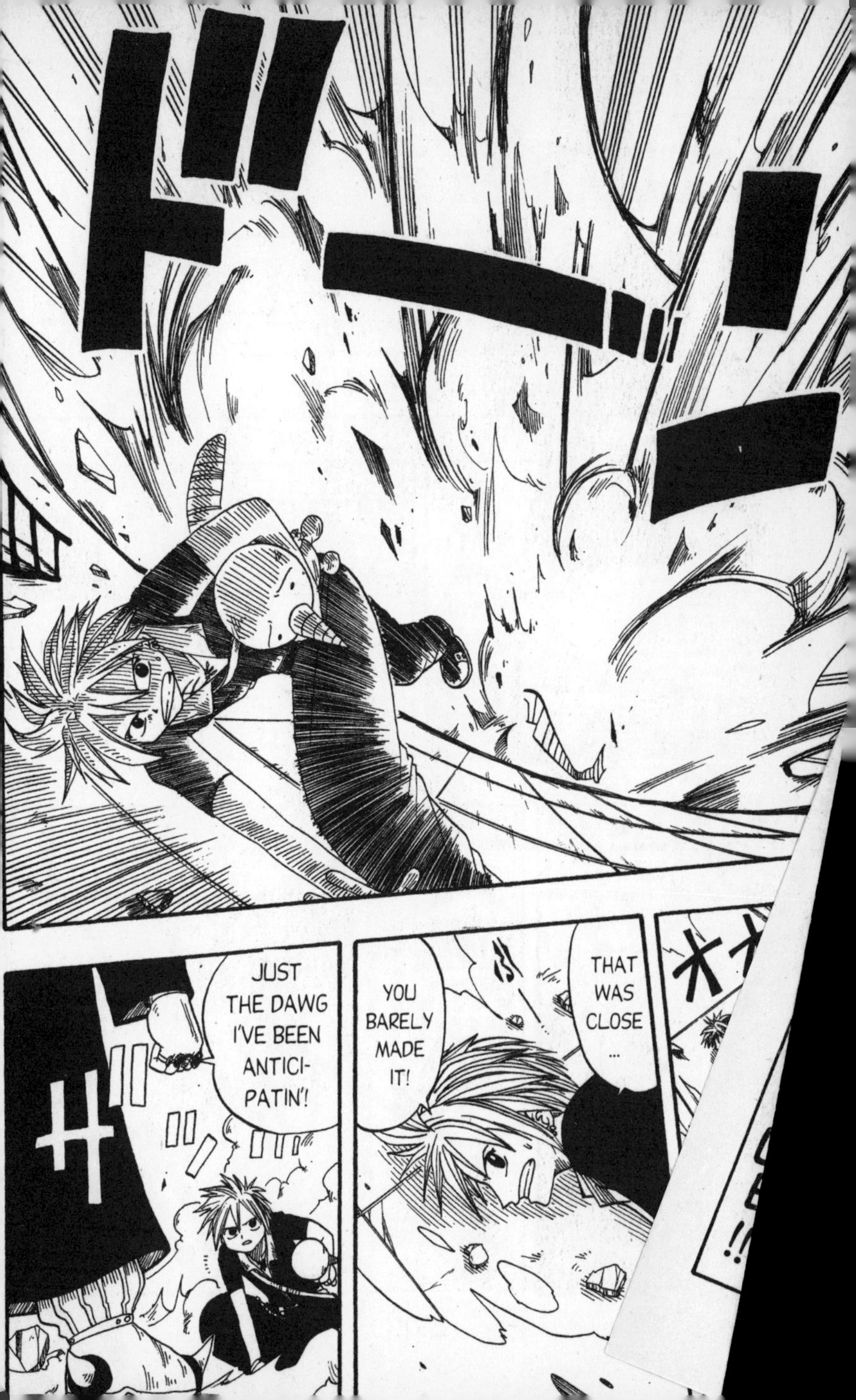
THAT WAS CLOSE ...
YOU BARELY MADE IT!
JUST THE DAWG I'VE BEEN ANTICI-PATIN'!

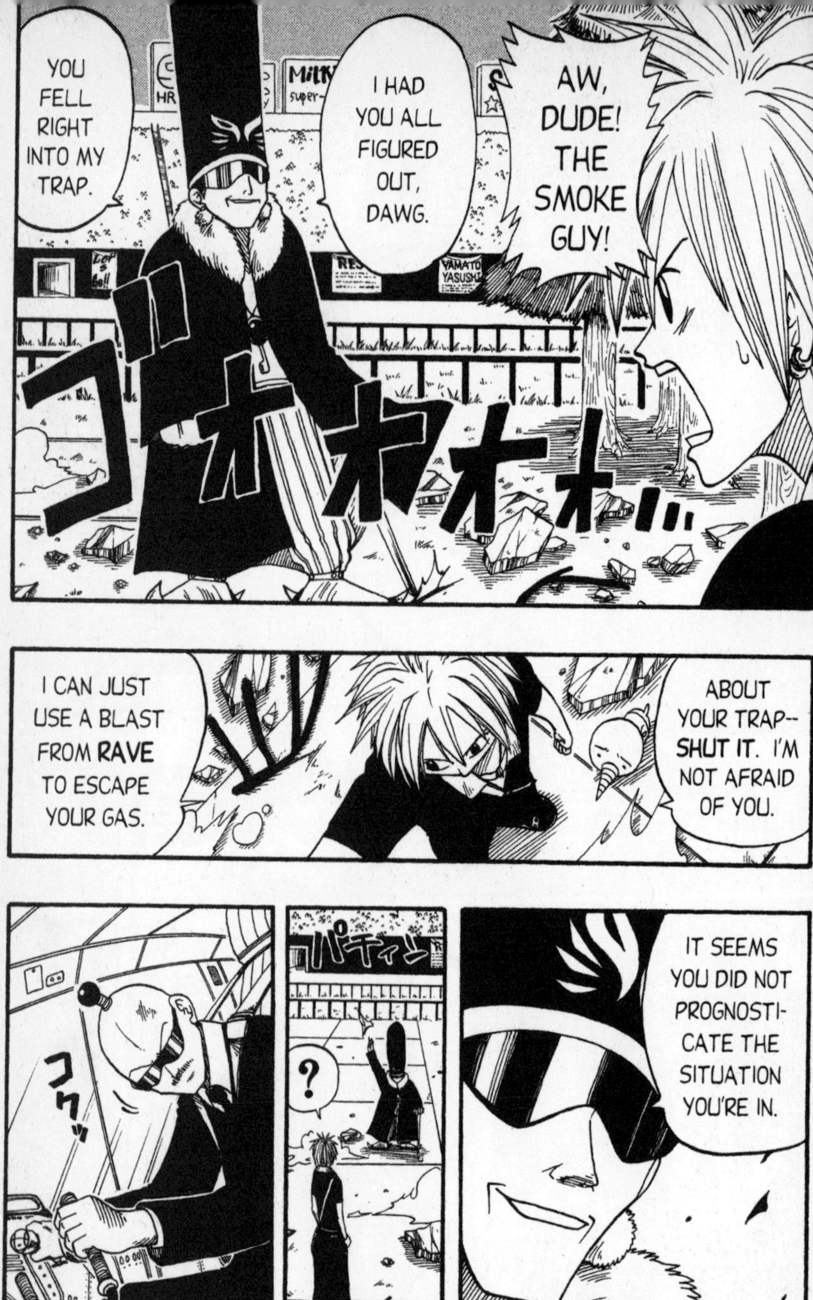
AW, DUDE! THE SMOKE GUY!
I HAD YOU ALL FIGURED OUT, DAWG.
YOU FELL RIGHT INTO MY TRAP.
YAMATO YASUSHI
ABOUT YOUR TRAP-- SHUT IT. I'M NOT AFRAID OF YOU.
I CAN JUST USE A BLAST FROM RAVE TO ESCAPE YOUR GAS.
IT SEEMS YOU DID NOT PROGNOSTI-CATE THE SITUATION YOU'RE IN.
?

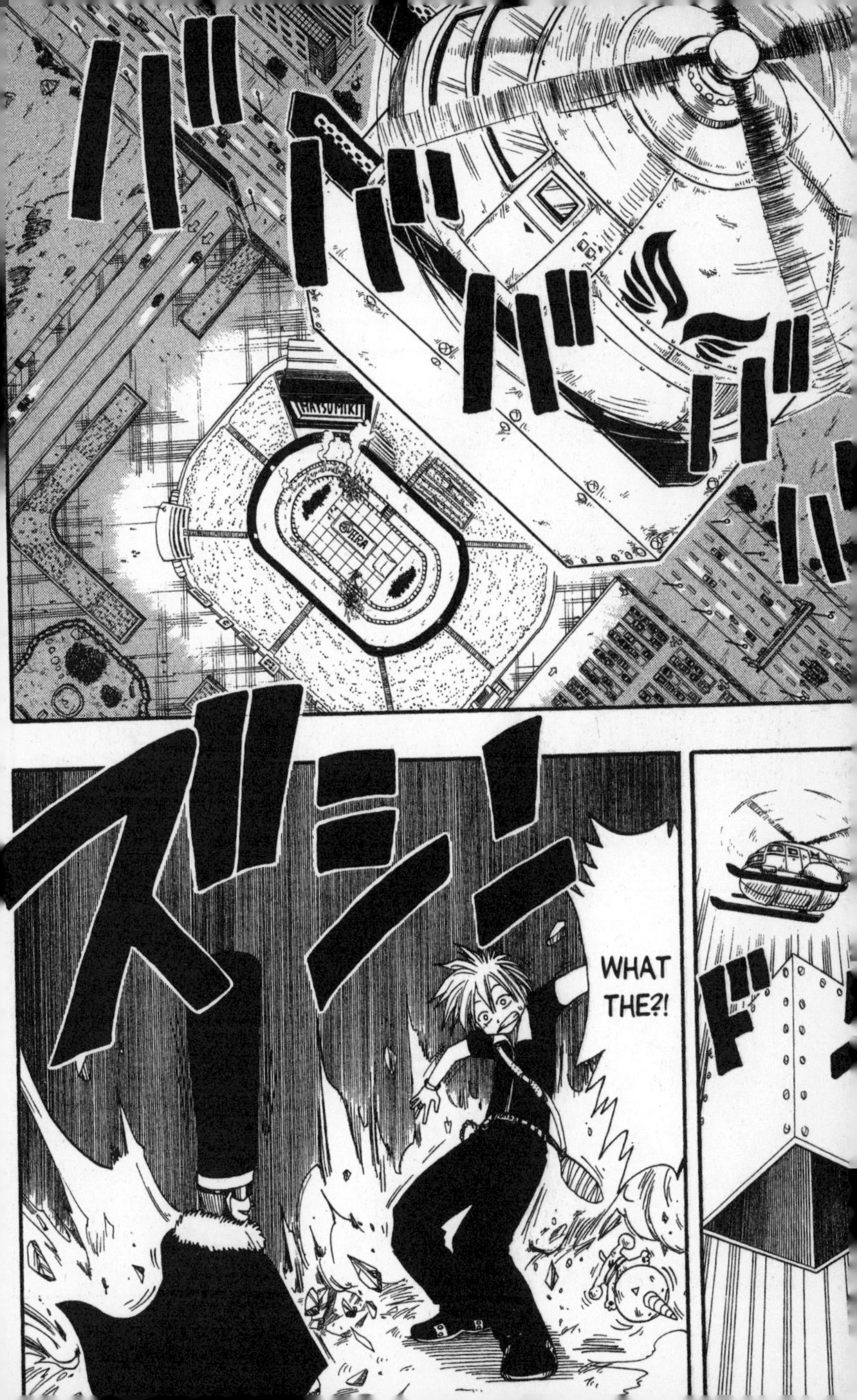
HATSUMIRI
WHAT THE?!

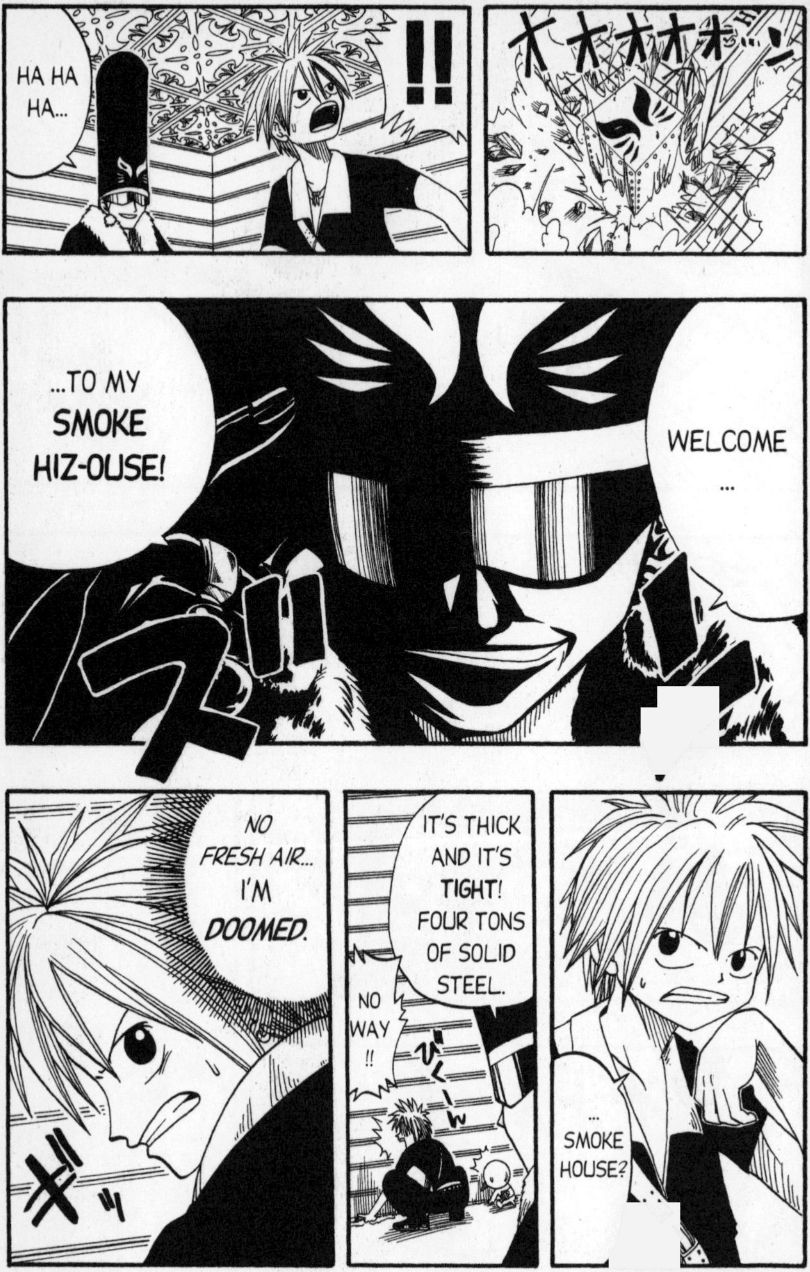
!!
HA HA HA...
WELCOME ...
...TO MY SMOKE HIZ-OUSE!
... SMOKE HOUSE?
IT'S THICK AND IT'S TIGHT! FOUR TONS OF SOLID STEEL.
NO WAY !!
NO FRESH AIR... I'M DOOMED.

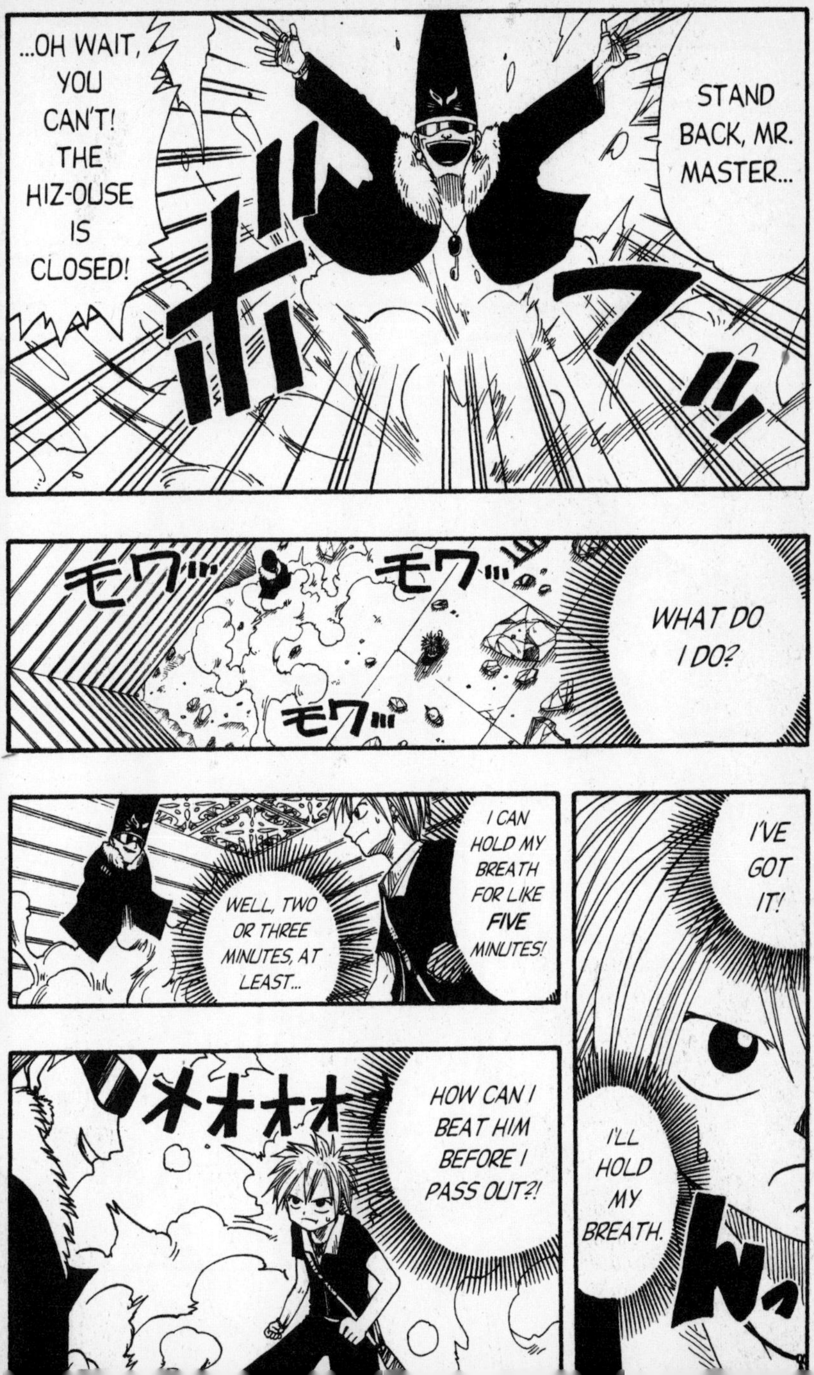
STAND BACK, MR. MASTER...
...OH WAIT, YOU CAN'T! THE HIZ-OUSE IS CLOSED!
WHAT DO I DO?
I'VE GOT IT!
I'LL HOLD MY BREATH.
I CAN HOLD MY BREATH FOR LIKE FIVE MINUTES!
WELL, TWO OR THREE MINUTES, AT LEAST...
オオオオ
HOW CAN I BEAT HIM BEFORE I PASS OUT?!

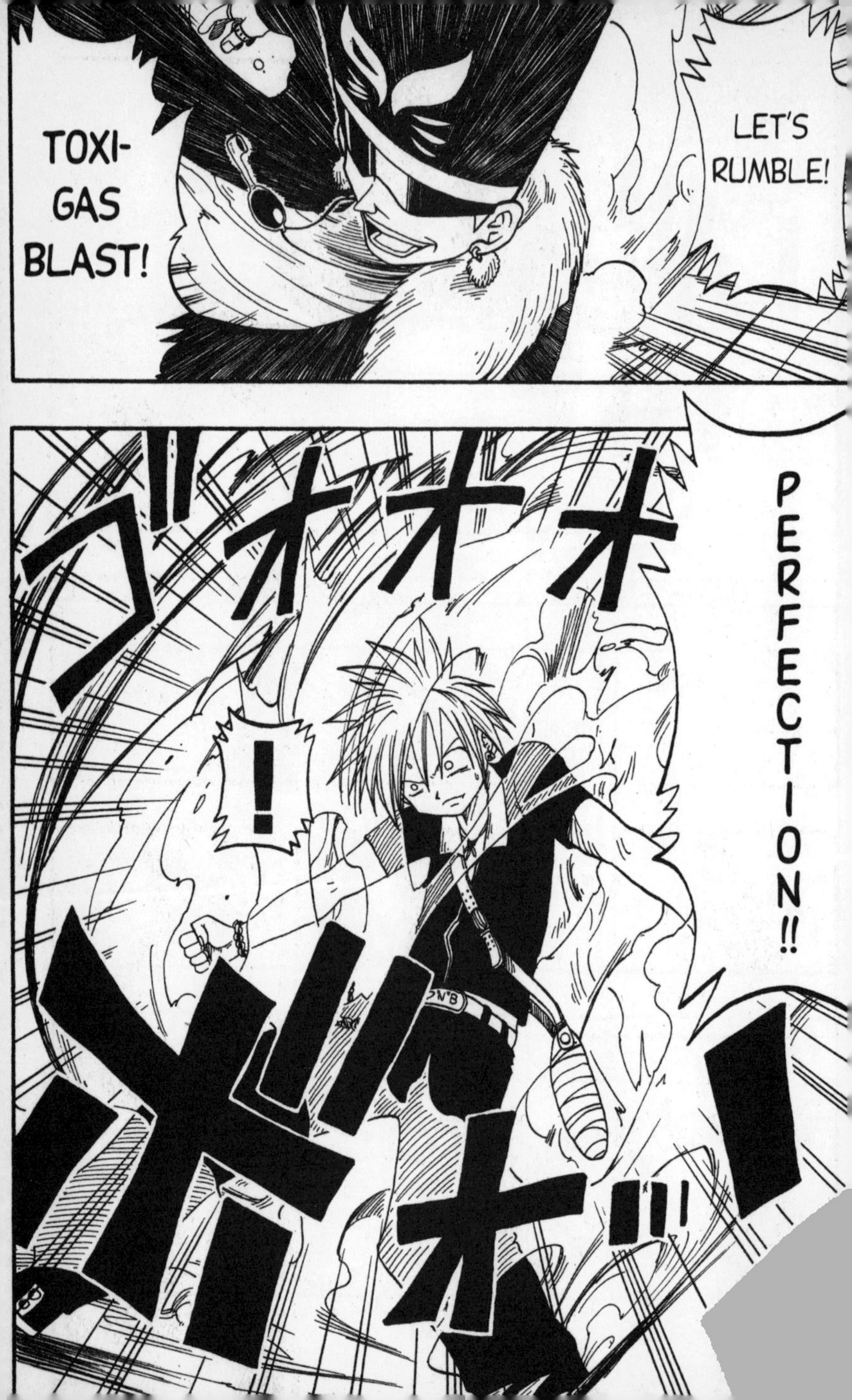
LET'S RUMBLE!
TOXI-GAS BLAST!
PERFECTION!!
!

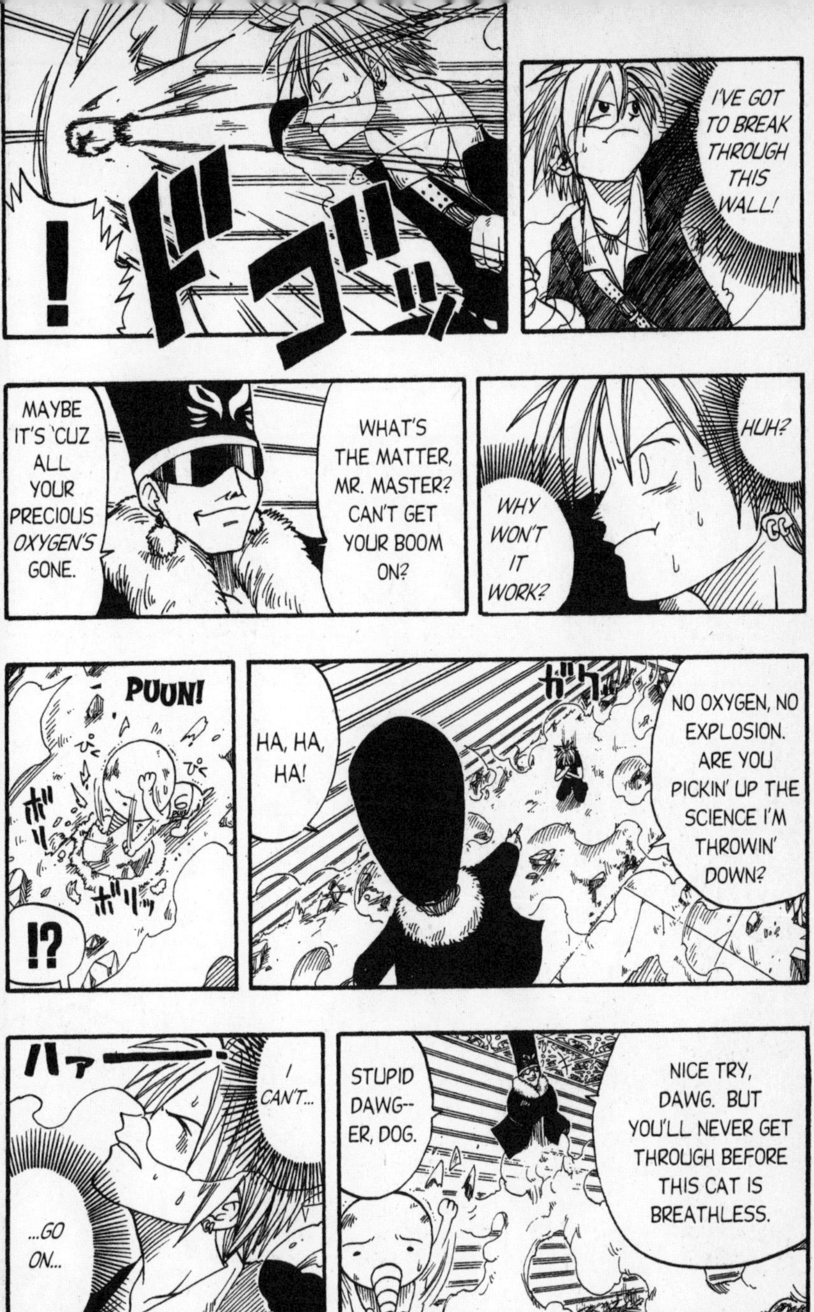
I'VE GOT TO BREAK THROUGH THIS WALL!
!
ドゴッ
HUH?
WHY WON'T IT WORK?
WHAT'S THE MATTER, MR. MASTER? CAN'T GET YOUR BOOM ON?
MAYBE IT'S 'CUZ ALL YOUR PRECIOUS OXYGEN'S GONE.
ガク
NO OXYGEN, NO EXPLOSION. ARE YOU PICKIN' UP THE SCIENCE I'M THROWIN' DOWN?
HA, HA, HA!
PUUN!
ぷく
ぷく
ボリ
ボリッ
!?
NICE TRY, DAWG. BUT YOU'LL NEVER GET THROUGH BEFORE THIS CAT IS BREATHLESS.
STUPID DAWG-ER, DOG.
ハァーー
I CAN'T...
...GO ON...

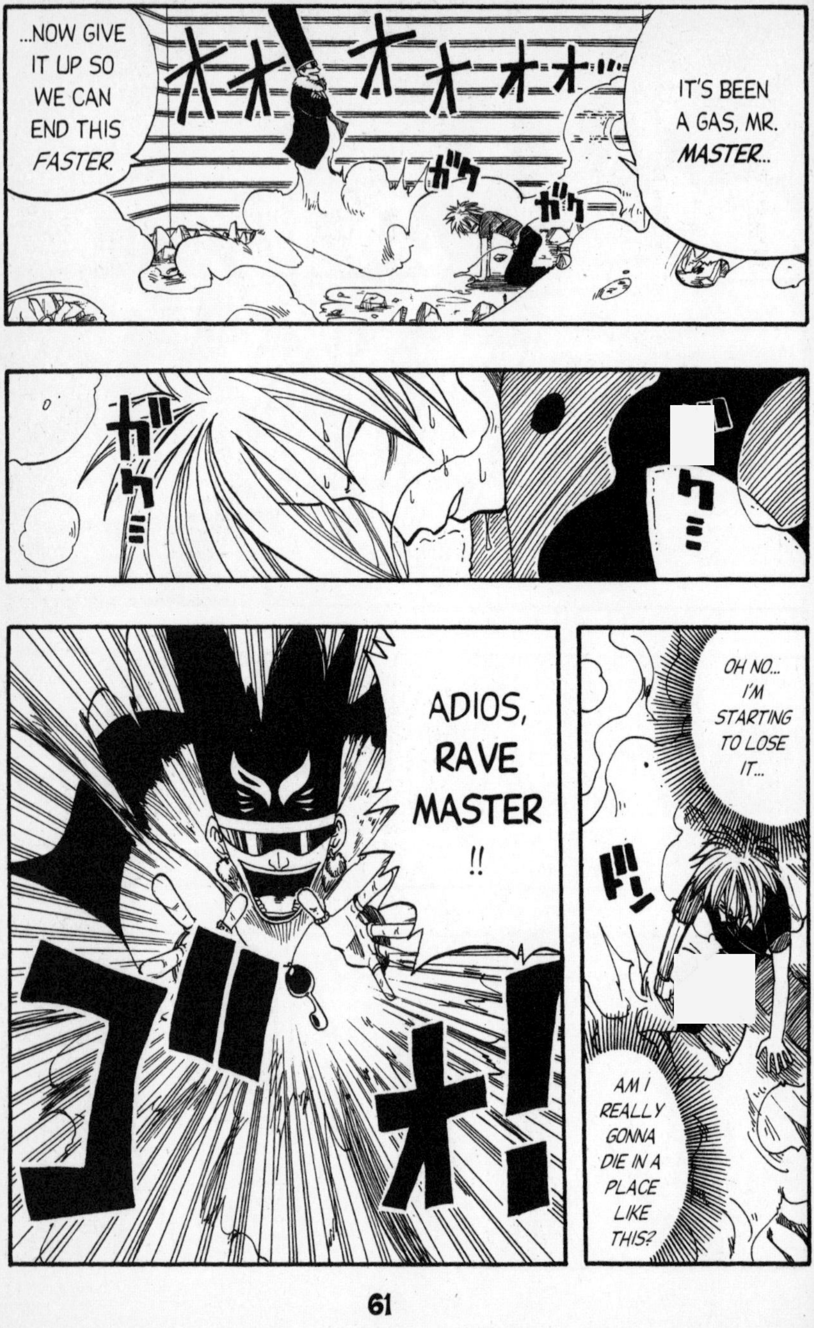
IT'S BEEN A GAS, MR. MASTER...
...NOW GIVE IT UP SO WE CAN END THIS FASTER.
OH NO... I'M STARTING TO LOSE IT...
AM I REALLY GONNA DIE IN A PLACE LIKE THIS?
ADIOS, RAVE MASTER!!

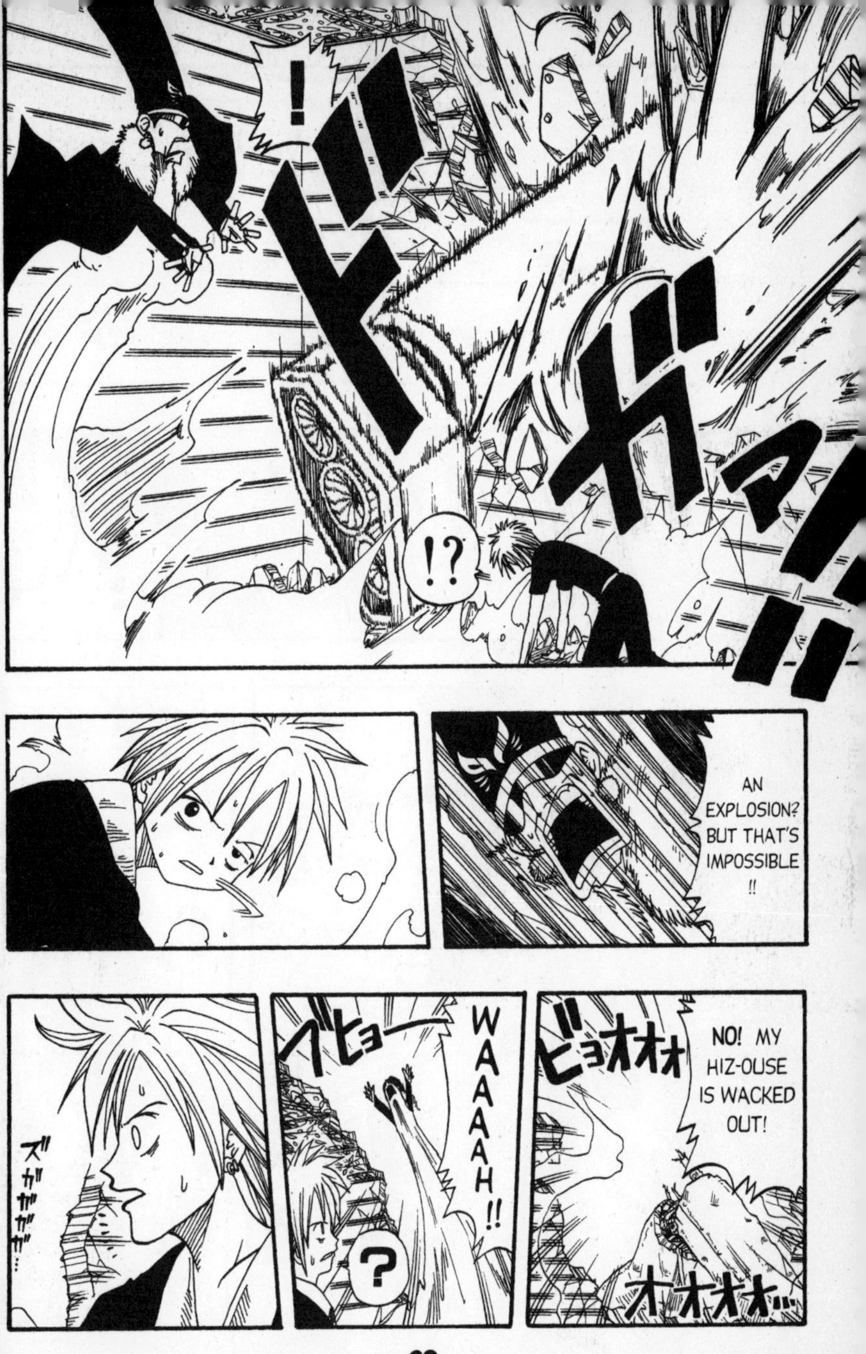
!
ドガァ!!
!?
AN EXPLOSION? BUT THAT'S IMPOSSIBLE !!
ビョオオオ
NO! MY HIZ-OUSE IS WACKED OUT!
オオオオ
ビュー
WAAAAH!!
?
ズガガガガ…

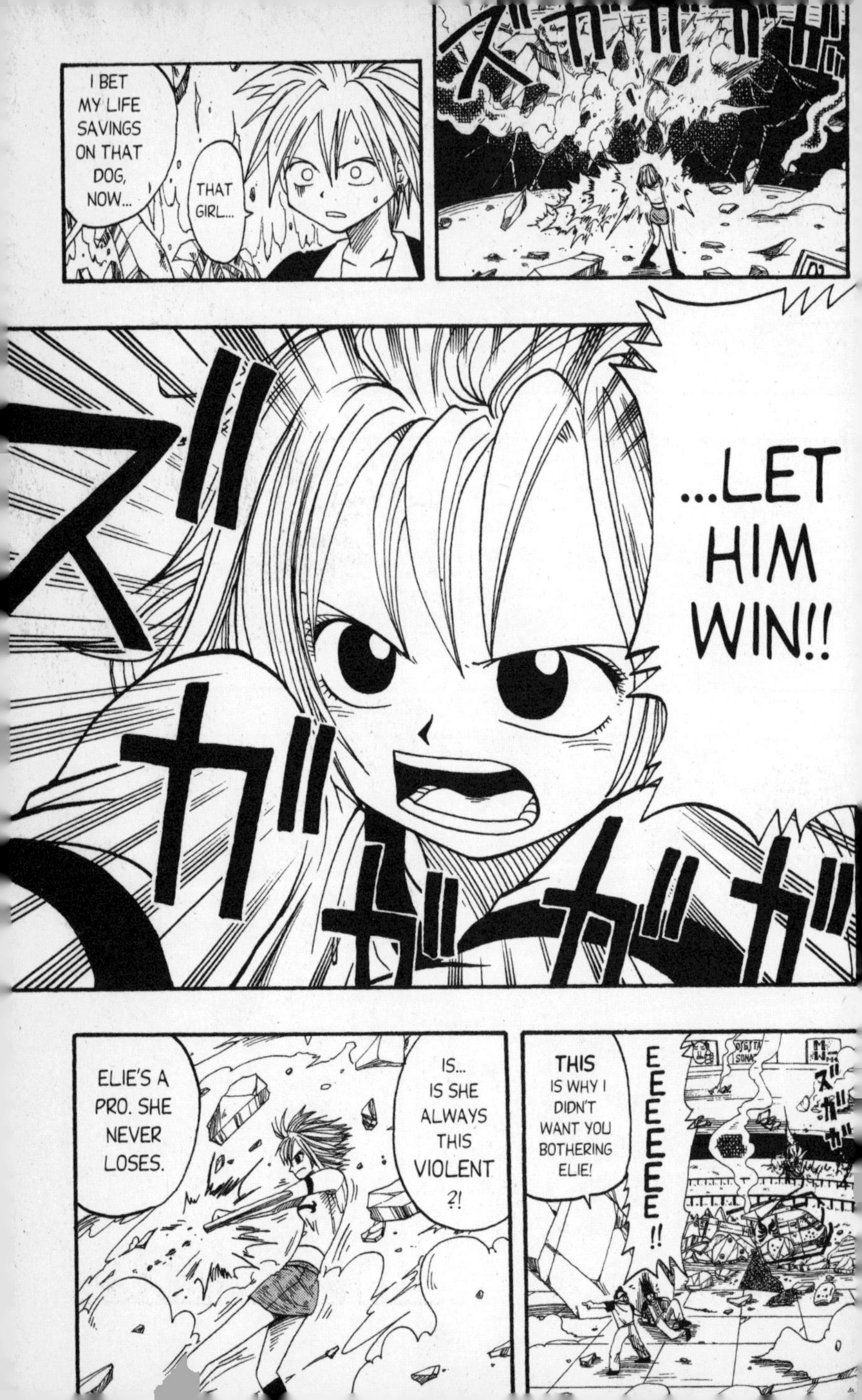
THAT GIRL...
I BET MY LIFE SAVINGS ON THAT DOG, NOW...
...LET HIM WIN!!
EEEEEE!!
THIS IS WHY I DIDN'T WANT YOU BOTHERING ELIE!
IS... IS SHE ALWAYS THIS VIOLENT?!
ELIE'S A PRO. SHE NEVER LOSES.

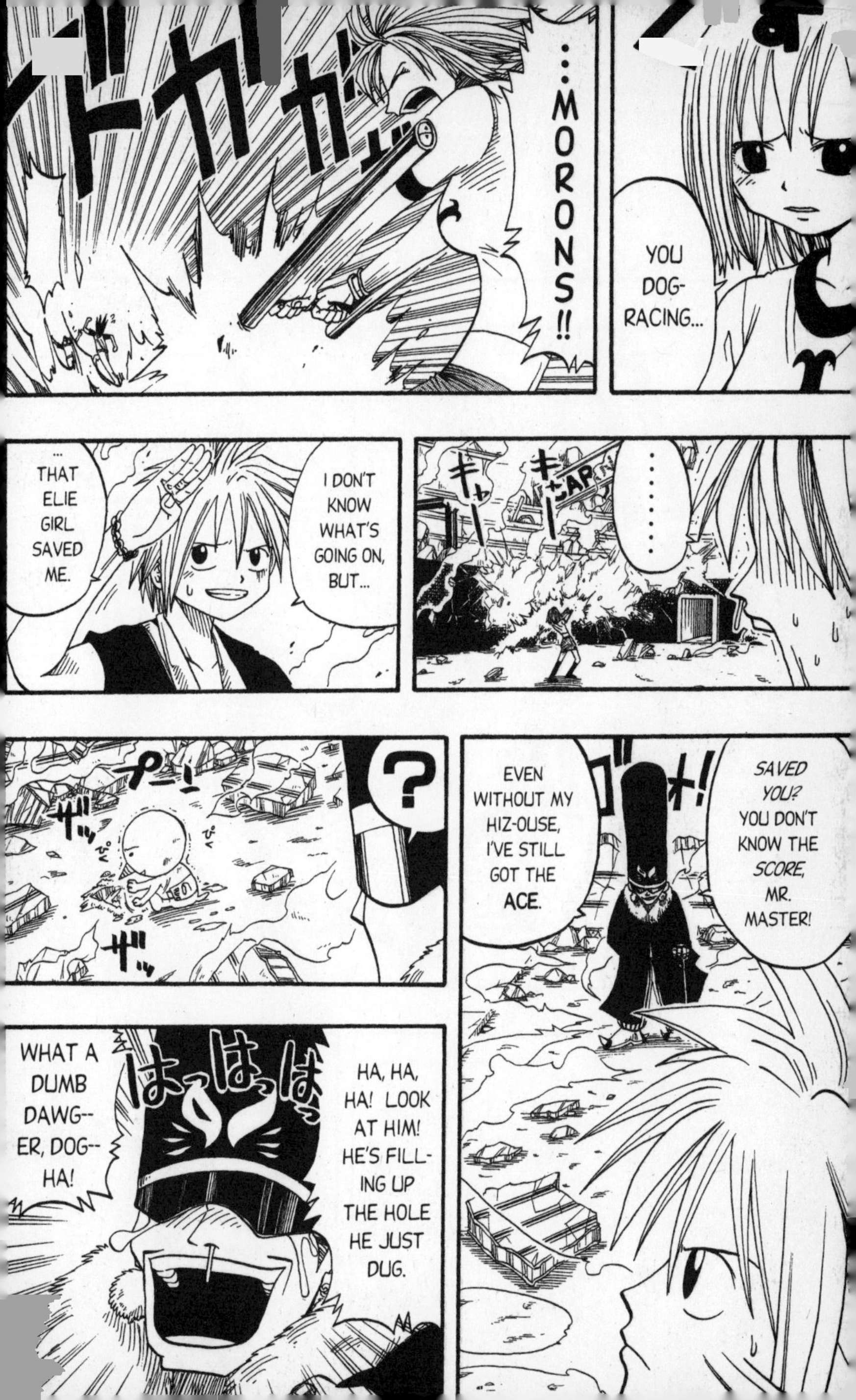
YOU DOG-RACING...
...MORONS!!
......
I DON'T KNOW WHAT'S GOING ON, BUT...
...THAT ELIE GIRL SAVED ME.
SAVED YOU!? YOU DON'T KNOW THE SCORE, MR. MASTER!
EVEN WITHOUT MY HIZ-OUSE, I'VE STILL GOT THE ACE.
?
HA, HA, HA! LOOK AT HIM! HE'S FILL-ING UP THE HOLE HE JUST DUG.
WHAT A DUMB DAWG--ER, DOG--HA!

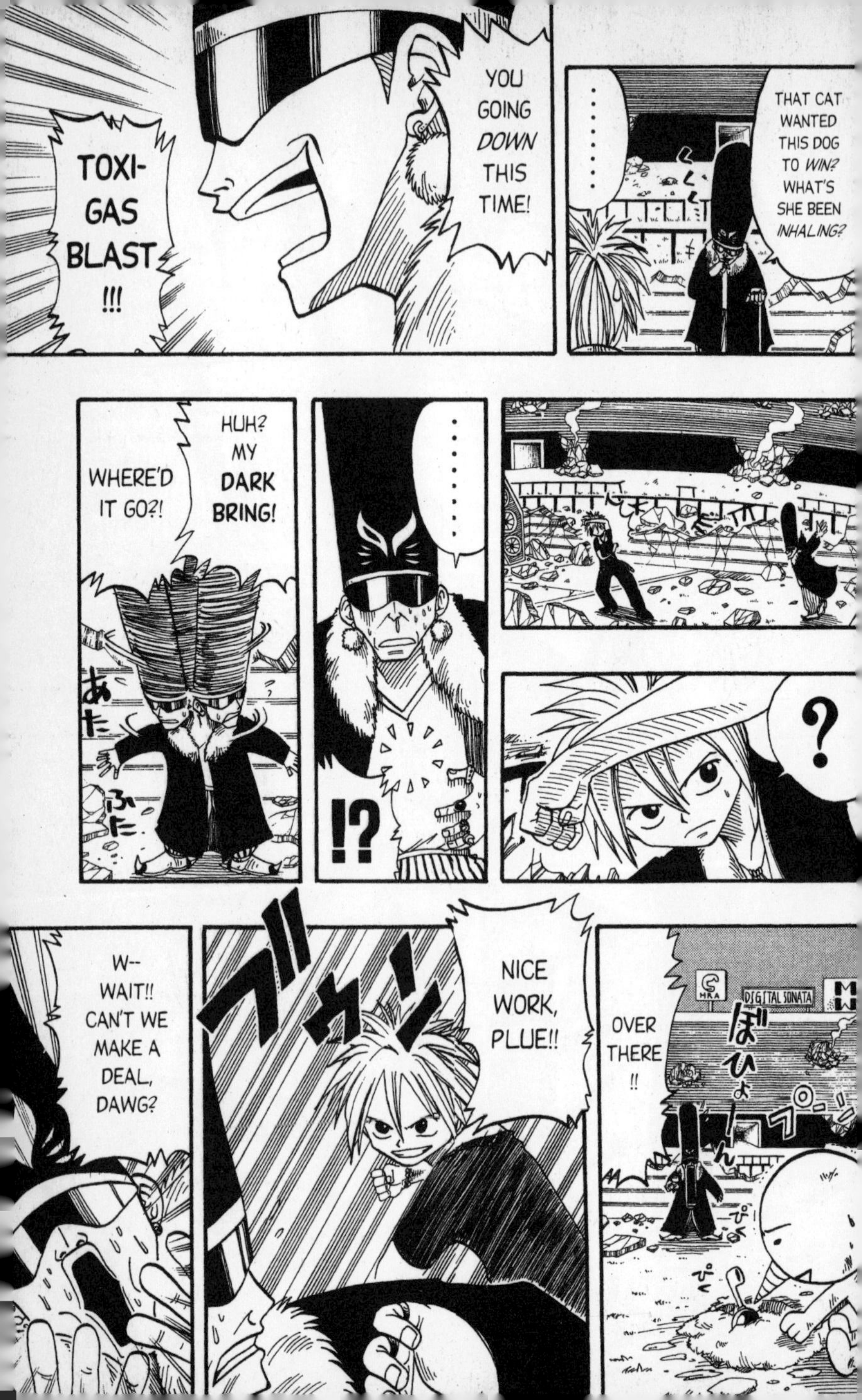
THAT CAT WANTED THIS DOG TO *WIN?* WHAT'S SHE BEEN *INHALING?*
......
YOU GOING *DOWN* THIS TIME!
TOXI-GAS BLAST!!!
?
......
!?
HUH? MY **DARK BRING!**
WHERE'D IT GO?!
あた
ふた
DIGITAL SONATA
OVER THERE!!
NICE WORK, PLUE!!
W-- WAIT!! CAN'T WE MAKE A DEAL, DAWG?

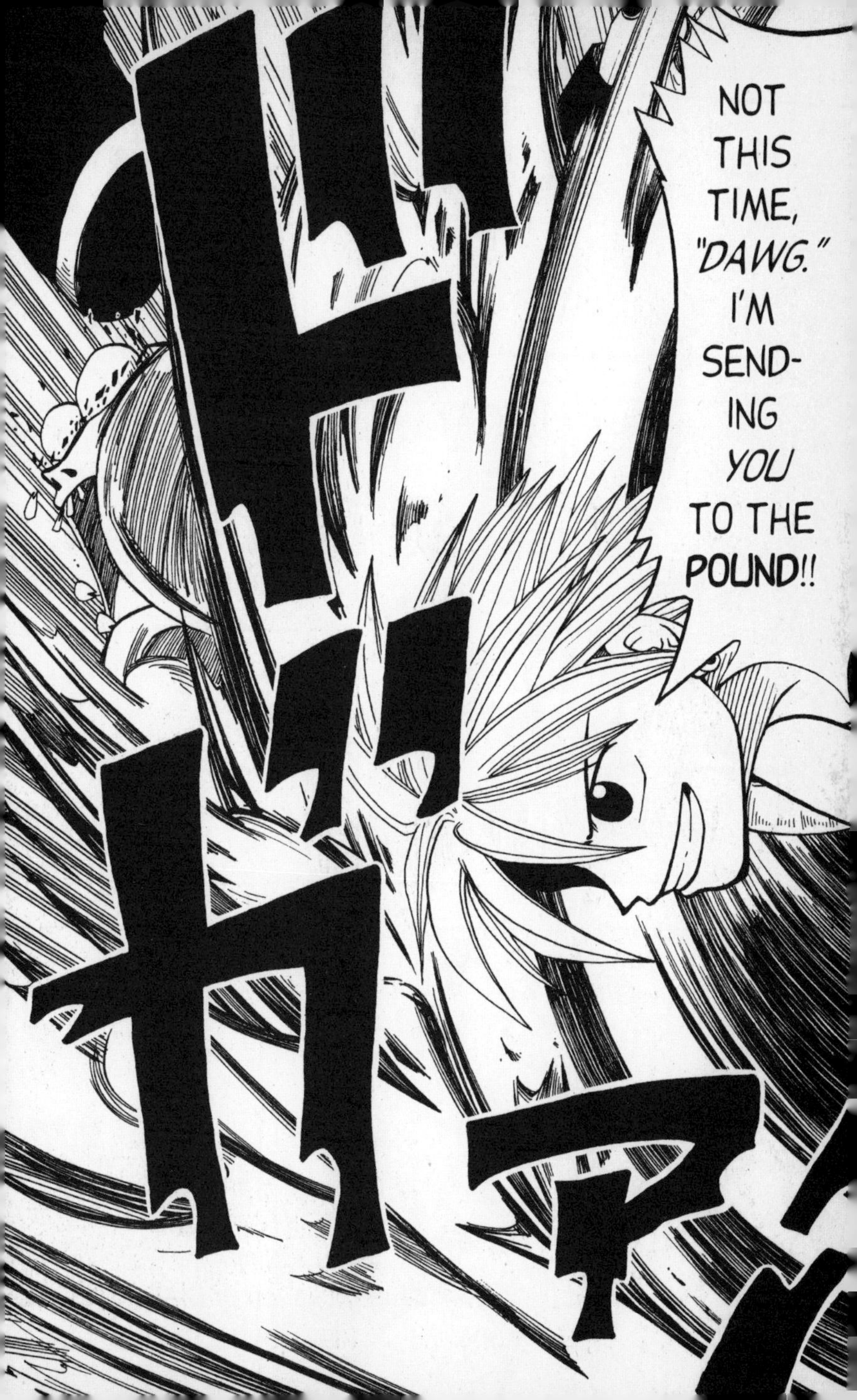
NOT THIS TIME, "DAWG." I'M SEND-ING YOU TO THE POUND!!

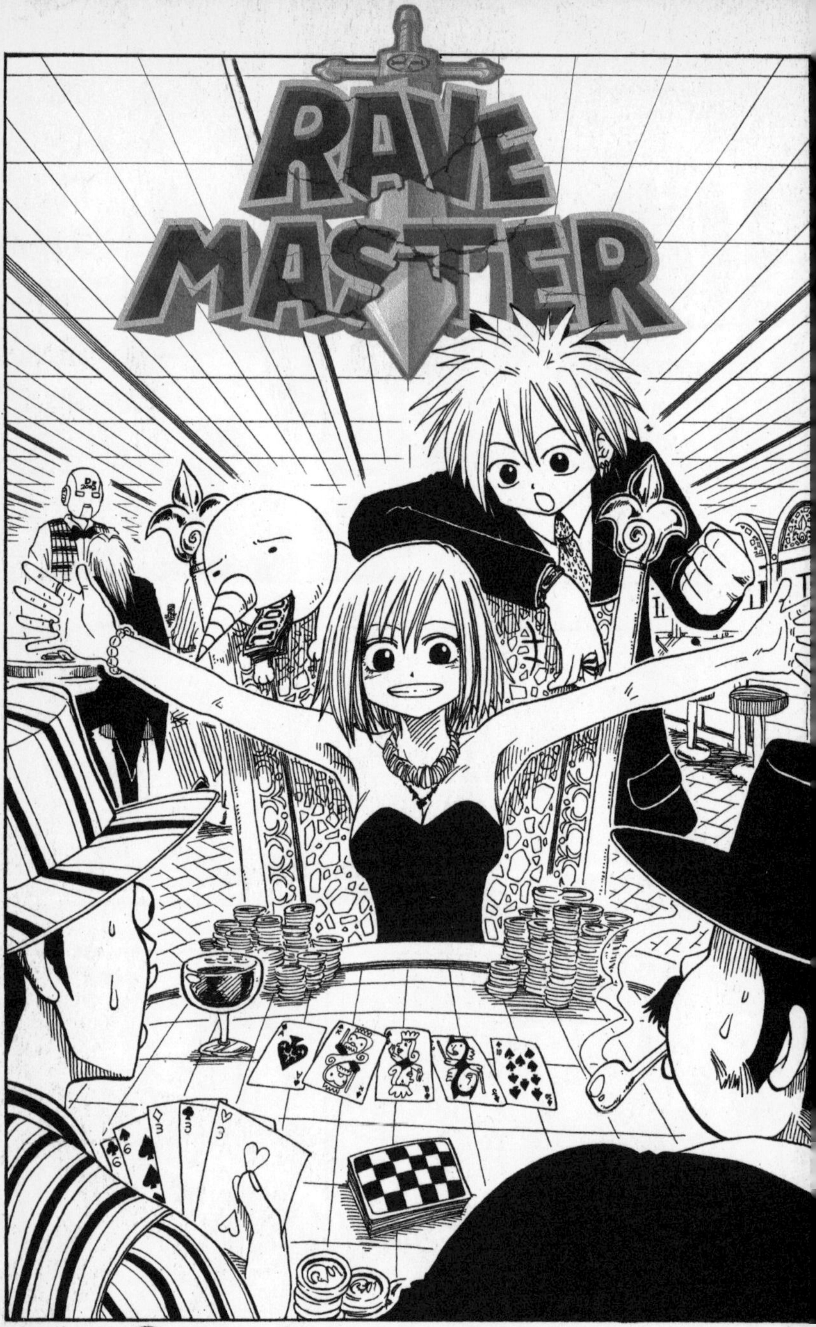
RAVE MASTER

RAVE 8 ✠ THE MAGIC OF A SMILE

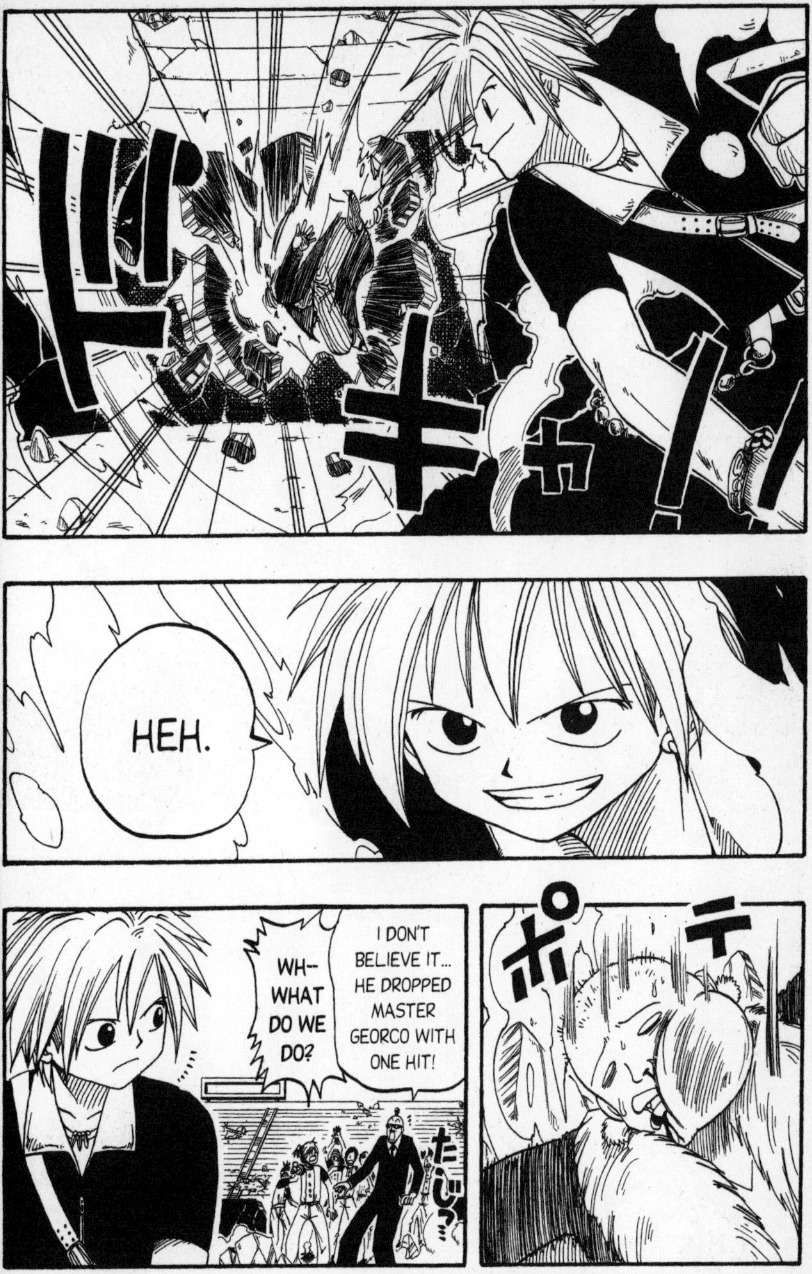
ドギャ!
HEH.
ポテ
I DON'T BELIEVE IT... HE DROPPED MASTER GEORCO WITH ONE HIT!
WH- WHAT DO WE DO?
たじっ…

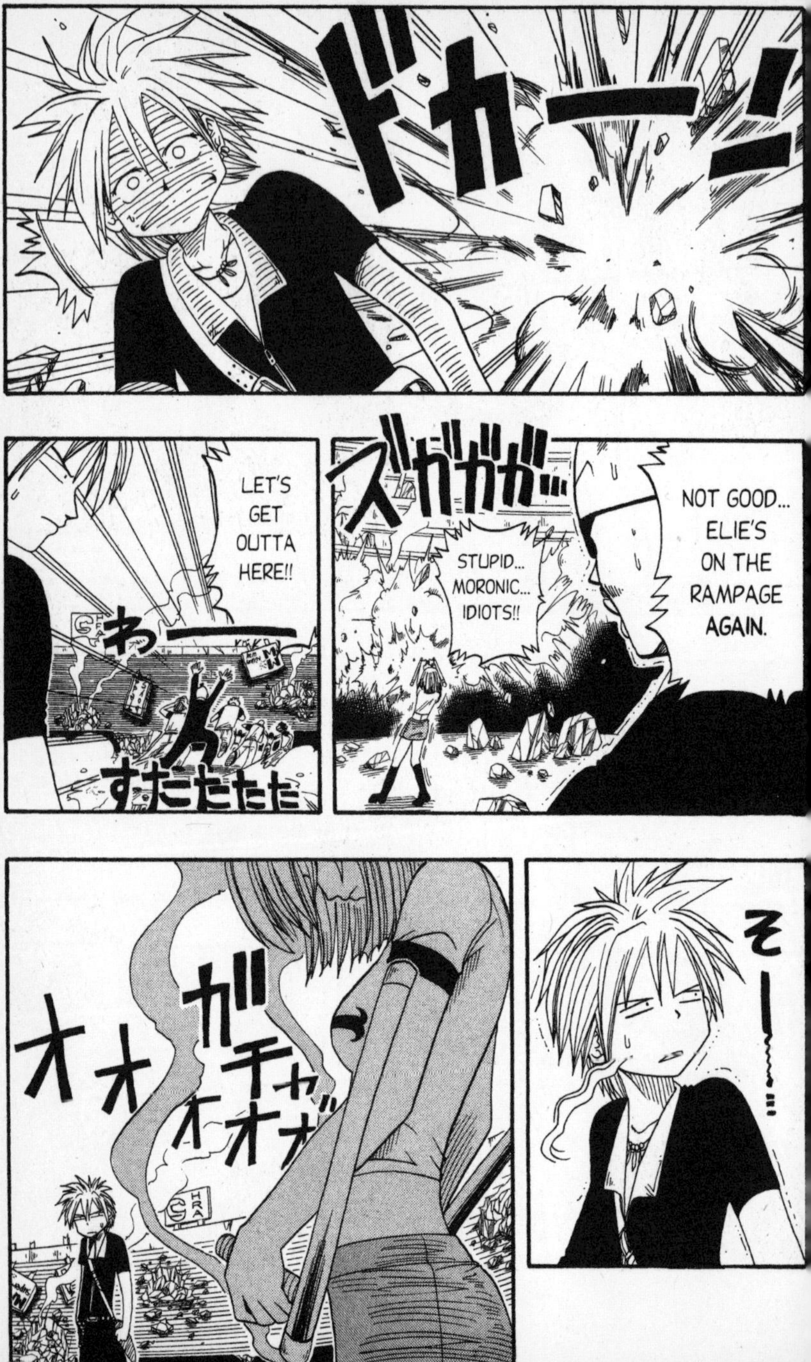
ドカーン
ズガガガ
NOT GOOD... ELIE'S ON THE RAMPAGE AGAIN.
STUPID... MORONIC... IDIOTS!!
LET'S GET OUTTA HERE!!
わー
すたたたたた
そー
ガチャ
オオオオオ

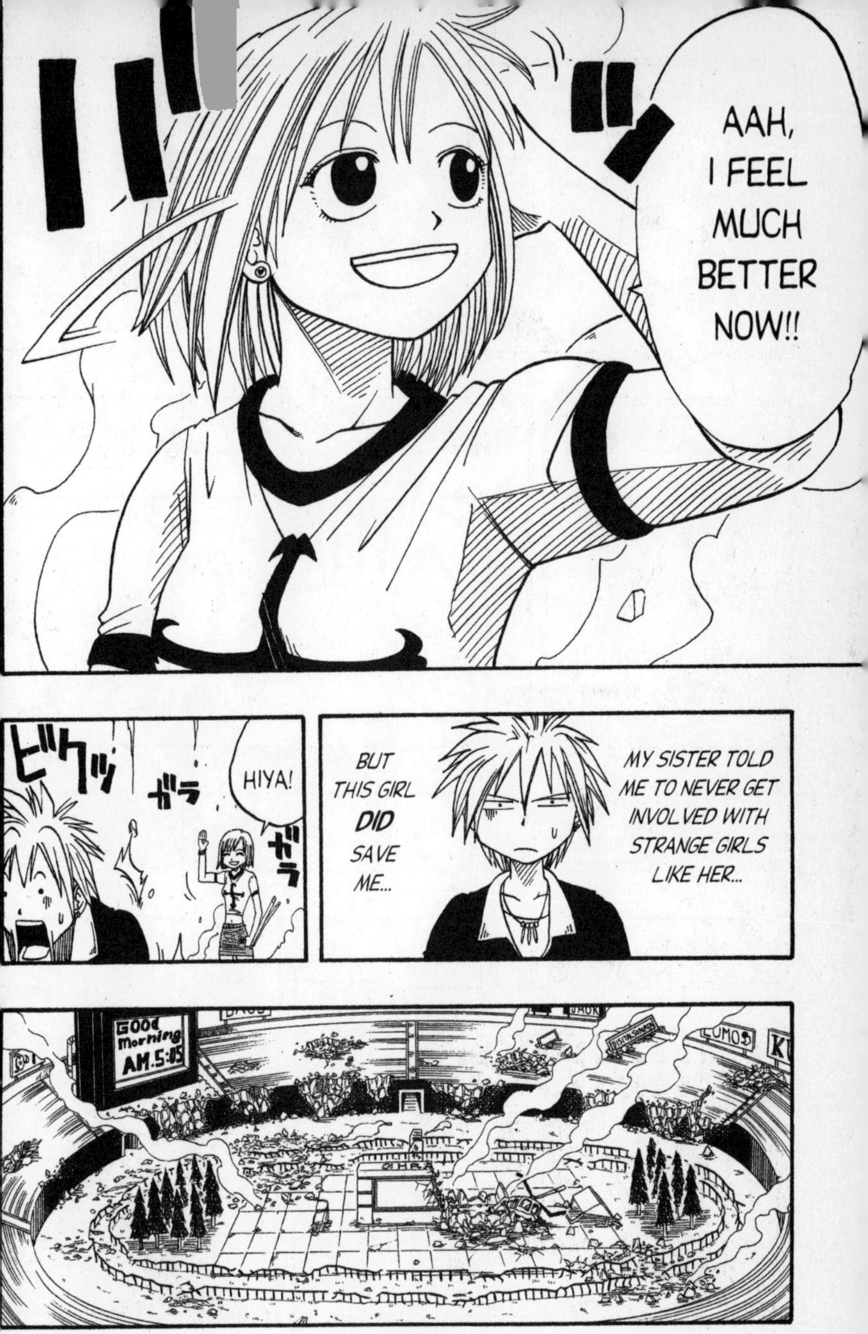
AAH, I FEEL MUCH BETTER NOW!!
MY SISTER TOLD ME TO NEVER GET INVOLVED WITH STRANGE GIRLS LIKE HER...
BUT THIS GIRL DID SAVE ME...
HIYA!
ガラ
ガラ
ビクッ
GOOD Morning
AM.5:05
LUMOS

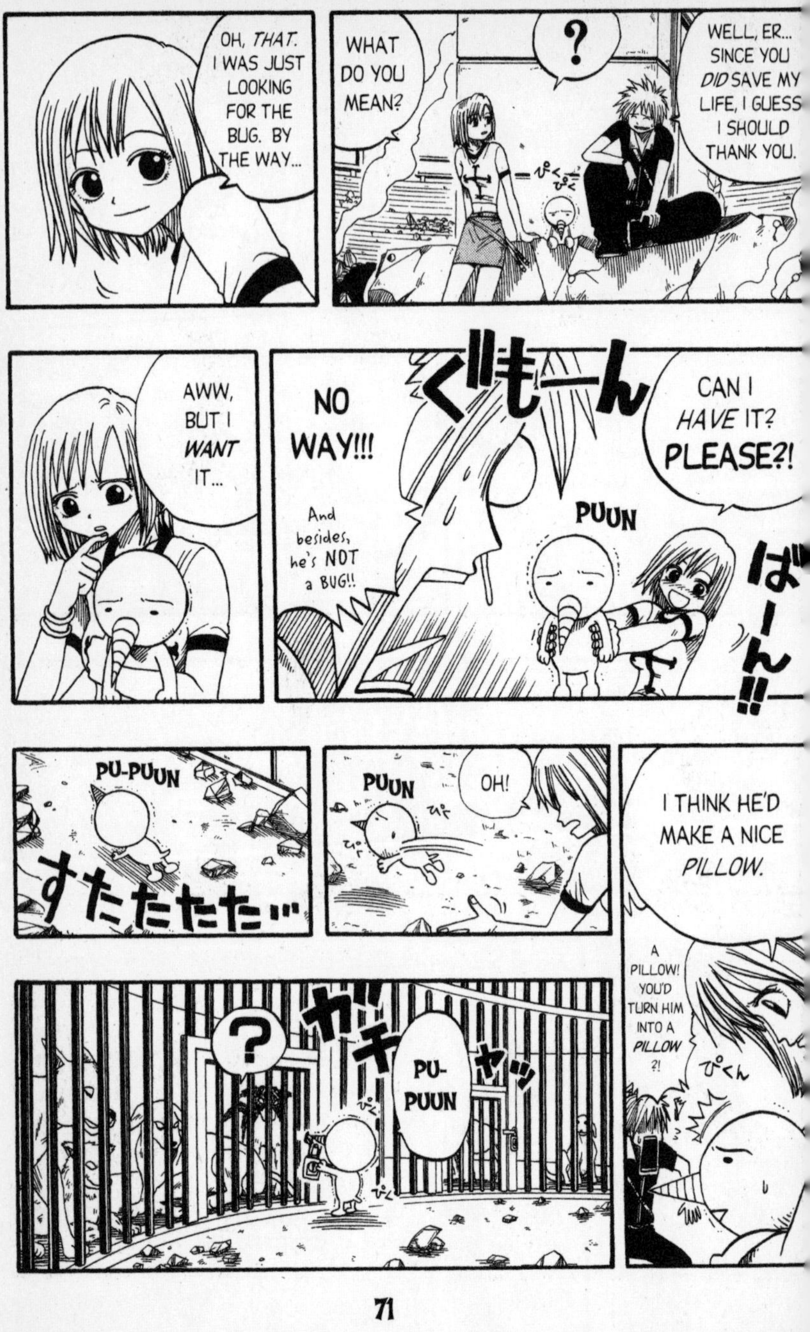
WELL, ER... SINCE YOU *DID* SAVE MY LIFE, I GUESS I SHOULD THANK YOU.
?
WHAT DO YOU MEAN?
ぴくぴく
OH, *THAT*. I WAS JUST LOOKING FOR THE BUG. BY THE WAY...
CAN I *HAVE* IT? PLEASE?!
ぐもーん
NO WAY!!!
ばーん!!
PUUN
And besides, he's NOT a BUG!!
AWW, BUT I *WANT* IT...
I THINK HE'D MAKE A NICE *PILLOW*.
A PILLOW! YOU'D TURN HIM INTO A *PILLOW*?!
ぴくん
OH!
PUUN
PU-PUUN
すたたたたッ
ガチャッ
PU-PUUN
?

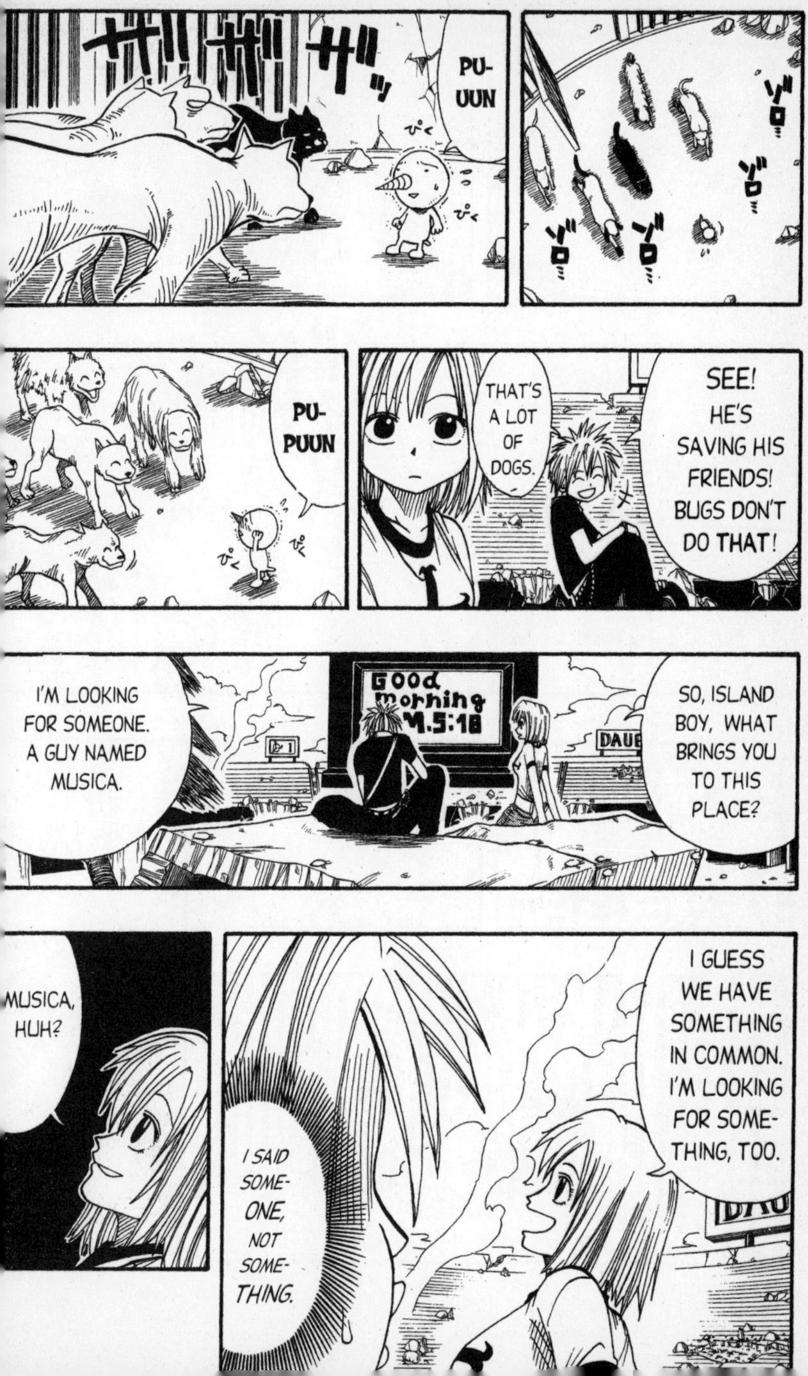
ゾロ
ゾロ
ゾロ
ゾロ
ザザザッ
PU-UUN
ぴく
ぴく
SEE! HE'S SAVING HIS FRIENDS! BUGS DON'T DO THAT!
THAT'S A LOT OF DOGS.
PU-PUUN
ぴく
ぴく
SO, ISLAND BOY, WHAT BRINGS YOU TO THIS PLACE?
Good morning
I'M LOOKING FOR SOMEONE. A GUY NAMED MUSICA.
I GUESS WE HAVE SOMETHING IN COMMON. I'M LOOKING FOR SOMETHING, TOO.
I SAID SOMEONE, NOT SOMETHING.
MUSICA, HUH?

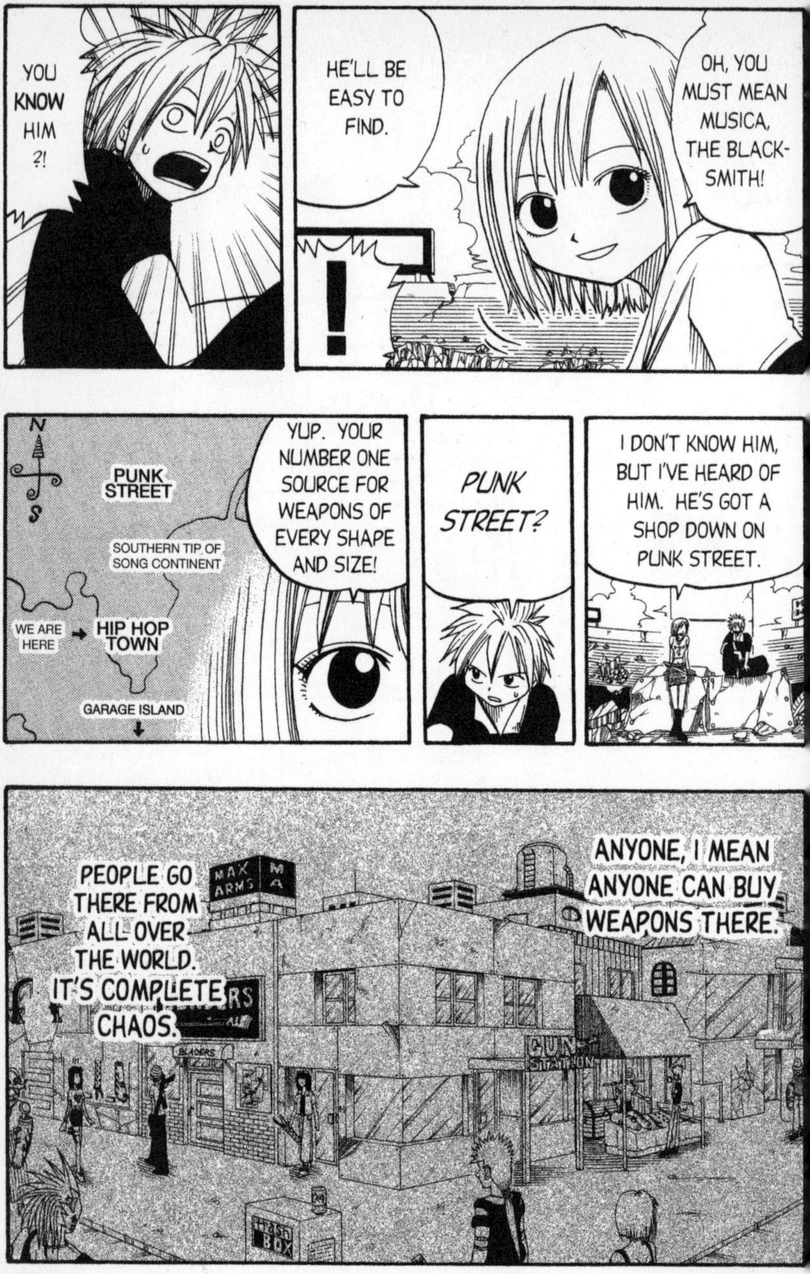
OH, YOU MUST MEAN MUSICA, THE BLACK-SMITH!
HE'LL BE EASY TO FIND.
!
YOU KNOW HIM ?!
I DON'T KNOW HIM, BUT I'VE HEARD OF HIM. HE'S GOT A SHOP DOWN ON PUNK STREET.
PUNK STREET?
YUP. YOUR NUMBER ONE SOURCE FOR WEAPONS OF EVERY SHAPE AND SIZE!
N
S
PUNK STREET
SOUTHERN TIP OF SONG CONTINENT
WE ARE HERE
HIP HOP TOWN
GARAGE ISLAND
ANYONE, I MEAN ANYONE CAN BUY WEAPONS THERE.
PEOPLE GO THERE FROM ALL OVER THE WORLD. IT'S COMPLETE CHAOS.
MAX ARMS
GUN STATION
BLADERS
TRASH BOX

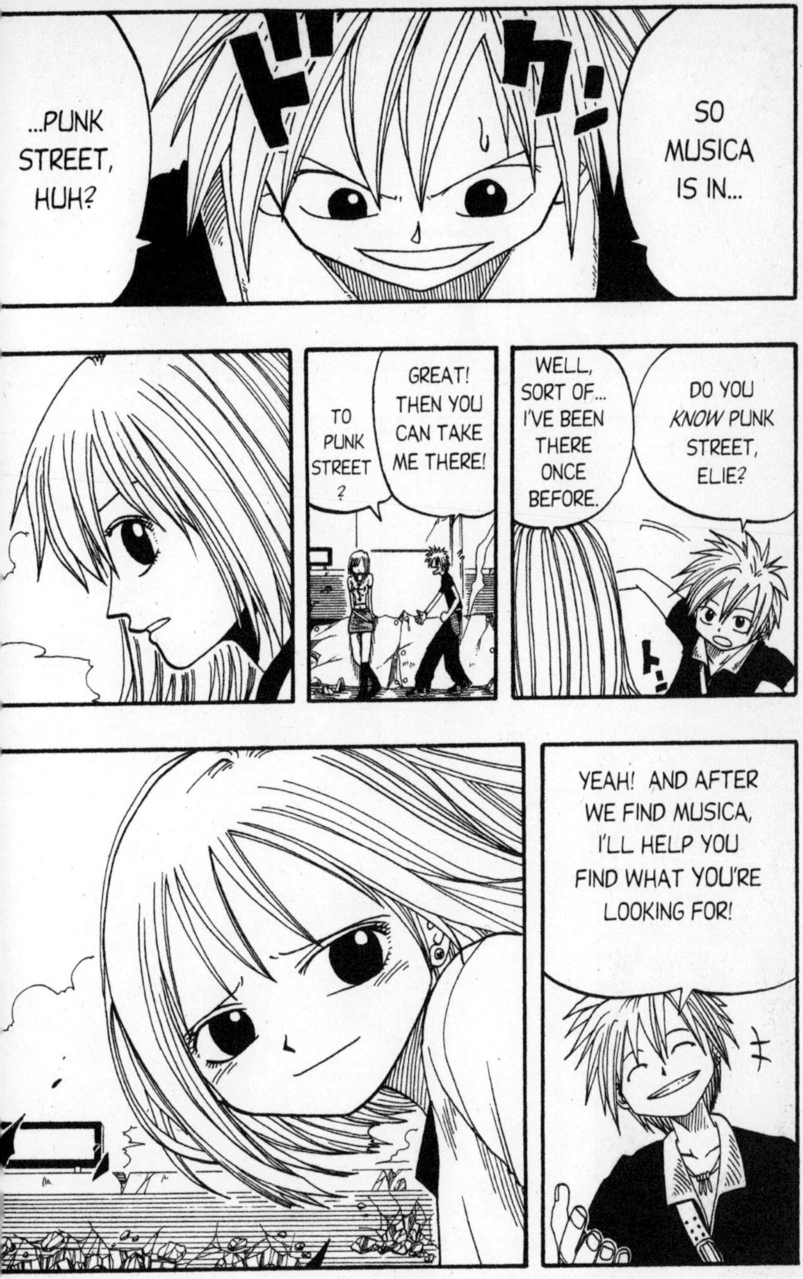

SO MUSICA IS IN...
...PUNK STREET, HUH?
DO YOU *KNOW* PUNK STREET, ELIE?
WELL, SORT OF... I'VE BEEN THERE ONCE BEFORE.
GREAT! THEN YOU CAN TAKE ME THERE!
TO PUNK STREET ?
YEAH! AND AFTER WE FIND MUSICA, I'LL HELP YOU FIND WHAT YOU'RE LOOKING FOR!

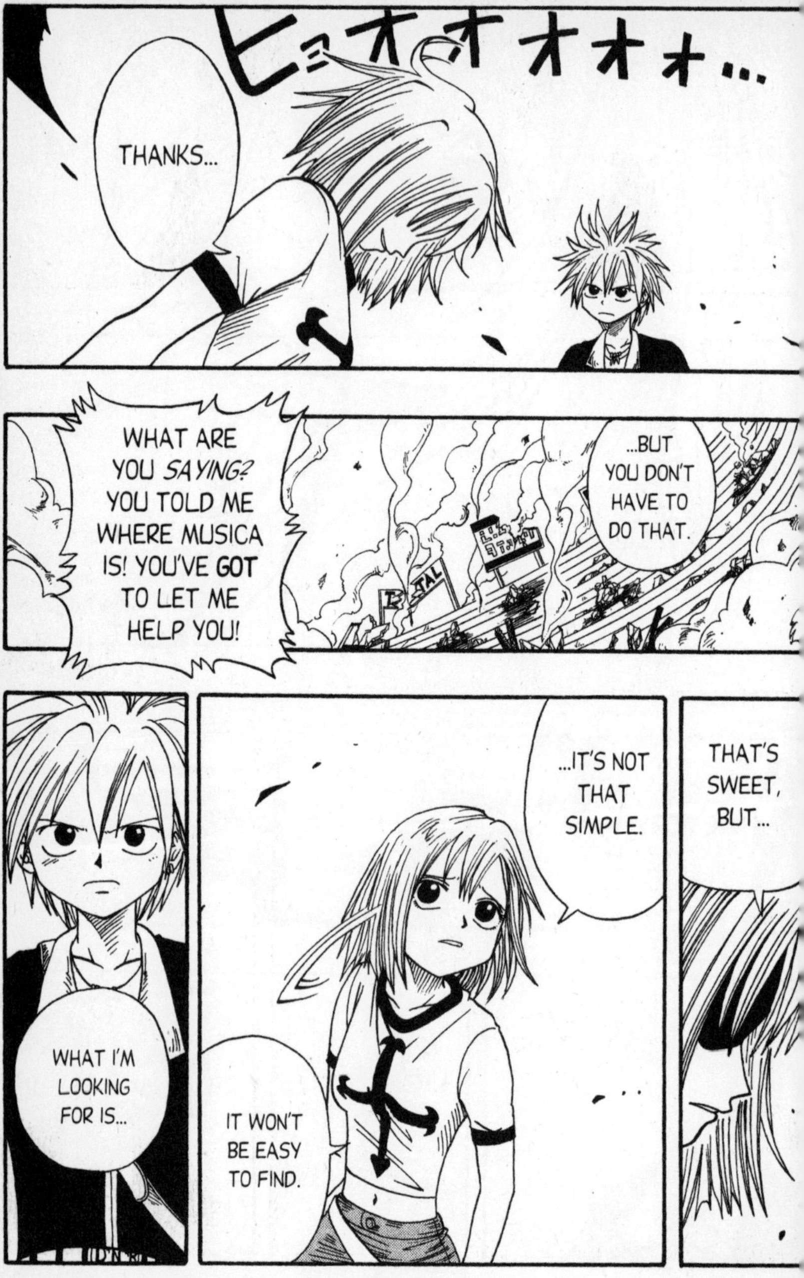
ヒョオオオオォ…
THANKS...
...BUT YOU DON'T HAVE TO DO THAT.
WHAT ARE YOU *SAYING?* YOU TOLD ME WHERE MUSICA IS! YOU'VE **GOT** TO LET ME HELP YOU!
THAT'S SWEET, BUT...
...IT'S NOT THAT SIMPLE.
IT WON'T BE EASY TO FIND.
WHAT I'M LOOKING FOR IS...

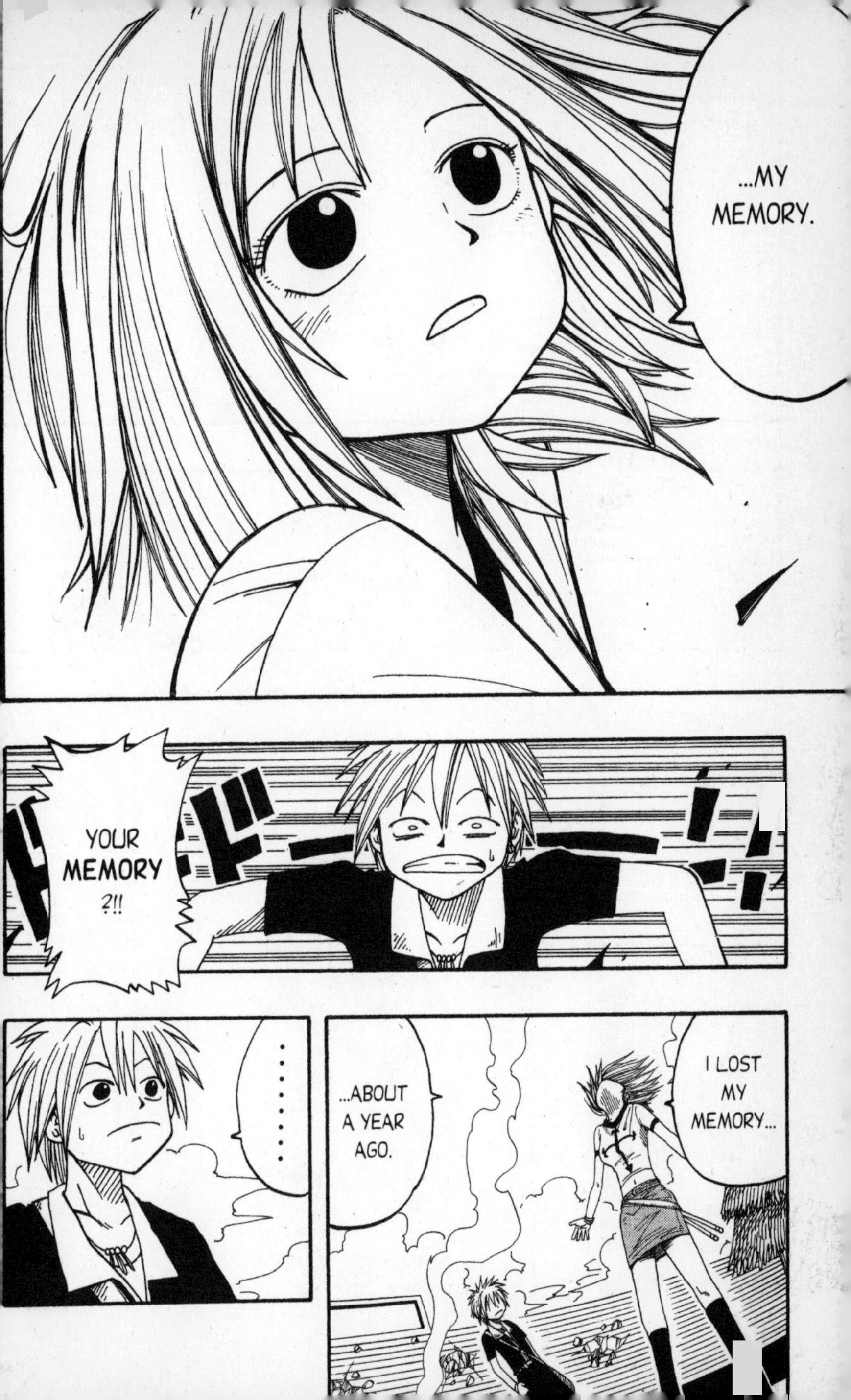
...MY MEMORY.
YOUR MEMORY ?!!
I LOST MY MEMORY...
...ABOUT A YEAR AGO.
....

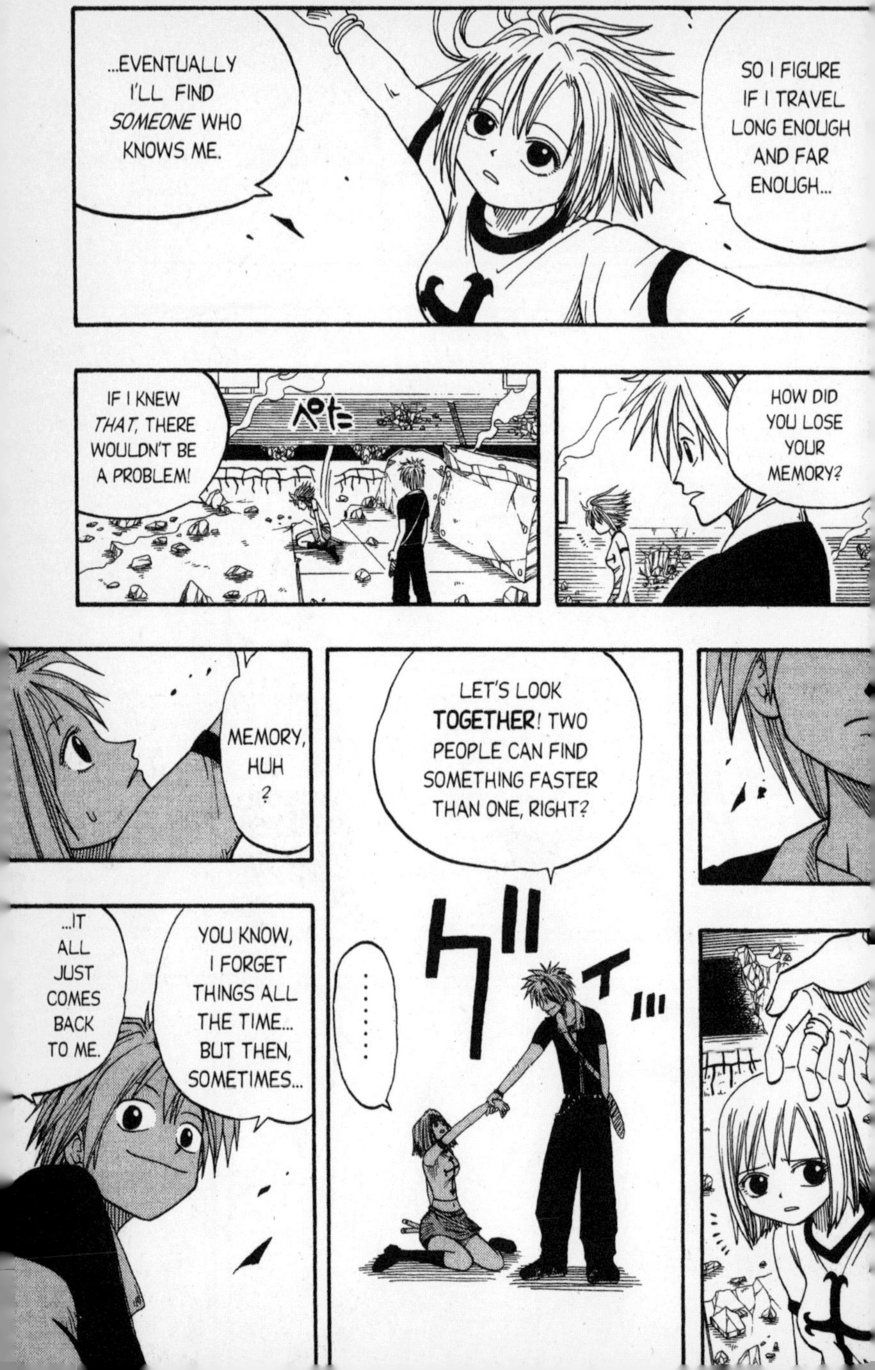
SO I FIGURE IF I TRAVEL LONG ENOUGH AND FAR ENOUGH...
...EVENTUALLY I'LL FIND *SOMEONE* WHO KNOWS ME.
HOW DID YOU LOSE YOUR MEMORY?
ぺた
IF I KNEW *THAT*, THERE WOULDN'T BE A PROBLEM!
LET'S LOOK **TOGETHER**! TWO PEOPLE CAN FIND SOMETHING FASTER THAN ONE, RIGHT?
グイッ
....
MEMORY, HUH ?
YOU KNOW, I FORGET THINGS ALL THE TIME... BUT THEN, SOMETIMES...
...IT ALL JUST COMES BACK TO ME.

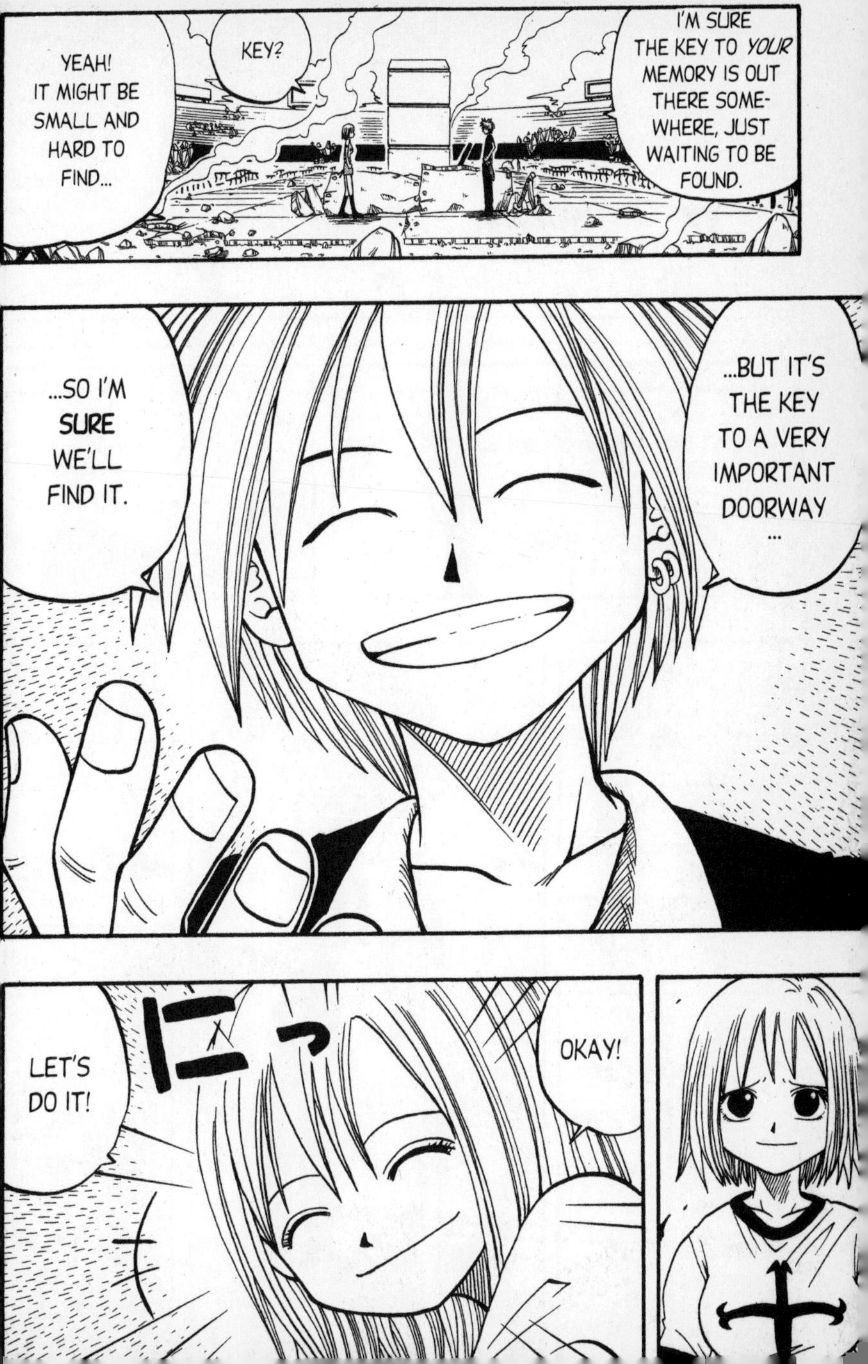
I'M SURE THE KEY TO *YOUR* MEMORY IS OUT THERE SOME-WHERE, JUST WAITING TO BE FOUND.
KEY?
YEAH! IT MIGHT BE SMALL AND HARD TO FIND...
...BUT IT'S THE KEY TO A VERY IMPORTANT DOORWAY ...
...SO I'M **SURE** WE'LL FIND IT.
OKAY!
ニッ
LET'S DO IT!

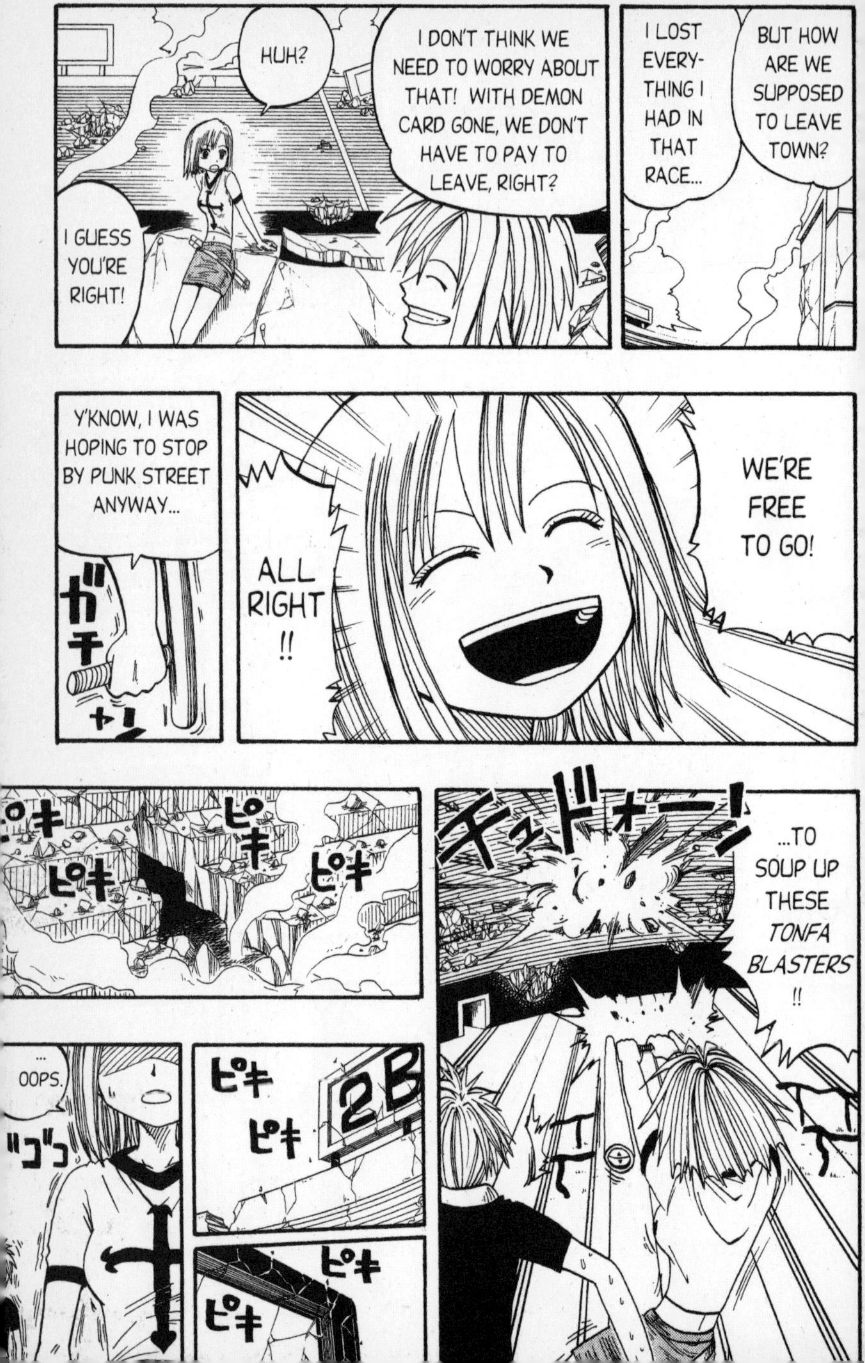
BUT HOW ARE WE SUPPOSED TO LEAVE TOWN?
I LOST EVERY-THING I HAD IN THAT RACE...
I DON'T THINK WE NEED TO WORRY ABOUT THAT! WITH DEMON CARD GONE, WE DON'T HAVE TO PAY TO LEAVE, RIGHT?
HUH?
I GUESS YOU'RE RIGHT!
WE'RE FREE TO GO!
ALL RIGHT !!
Y'KNOW, I WAS HOPING TO STOP BY PUNK STREET ANYWAY...
ガチ
...TO SOUP UP THESE *TONFA BLASTERS* !!
ピキ
ピキ
ピキ
ピキ
ピキ
ピキ
2B
ピキ
ピキ
... OOPS.

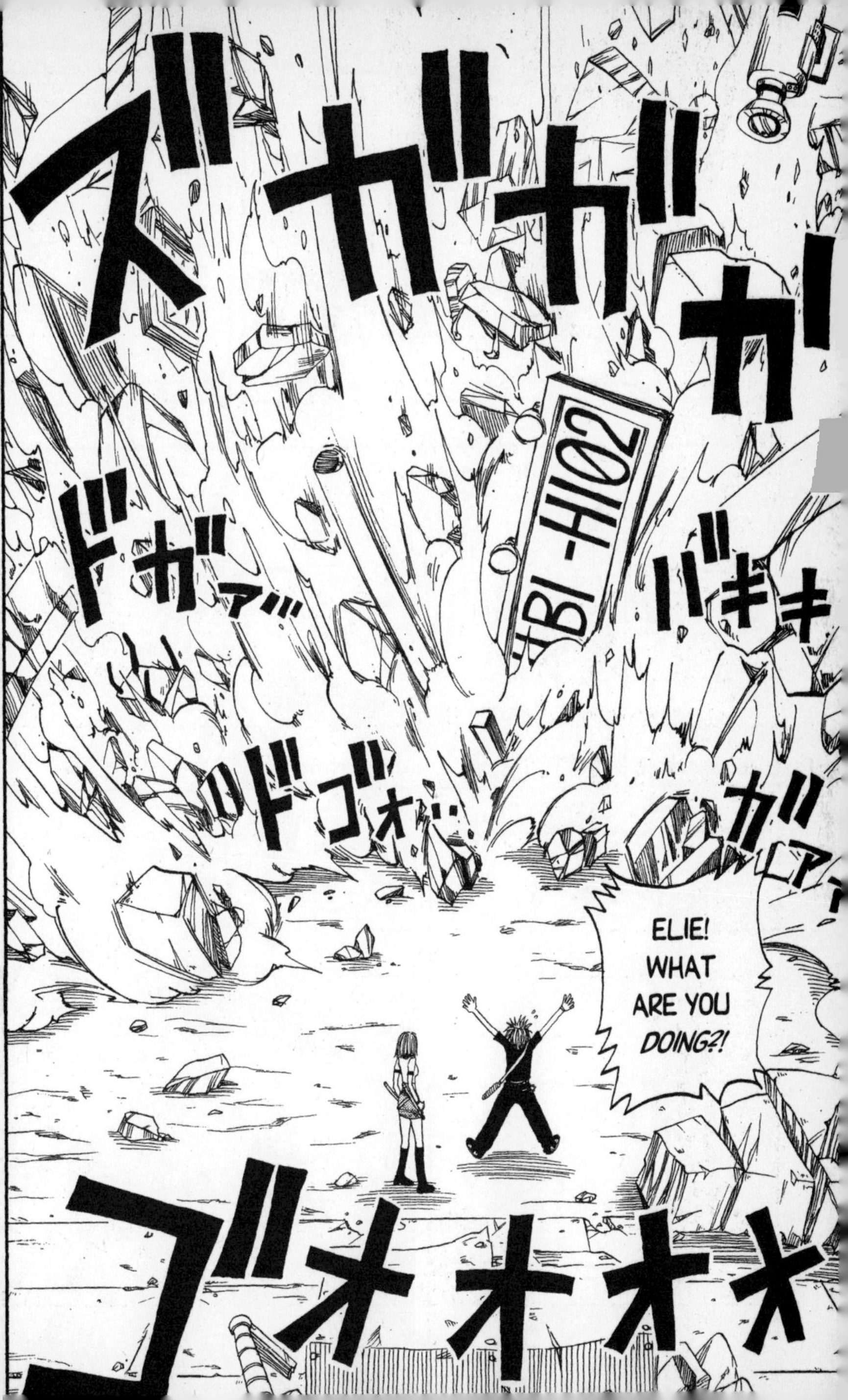
ズガガガ
ドガァ
バキキ
ドゴォ
ガァ
ELIE! WHAT ARE YOU DOING?!
ゴオオオ

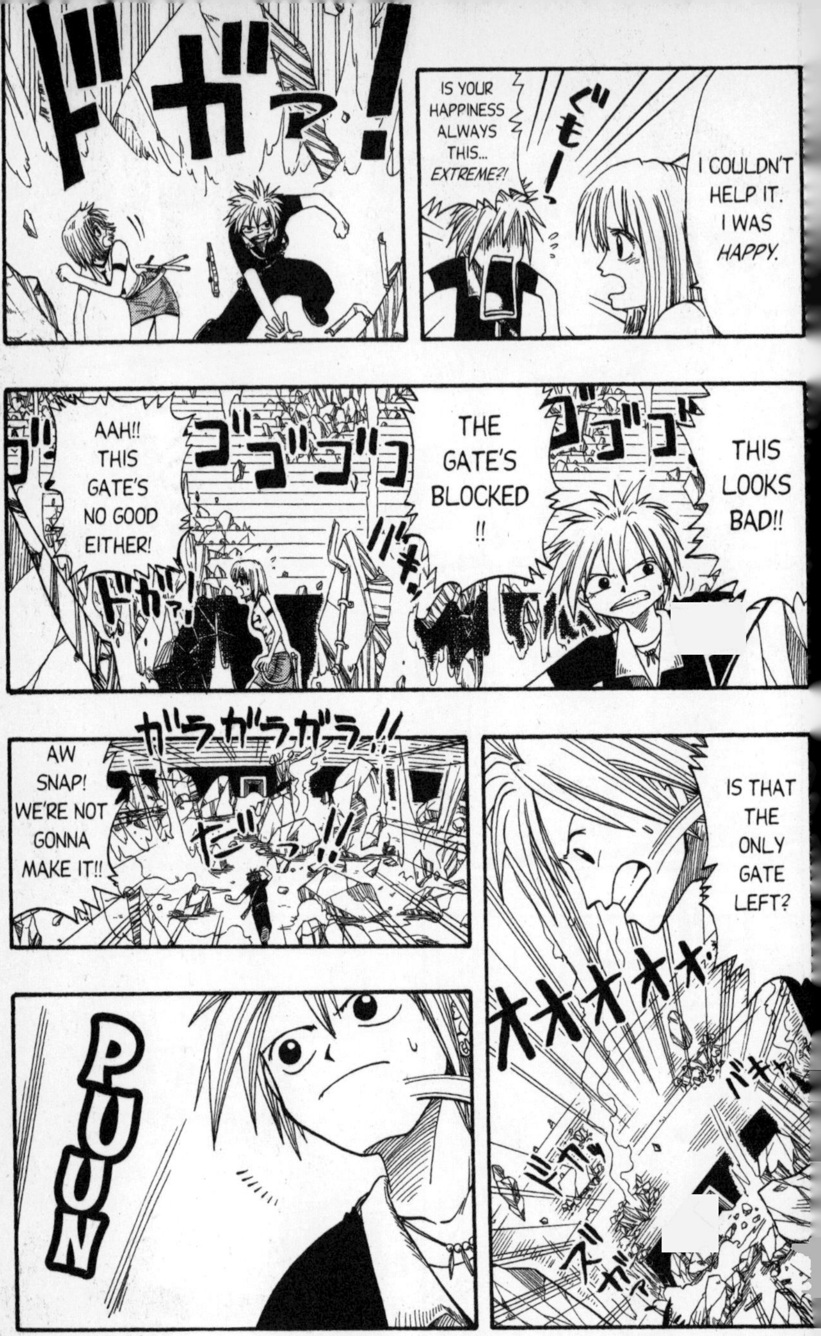
I COULDN'T HELP IT. I WAS *HAPPY.*
ぐもー!
IS YOUR HAPPINESS ALWAYS THIS... *EXTREME?!*
ドガァ!
THIS LOOKS BAD!!
THE GATE'S BLOCKED !!
バキッ
ゴゴゴゴ
AAH!! THIS GATE'S NO GOOD EITHER!
ドガァ!
IS THAT THE ONLY GATE LEFT?
オオオオオ
ガラガラガラ!!
AW SNAP! WE'RE NOT GONNA MAKE IT!!
だっ!!
PUUN

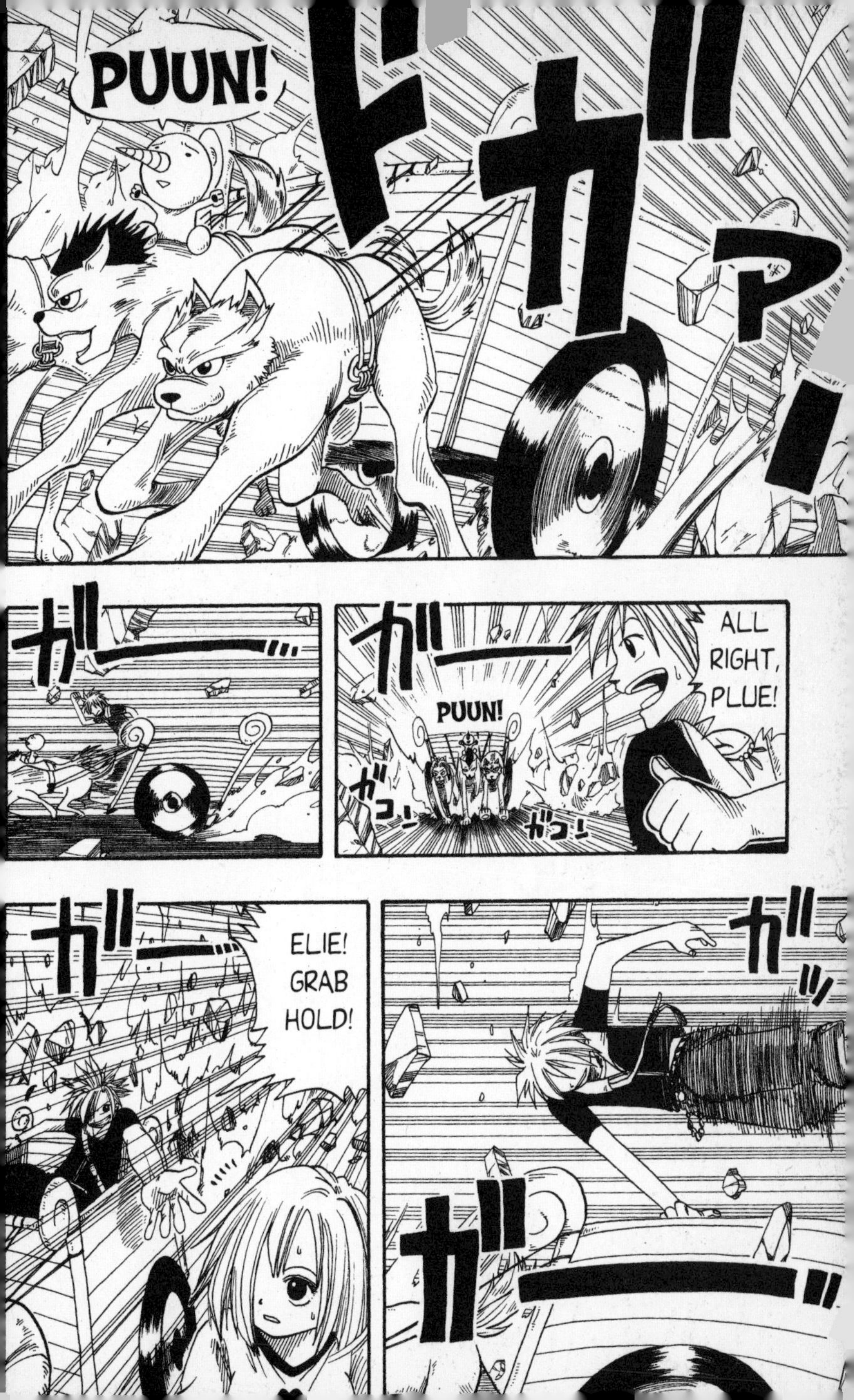
PUUN!
ドガァ！
ALL RIGHT, PLUE!
PUUN!
ガー
ガー
ガッ
ガー
ELIE! GRAB HOLD!
ガー

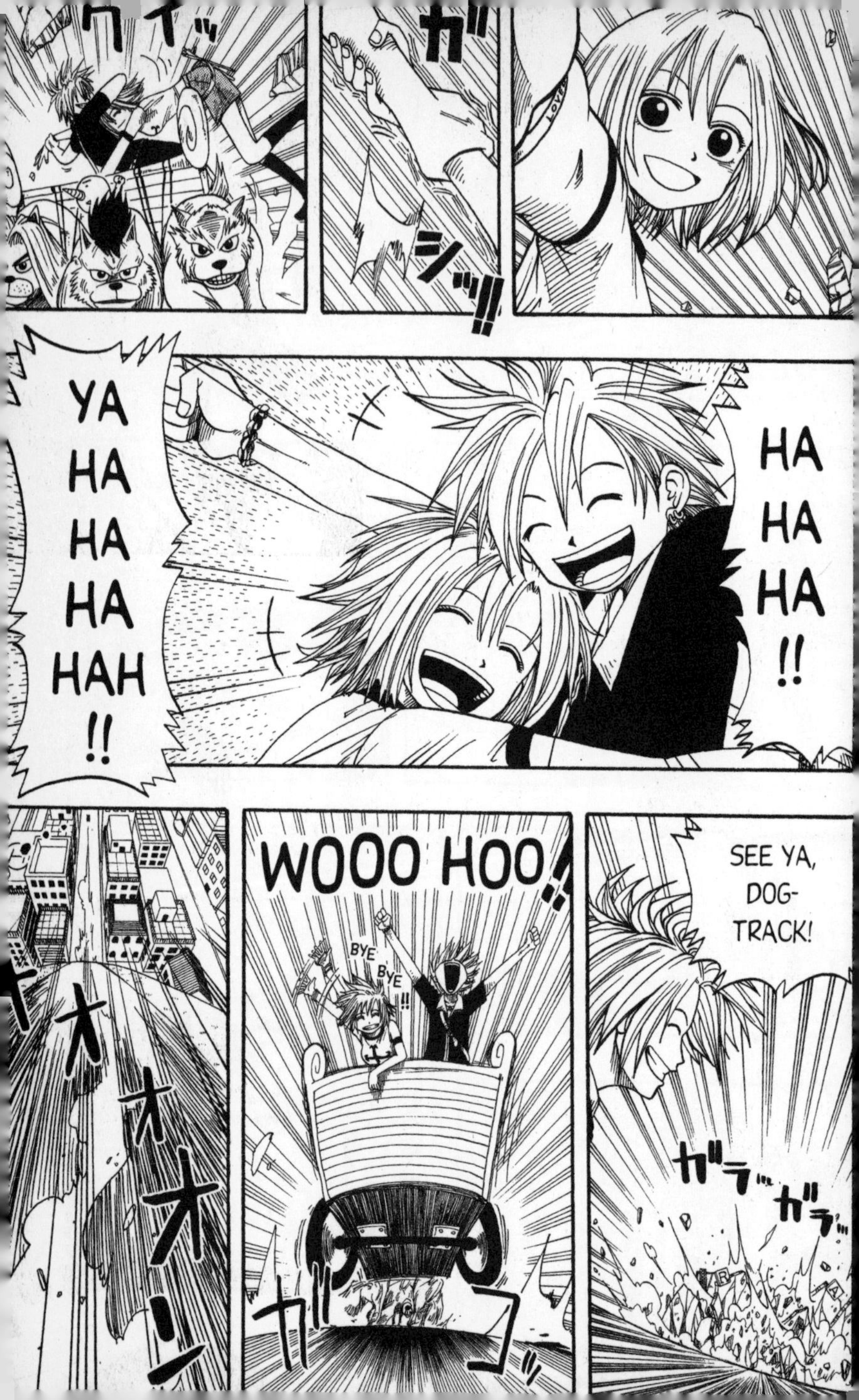
ガッ
HA HA HA!!
YA HA HA HA HAH!!
SEE YA, DOG-TRACK!
WOOO HOO!!
BYE BYE!!

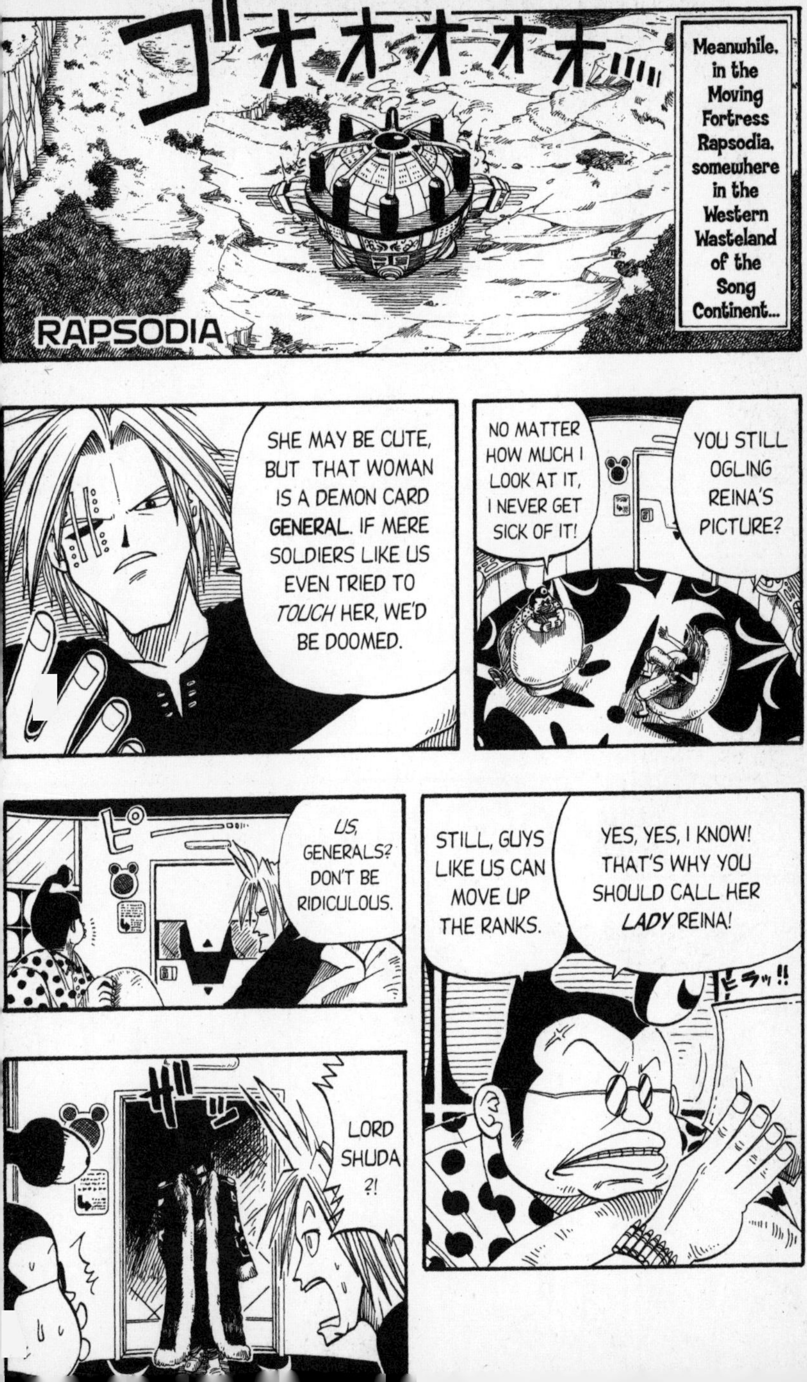
Meanwhile, in the Moving Fortress Rapsodia, somewhere in the Western Wasteland of the Song Continent...
ゴオオオオオ
RAPSODIA
YOU STILL OGLING REINA'S PICTURE?
NO MATTER HOW MUCH I LOOK AT IT, I NEVER GET SICK OF IT!
SHE MAY BE CUTE, BUT THAT WOMAN IS A DEMON CARD GENERAL. IF MERE SOLDIERS LIKE US EVEN TRIED TO TOUCH HER, WE'D BE DOOMED.
YES, YES, I KNOW! THAT'S WHY YOU SHOULD CALL HER LADY REINA!
STILL, GUYS LIKE US CAN MOVE UP THE RANKS.
US, GENERALS? DON'T BE RIDICULOUS.
ピー
LORD SHUDA?!

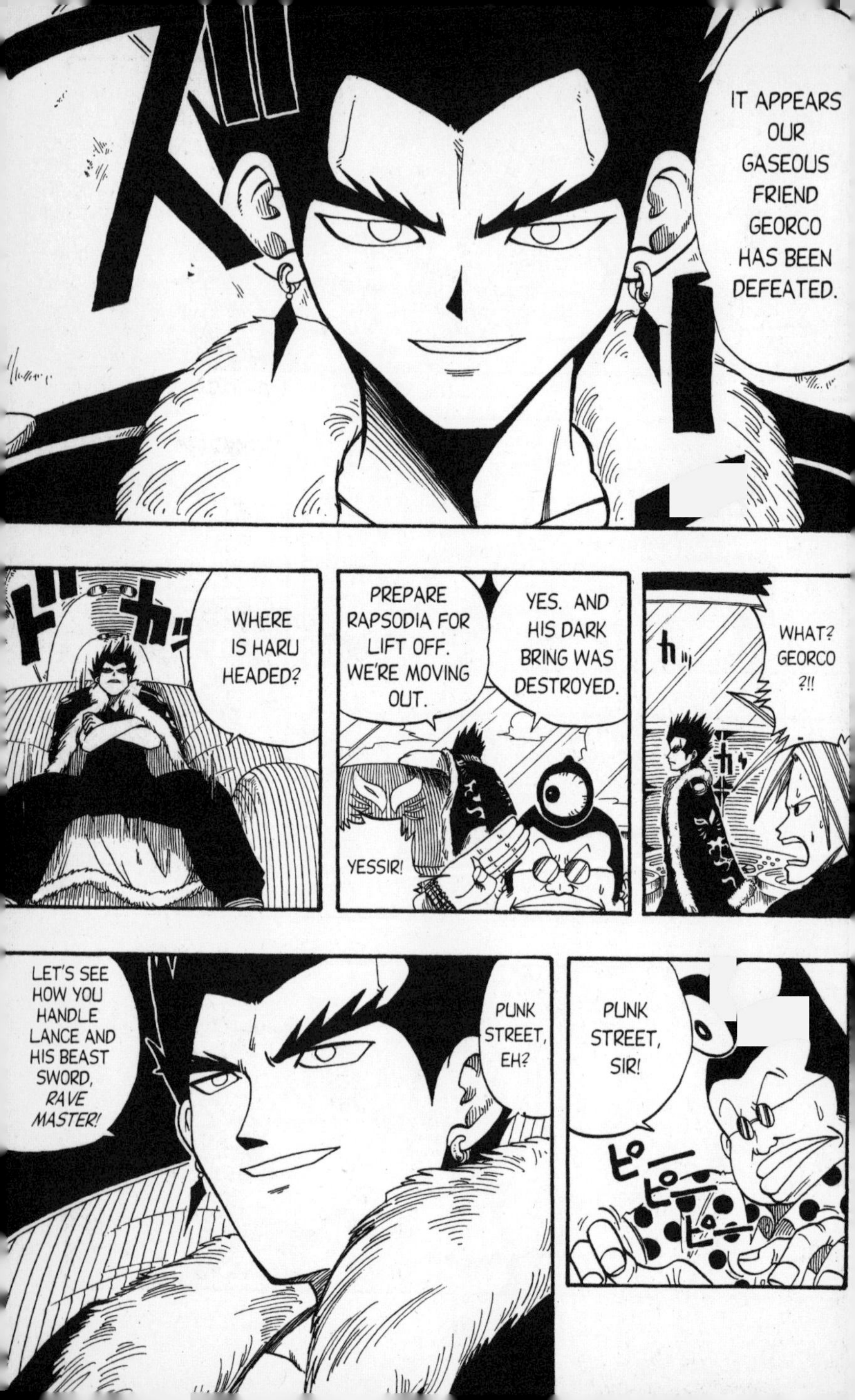
IT APPEARS OUR GASEOUS FRIEND GEORCO HAS BEEN DEFEATED.
WHAT? GEORCO ?!!
YES. AND HIS DARK BRING WAS DESTROYED.
PREPARE RAPSODIA FOR LIFT OFF. WE'RE MOVING OUT.
YESSIR!
WHERE IS HARU HEADED?
PUNK STREET, SIR!
PUNK STREET, EH?
LET'S SEE HOW YOU HANDLE LANCE AND HIS BEAST SWORD, *RAVE MASTER!*

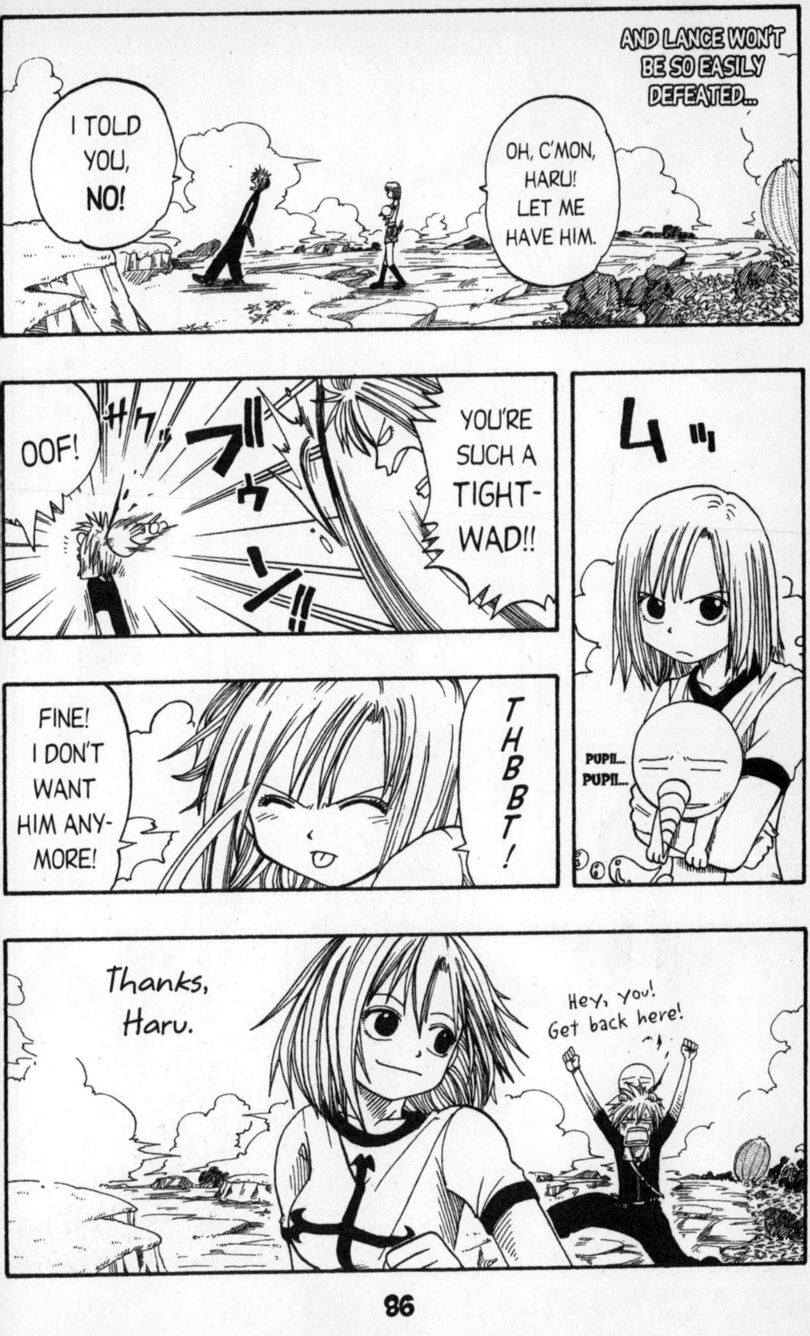

AND LANCE WON'T BE SO EASILY DEFEATED...
OH, C'MON, HARU! LET ME HAVE HIM.
I TOLD YOU, NO!
ムッ
PUPII... PUPII...
YOU'RE SUCH A TIGHT-WAD!!
ブゥーン!!
サクッ
OOF!
THBBT!
FINE! I DON'T WANT HIM ANY-MORE!
Hey, you! Get back here!
Thanks, Haru.

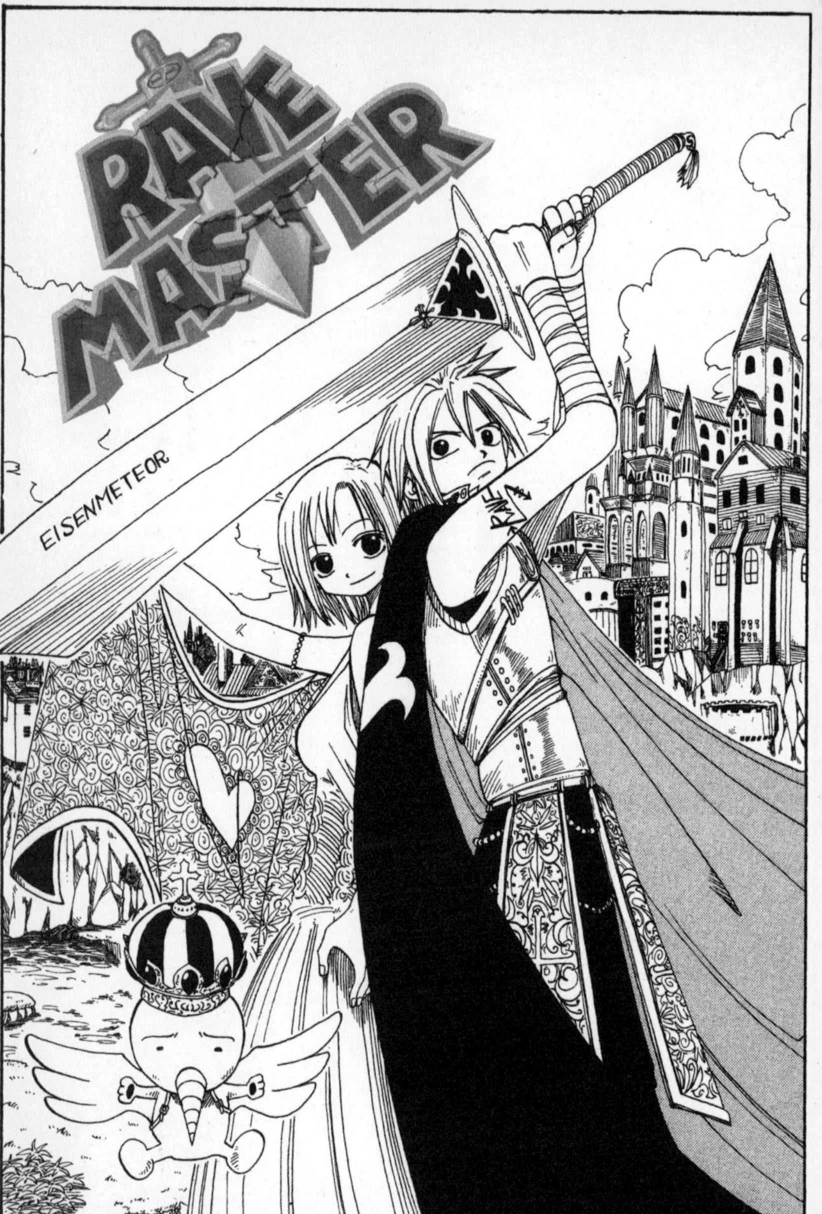
RAVE MASTER
EISENMETEOR
RAVE

RAVE 9 ✠ THE LEGENDARY BLACKSMITH

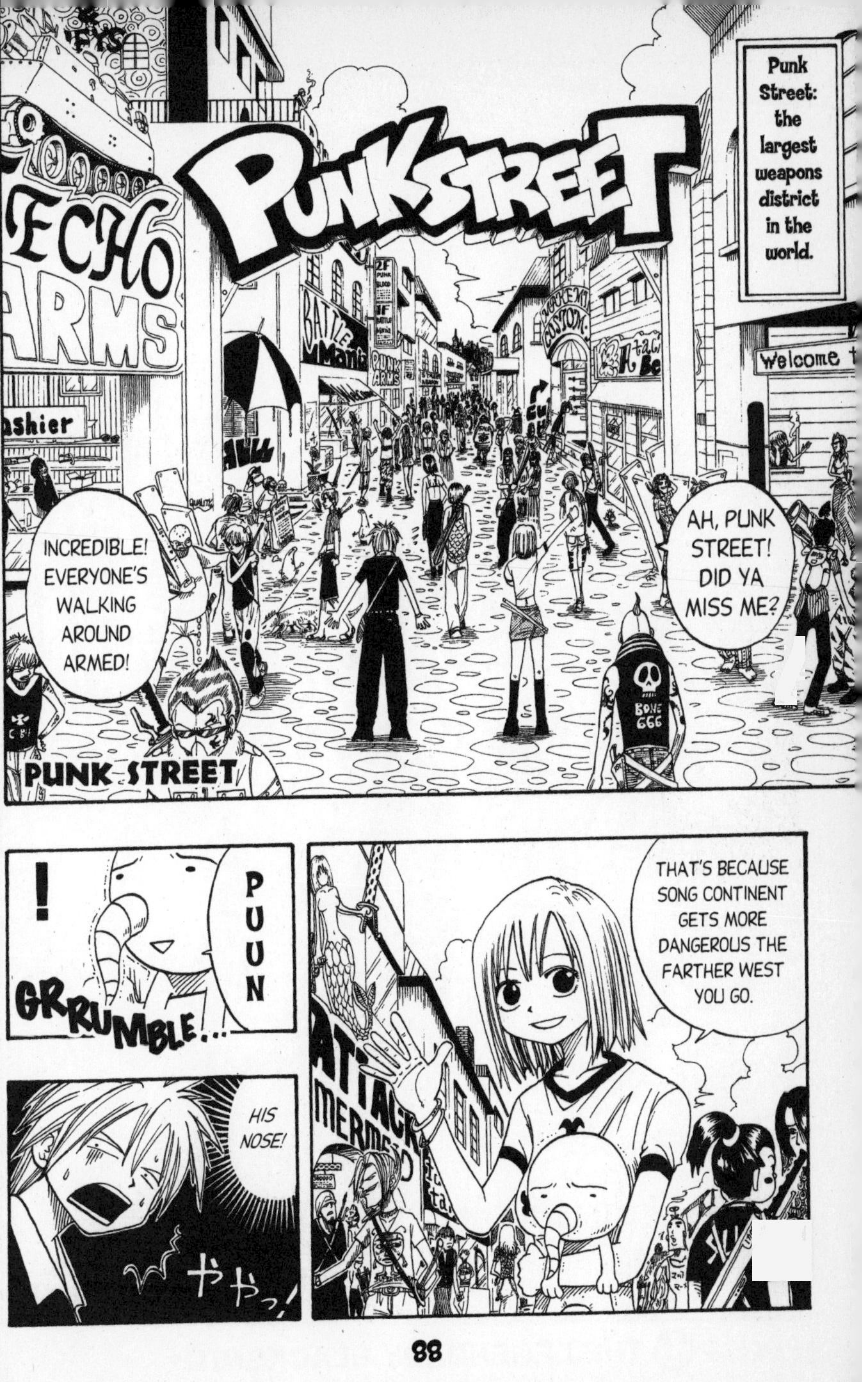

Punk Street: the largest weapons district in the world.
PUNKSTREET
AH, PUNK STREET! DID YA MISS ME?
INCREDIBLE! EVERYONE'S WALKING AROUND ARMED!
ECHO ARMS
Welcome
PUNK STREET
THAT'S BECAUSE SONG CONTINENT GETS MORE DANGEROUS THE FARTHER WEST YOU GO.
PUUN
!
GRRUMBLE...
HIS NOSE!

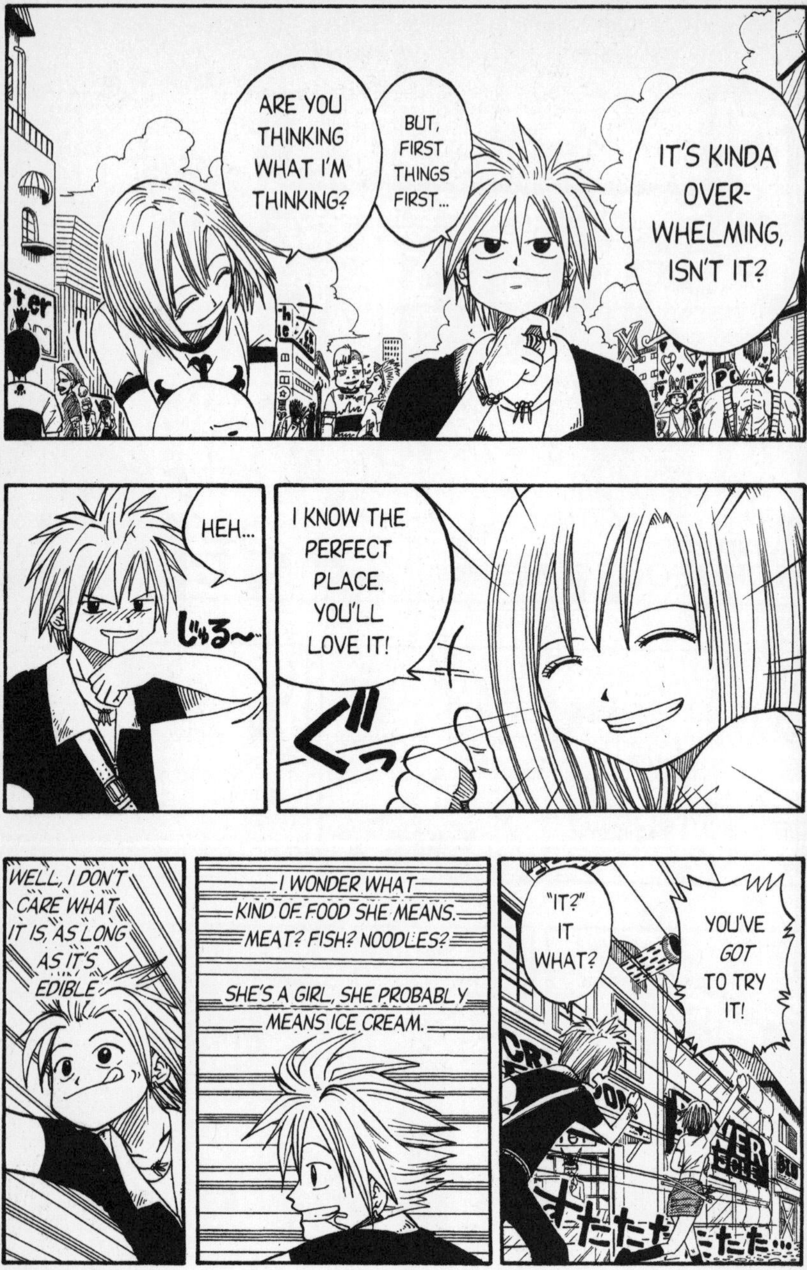
IT'S KINDA OVER-WHELMING, ISN'T IT?
BUT, FIRST THINGS FIRST...
ARE YOU THINKING WHAT I'M THINKING?
I KNOW THE PERFECT PLACE. YOU'LL LOVE IT!
ぐっ
HEH...
じゅる～
YOU'VE GOT TO TRY IT!
"IT?" IT WHAT?
たたた たたた…
I WONDER WHAT KIND OF FOOD SHE MEANS. MEAT? FISH? NOODLES?
SHE'S A GIRL, SHE PROBABLY MEANS ICE CREAM.
WELL, I DON'T CARE WHAT IT IS, AS LONG AS IT'S EDIBLE.

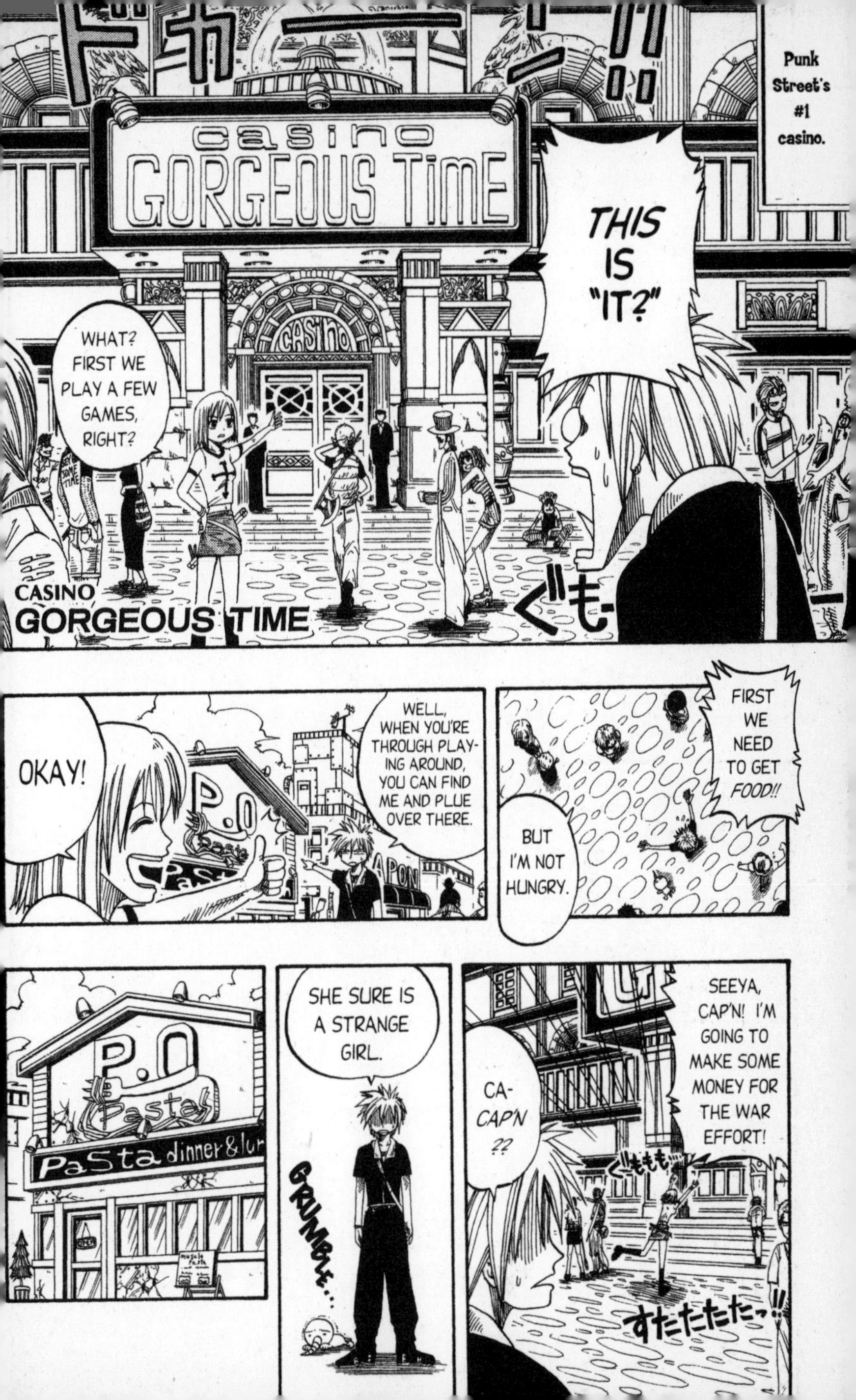
Punk Street's #1 casino.
casino GORGEOUS TimE
THIS IS "IT?"
WHAT? FIRST WE PLAY A FEW GAMES, RIGHT?
CASINO GORGEOUS TIME
ぐも
FIRST WE NEED TO GET FOOD!!
BUT I'M NOT HUNGRY.
WELL, WHEN YOU'RE THROUGH PLAYING AROUND, YOU CAN FIND ME AND PLUE OVER THERE.
OKAY!
SEEYA, CAP'N! I'M GOING TO MAKE SOME MONEY FOR THE WAR EFFORT!
CA-CAP'N ??
ぐももも
すたたたたっ!!
SHE SURE IS A STRANGE GIRL.
GRUMBLE...
P.O Pasta
PaSta dinner &lu

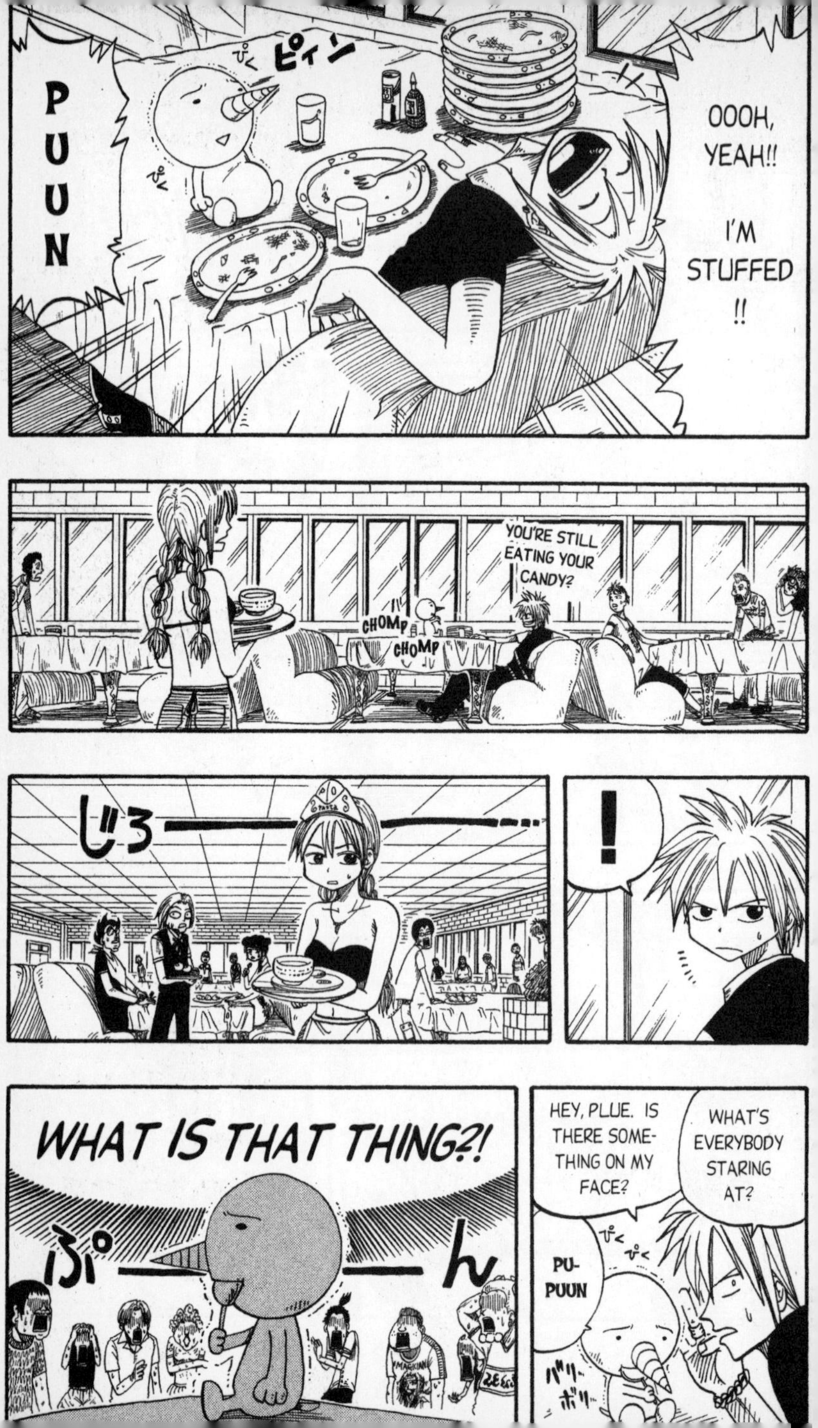

OOOH, YEAH!!
I'M STUFFED!!
ピィン
ぴく
ぴく
PUUN
YOU'RE STILL EATING YOUR CANDY?
CHOMP
CHOMP
!
じろ
WHAT'S EVERYBODY STARING AT?
HEY, PLUE. IS THERE SOME-THING ON MY FACE?
ぴく ぴく
PU-PUUN
バリ
ボリ
WHAT IS THAT THING?!
ぷ
ん

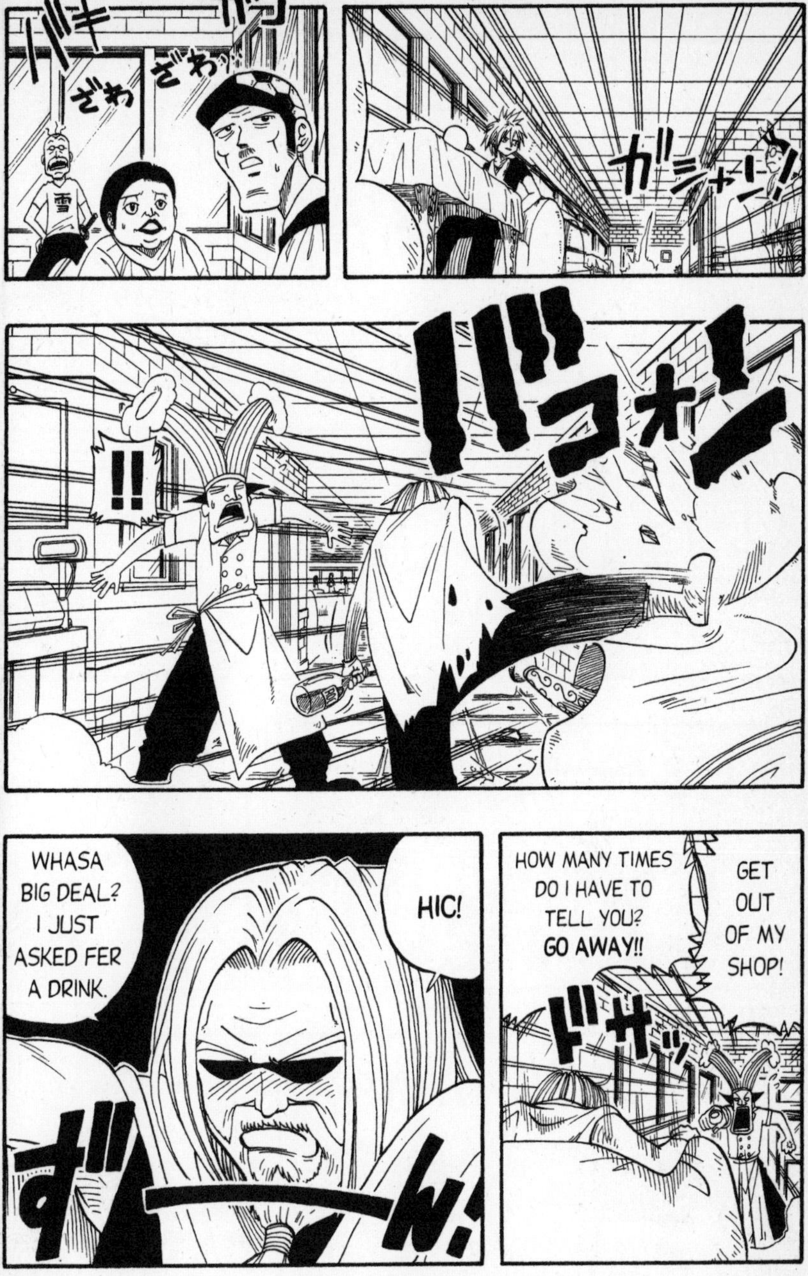
ガシャーン!
ガコ
バキ
ざわ…
ざわ
バコォン
!!
HOW MANY TIMES DO I HAVE TO TELL YOU? GO AWAY!!
GET OUT OF MY SHOP!
ドサッ
HIC!
WHASA BIG DEAL? I JUST ASKED FER A DRINK.
ずん

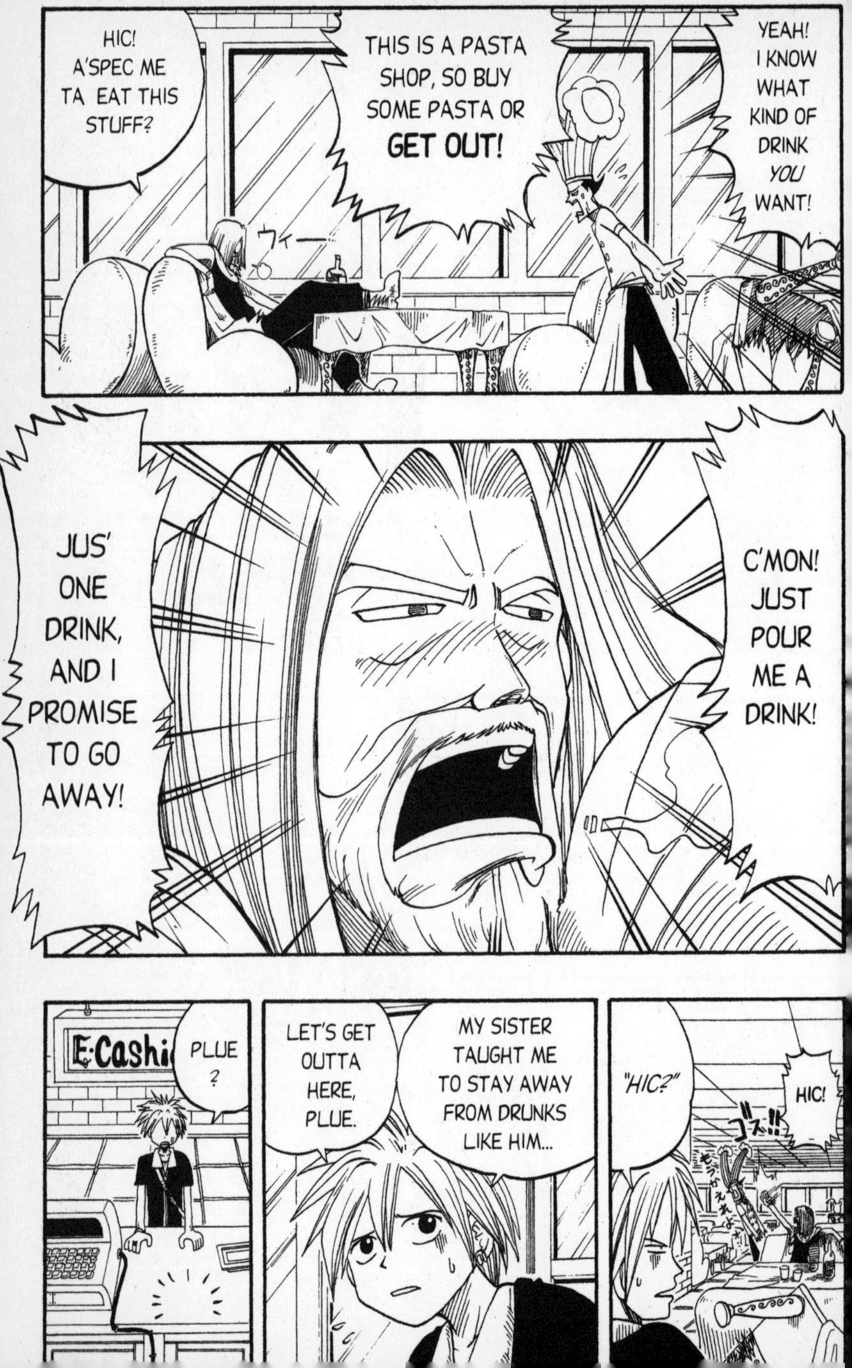
YEAH! I KNOW WHAT KIND OF DRINK *YOU* WANT!
THIS IS A PASTA SHOP, SO BUY SOME PASTA OR **GET OUT!**
ウィー
HIC! A'SPEC ME TA EAT THIS STUFF?
C'MON! JUST POUR ME A DRINK!
JUS' ONE DRINK, AND I PROMISE TO GO AWAY!
HIC!
ゴズ!!
"HIC?"
MY SISTER TAUGHT ME TO STAY AWAY FROM DRUNKS LIKE HIM...
LET'S GET OUTTA HERE, PLUE.
E:Cashi
PLUE ?

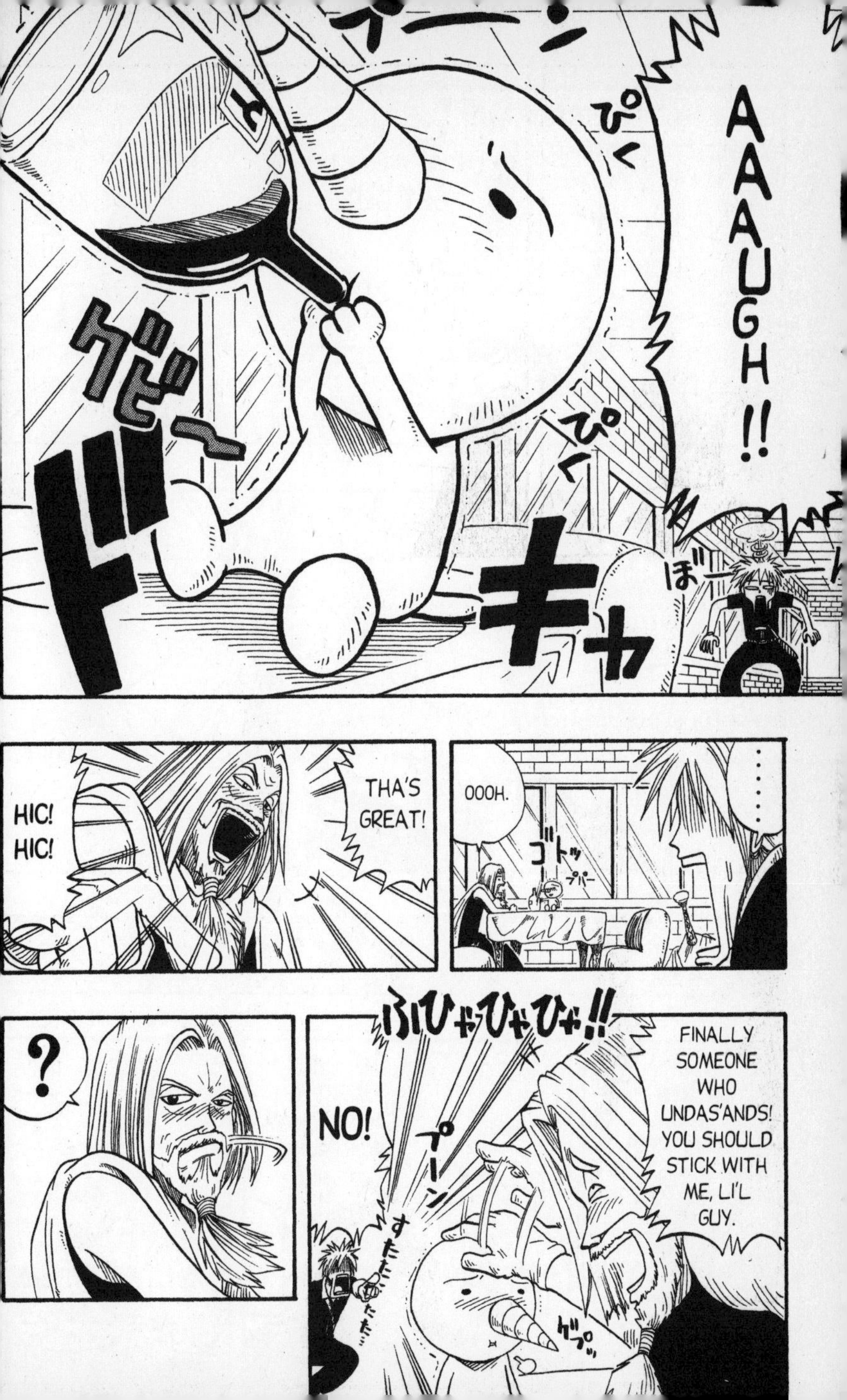
AAAUGH!!
. . . . .
OOOH.
THA'S GREAT!
HIC! HIC!
FINALLY SOMEONE WHO UNDAS'ANDS! YOU SHOULD STICK WITH ME, LI'L GUY.
ふひゃひゃひゃ!!
NO!
?

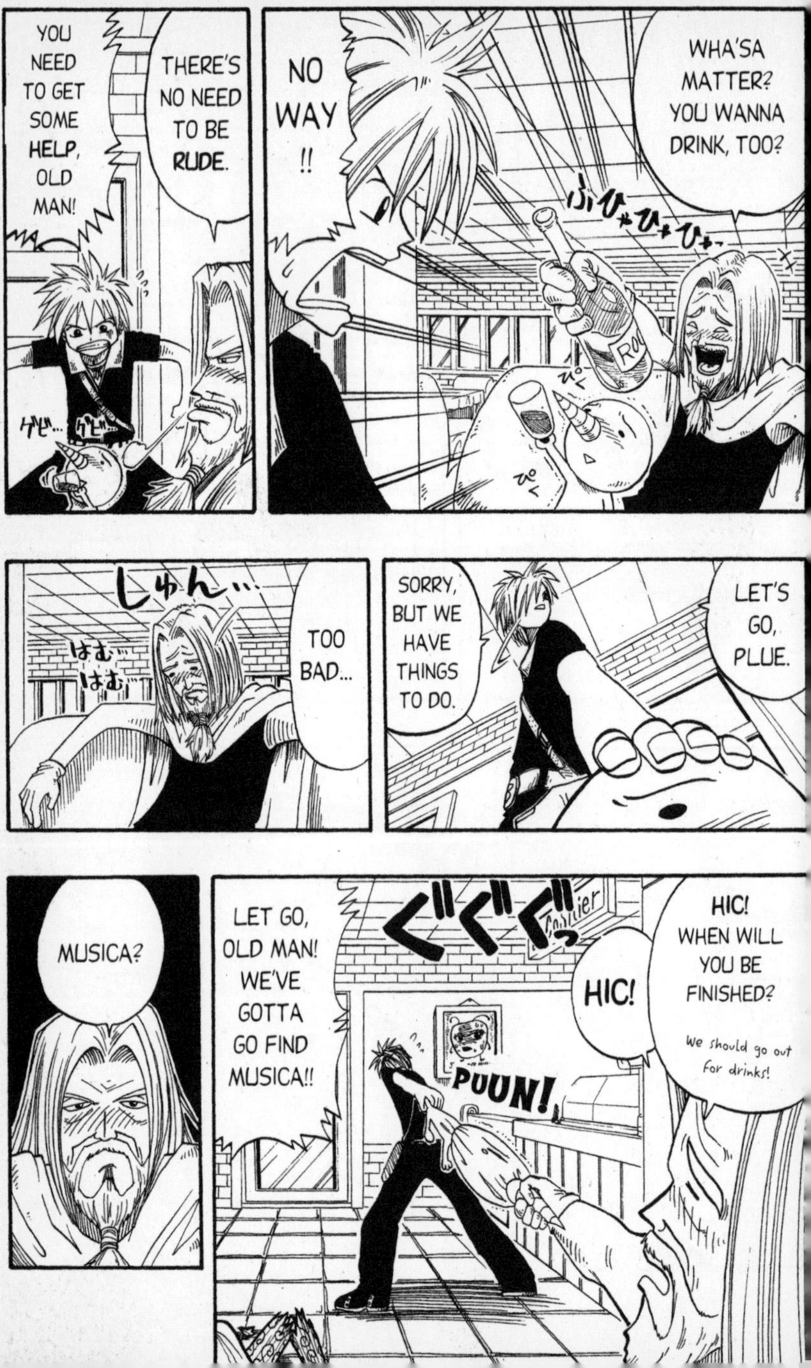
WHA'SA MATTER? YOU WANNA DRINK, TOO?
ふひゃひゃひゃ
NO WAY!!
THERE'S NO NEED TO BE RUDE.
YOU NEED TO GET SOME HELP, OLD MAN!
LET'S GO, PLUE.
SORRY, BUT WE HAVE THINGS TO DO.
TOO BAD...
しゅん…
はむ はむ
HIC! WHEN WILL YOU BE FINISHED?
We should go out for drinks!
HIC!
ぐぐぐっ
LET GO, OLD MAN! WE'VE GOTTA GO FIND MUSICA!!
PUUN!
MUSICA?

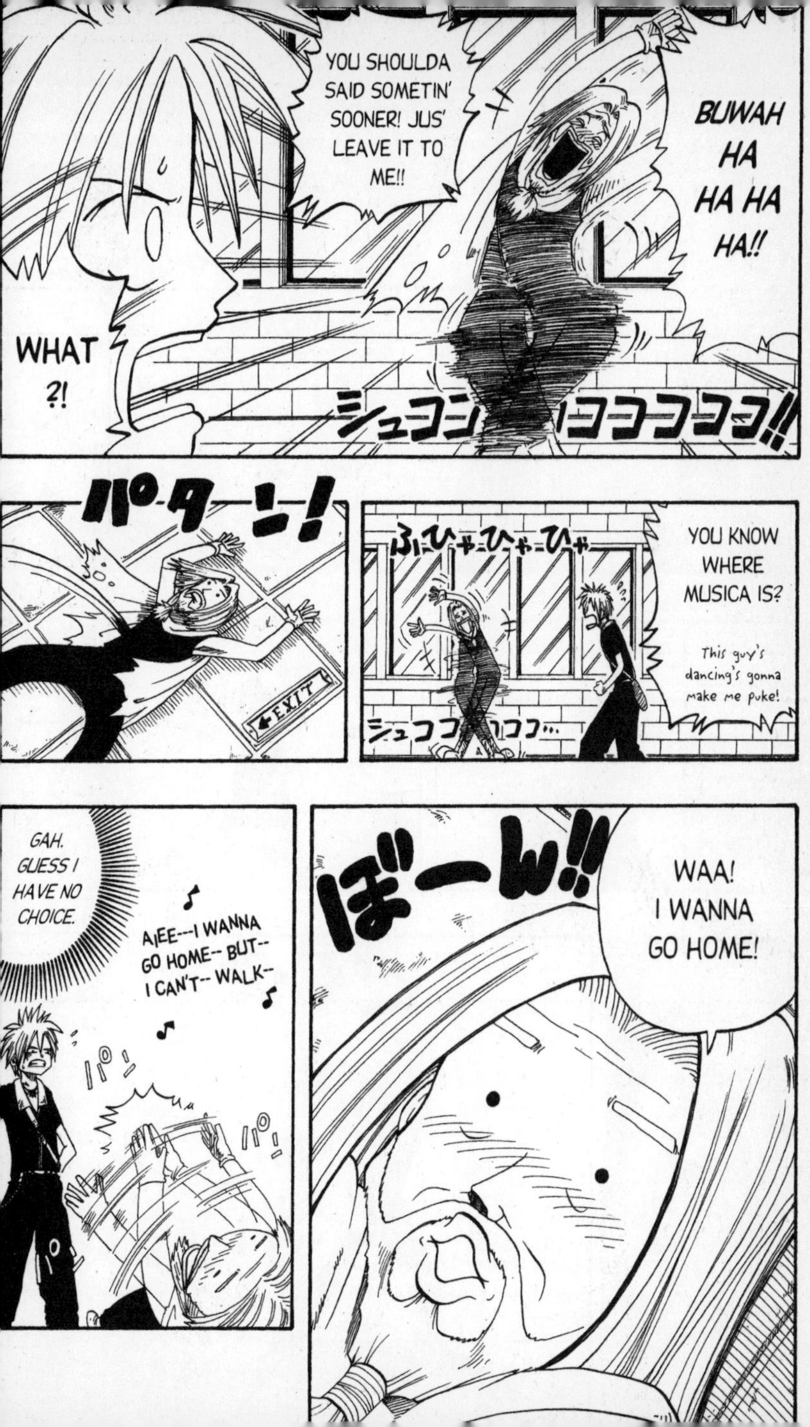
YOU SHOULDA SAID SOMETIN' SOONER! JUS' LEAVE IT TO ME!!
BUWAH HA HA HA HA!!
シュコン
WHAT ?!
ふひゃひゃひゃ
YOU KNOW WHERE MUSICA IS?
This guy's dancing's gonna make me puke!
パターン!
EXIT
ぼーん!!
WAA! I WANNA GO HOME!
GAH. GUESS I HAVE NO CHOICE.
AIEE---I WANNA GO HOME-- BUT-- I CAN'T-- WALK--

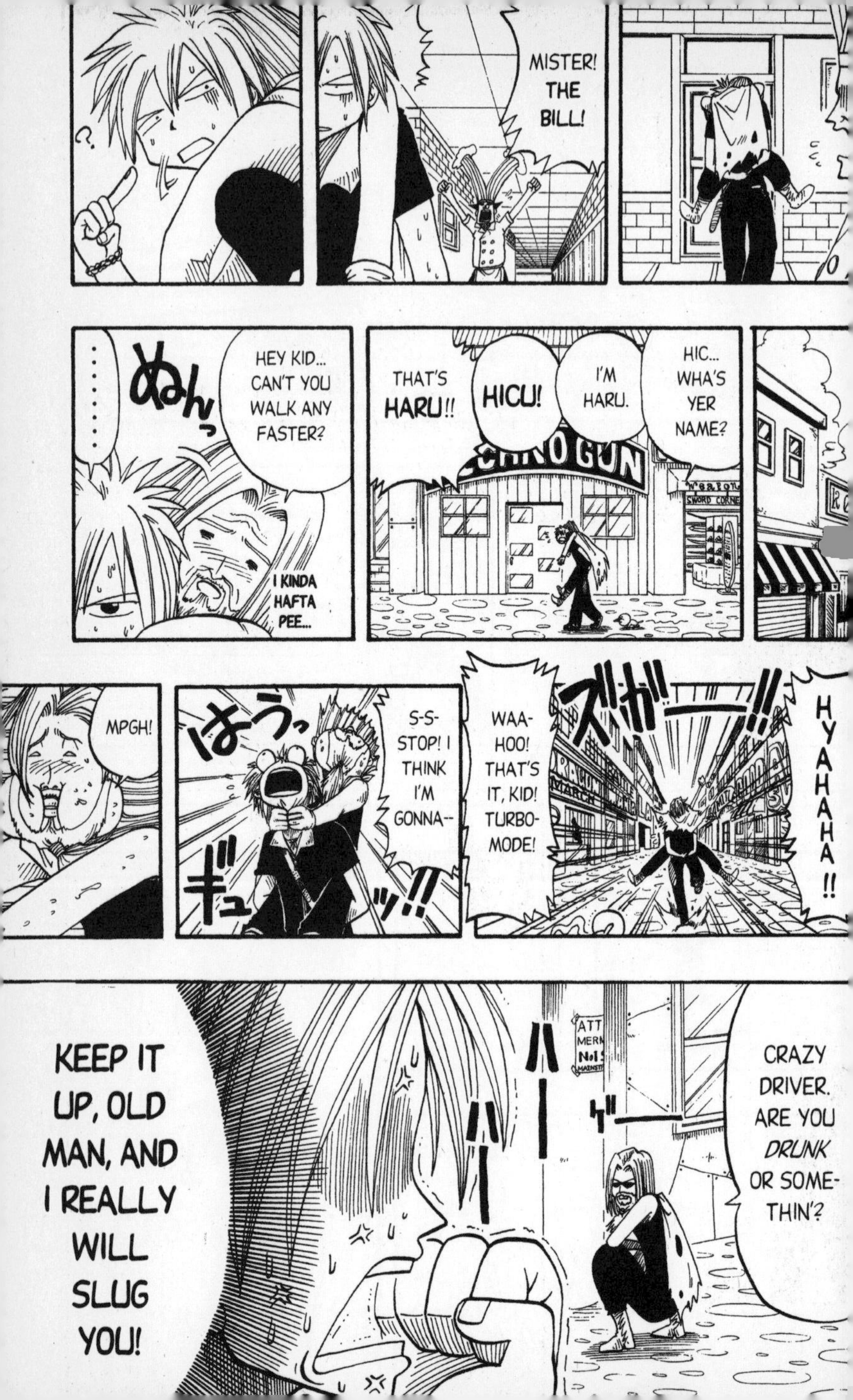
MISTER! THE BILL!
HIC... WHA'S YER NAME?
I'M HARU.
HICU!
THAT'S HARU!!
HEY KID... CAN'T YOU WALK ANY FASTER?
ぬんっ
....
I KINDA HAFTA PEE...
HYAHAHAHA!!
ズガーーー!!
WAA-HOO! THAT'S IT, KID! TURBO-MODE!
S-S-STOP! I THINK I'M GONNA--
はうっ
ギュッ!!
MPGH!
CRAZY DRIVER. ARE YOU *DRUNK* OR SOMETHIN'?
ハーハー
ゲー
KEEP IT UP, OLD MAN, AND I REALLY WILL SLUG YOU!

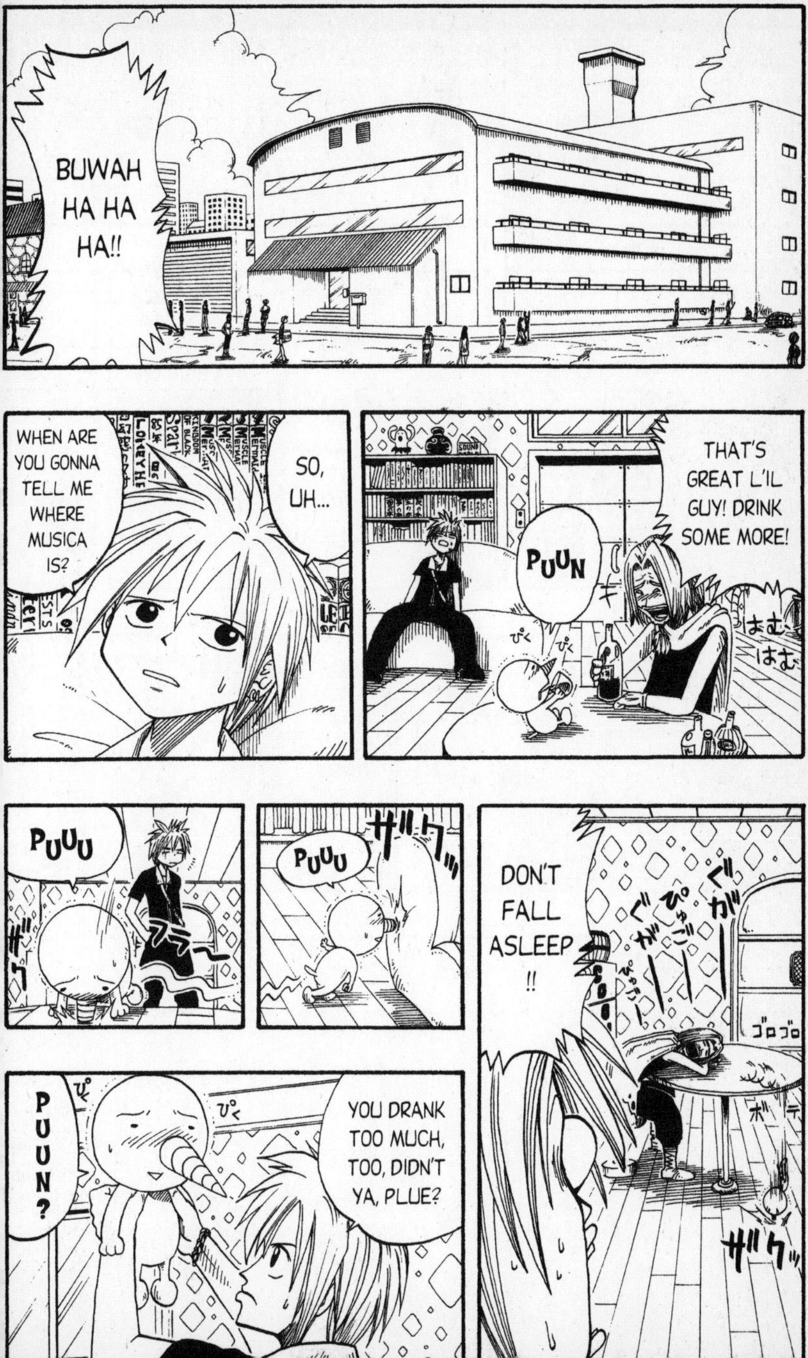
BUWAH HA HA HA!!
THAT'S GREAT L'IL GUY! DRINK SOME MORE!
PUUN
はむ はむ
ぴく ぴく
SO, UH...
WHEN ARE YOU GONNA TELL ME WHERE MUSICA IS?
DON'T FALL ASLEEP!!
ぐがー
ぴゅごー
ぐがー
ゴロゴロ
ボテ
ザクッ
PUUU
ザクッ
PUUU
フラ〜
ザク
YOU DRANK TOO MUCH, TOO, DIDN'T YA, PLUE?
ぴく
PUUUN?

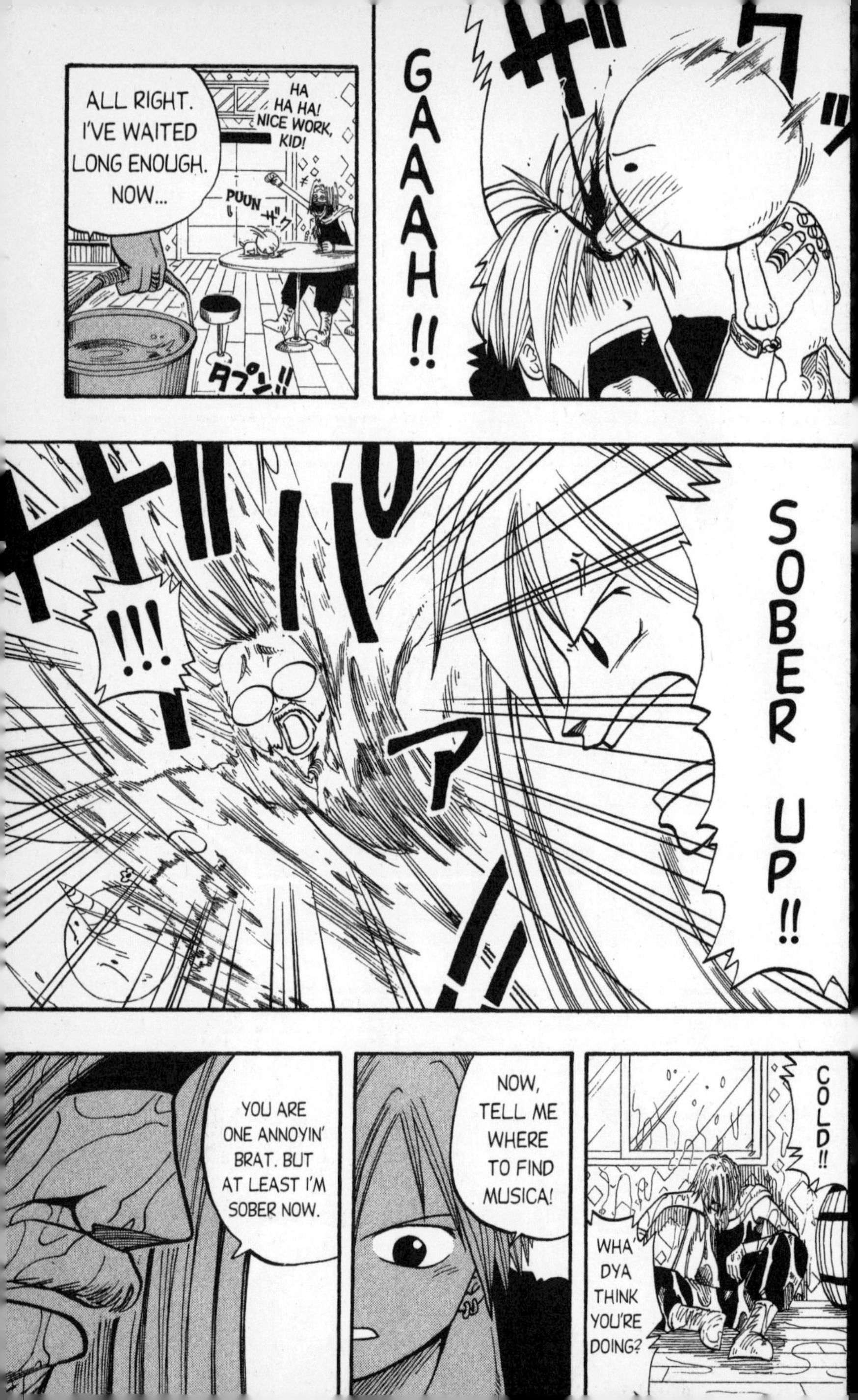

GAAAH!!
HA HA HA! NICE WORK, KID!
ALL RIGHT. I'VE WAITED LONG ENOUGH. NOW...
PUUN
SOBER UP!!
!!!
COLD!!
WHA' DYA THINK YOU'RE DOING?
NOW, TELL ME WHERE TO FIND MUSICA!
YOU ARE ONE ANNOYIN' BRAT. BUT AT LEAST I'M SOBER NOW.

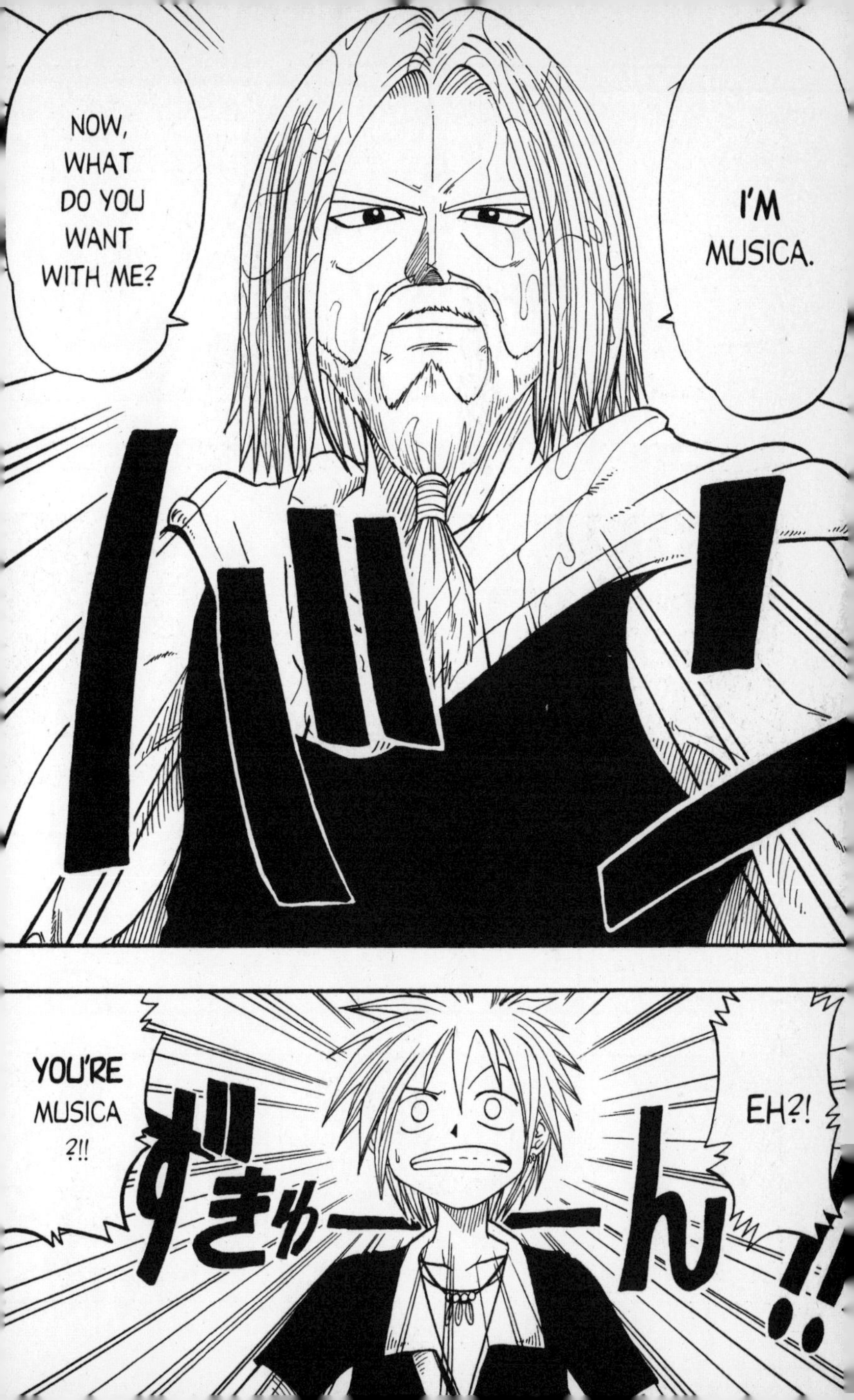
I'M MUSICA.
NOW, WHAT DO YOU WANT WITH ME?
EH?!
YOU'RE MUSICA ?!!
ずぎゃーーん!!

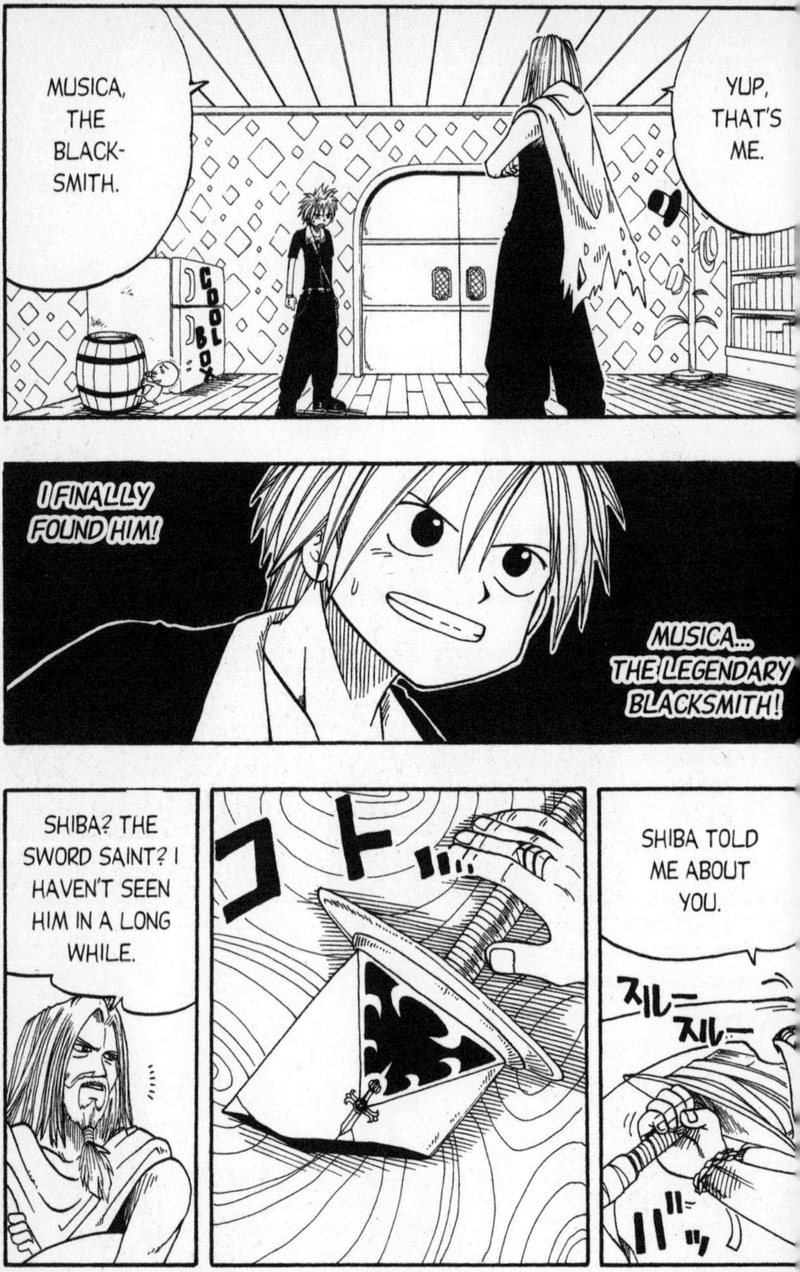
YUP, THAT'S ME.
MUSICA, THE BLACKSMITH.
COOL BOX
I FINALLY FOUND HIM!
MUSICA... THE LEGENDARY BLACKSMITH!
SHIBA TOLD ME ABOUT YOU.
スルー スルー
バッ
コト
SHIBA? THE SWORD SAINT? I HAVEN'T SEEN HIM IN A LONG WHILE.

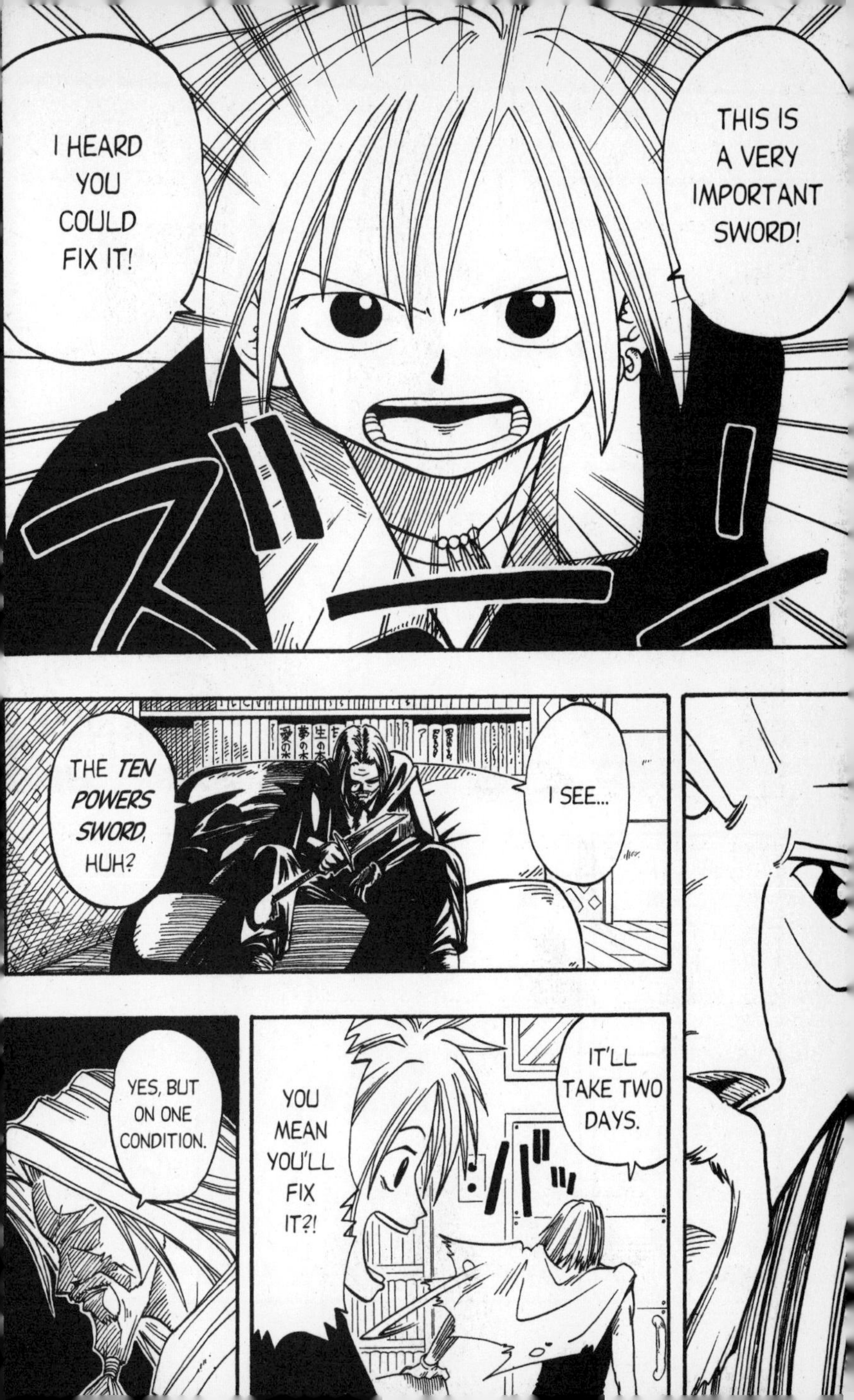
THIS IS A VERY IMPORTANT SWORD!
I HEARD YOU COULD FIX IT!
I SEE...
THE *TEN POWERS SWORD*, HUH?
IT'LL TAKE TWO DAYS.
YOU MEAN YOU'LL FIX IT?!
YES, BUT ON ONE CONDITION.

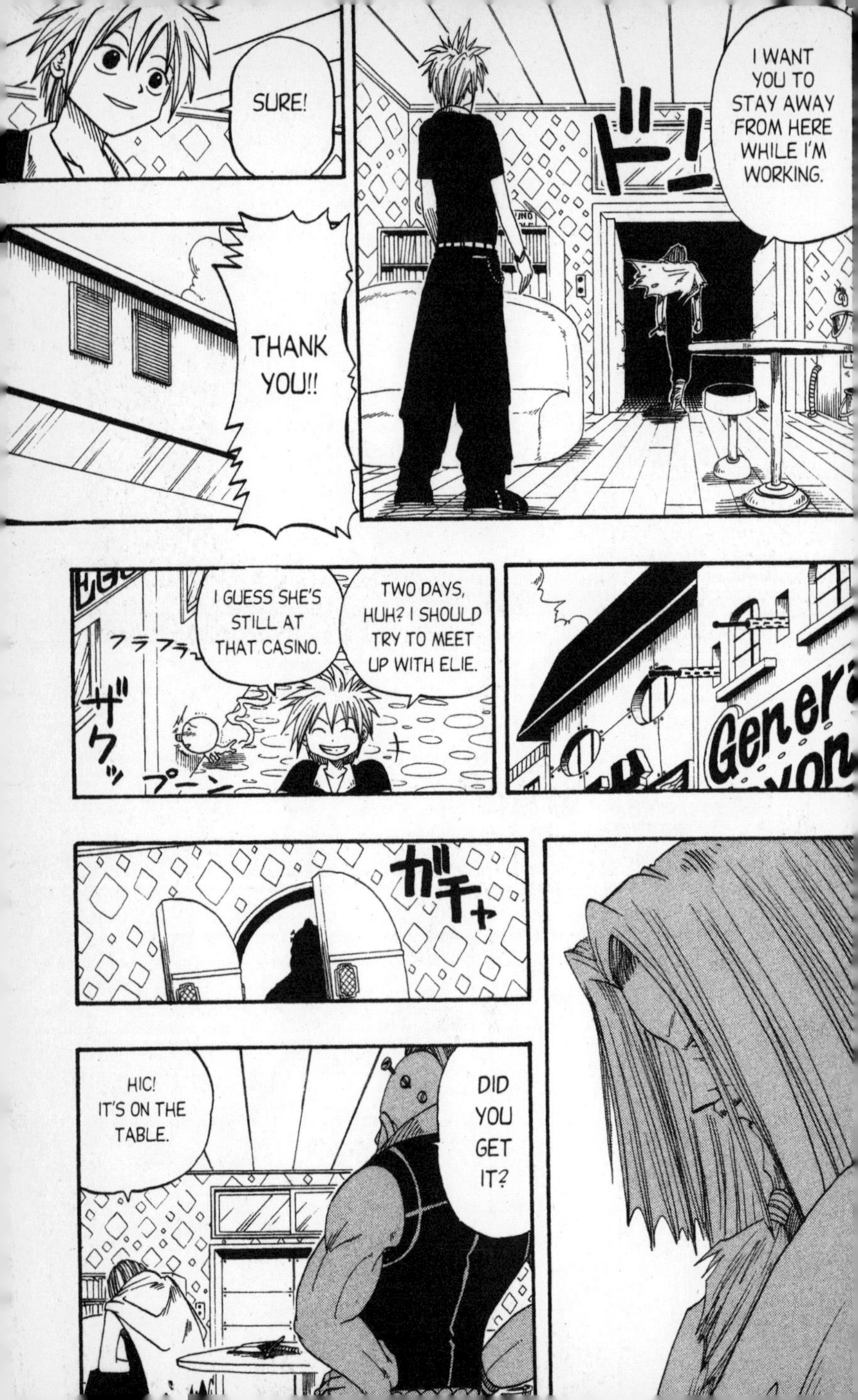

I WANT YOU TO STAY AWAY FROM HERE WHILE I'M WORKING.
ドーン
SURE!
THANK YOU!!
TWO DAYS, HUH? I SHOULD TRY TO MEET UP WITH ELIE.
I GUESS SHE'S STILL AT THAT CASINO.
フラフラ
ザクッ
プーン
ガチャ
DID YOU GET IT?
HIC! IT'S ON THE TABLE.

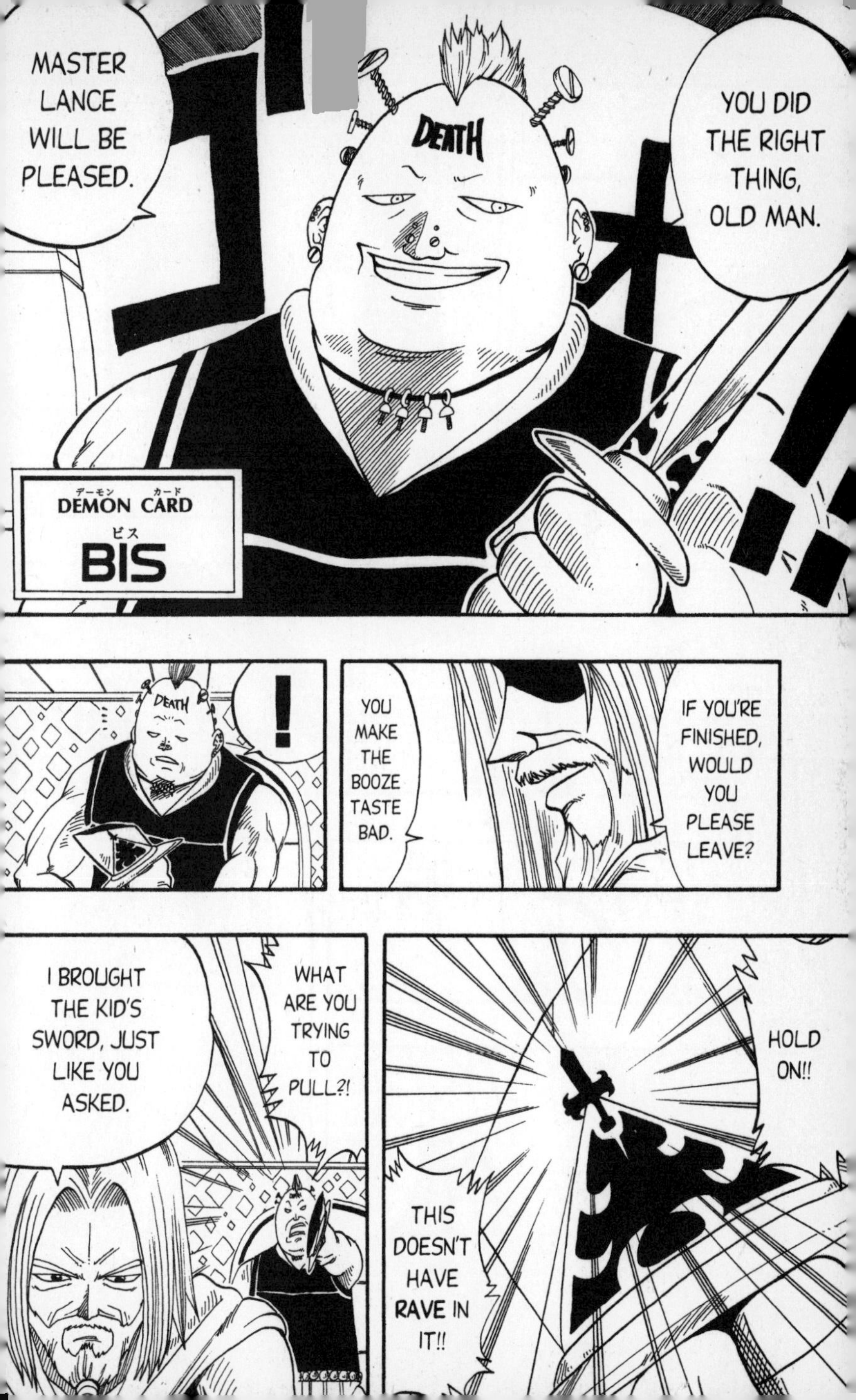
YOU DID THE RIGHT THING, OLD MAN.
MASTER LANCE WILL BE PLEASED.
デーモン カード
DEMON CARD
ビス
BIS
IF YOU'RE FINISHED, WOULD YOU PLEASE LEAVE?
YOU MAKE THE BOOZE TASTE BAD.
!
HOLD ON!!
THIS DOESN'T HAVE **RAVE** IN IT!!
WHAT ARE YOU TRYING TO PULL?!
I BROUGHT THE KID'S SWORD, JUST LIKE YOU ASKED.

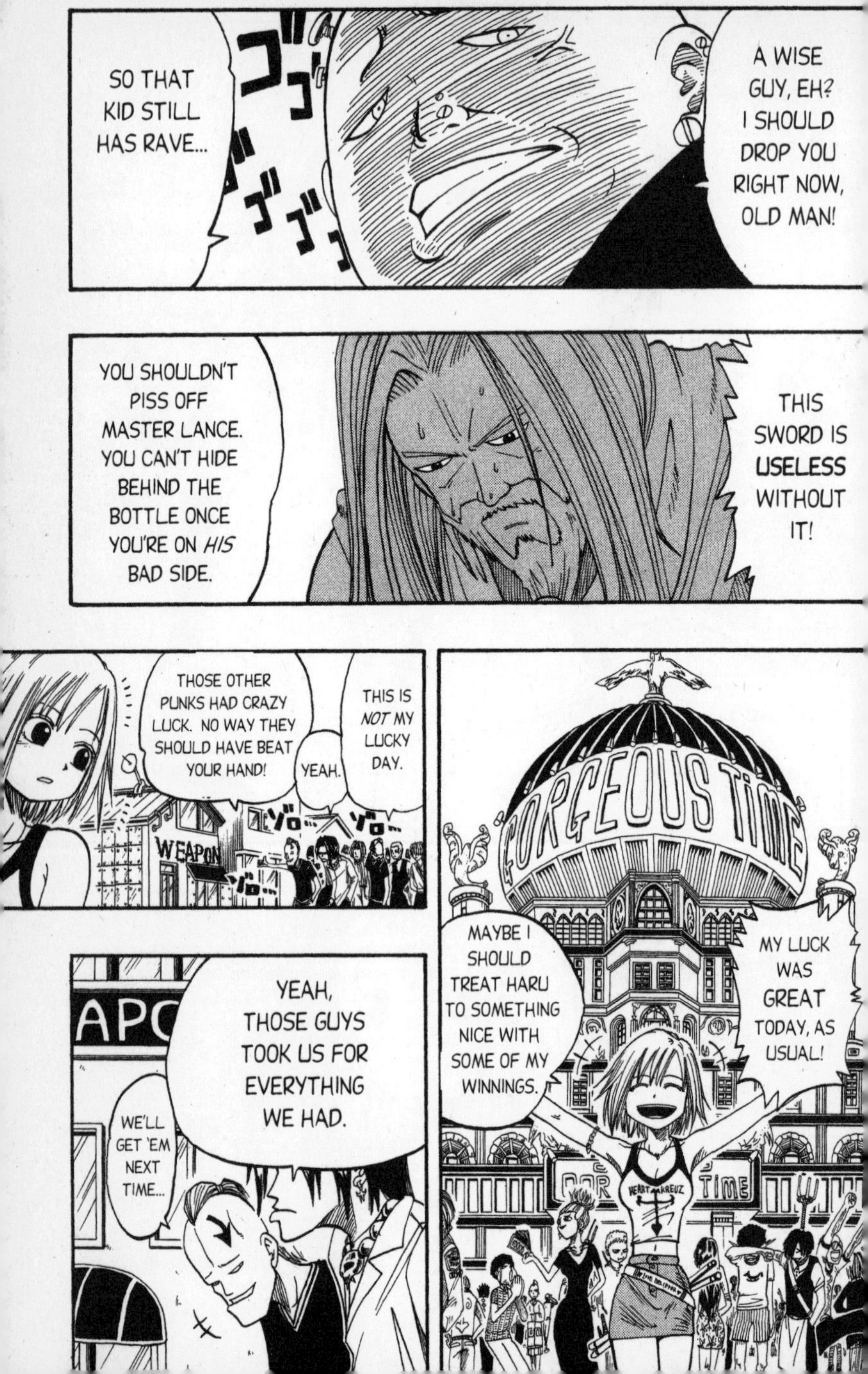
A WISE GUY, EH? I SHOULD DROP YOU RIGHT NOW, OLD MAN!
SO THAT KID STILL HAS RAVE...
THIS SWORD IS **USELESS** WITHOUT IT!
YOU SHOULDN'T PISS OFF MASTER LANCE. YOU CAN'T HIDE BEHIND THE BOTTLE ONCE YOU'RE ON *HIS* BAD SIDE.
GORGEOUS TIME
MY LUCK WAS GREAT TODAY, AS USUAL!
MAYBE I SHOULD TREAT HARU TO SOMETHING NICE WITH SOME OF MY WINNINGS.
THIS IS *NOT* MY LUCKY DAY.
YEAH.
THOSE OTHER PUNKS HAD CRAZY LUCK. NO WAY THEY SHOULD HAVE BEAT YOUR HAND!
WEAPON
YEAH, THOSE GUYS TOOK US FOR EVERYTHING WE HAD.
WE'LL GET 'EM NEXT TIME...

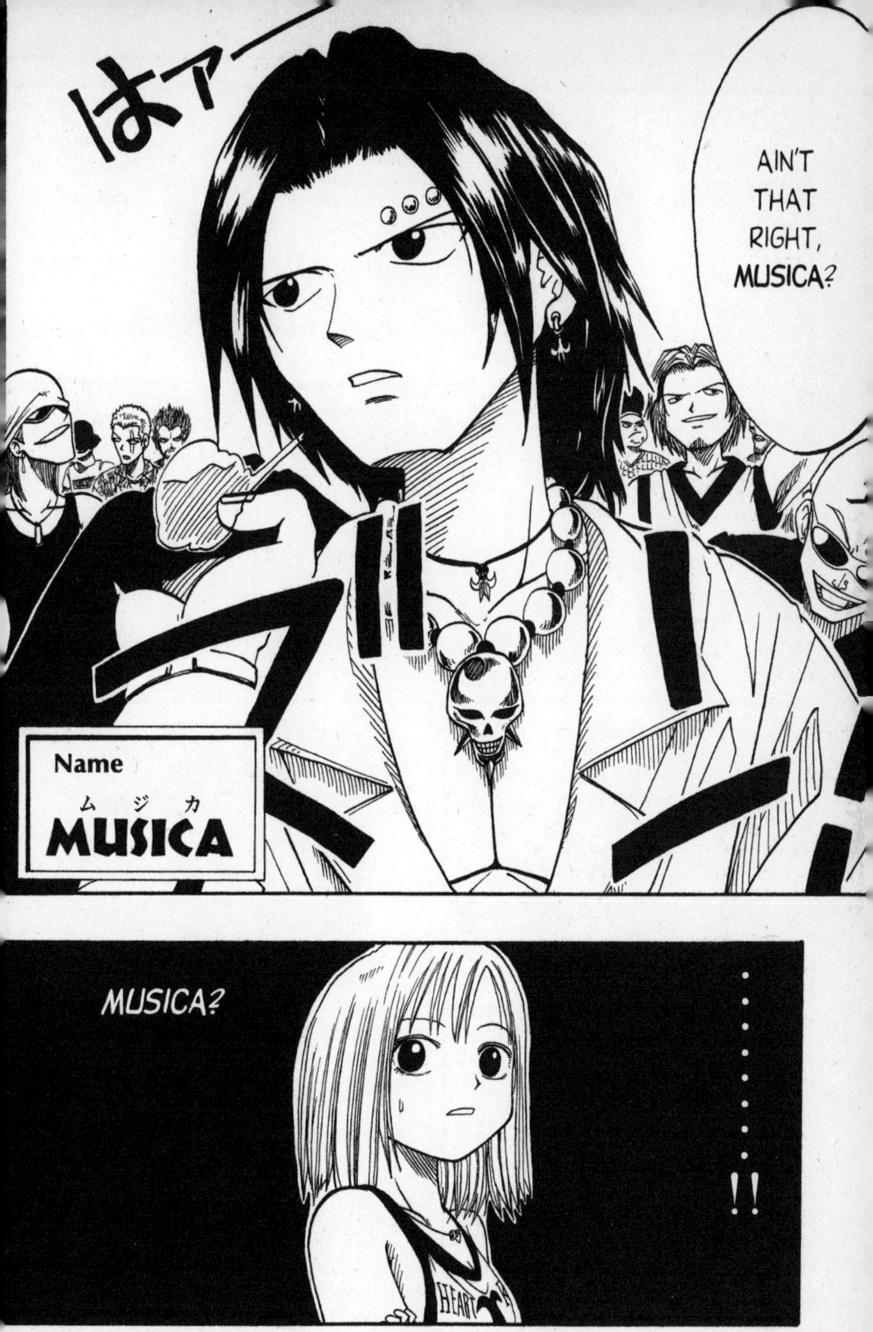

AIN'T THAT RIGHT, MUSICA?
はァー
Name
ムジカ
MUSICA
.......!!
MUSICA?

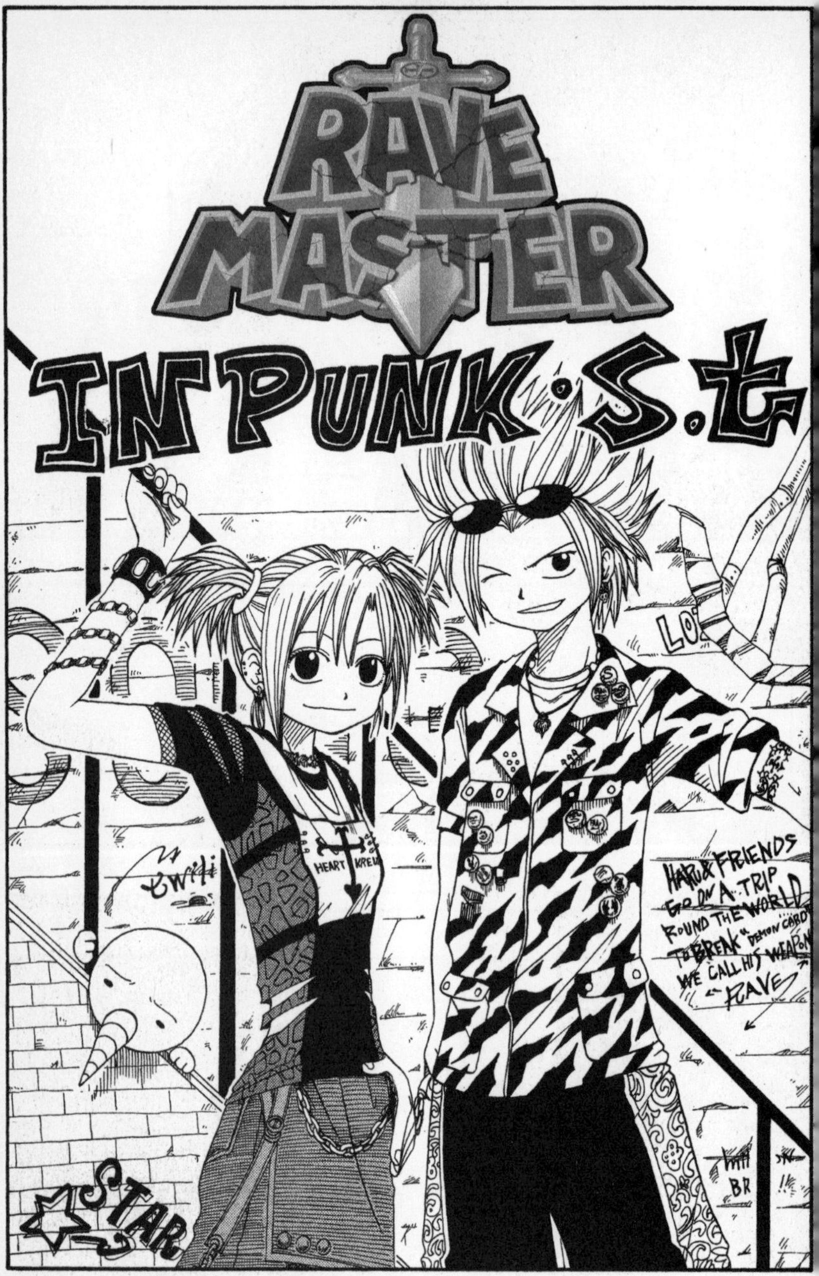
RAVE MASTER
IN PUNK S.t
HEART KREW
HARU & FRIENDS GO ON A TRIP ROUND THE WORLD TO BREAK "DEMON CARD"... WE CALL HIS WEAPON RAVE
STAR

RAVE 10 ✚ WANDERING FALLEN ANGEL

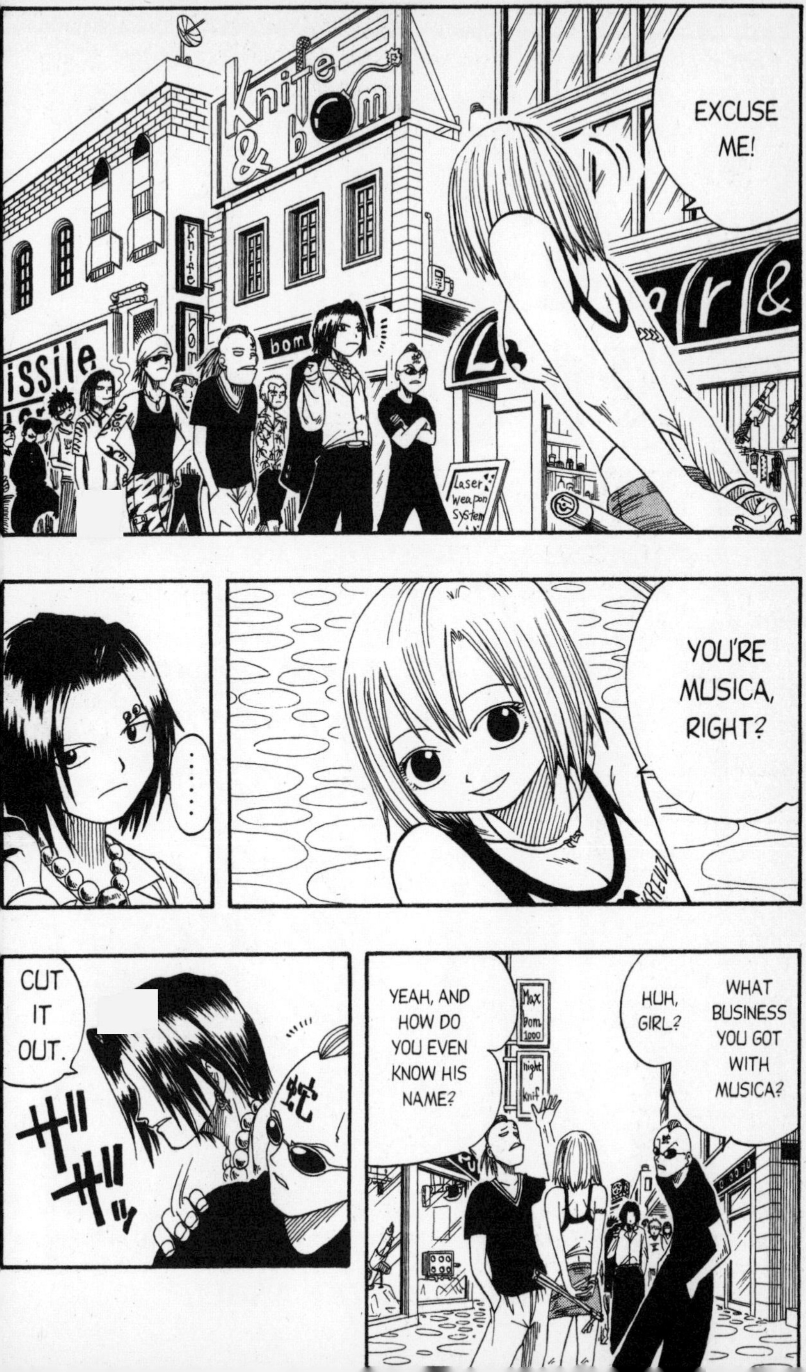
Knife & bom
Knife
bom
issile
Laser weapon system
EXCUSE ME!
YOU'RE MUSICA, RIGHT?
......
WHAT BUSINESS YOU GOT WITH MUSICA?
HUH, GIRL?
YEAH, AND HOW DO YOU EVEN KNOW HIS NAME?
CUT IT OUT.

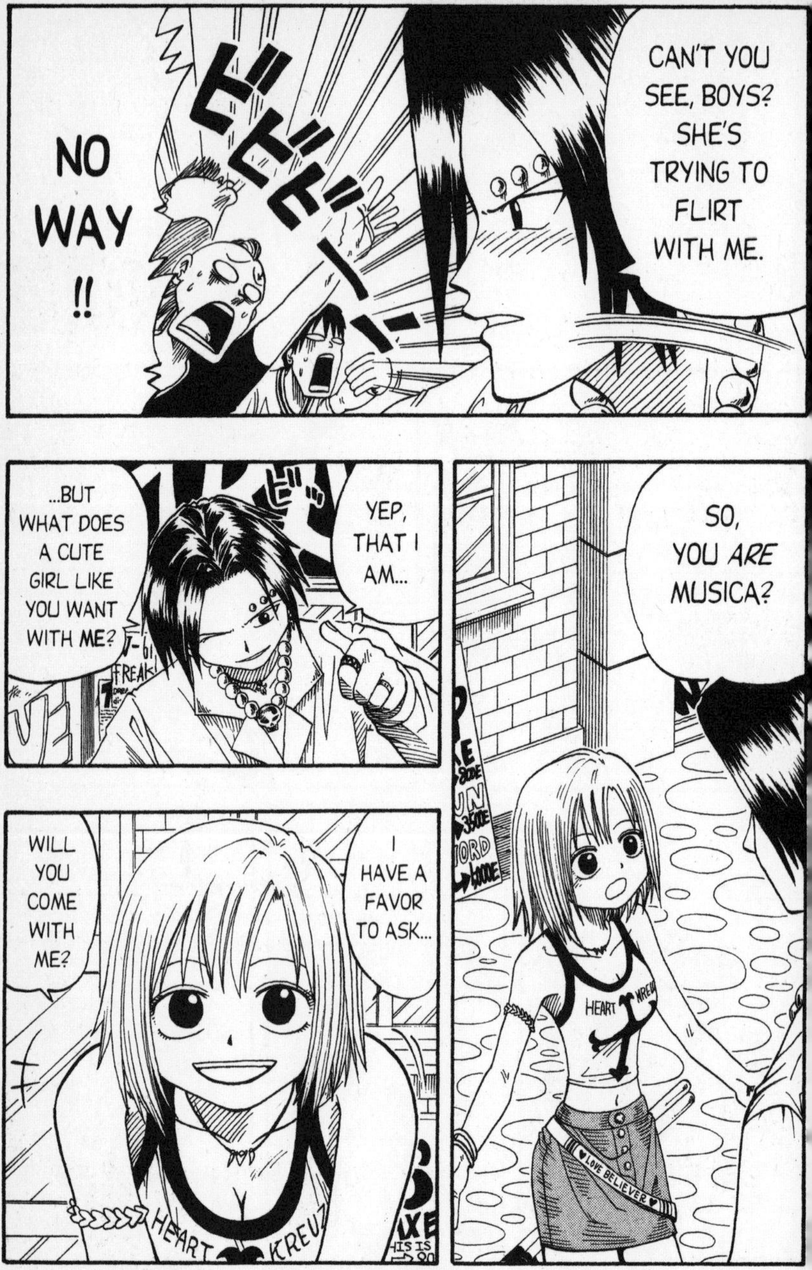
CAN'T YOU SEE, BOYS? SHE'S TRYING TO FLIRT WITH ME.
NO WAY !!
SO, YOU *ARE* MUSICA?
YEP, THAT I AM...
...BUT WHAT DOES A CUTE GIRL LIKE YOU WANT WITH ME?
I HAVE A FAVOR TO ASK...
WILL YOU COME WITH ME?

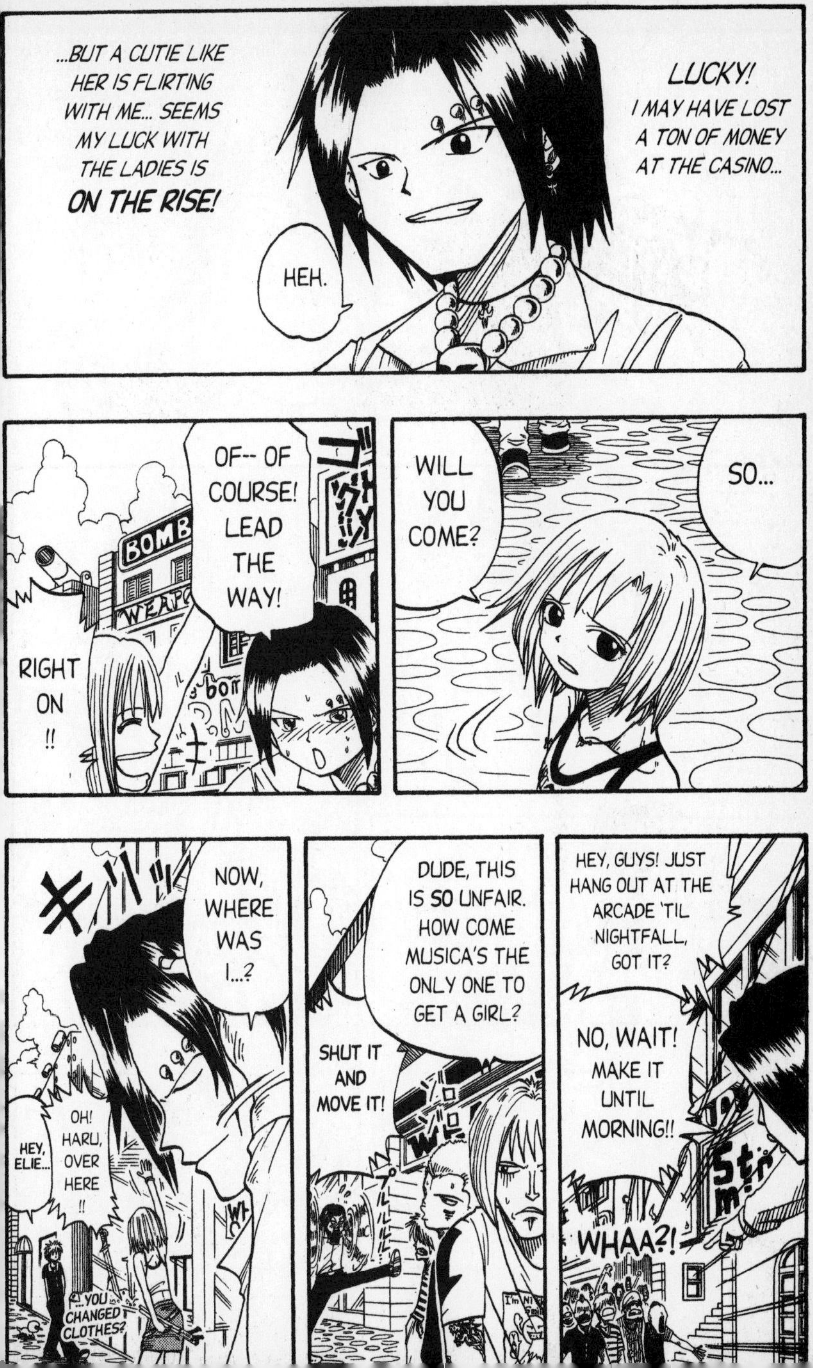
LUCKY! I MAY HAVE LOST A TON OF MONEY AT THE CASINO...
...BUT A CUTIE LIKE HER IS FLIRTING WITH ME... SEEMS MY LUCK WITH THE LADIES IS ON THE RISE!
HEH.
SO...
WILL YOU COME?
OF-- OF COURSE! LEAD THE WAY!
RIGHT ON!!
BOMB
HEY, GUYS! JUST HANG OUT AT THE ARCADE 'TIL NIGHTFALL, GOT IT?
NO, WAIT! MAKE IT UNTIL MORNING!!
WHAA?!
DUDE, THIS IS SO UNFAIR. HOW COME MUSICA'S THE ONLY ONE TO GET A GIRL?
SHUT IT AND MOVE IT!
NOW, WHERE WAS I...?
OH! HARU, OVER HERE!!
HEY, ELIE...
...YOU CHANGED CLOTHES?

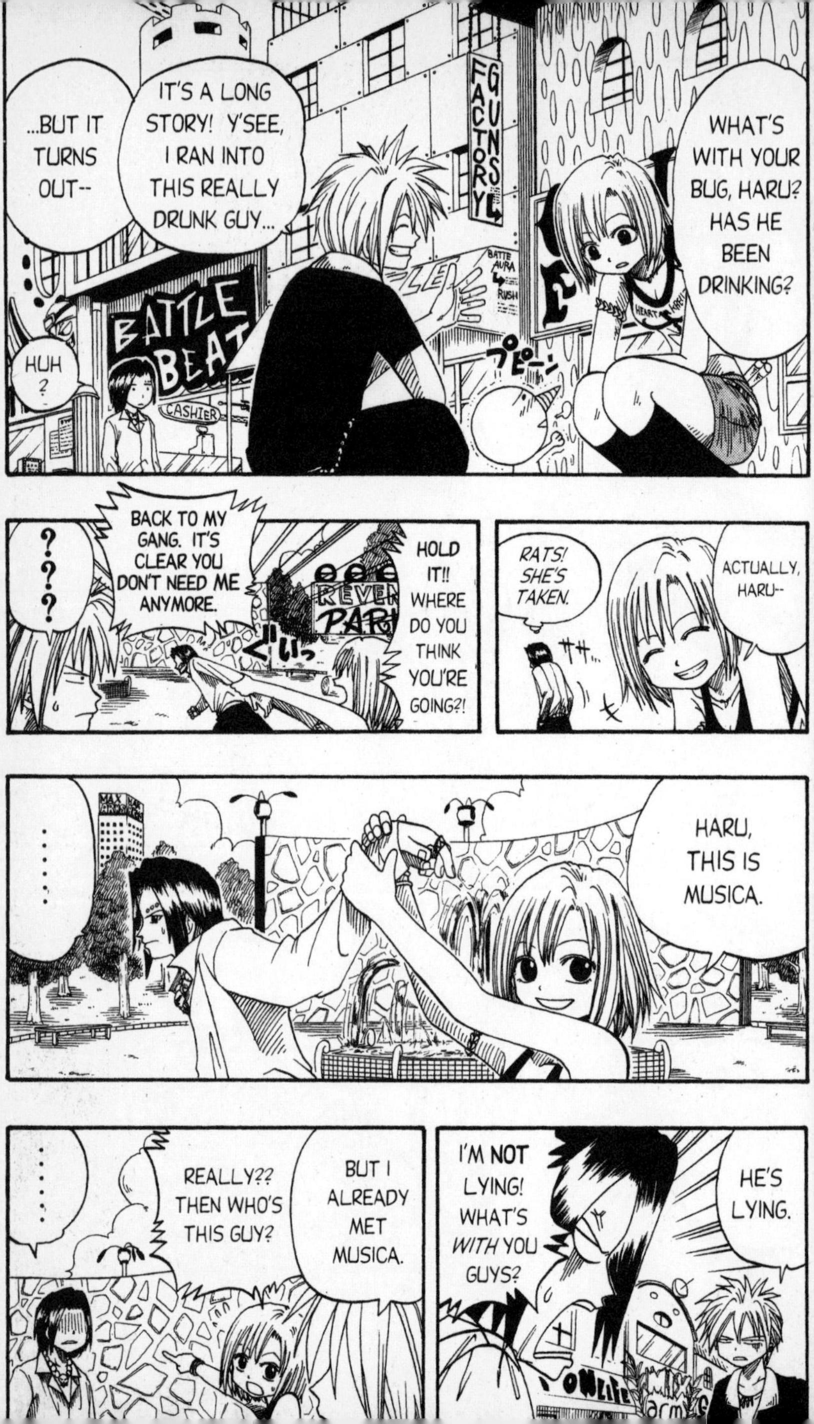
WHAT'S WITH YOUR BUG, HARU? HAS HE BEEN DRINKING?
GUNS
FACTORY
IT'S A LONG STORY! Y'SEE, I RAN INTO THIS REALLY DRUNK GUY...
...BUT IT TURNS OUT--
BATTLE BEAT
CASHIER
HUH ?
ACTUALLY, HARU--
RATS! SHE'S TAKEN.
HOLD IT!! WHERE DO YOU THINK YOU'RE GOING?!
BACK TO MY GANG. IT'S CLEAR YOU DON'T NEED ME ANYMORE.
???
HARU, THIS IS MUSICA.
......
HE'S LYING.
I'M **NOT** LYING! WHAT'S *WITH* YOU GUYS?
BUT I ALREADY MET MUSICA.
REALLY?? THEN WHO'S THIS GUY?
......

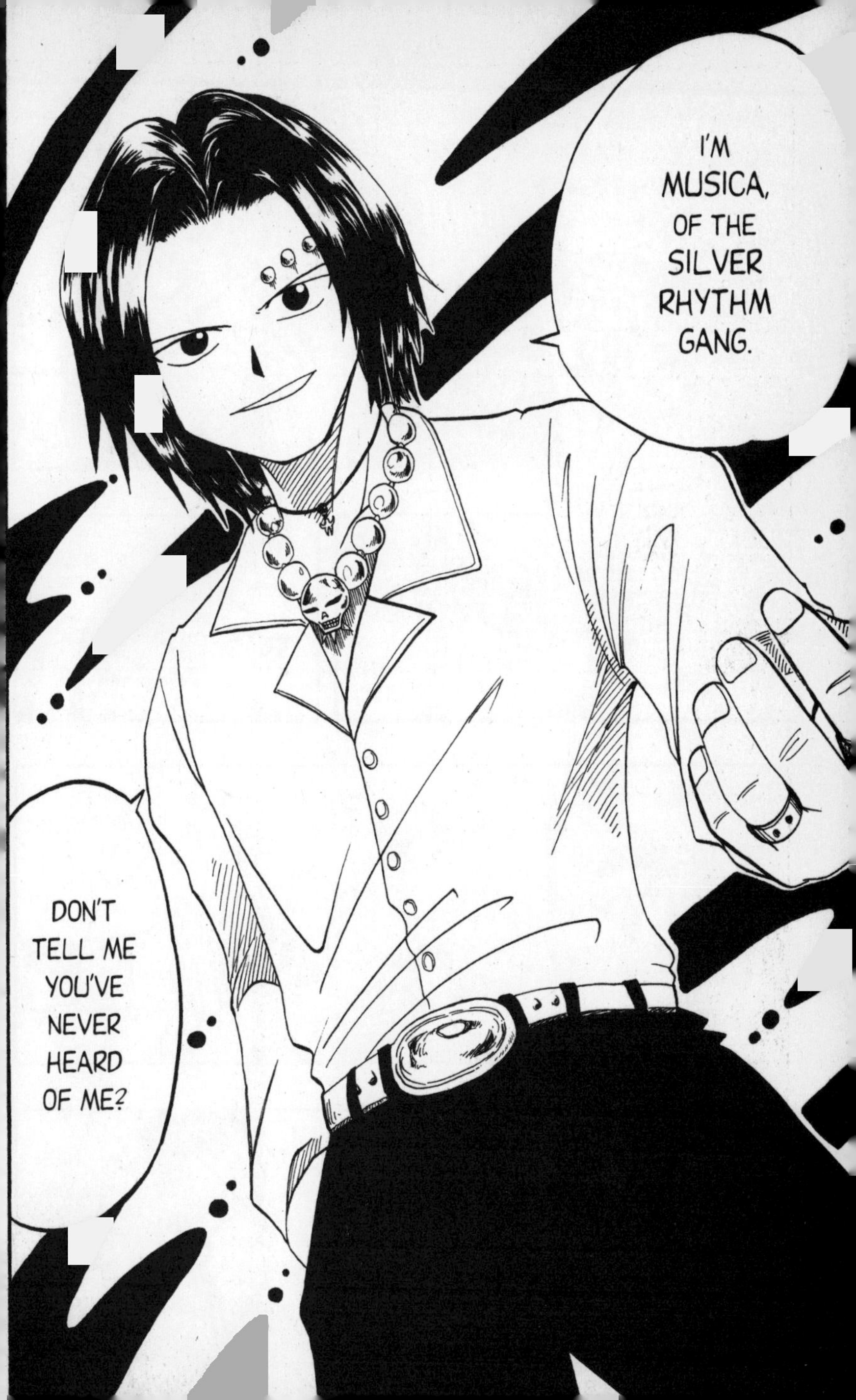
I'M MUSICA, OF THE SILVER RHYTHM GANG.
DON'T TELL ME YOU'VE NEVER HEARD OF ME?

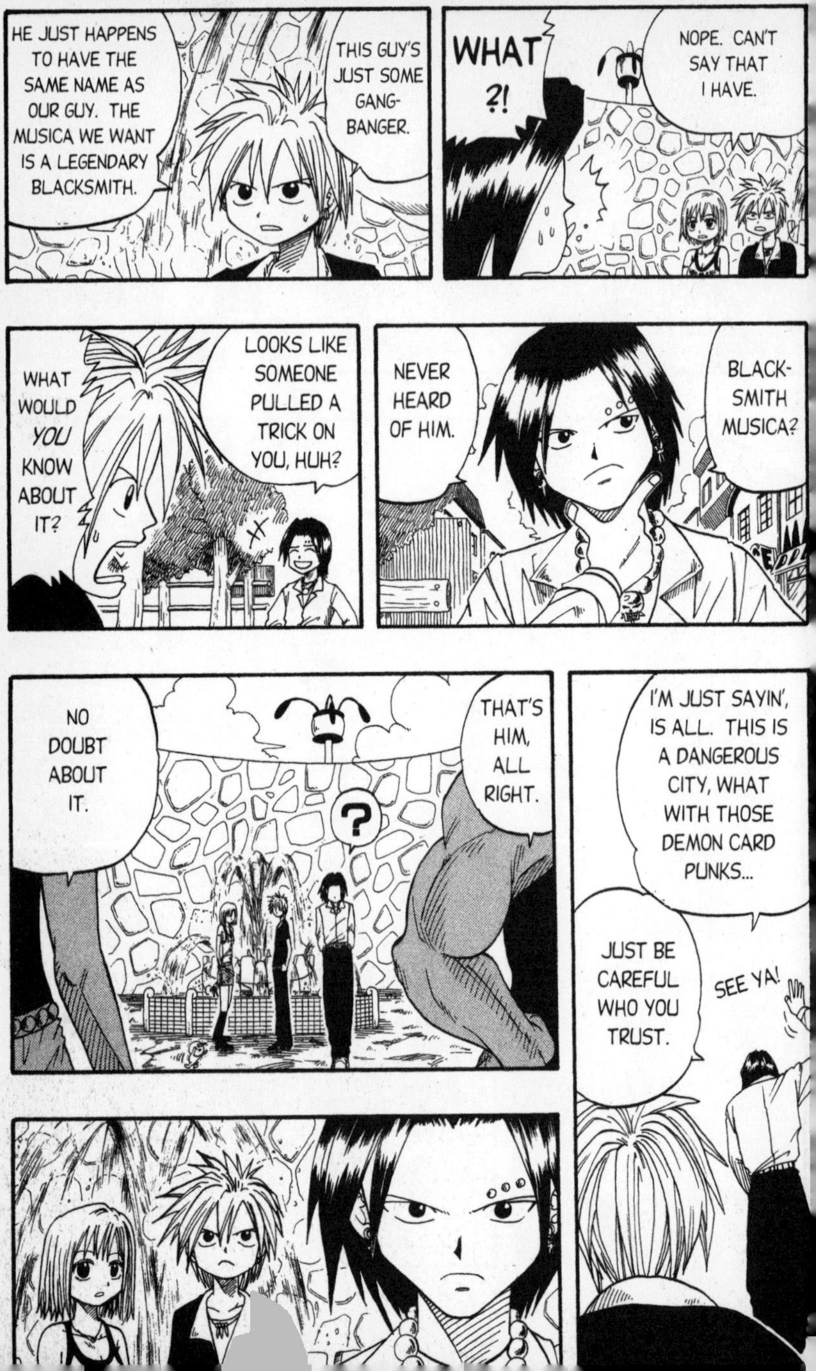
NOPE. CAN'T SAY THAT I HAVE.
WHAT?!
THIS GUY'S JUST SOME GANG-BANGER.
HE JUST HAPPENS TO HAVE THE SAME NAME AS OUR GUY. THE MUSICA WE WANT IS A LEGENDARY BLACKSMITH.
BLACK-SMITH MUSICA?
NEVER HEARD OF HIM.
LOOKS LIKE SOMEONE PULLED A TRICK ON YOU, HUH?
WHAT WOULD YOU KNOW ABOUT IT?
I'M JUST SAYIN', IS ALL. THIS IS A DANGEROUS CITY, WHAT WITH THOSE DEMON CARD PUNKS...
SEE YA!
JUST BE CAREFUL WHO YOU TRUST.
THAT'S HIM, ALL RIGHT.
NO DOUBT ABOUT IT.
?

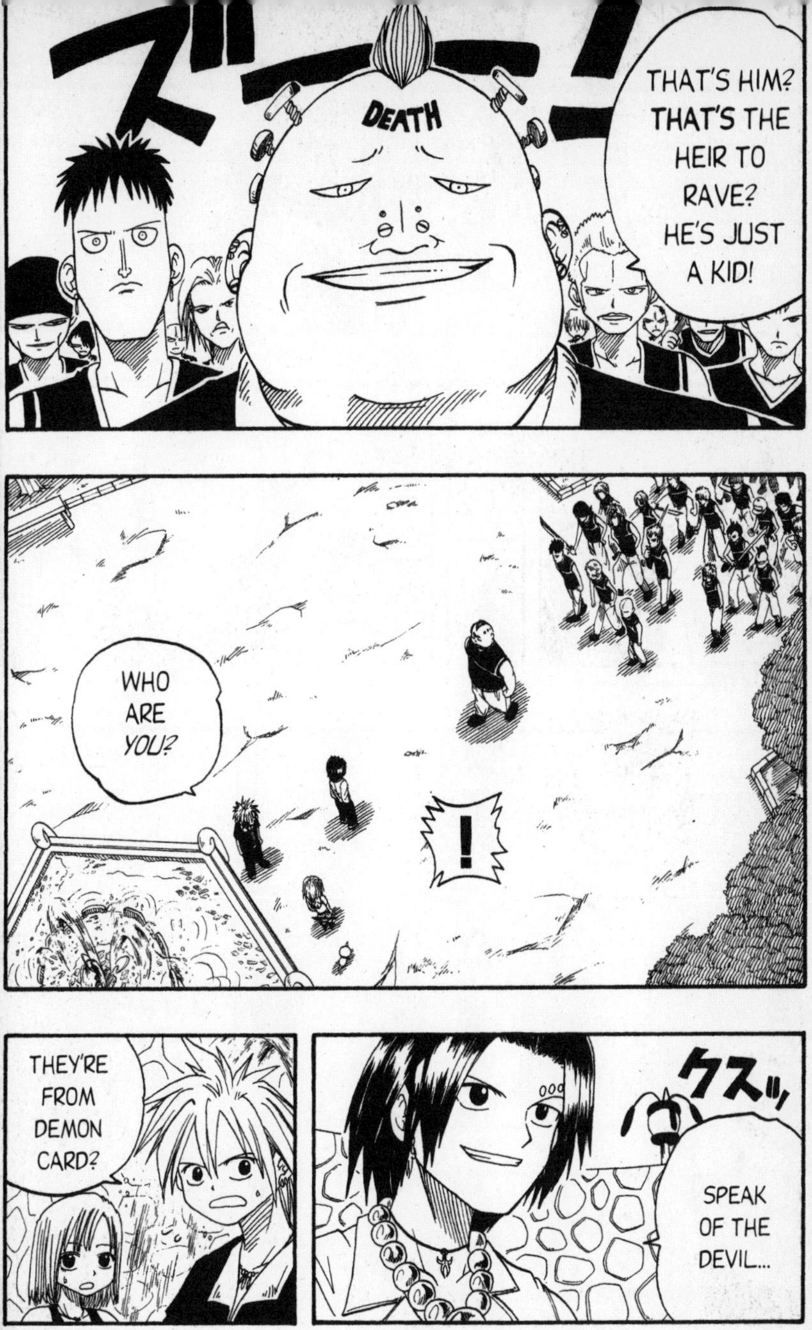
DEATH
THAT'S HIM? THAT'S THE HEIR TO RAVE? HE'S JUST A KID!
WHO ARE *YOU*?
!
クスッ
SPEAK OF THE DEVIL...
THEY'RE FROM DEMON CARD?

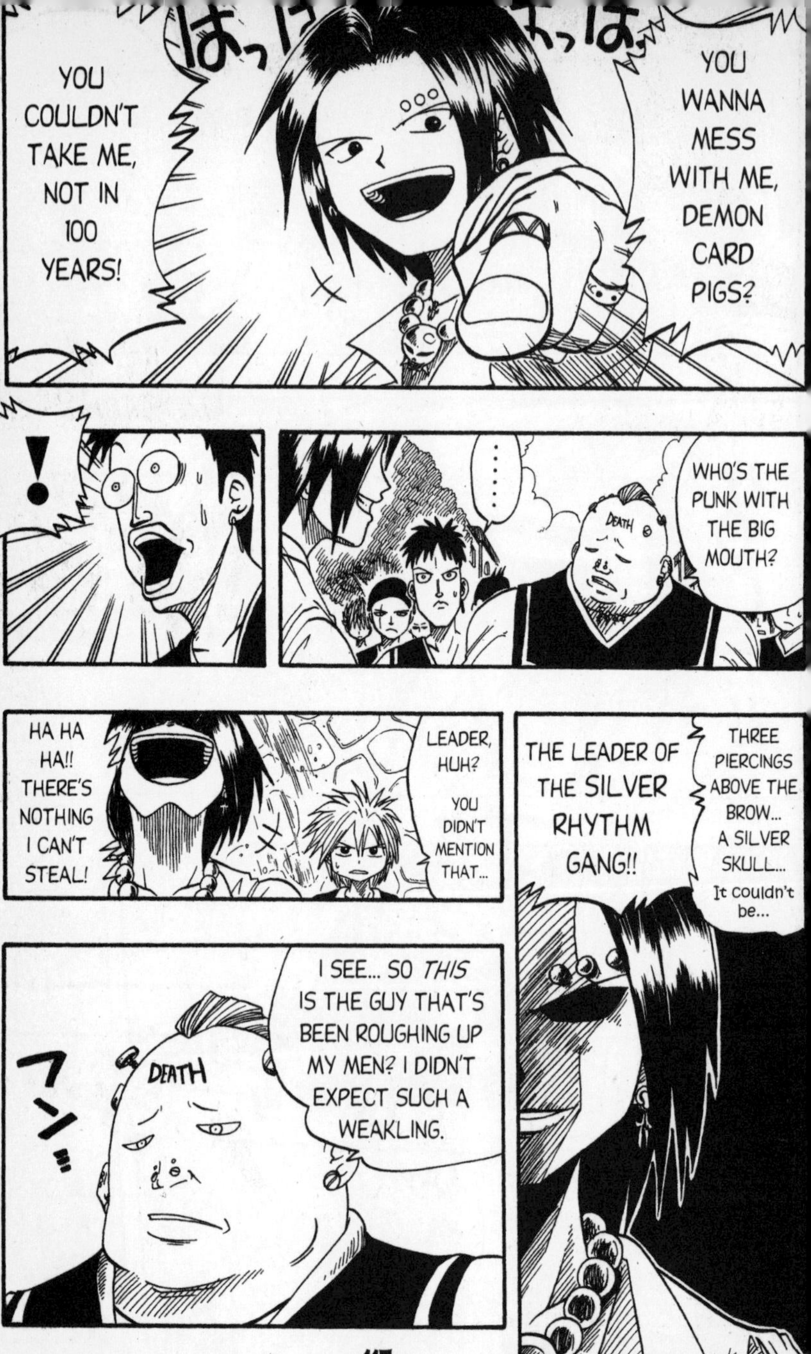

YOU WANNA MESS WITH ME, DEMON CARD PIGS?
YOU COULDN'T TAKE ME, NOT IN 100 YEARS!
WHO'S THE PUNK WITH THE BIG MOUTH?
......
!
THREE PIERCINGS ABOVE THE BROW... A SILVER SKULL... It couldn't be...
THE LEADER OF THE SILVER RHYTHM GANG!!
LEADER, HUH? YOU DIDN'T MENTION THAT...
HA HA HA!! THERE'S NOTHING I CAN'T STEAL!
I SEE... SO *THIS* IS THE GUY THAT'S BEEN ROUGHING UP MY MEN? I DIDN'T EXPECT SUCH A WEAKLING.
フン

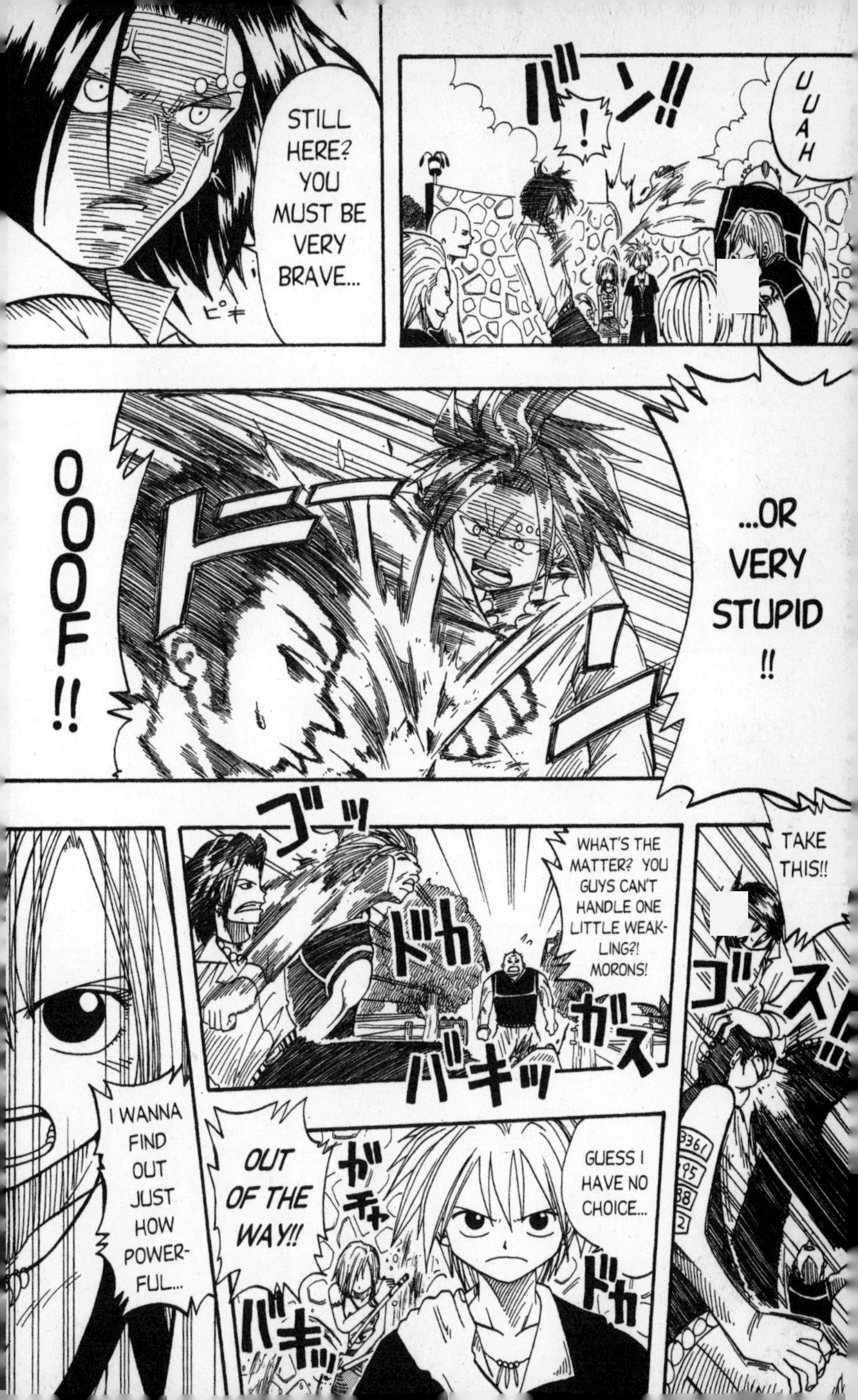
UUAH
バン!!
!
STILL HERE? YOU MUST BE VERY BRAVE...
ピキ
...OR VERY STUPID!!
OOOOF!!
TAKE THIS!!
ゴス!!
ゴッ
WHAT'S THE MATTER? YOU GUYS CAN'T HANDLE ONE LITTLE WEAK-LING?! MORONS!
ドカ
ガス
バキッ
GUESS I HAVE NO CHOICE...
ドカ
OUT OF THE WAY!!
ガチャ
バキッ
I WANNA FIND OUT JUST HOW POWER-FUL...

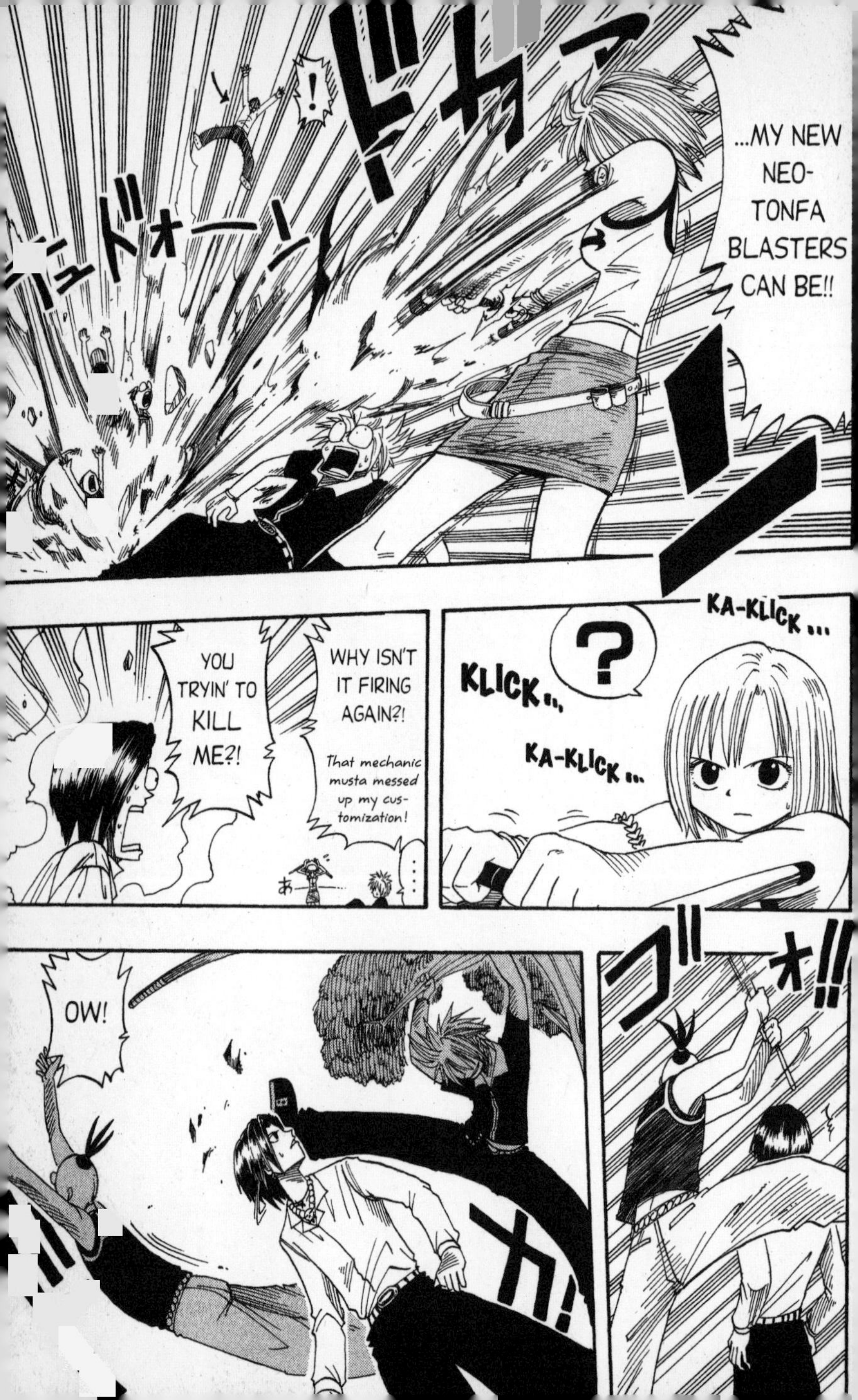

...MY NEW NEO-TONFA BLASTERS CAN BE!!
KA-KLICK...
?
KLICK...
KA-KLICK...
WHY ISN'T IT FIRING AGAIN?!
That mechanic musta messed up my cus-tomization!
YOU TRYIN' TO KILL ME?!
あ
OW!

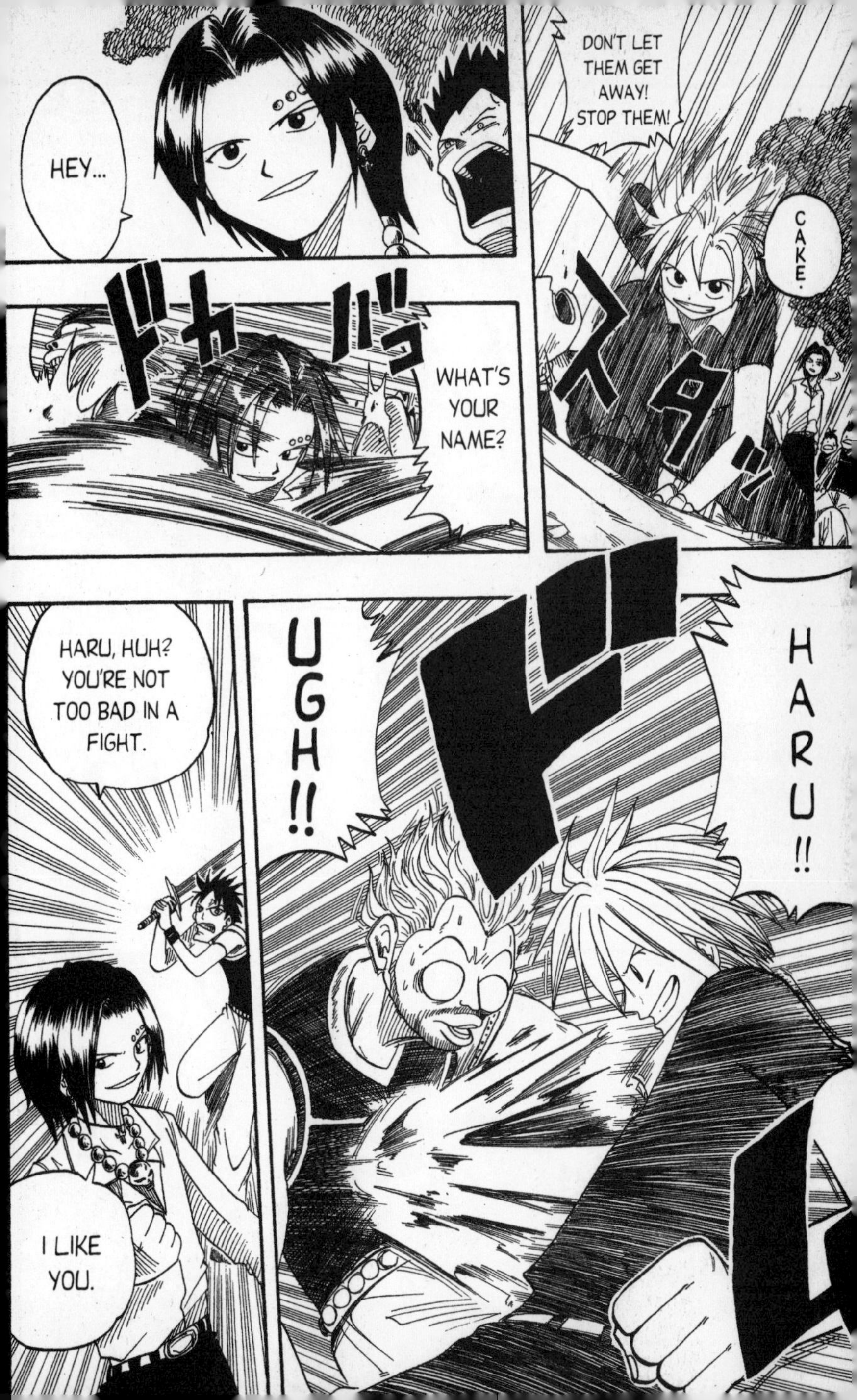
DON'T LET THEM GET AWAY! STOP THEM!
CAKE.
HEY...
WHAT'S YOUR NAME?
HARU!!
UGH!!
HARU, HUH? YOU'RE NOT TOO BAD IN A FIGHT.
I LIKE YOU.

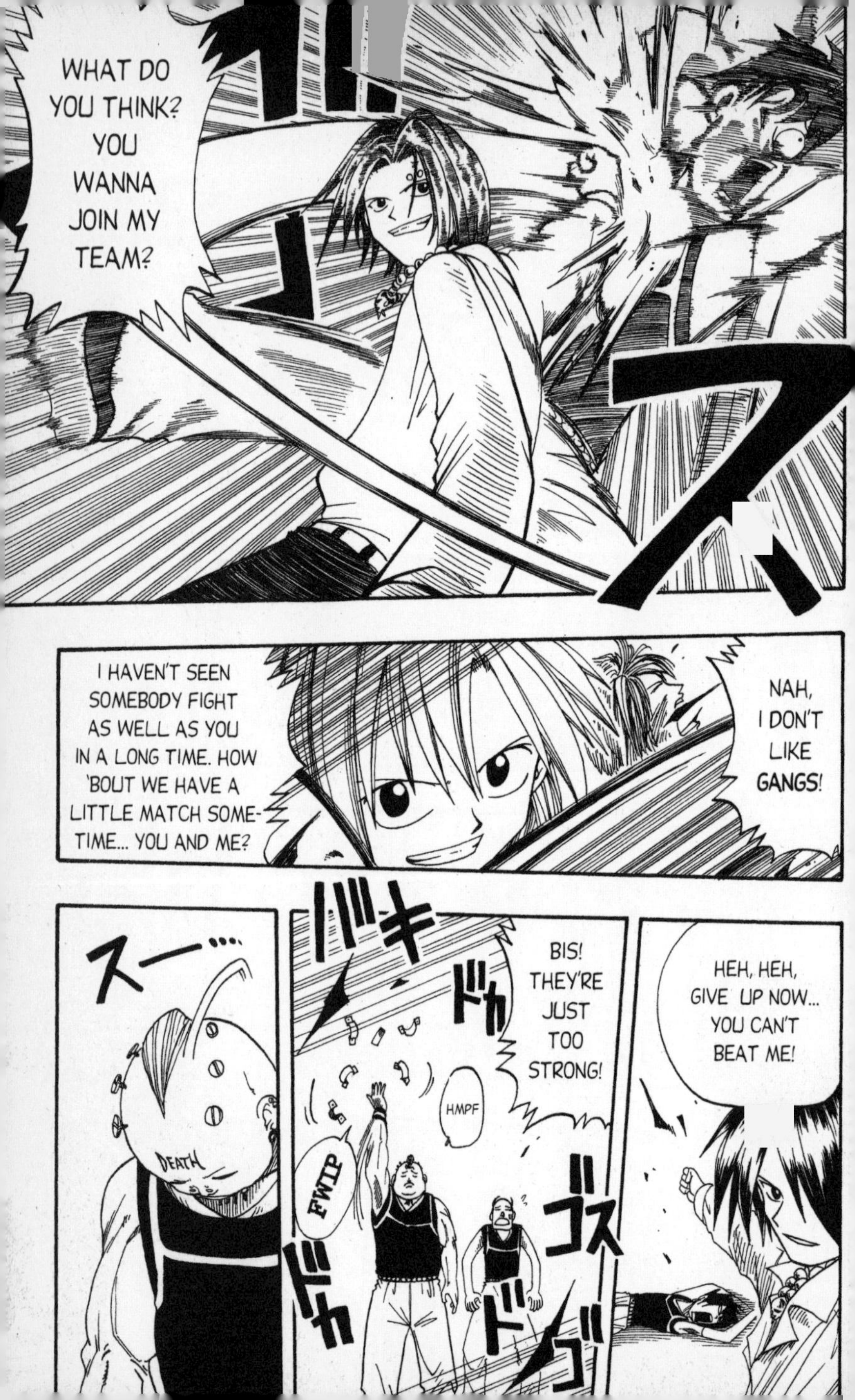
WHAT DO YOU THINK? YOU WANNA JOIN MY TEAM?
NAH, I DON'T LIKE GANGS!
I HAVEN'T SEEN SOMEBODY FIGHT AS WELL AS YOU IN A LONG TIME. HOW 'BOUT WE HAVE A LITTLE MATCH SOME-TIME... YOU AND ME?
HEH, HEH, GIVE UP NOW... YOU CAN'T BEAT ME!
バキ
BIS! THEY'RE JUST TOO STRONG!
ドカ
HMPF
FWIP
ゴス
ドカ
スー…
DEATH

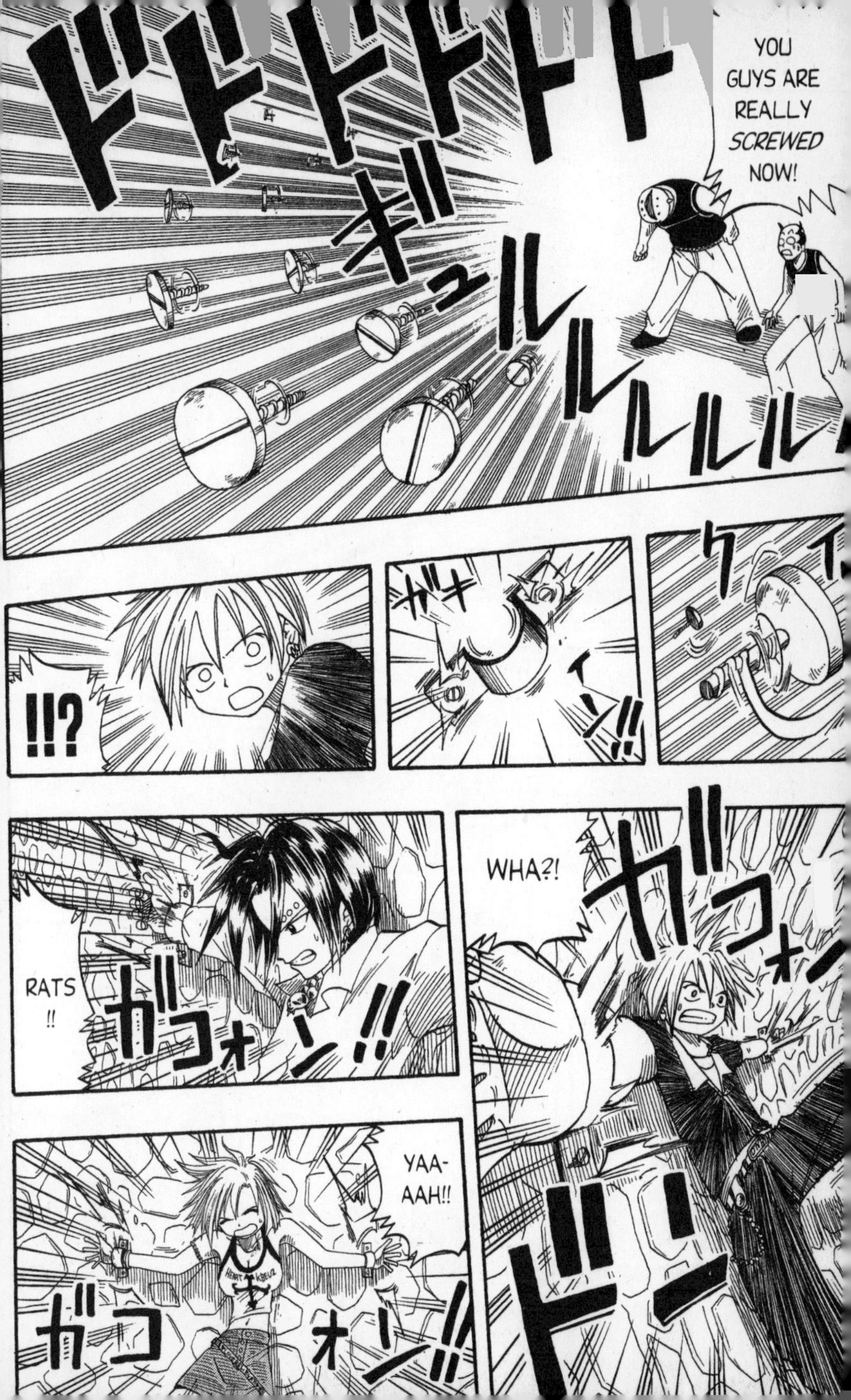
YOU GUYS ARE REALLY SCREWED NOW!
!!?
WHA?!
RATS!!
YAA-AAH!!

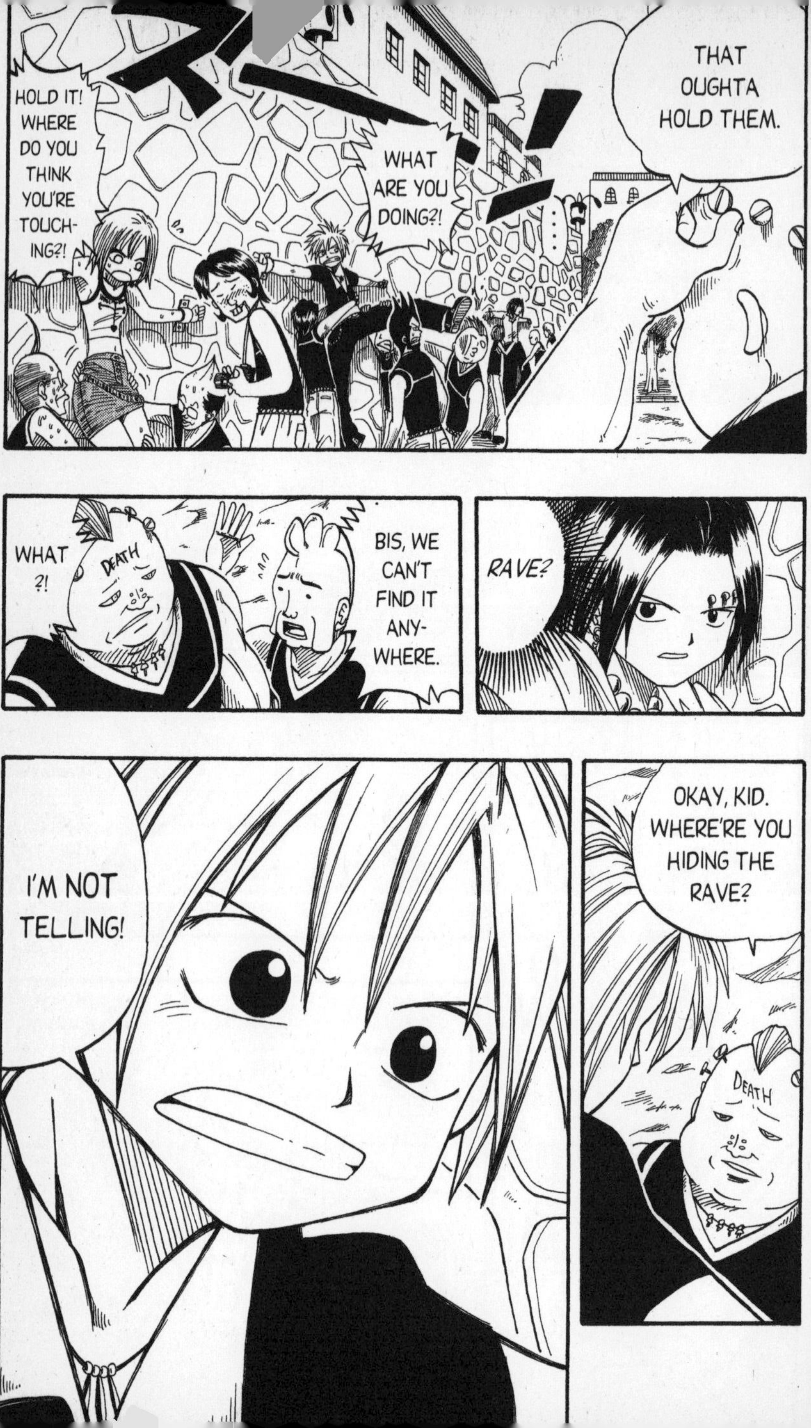
THAT OUGHTA HOLD THEM.
WHAT ARE YOU DOING?!
HOLD IT! WHERE DO YOU THINK YOU'RE TOUCHING?!
RAVE?
BIS, WE CAN'T FIND IT ANYWHERE.
WHAT ?!
DEATH
OKAY, KID. WHERE'RE YOU HIDING THE RAVE?
DEATH
I'M NOT TELLING!

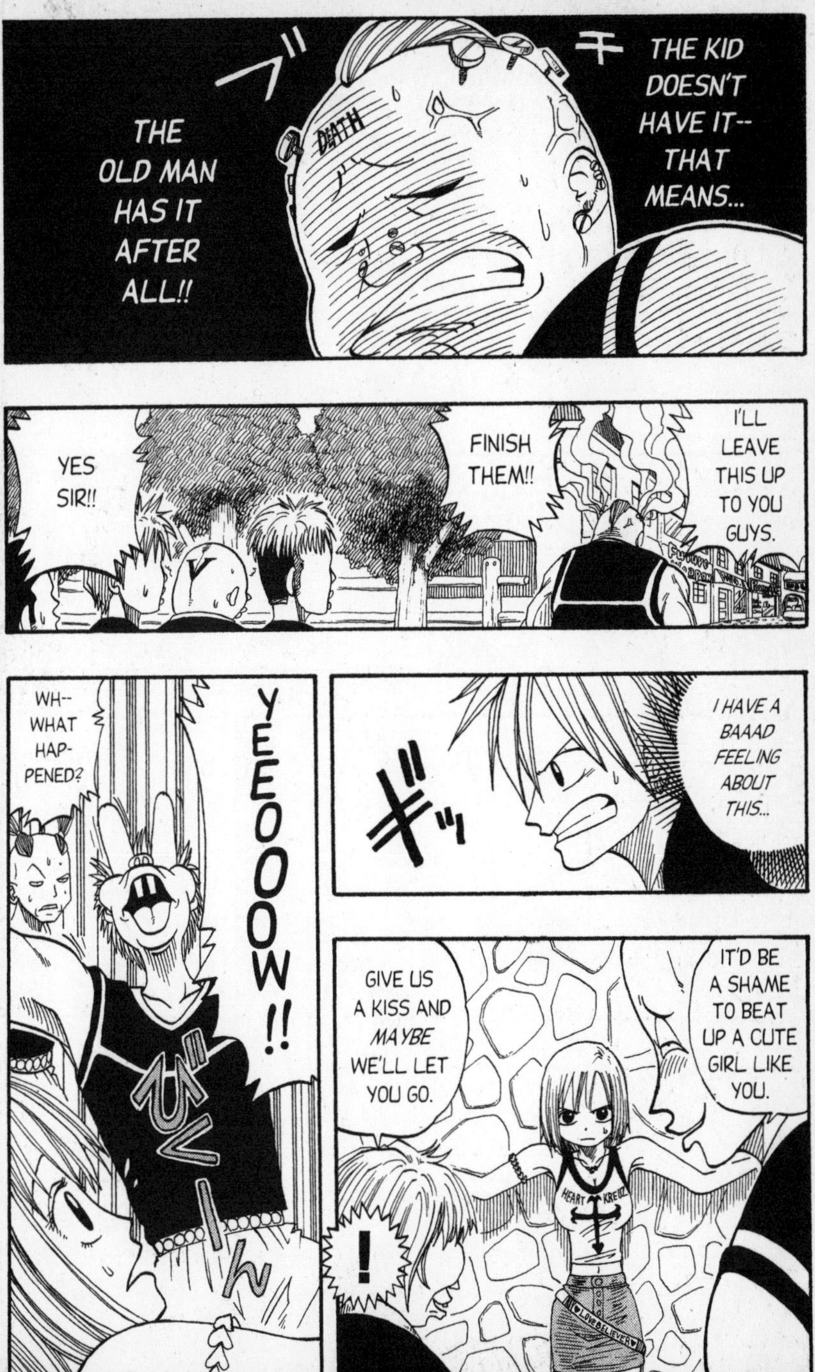
THE KID DOESN'T HAVE IT-- THAT MEANS...
THE OLD MAN HAS IT AFTER ALL!!
I'LL LEAVE THIS UP TO YOU GUYS.
FINISH THEM!!
YES SIR!!
I HAVE A BAAAD FEELING ABOUT THIS...
IT'D BE A SHAME TO BEAT UP A CUTE GIRL LIKE YOU.
GIVE US A KISS AND *MAYBE* WE'LL LET YOU GO.
!
YEEOOOOW!!
WH-- WHAT HAP-PENED?

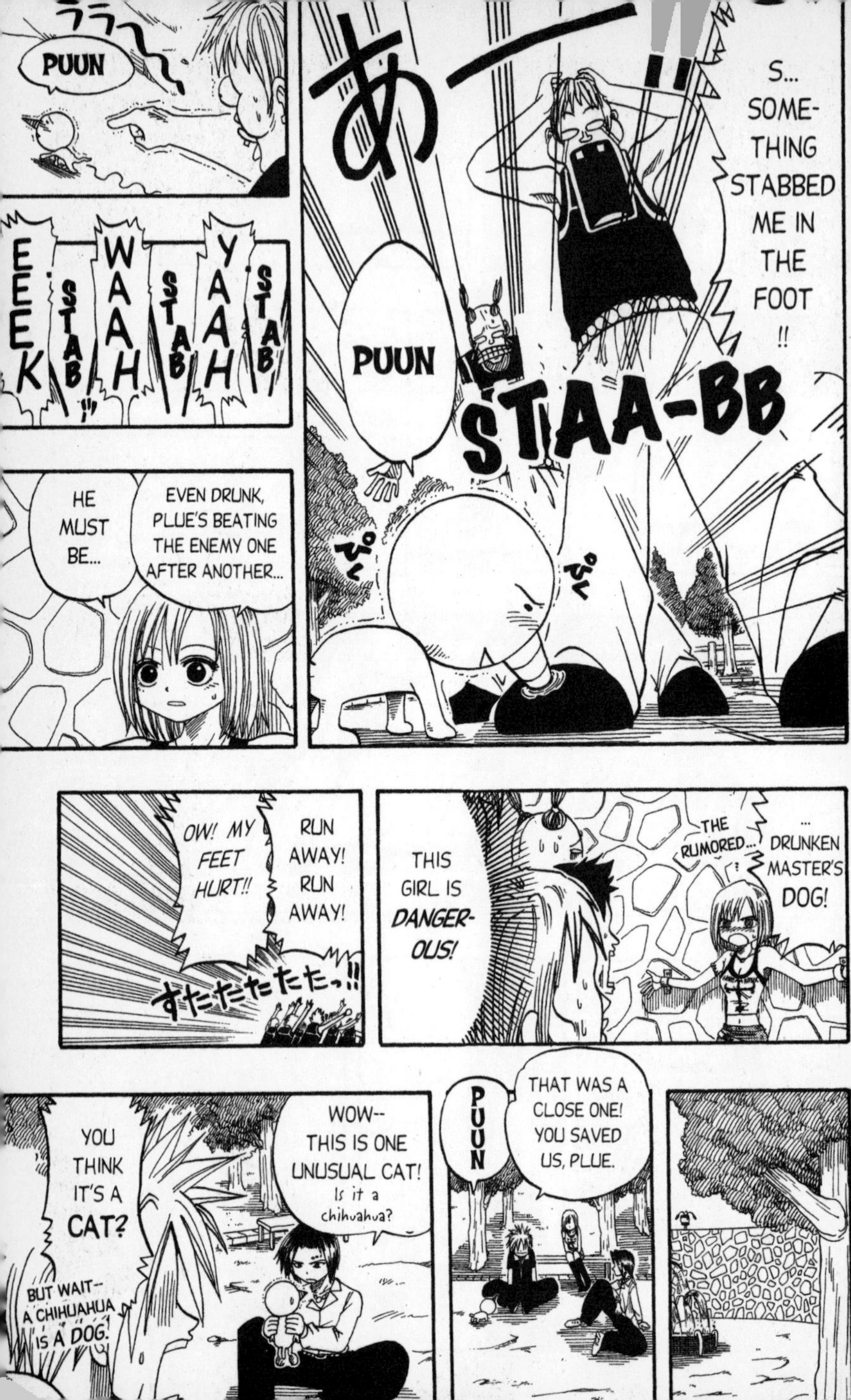
あー!!
S... SOMETHING STABBED ME IN THE FOOT!!
PUUN
STAA-BB
ぴく
ぴく
フラ~
PUUN
STAB
YAAH
STAB
WAAH
STAB
EEEK
EVEN DRUNK, PLUE'S BEATING THE ENEMY ONE AFTER ANOTHER...
HE MUST BE...
THE RUMORED...
...DRUNKEN MASTER'S DOG!
THIS GIRL IS DANGEROUS!
RUN AWAY! RUN AWAY!
OW! MY FEET HURT!!
すたたたたたっ!!
PUUN
THAT WAS A CLOSE ONE! YOU SAVED US, PLUE.
WOW-- THIS IS ONE UNUSUAL CAT! Is it a chihuahua?
YOU THINK IT'S A CAT?
BUT WAIT-- A CHIHUAHUA IS A DOG.

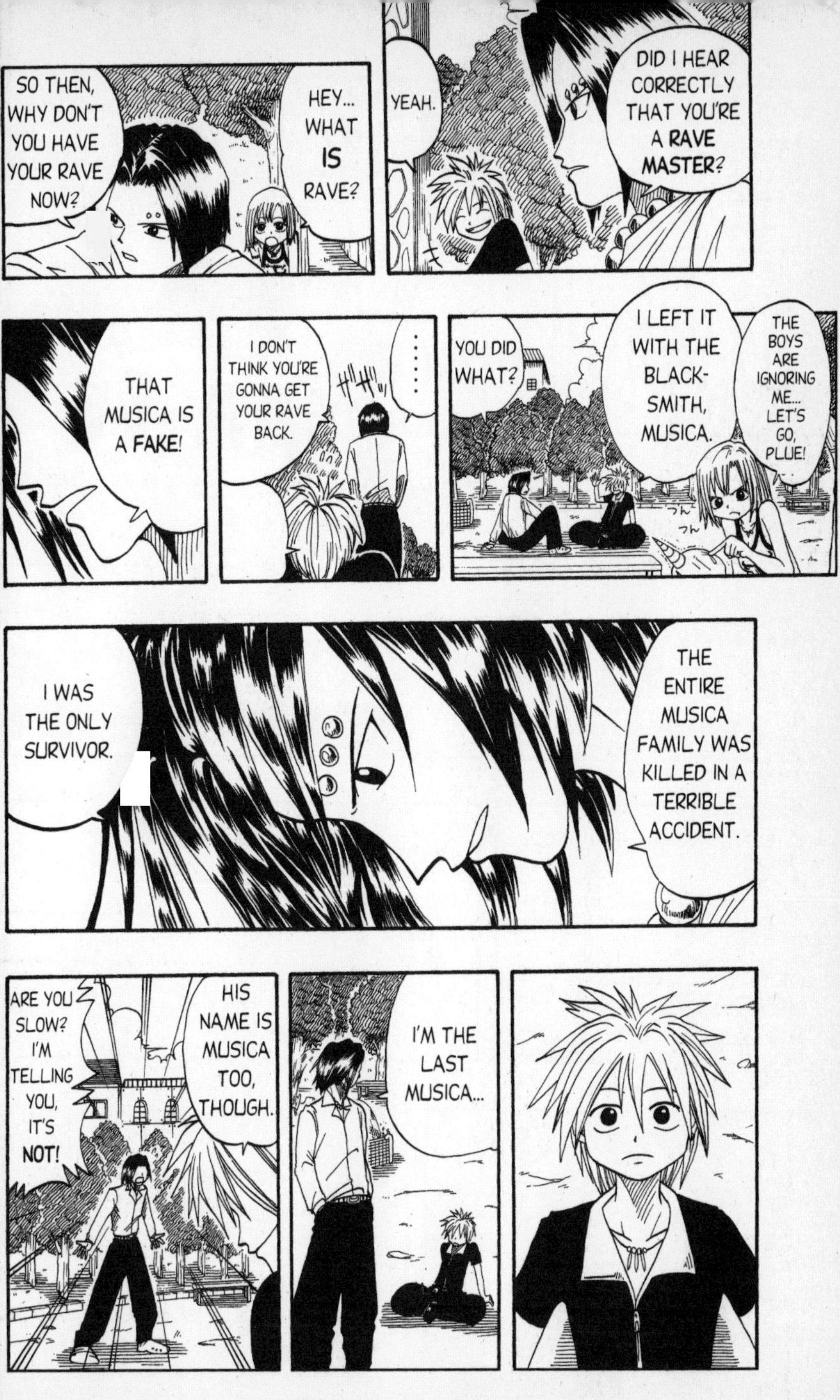
DID I HEAR CORRECTLY THAT YOU'RE A RAVE MASTER?
YEAH.
HEY... WHAT IS RAVE?
SO THEN, WHY DON'T YOU HAVE YOUR RAVE NOW?
THE BOYS ARE IGNORING ME... LET'S GO, PLUE!
I LEFT IT WITH THE BLACK-SMITH, MUSICA.
YOU DID WHAT?
......
I DON'T THINK YOU'RE GONNA GET YOUR RAVE BACK.
THAT MUSICA IS A FAKE!
THE ENTIRE MUSICA FAMILY WAS KILLED IN A TERRIBLE ACCIDENT.
I WAS THE ONLY SURVIVOR.
I'M THE LAST MUSICA...
HIS NAME IS MUSICA TOO, THOUGH.
ARE YOU SLOW? I'M TELLING YOU, IT'S NOT!

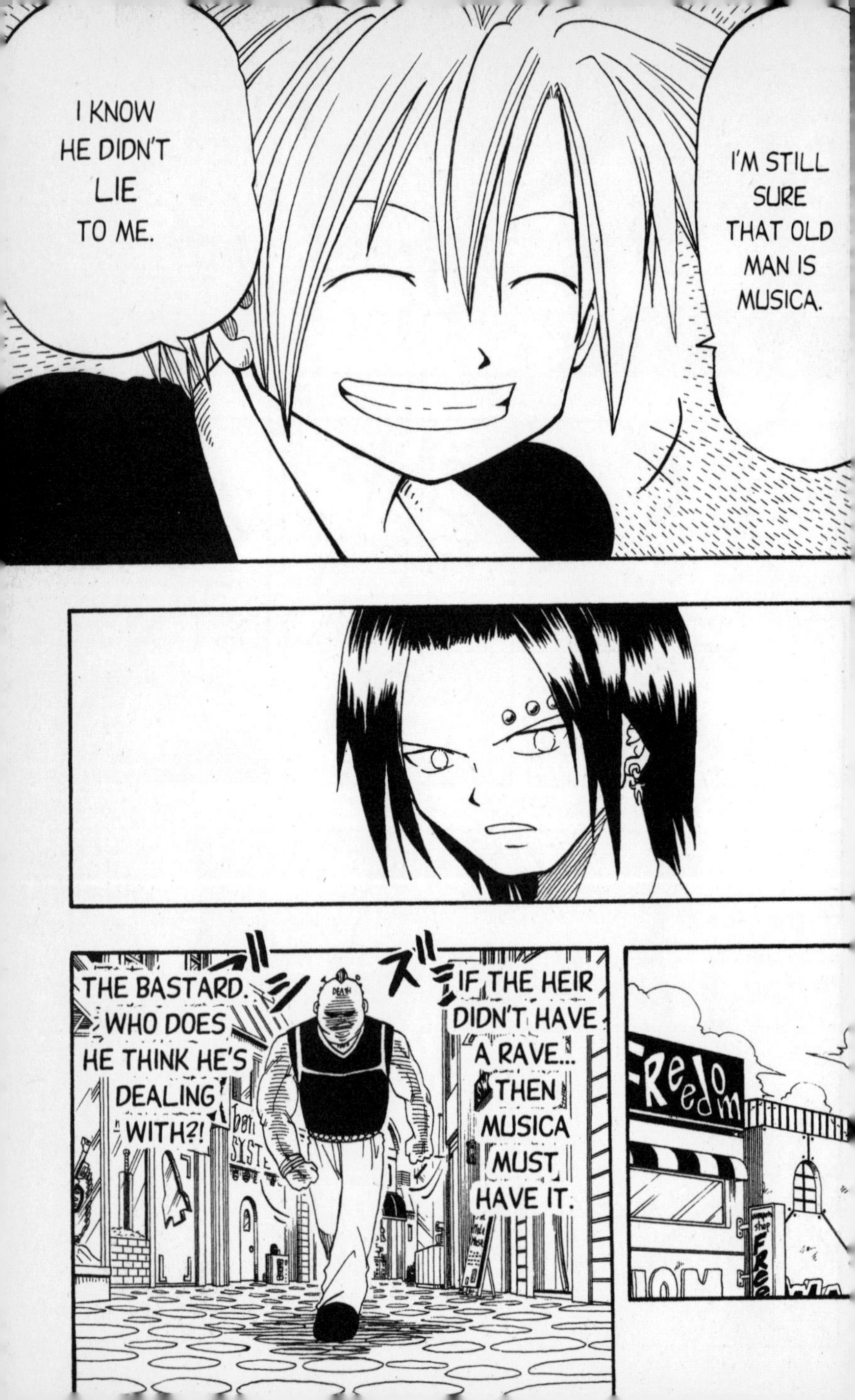
I'M STILL SURE THAT OLD MAN IS MUSICA.
I KNOW HE DIDN'T LIE TO ME.
Freedom
IF THE HEIR DIDN'T HAVE A RAVE... THEN MUSICA MUST HAVE IT.
ズシ
ズシ
THE BASTARD. WHO DOES HE THINK HE'S DEALING WITH?!

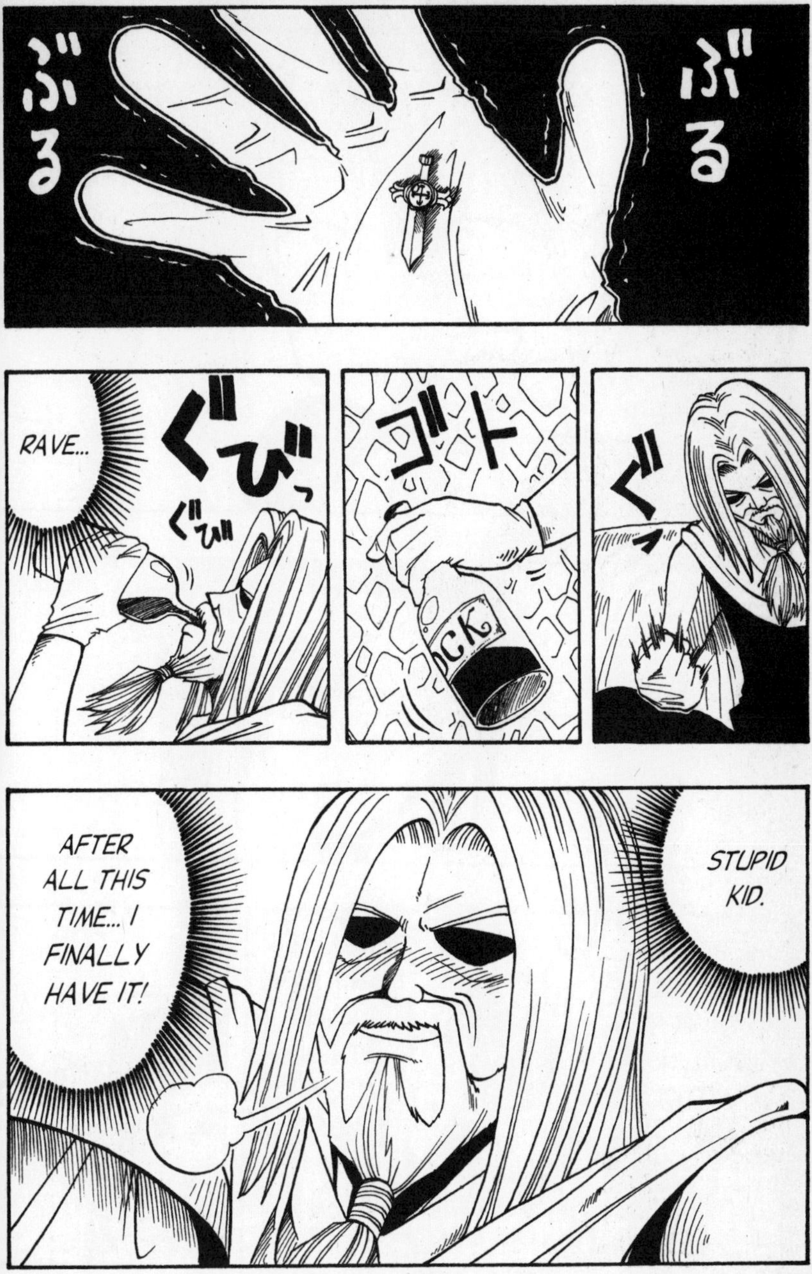

ぶる
ぶる
ぐっ
ゴト
ぐびっ
ぐび
RAVE...
STUPID KID.
AFTER ALL THIS TIME... I FINALLY HAVE IT!

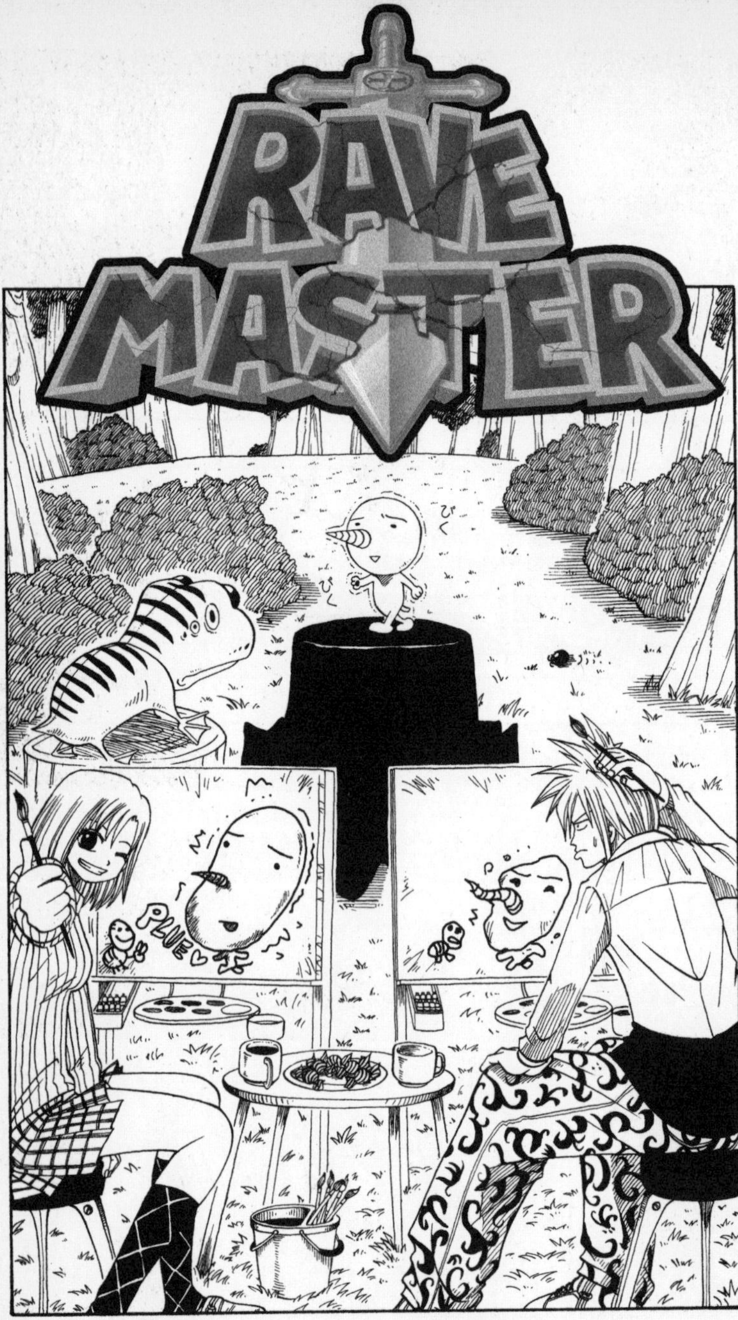
RAVE MASTER
PLUE

RAVE 11 ✠ FROM THE BROKEN DOOR

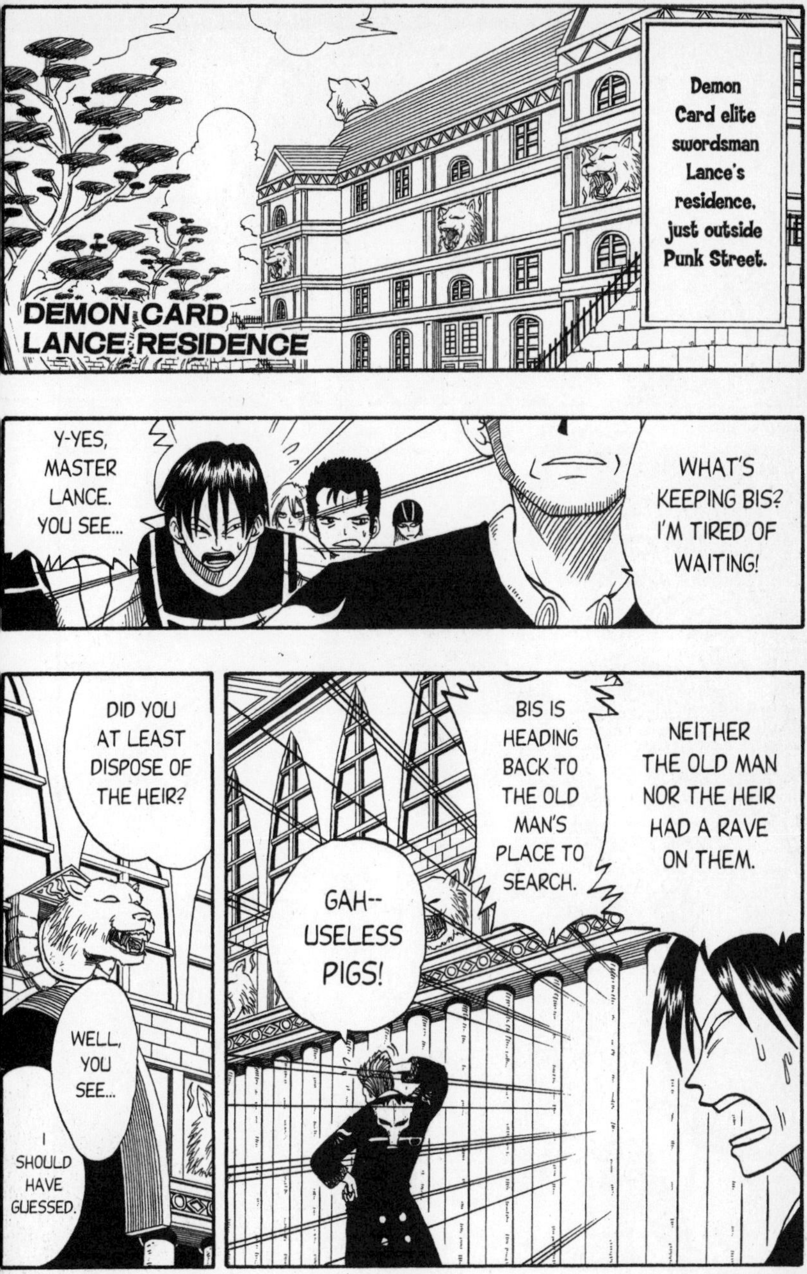
Demon Card elite swordsman Lance's residence, just outside Punk Street.
DEMON CARD LANCE RESIDENCE
WHAT'S KEEPING BIS? I'M TIRED OF WAITING!
Y-YES, MASTER LANCE. YOU SEE...
NEITHER THE OLD MAN NOR THE HEIR HAD A RAVE ON THEM.
BIS IS HEADING BACK TO THE OLD MAN'S PLACE TO SEARCH.
GAH-- USELESS PIGS!
DID YOU AT LEAST DISPOSE OF THE HEIR?
WELL, YOU SEE...
I SHOULD HAVE GUESSED.

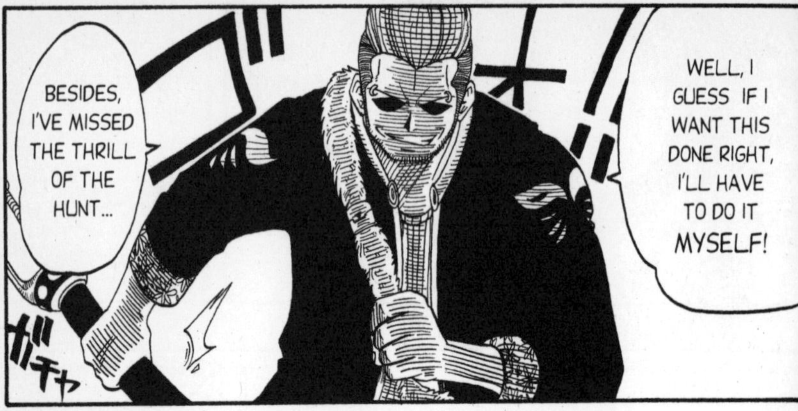
WELL, I GUESS IF I WANT THIS DONE RIGHT, I'LL HAVE TO DO IT MYSELF!
BESIDES, I'VE MISSED THE THRILL OF THE HUNT...
ガチャ

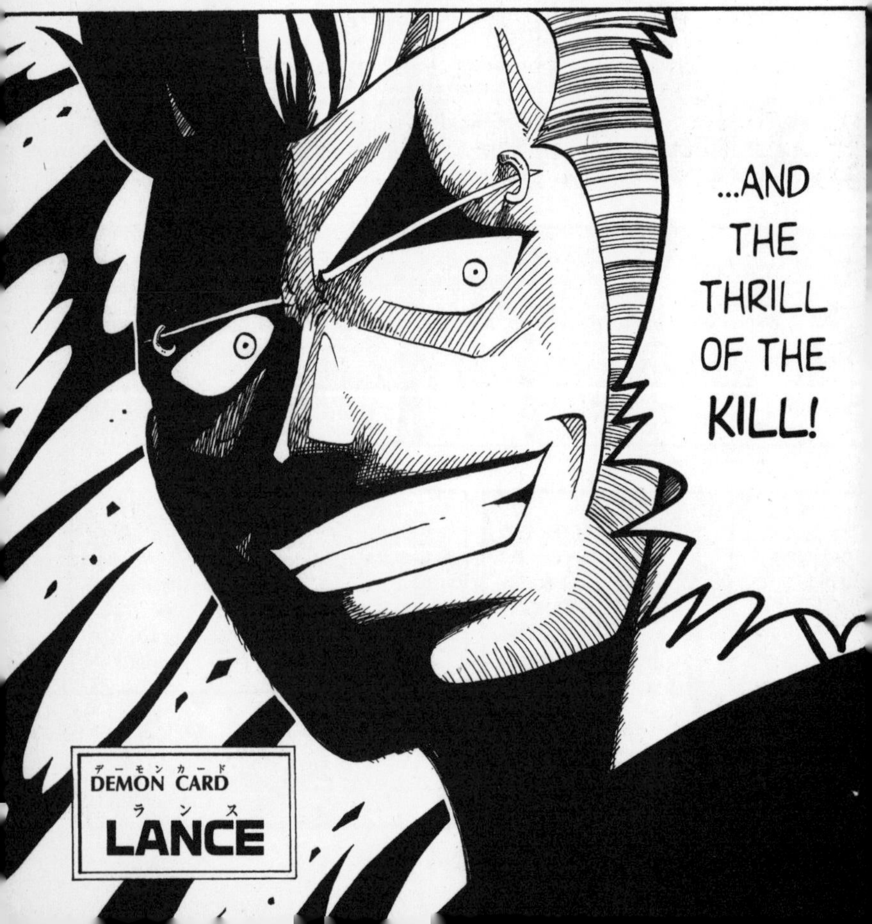
...AND THE THRILL OF THE KILL!
デーモンカード
DEMON CARD
ランス
LANCE

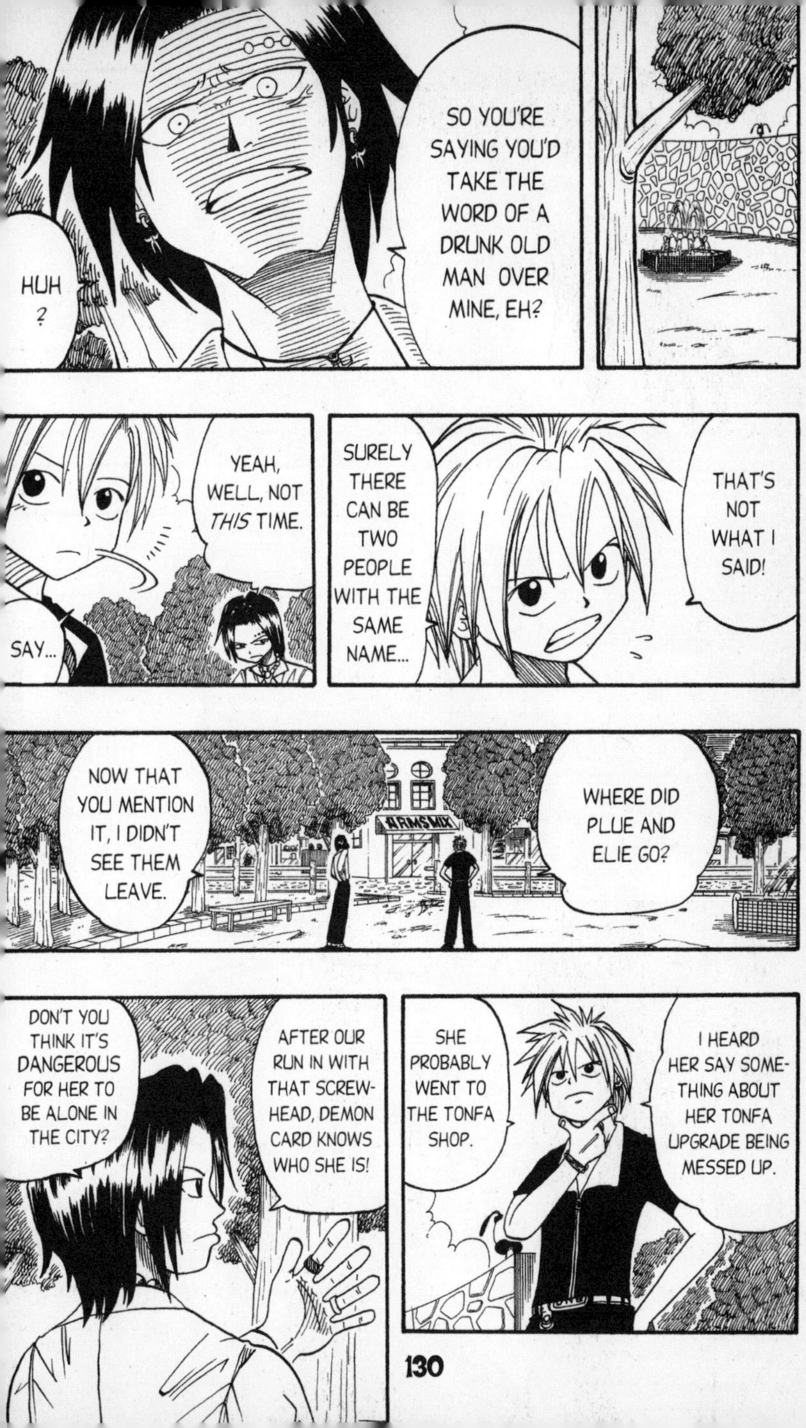
SO YOU'RE SAYING YOU'D TAKE THE WORD OF A DRUNK OLD MAN OVER MINE, EH?
HUH?
THAT'S NOT WHAT I SAID!
SURELY THERE CAN BE TWO PEOPLE WITH THE SAME NAME...
YEAH, WELL, NOT *THIS* TIME.
SAY...
WHERE DID PLUE AND ELIE GO?
ARMSMIX
NOW THAT YOU MENTION IT, I DIDN'T SEE THEM LEAVE.
I HEARD HER SAY SOME-THING ABOUT HER TONFA UPGRADE BEING MESSED UP.
SHE PROBABLY WENT TO THE TONFA SHOP.
AFTER OUR RUN IN WITH THAT SCREW-HEAD, DEMON CARD KNOWS WHO SHE IS!
DON'T YOU THINK IT'S DANGEROUS FOR HER TO BE ALONE IN THE CITY?

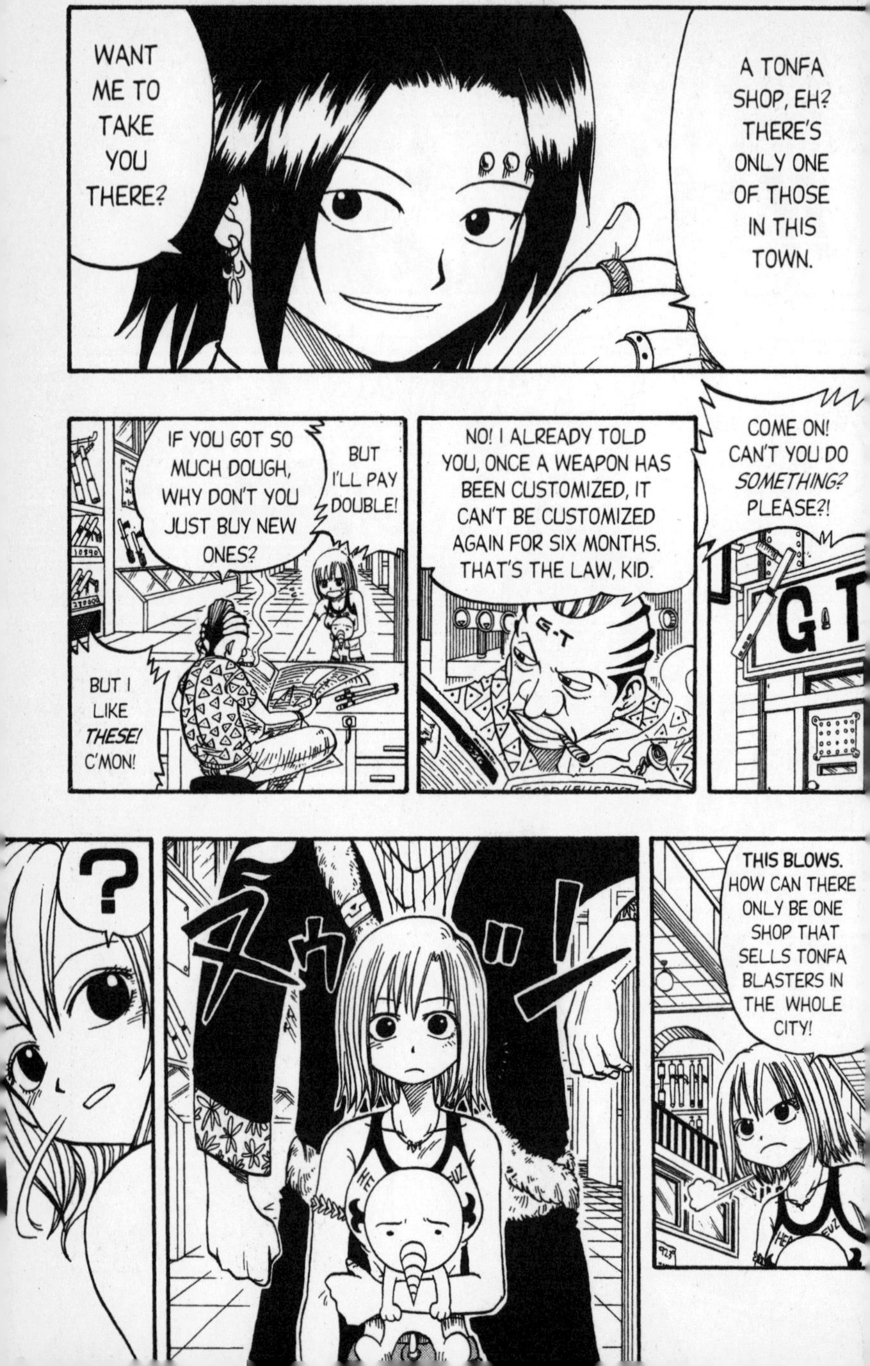
A TONFA SHOP, EH? THERE'S ONLY ONE OF THOSE IN THIS TOWN.
WANT ME TO TAKE YOU THERE?
COME ON! CAN'T YOU DO *SOMETHING?* PLEASE?!
NO! I ALREADY TOLD YOU, ONCE A WEAPON HAS BEEN CUSTOMIZED, IT CAN'T BE CUSTOMIZED AGAIN FOR SIX MONTHS. THAT'S THE LAW, KID.
BUT I'LL PAY DOUBLE!
IF YOU GOT SO MUCH DOUGH, WHY DON'T YOU JUST BUY NEW ONES?
BUT I LIKE *THESE!* C'MON!
G·T
THIS BLOWS. HOW CAN THERE ONLY BE ONE SHOP THAT SELLS TONFA BLASTERS IN THE WHOLE CITY!
?

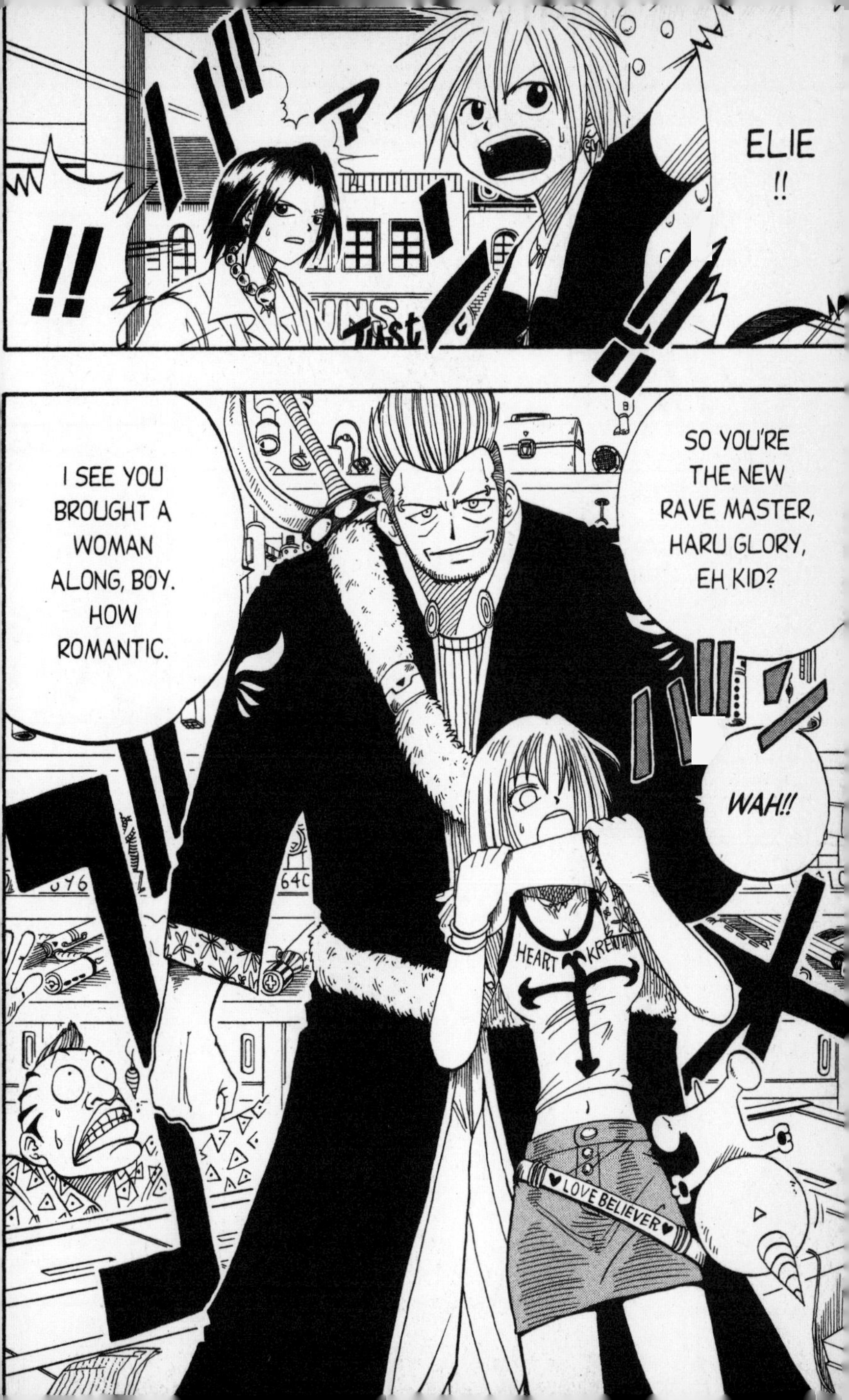
ELIE !!
SO YOU'RE THE NEW RAVE MASTER, HARU GLORY, EH KID?
WAH!!
I SEE YOU BROUGHT A WOMAN ALONG, BOY. HOW ROMANTIC.
LOVE BELIEVER

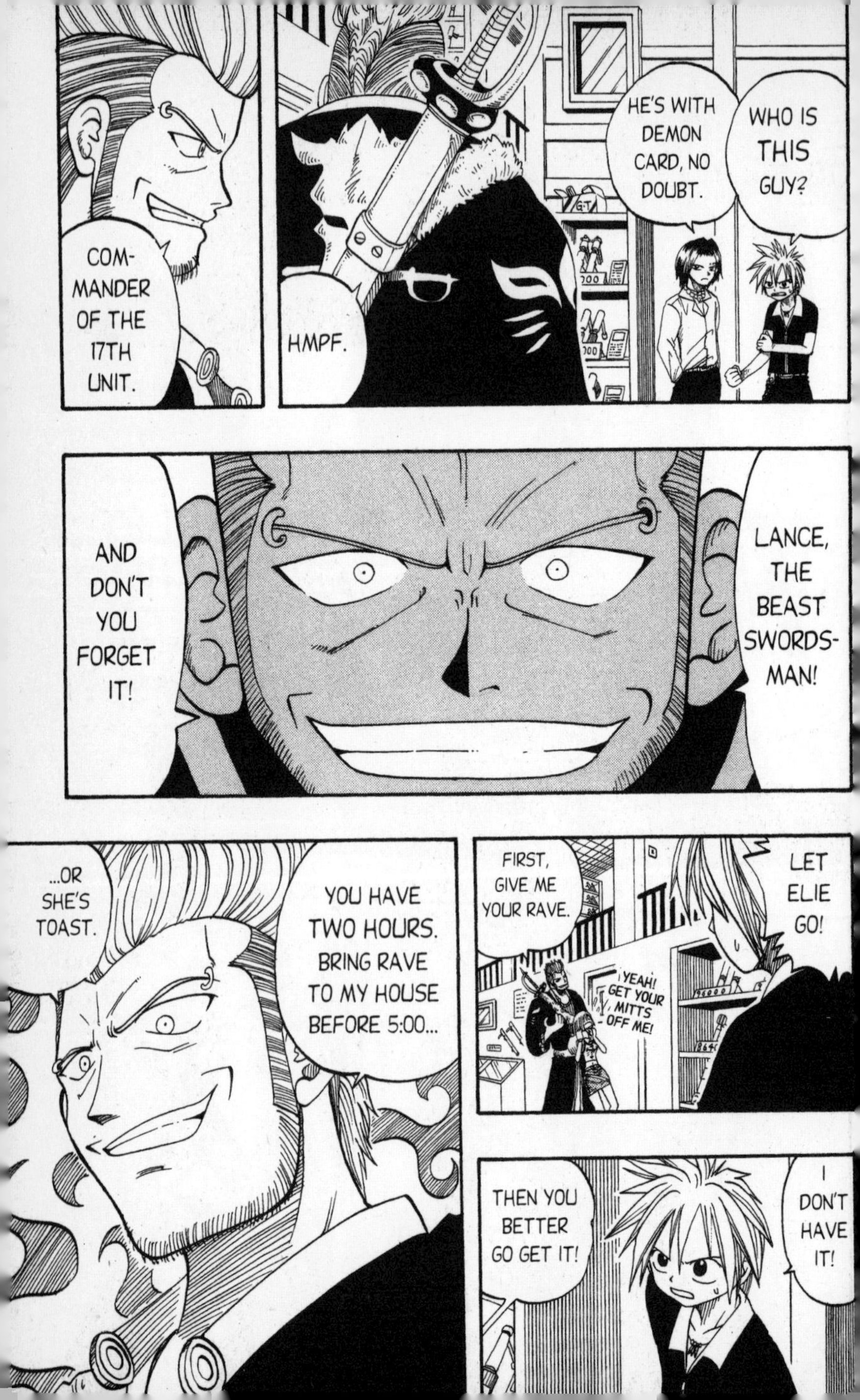
WHO IS THIS GUY?
HE'S WITH DEMON CARD, NO DOUBT.
HMPF.
COM-MANDER OF THE 17TH UNIT.
LANCE, THE BEAST SWORDS-MAN!
AND DON'T YOU FORGET IT!
LET ELIE GO!
FIRST, GIVE ME YOUR RAVE.
YEAH! GET YOUR MITTS OFF ME!
I DON'T HAVE IT!
THEN YOU BETTER GO GET IT!
YOU HAVE TWO HOURS. BRING RAVE TO MY HOUSE BEFORE 5:00...
...OR SHE'S TOAST.

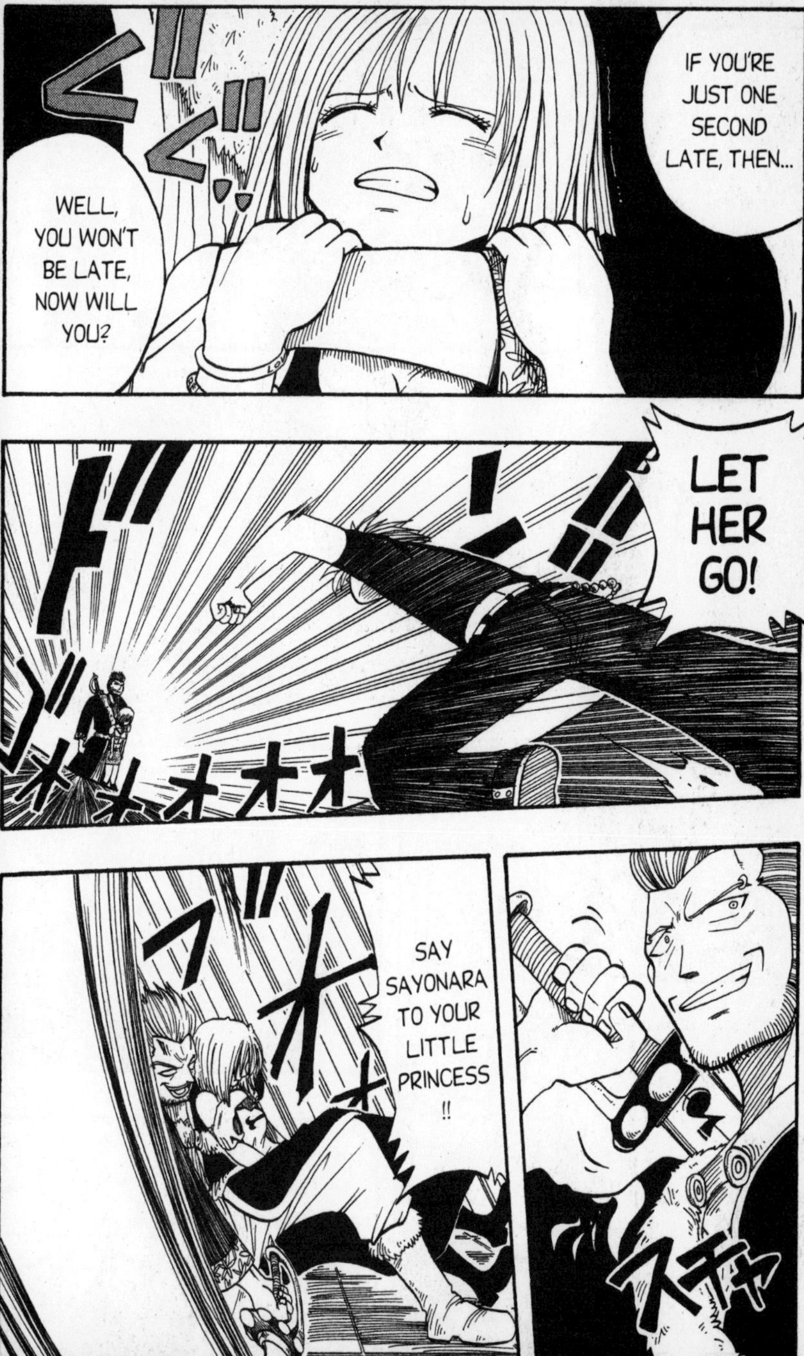
IF YOU'RE JUST ONE SECOND LATE, THEN...
WELL, YOU WON'T BE LATE, NOW WILL YOU?
LET HER GO!
SAY SAYONARA TO YOUR LITTLE PRINCESS !!

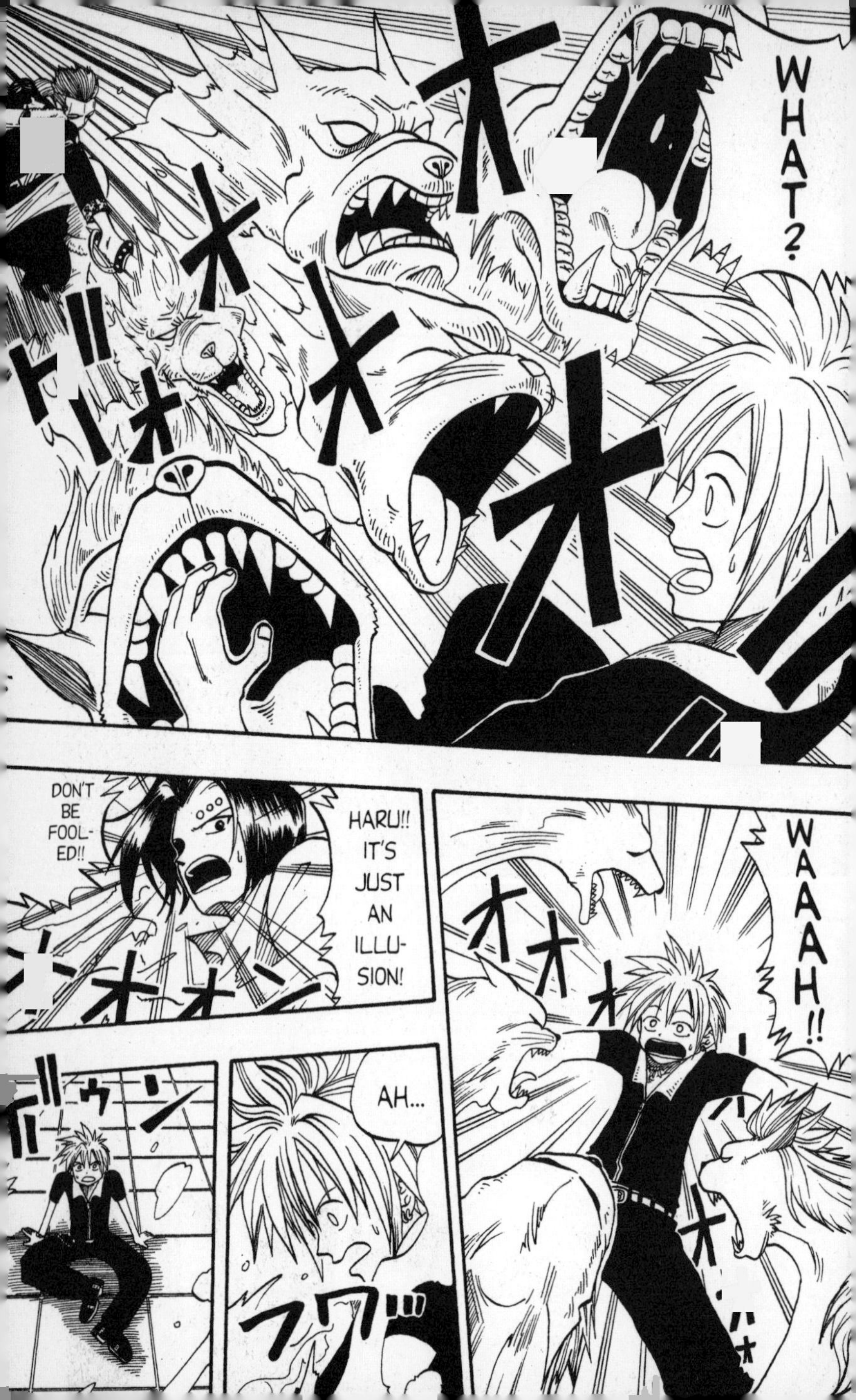
WHAT?
WAAAAH!!
HARU!! IT'S JUST AN ILLUSION!
DON'T BE FOOLED!!
AH...

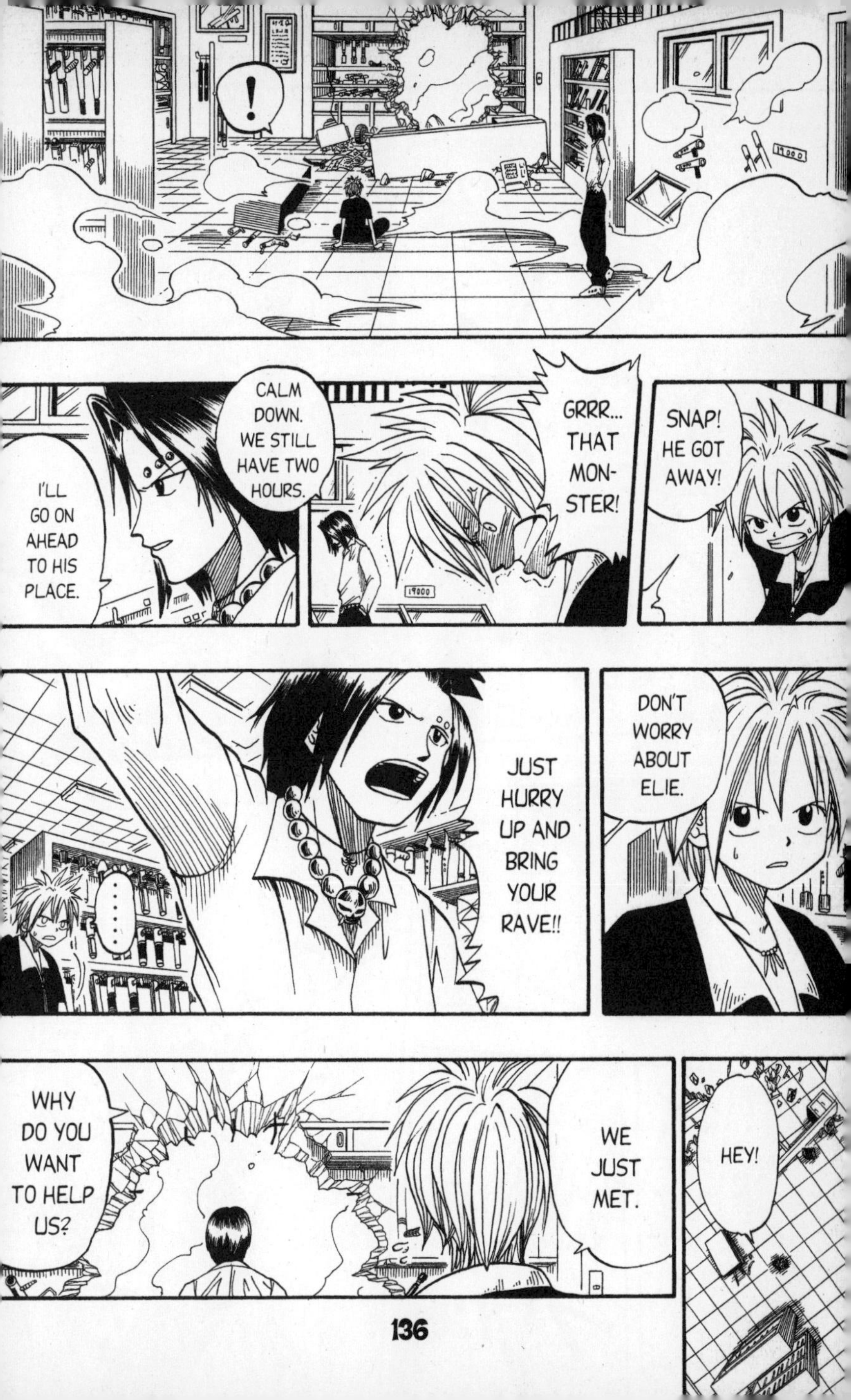
!
SNAP! HE GOT AWAY!
GRRR... THAT MON-STER!
CALM DOWN. WE STILL HAVE TWO HOURS.
I'LL GO ON AHEAD TO HIS PLACE.
DON'T WORRY ABOUT ELIE.
JUST HURRY UP AND BRING YOUR RAVE!!
......
HEY!
WE JUST MET.
WHY DO YOU WANT TO HELP US?

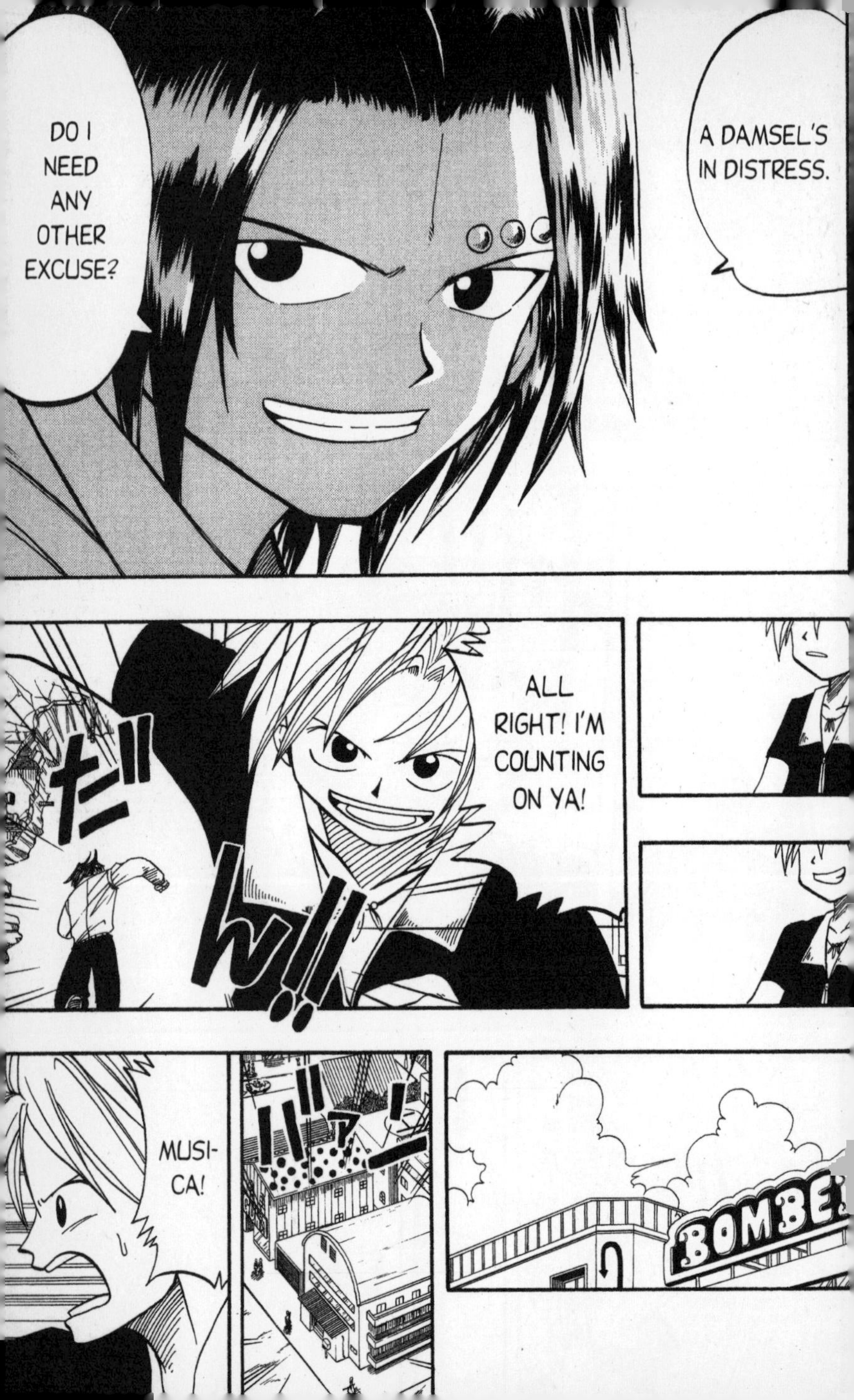
A DAMSEL'S IN DISTRESS.
DO I NEED ANY OTHER EXCUSE?
ALL RIGHT! I'M COUNTING ON YA!
MUSI-CA!

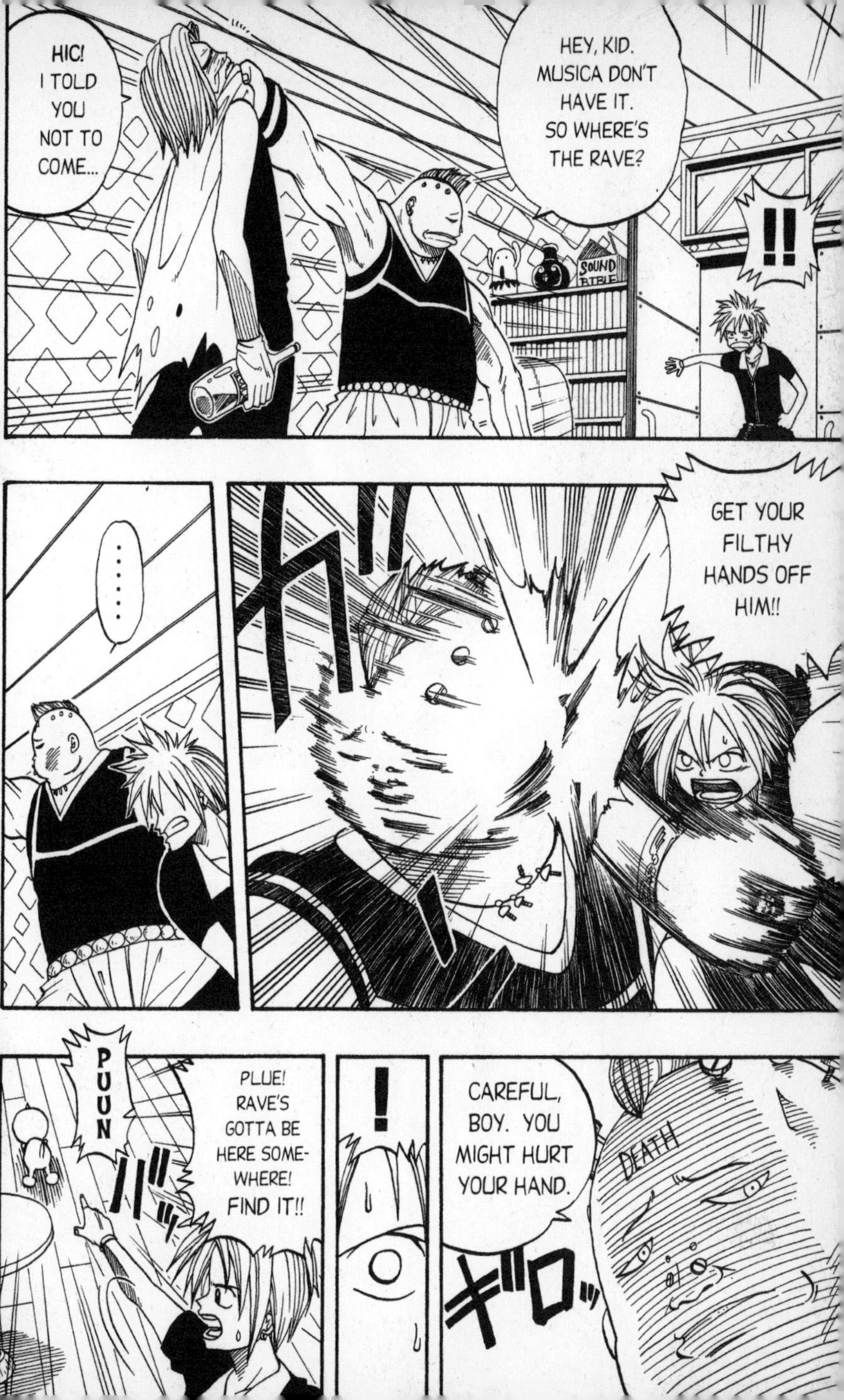
HEY, KID. MUSICA DON'T HAVE IT. SO WHERE'S THE RAVE?
!!
HIC! I TOLD YOU NOT TO COME...
GET YOUR FILTHY HANDS OFF HIM!!
......
CAREFUL, BOY. YOU MIGHT HURT YOUR HAND.
DEATH
!
PLUE! RAVE'S GOTTA BE HERE SOME-WHERE! FIND IT!!
PUUN

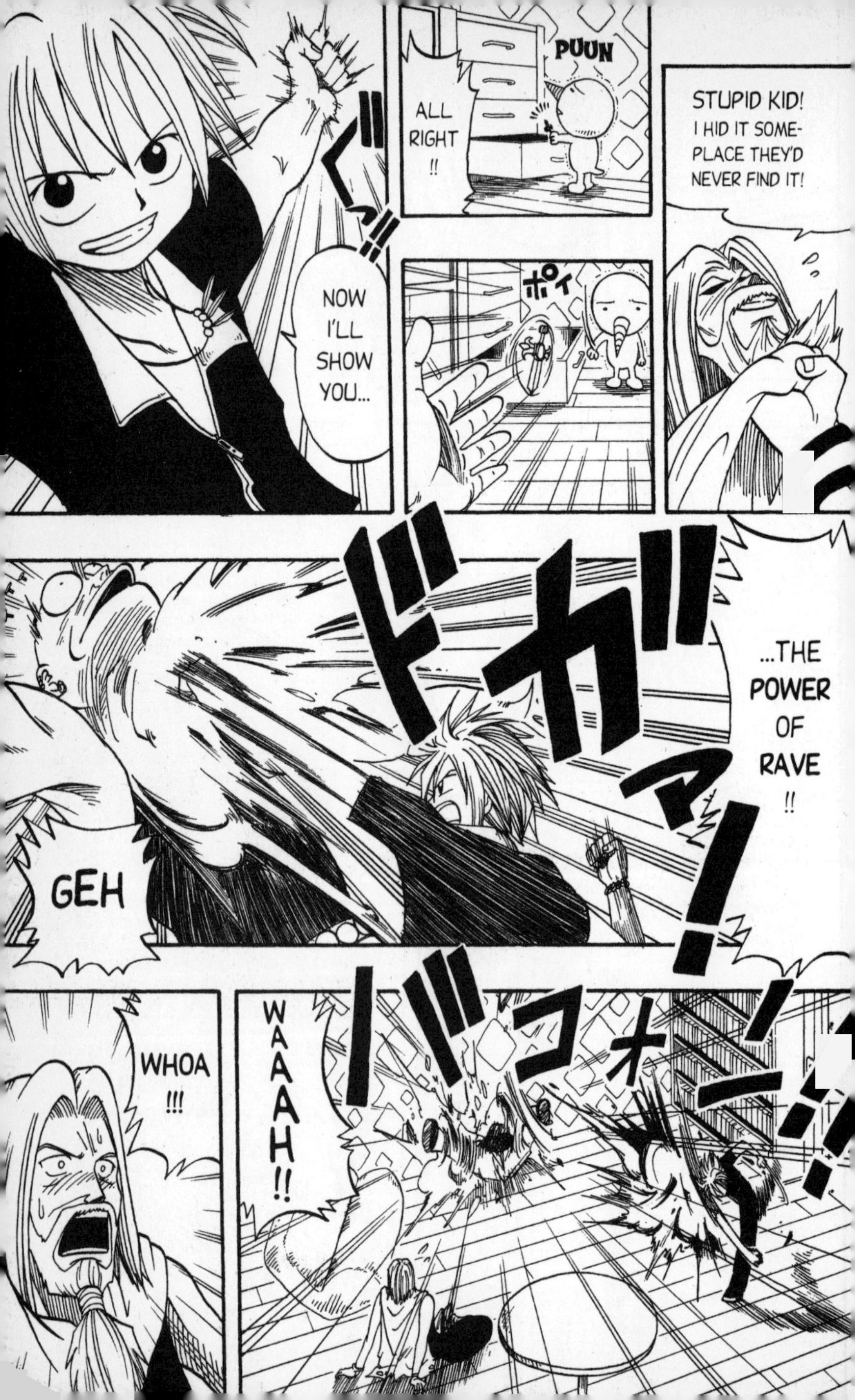
STUPID KID! I HID IT SOME-PLACE THEY'D NEVER FIND IT!
PUUN
ALL RIGHT !!
ポイ
NOW I'LL SHOW YOU...
...THE POWER OF RAVE !!
ドガァ!!
GEH
WAAAAH!!
ドゴォーン!!
WHOA !!!

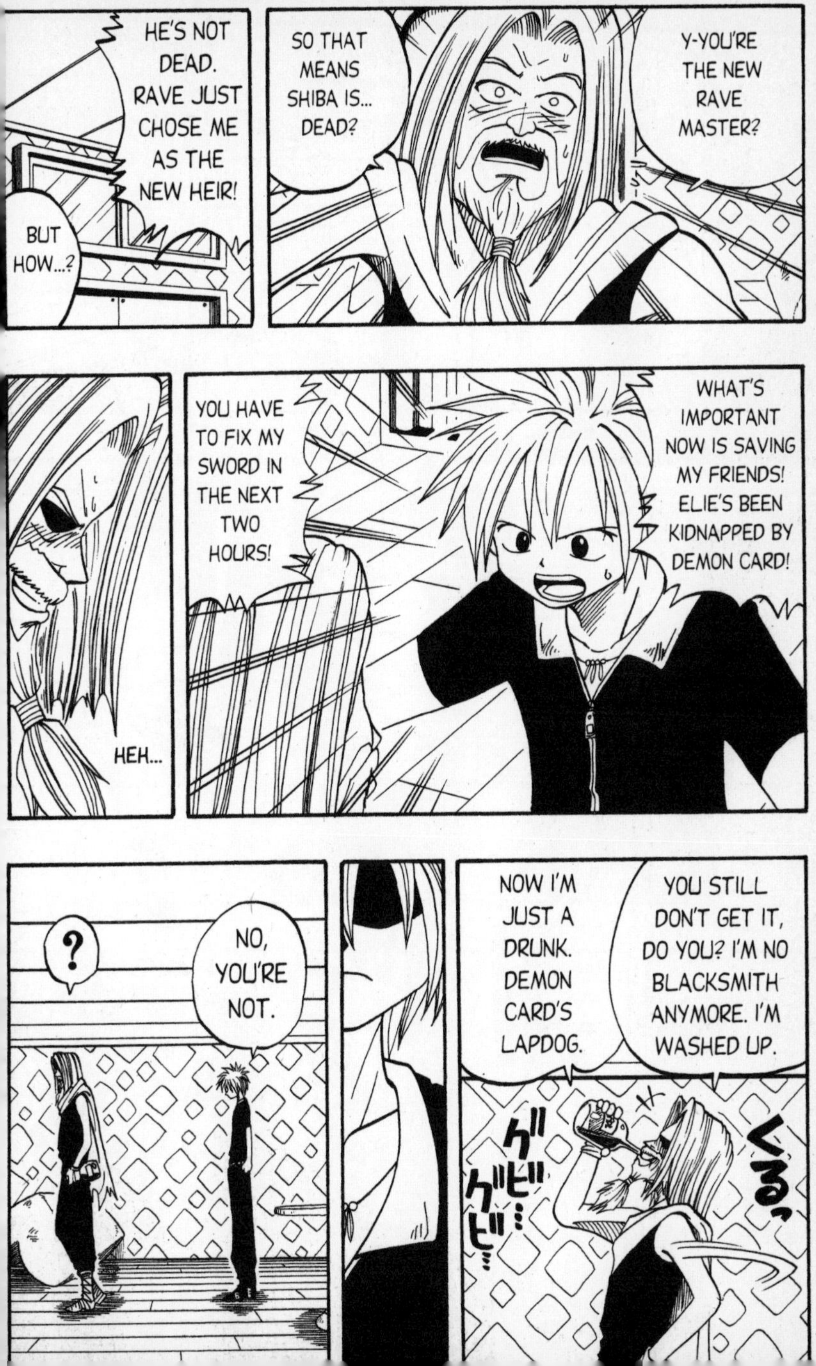
Y-YOU'RE THE NEW RAVE MASTER?
SO THAT MEANS SHIBA IS... DEAD?
HE'S NOT DEAD. RAVE JUST CHOSE ME AS THE NEW HEIR!
BUT HOW...?
WHAT'S IMPORTANT NOW IS SAVING MY FRIENDS! ELIE'S BEEN KIDNAPPED BY DEMON CARD!
YOU HAVE TO FIX MY SWORD IN THE NEXT TWO HOURS!
HEH...
YOU STILL DON'T GET IT, DO YOU? I'M NO BLACKSMITH ANYMORE. I'M WASHED UP.
NOW I'M JUST A DRUNK. DEMON CARD'S LAPDOG.
グビ…
グビ…
NO, YOU'RE NOT.
?

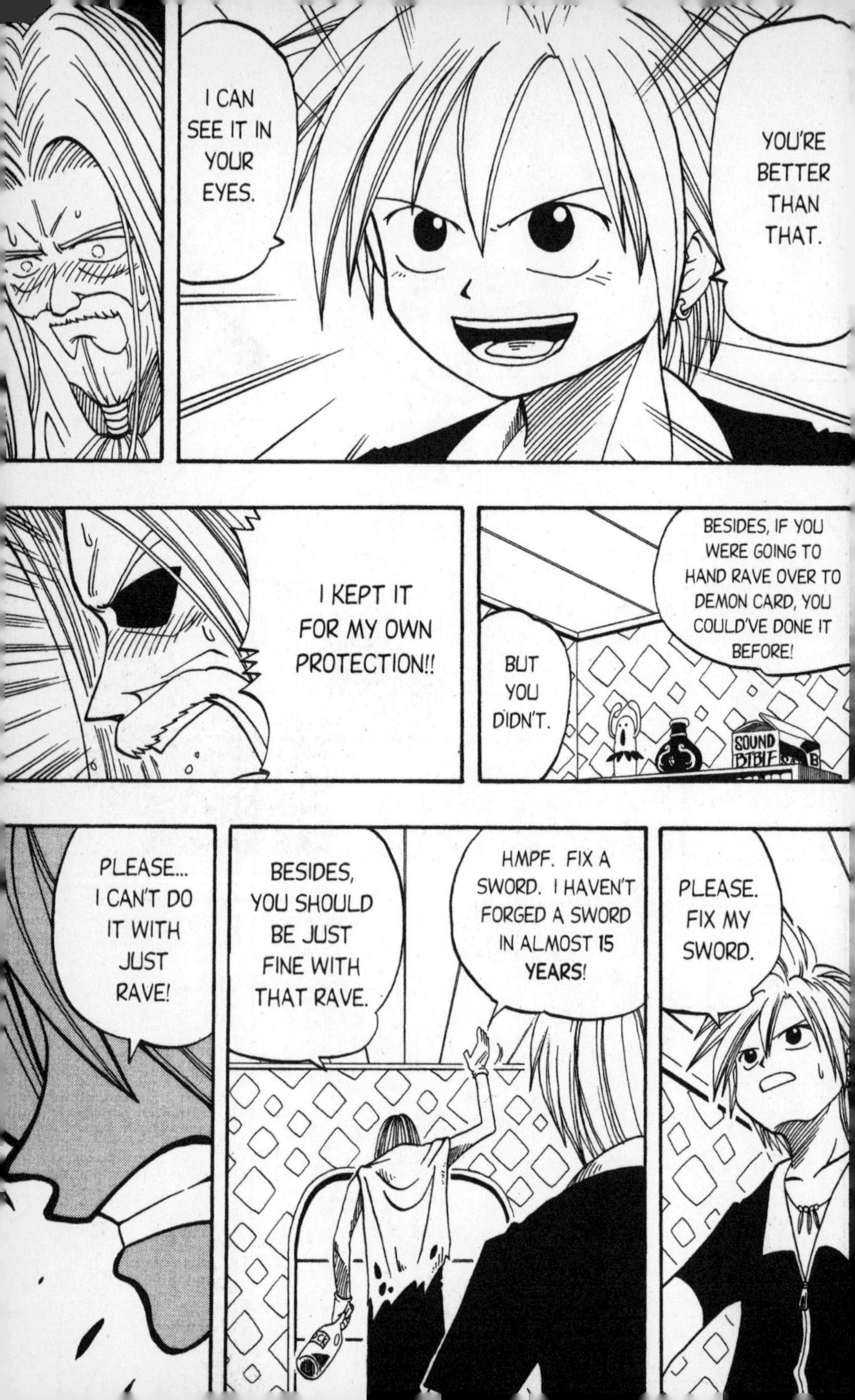
YOU'RE BETTER THAN THAT.
I CAN SEE IT IN YOUR EYES.
BESIDES, IF YOU WERE GOING TO HAND RAVE OVER TO DEMON CARD, YOU COULD'VE DONE IT BEFORE!
BUT YOU DIDN'T.
I KEPT IT FOR MY OWN PROTECTION!!
PLEASE. FIX MY SWORD.
HMPF. FIX A SWORD. I HAVEN'T FORGED A SWORD IN ALMOST 15 YEARS!
BESIDES, YOU SHOULD BE JUST FINE WITH THAT RAVE.
PLEASE... I CAN'T DO IT WITH JUST RAVE!

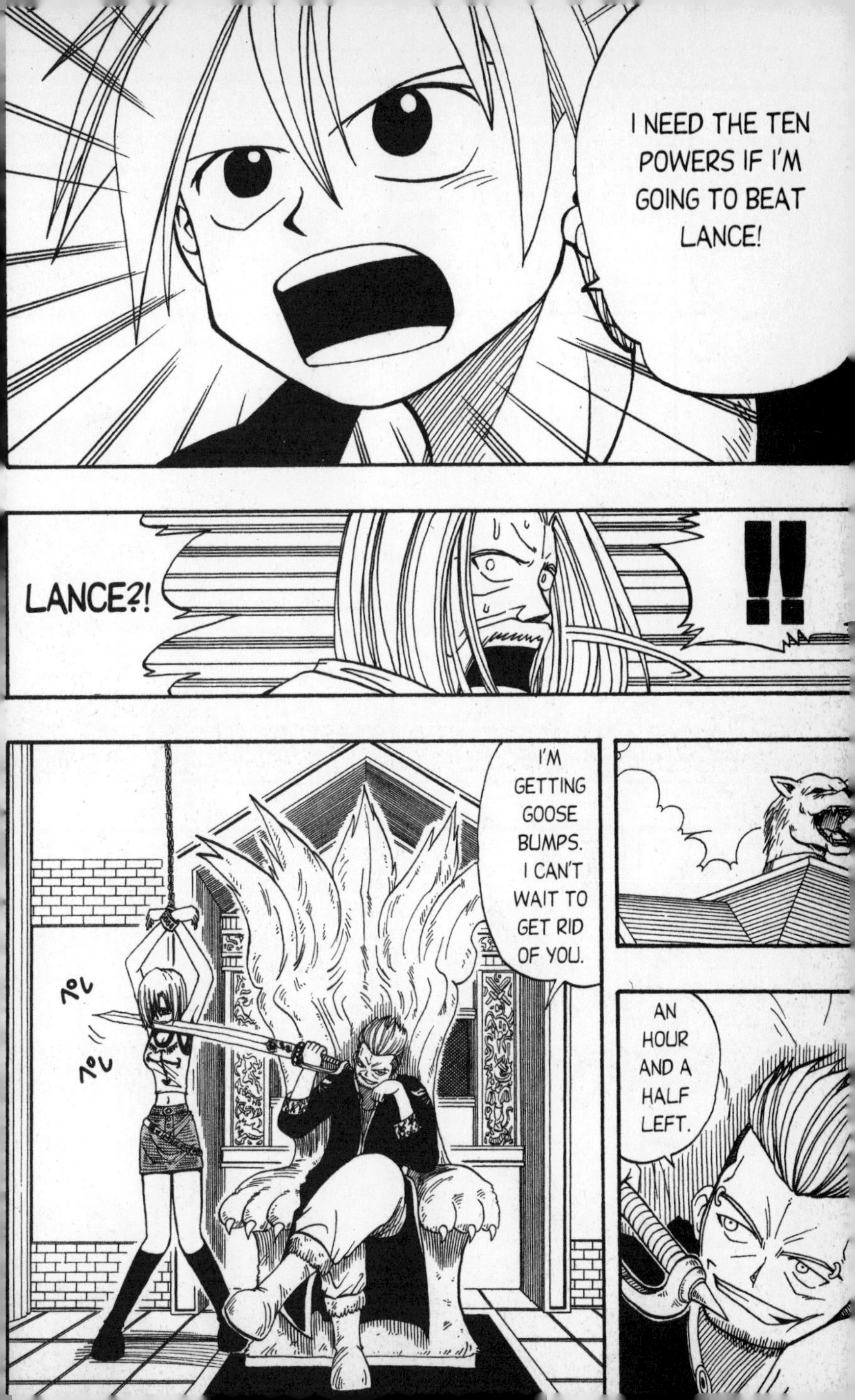

I NEED THE TEN POWERS IF I'M GOING TO BEAT LANCE!
LANCE?!
!!
AN HOUR AND A HALF LEFT.
I'M GETTING GOOSE BUMPS. I CAN'T WAIT TO GET RID OF YOU.
ぺし
ぺし

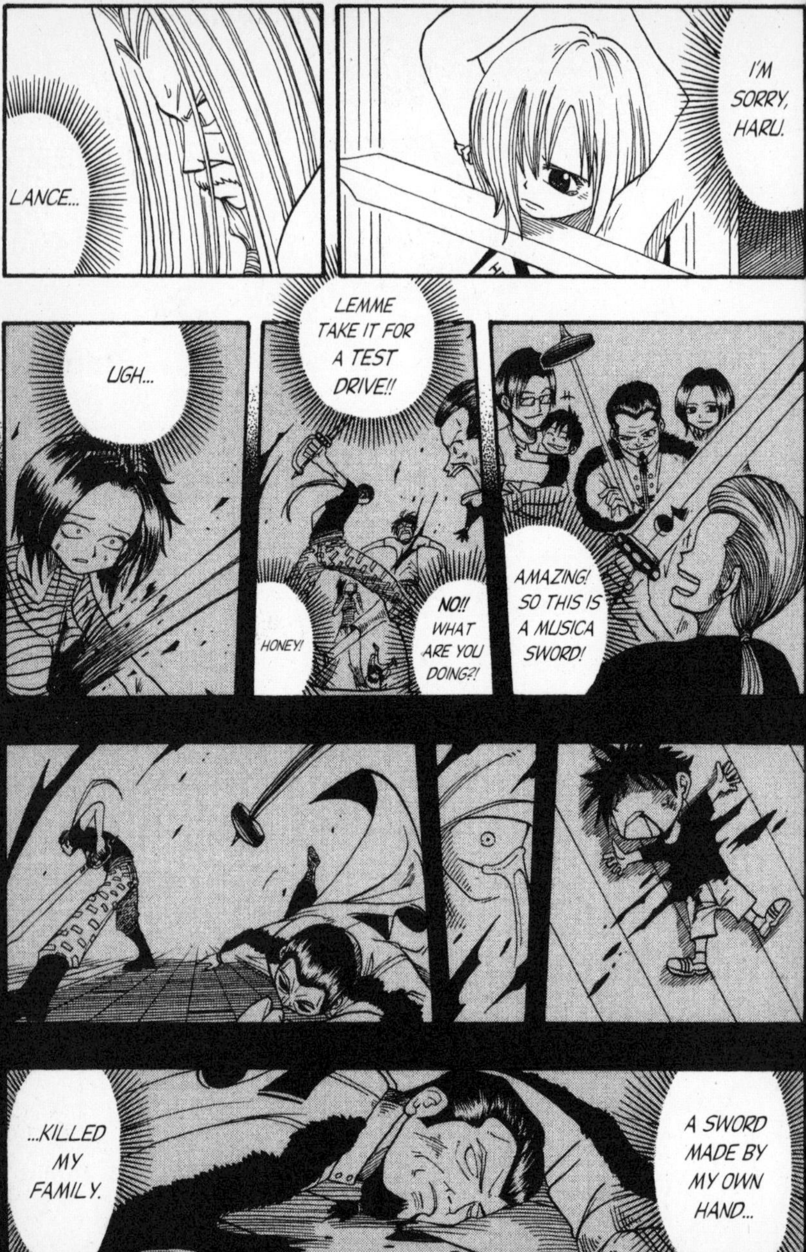
I'M SORRY, HARU.
LANCE...
AMAZING! SO THIS IS A MUSICA SWORD!
LEMME TAKE IT FOR A TEST DRIVE!!
NO!! WHAT ARE YOU DOING?!
HONEY!
UGH...
A SWORD MADE BY MY OWN HAND...
...KILLED MY FAMILY.

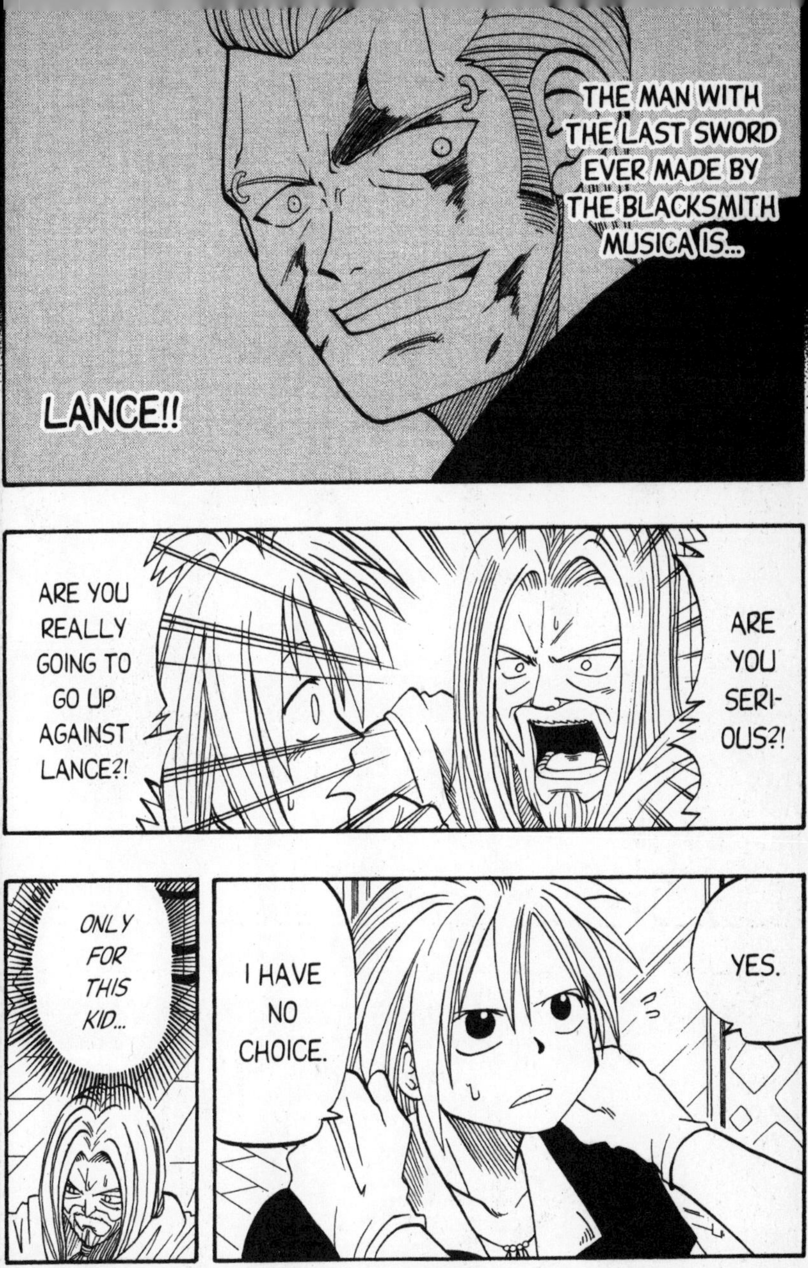
THE MAN WITH THE LAST SWORD EVER MADE BY THE BLACKSMITH MUSICA IS...
LANCE!!
ARE YOU SERI-OUS?!
ARE YOU REALLY GOING TO GO UP AGAINST LANCE?!
YES.
I HAVE NO CHOICE.
ONLY FOR THIS KID...

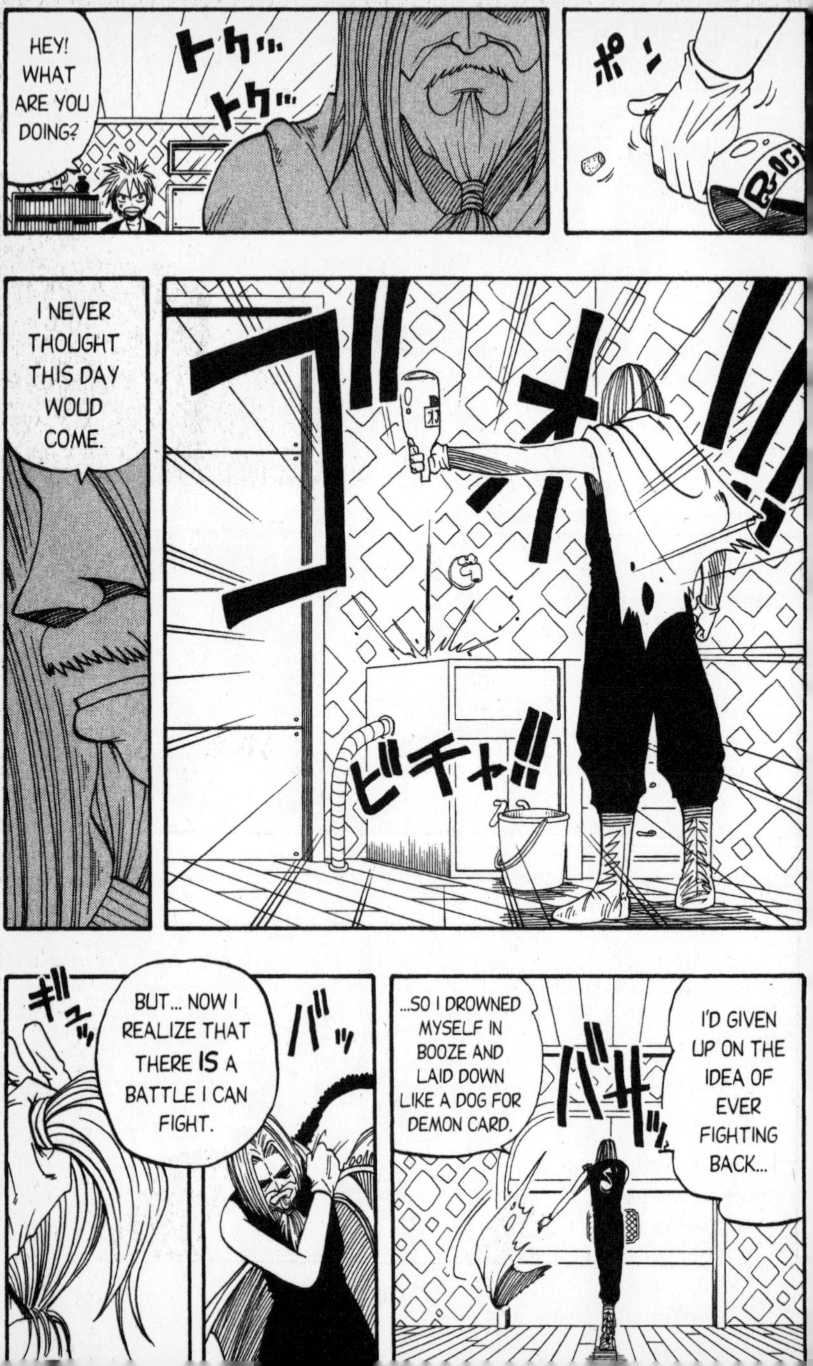
ポン
トクッ
トクッ
HEY! WHAT ARE YOU DOING?
ゴボッ!!
ビチャ!!
I NEVER THOUGHT THIS DAY WOUD COME.
I'D GIVEN UP ON THE IDEA OF EVER FIGHTING BACK...
...SO I DROWNED MYSELF IN BOOZE AND LAID DOWN LIKE A DOG FOR DEMON CARD.
バサッ
バッ
BUT... NOW I REALIZE THAT THERE **IS** A BATTLE I CAN FIGHT.
ギュッ

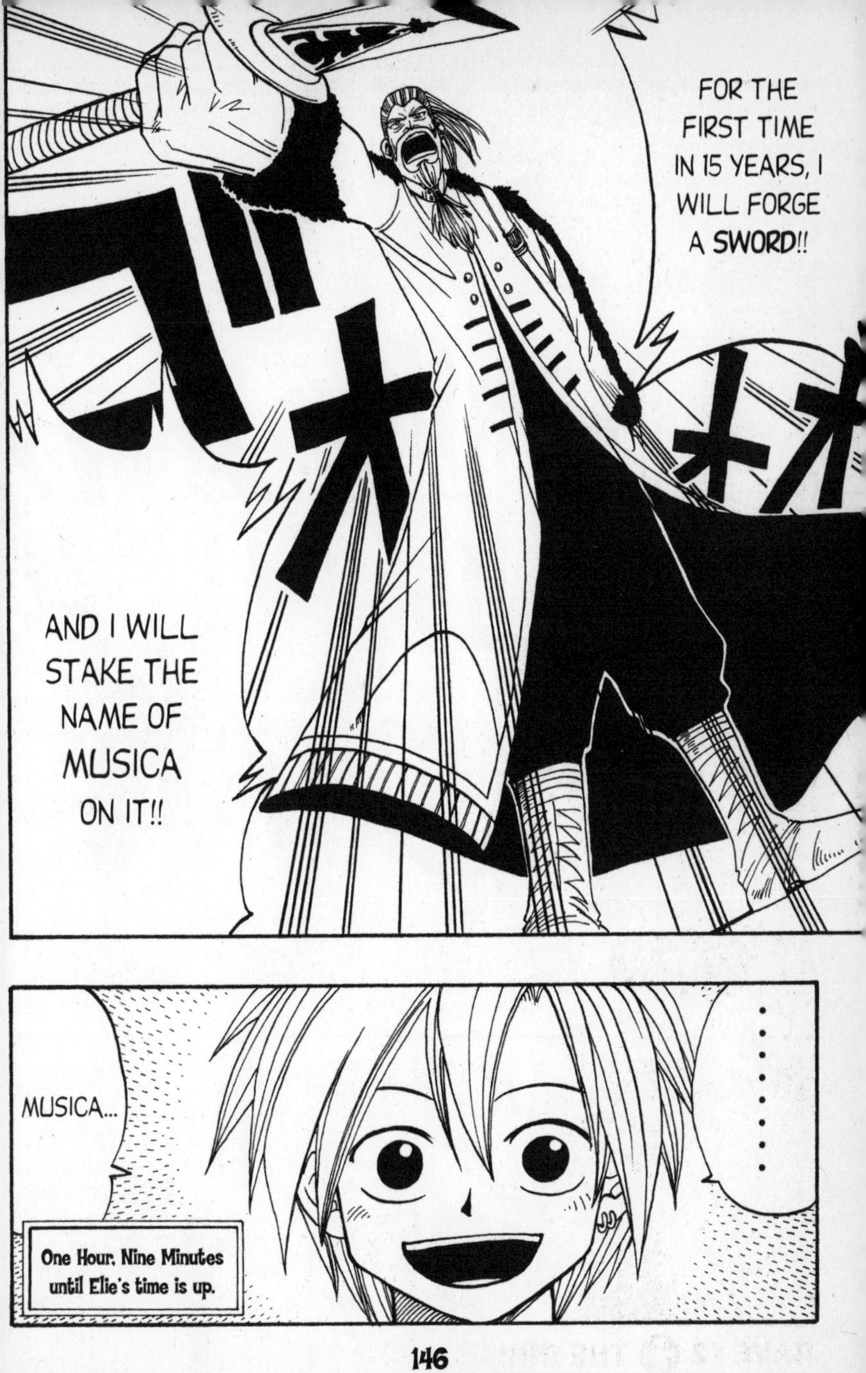
FOR THE FIRST TIME IN 15 YEARS, I WILL FORGE A SWORD!!
AND I WILL STAKE THE NAME OF MUSICA ON IT!!
....
MUSICA...
One Hour, Nine Minutes until Elie's time is up.

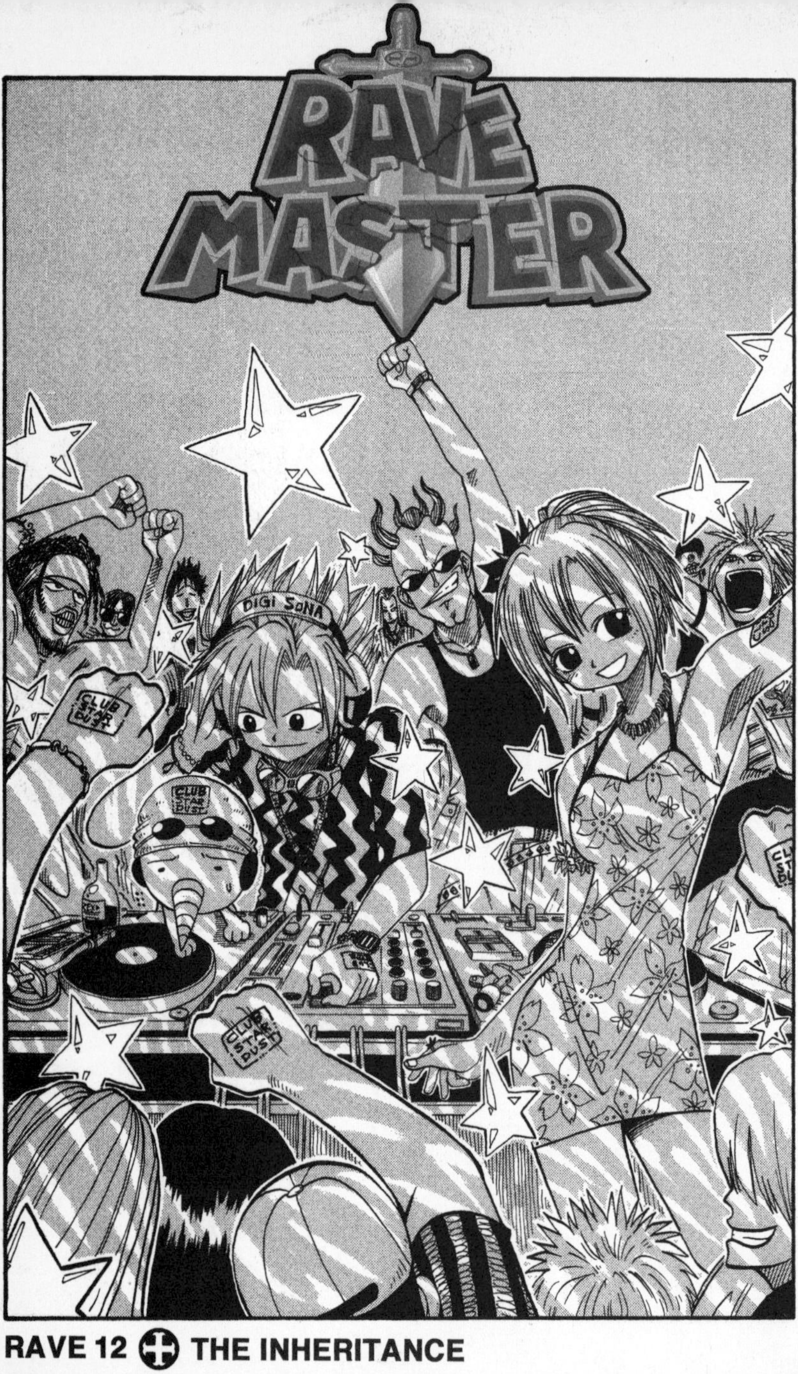
RAVE MASTER
DIGI SONA
CLUB STAR DUST

RAVE 12 ✠ THE INHERITANCE

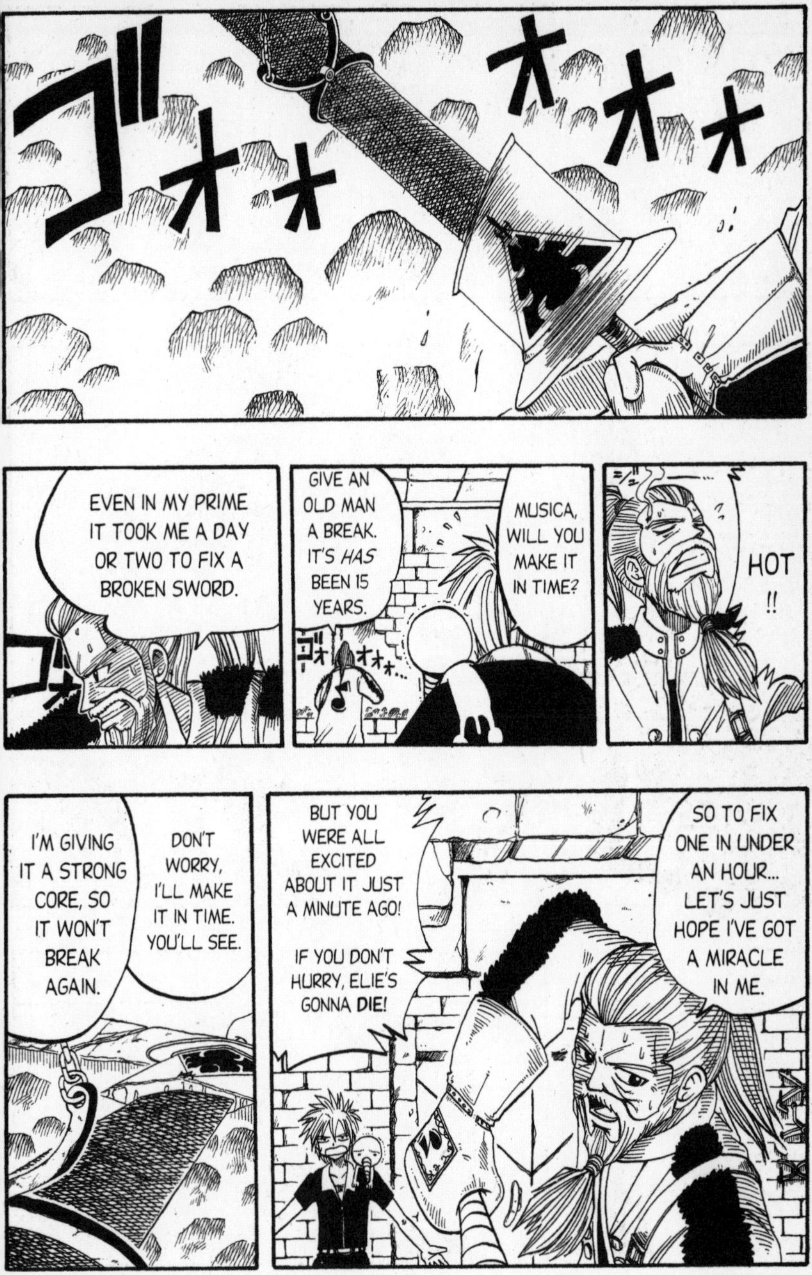
ゴオォ オオォ
HOT !!
MUSICA, WILL YOU MAKE IT IN TIME?
GIVE AN OLD MAN A BREAK. IT'S *HAS* BEEN 15 YEARS.
ゴオォオォ...
EVEN IN MY PRIME IT TOOK ME A DAY OR TWO TO FIX A BROKEN SWORD.
SO TO FIX ONE IN UNDER AN HOUR... LET'S JUST HOPE I'VE GOT A MIRACLE IN ME.
BUT YOU WERE ALL EXCITED ABOUT IT JUST A MINUTE AGO!
IF YOU DON'T HURRY, ELIE'S GONNA **DIE**!
DON'T WORRY, I'LL MAKE IT IN TIME. YOU'LL SEE.
I'M GIVING IT A STRONG CORE, SO IT WON'T BREAK AGAIN.

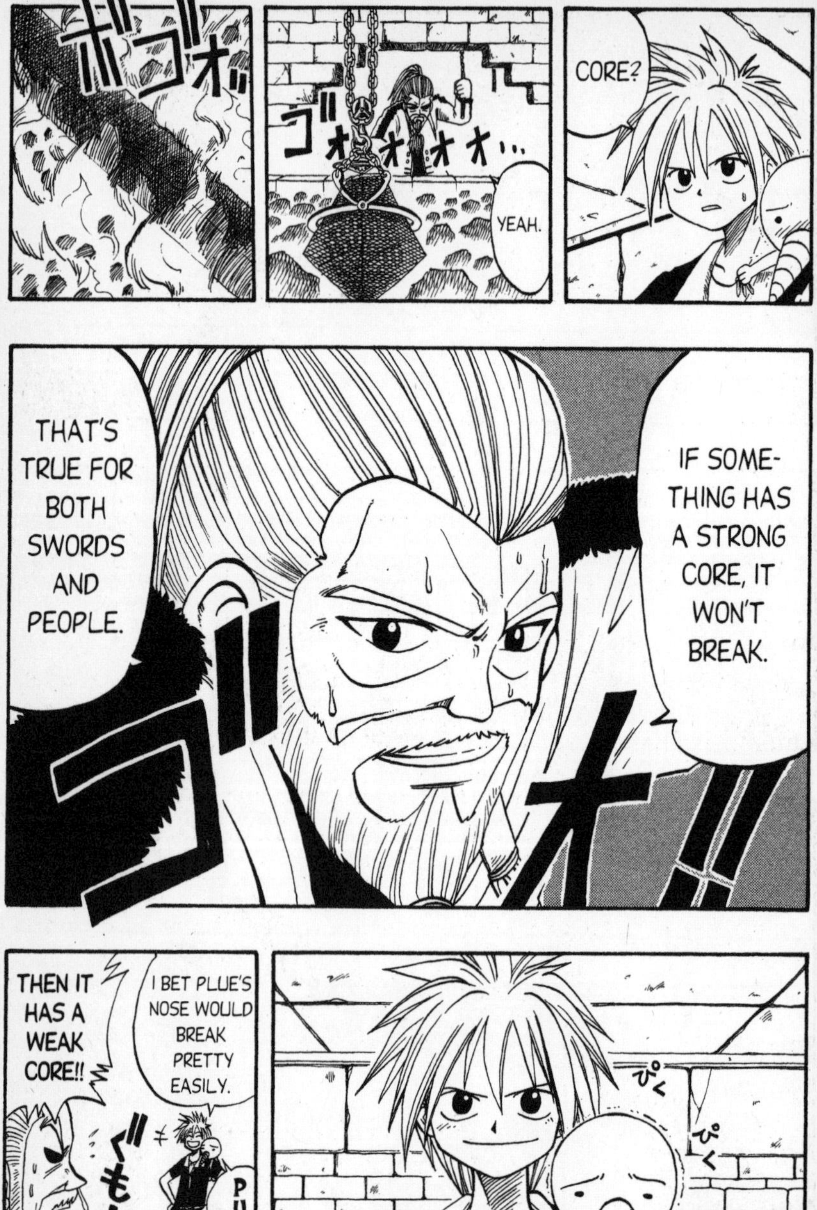
CORE?
YEAH.
ゴォォォォォ...
ボゴォォ
IF SOME-
THING HAS
A STRONG
CORE, IT
WON'T
BREAK.
THAT'S
TRUE FOR
BOTH
SWORDS
AND
PEOPLE.
ゴォ!!
ぴく
ぴく
I BET PLUE'S
NOSE WOULD
BREAK
PRETTY
EASILY.
THEN IT
HAS A
WEAK
CORE!!
ぐもー
PUUN

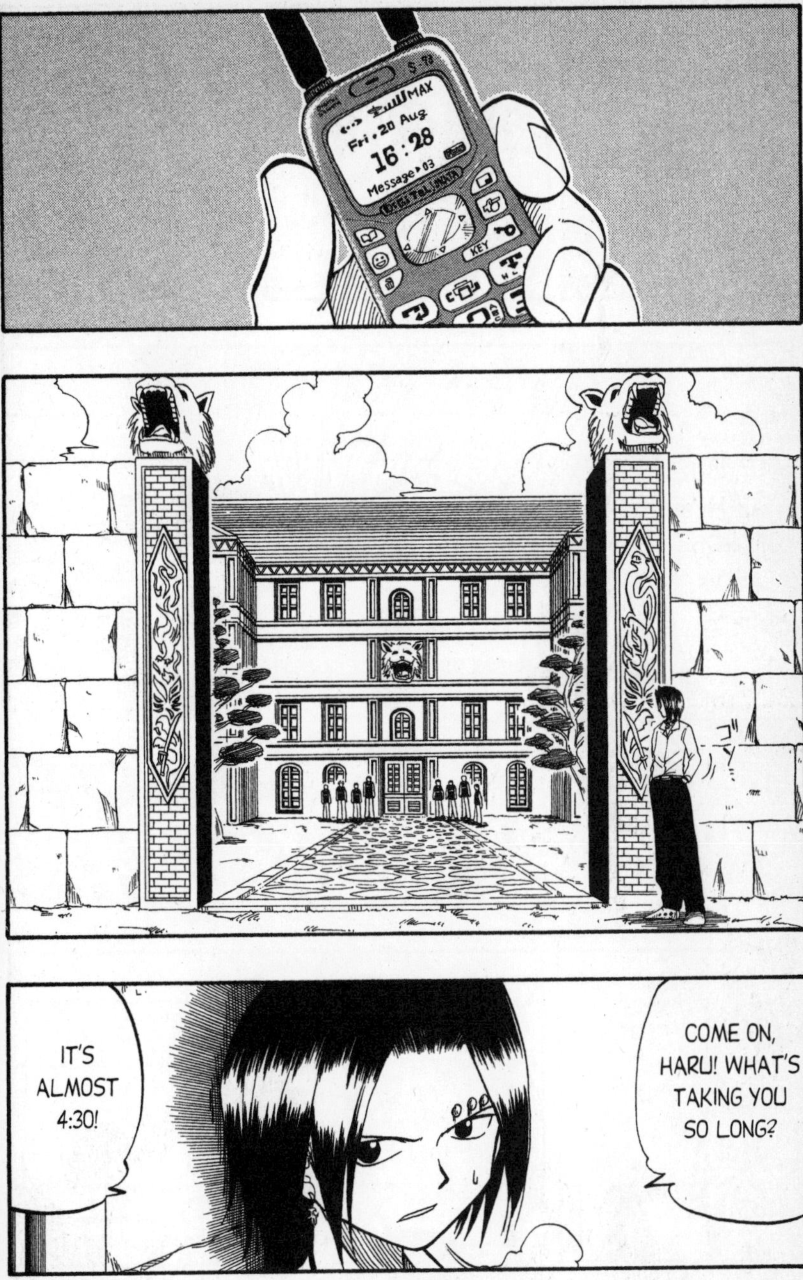
MAX
Fri, 20 Aug
16:28
Message 03
KEY
COME ON, HARU! WHAT'S TAKING YOU SO LONG?
IT'S ALMOST 4:30!

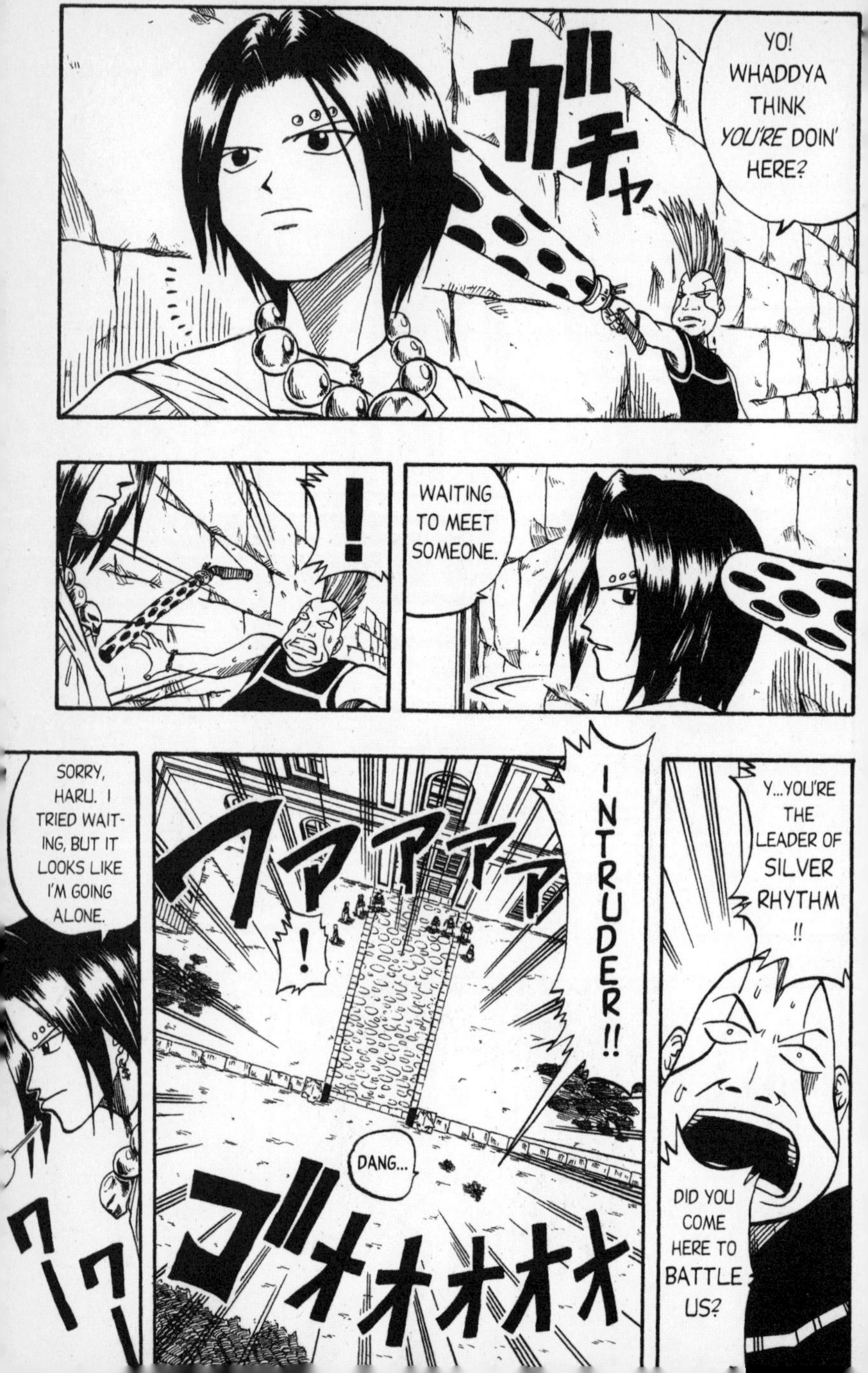
ガチャ
YO! WHADDYA THINK YOU'RE DOIN' HERE?
WAITING TO MEET SOMEONE.
!
Y...YOU'RE THE LEADER OF SILVER RHYTHM !!
DID YOU COME HERE TO BATTLE US?
INTRUDER!!
!
DANG...
ゴオオオオ
SORRY, HARU. I TRIED WAIT-ING, BUT IT LOOKS LIKE I'M GOING ALONE.
ワーワー

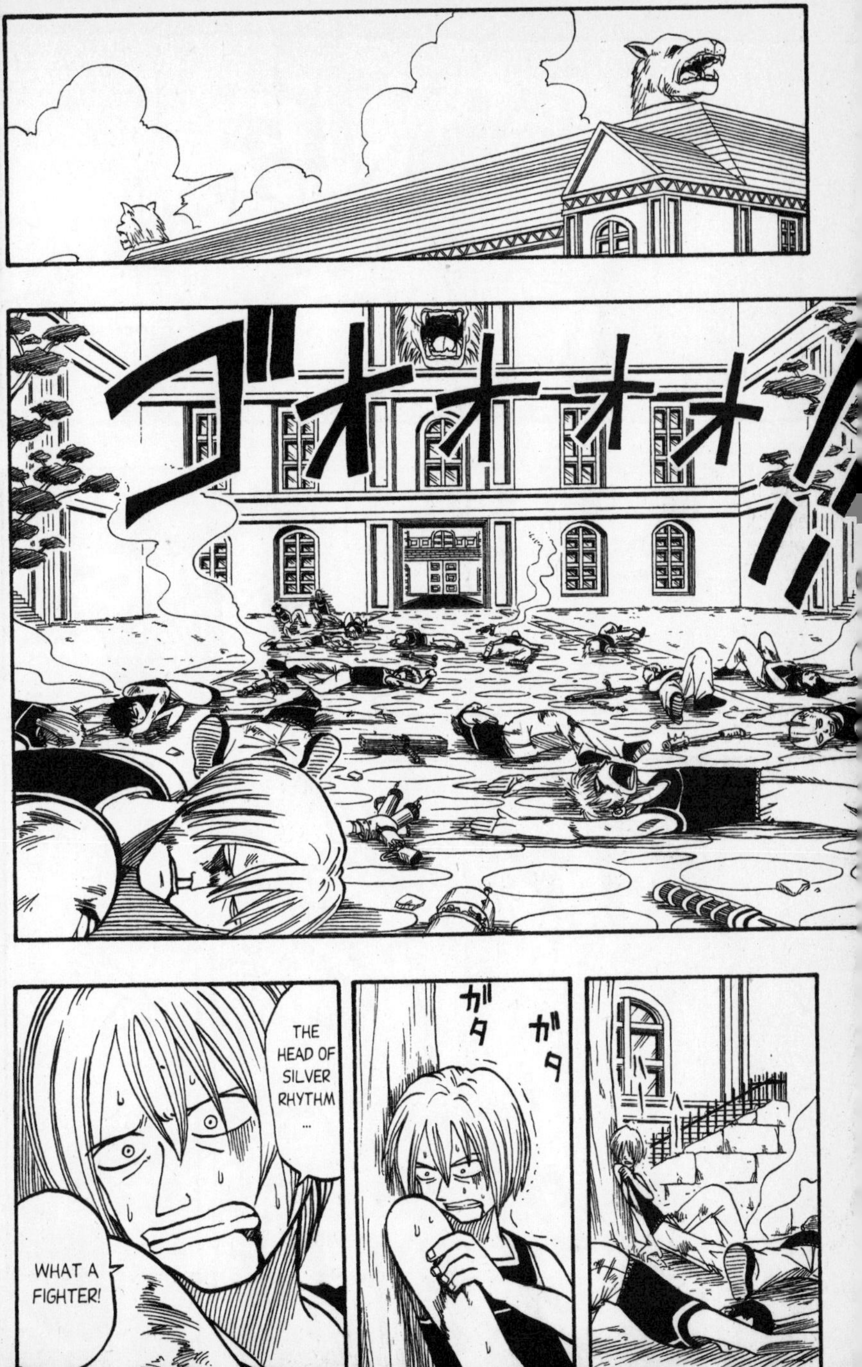
ゴオオオ!!
ガタ ガタ
THE HEAD OF SILVER RHYTHM ...
WHAT A FIGHTER!

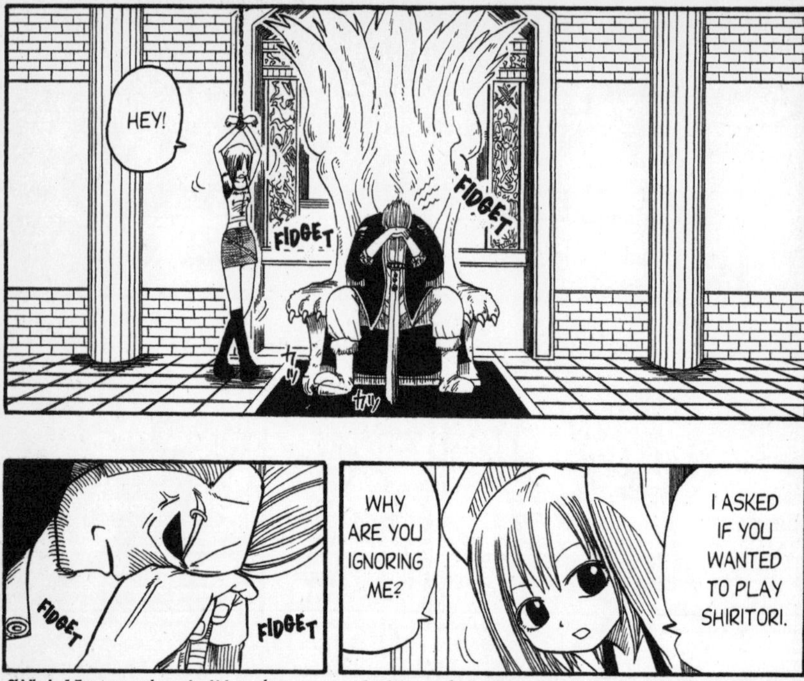
HEY!
FIDGET
FIDGET
I ASKED IF YOU WANTED TO PLAY SHIRITORI.
WHY ARE YOU IGNORING ME?
FIDGET
FIDGET

Shiritori- A Japanese word game in which one player names a word and the next player must say a word that starts with the first word's ending syllable. So in English, a game might go "sushi" --> "shindig" --> "igloo" "oozing" --> "ingot," et cetera...

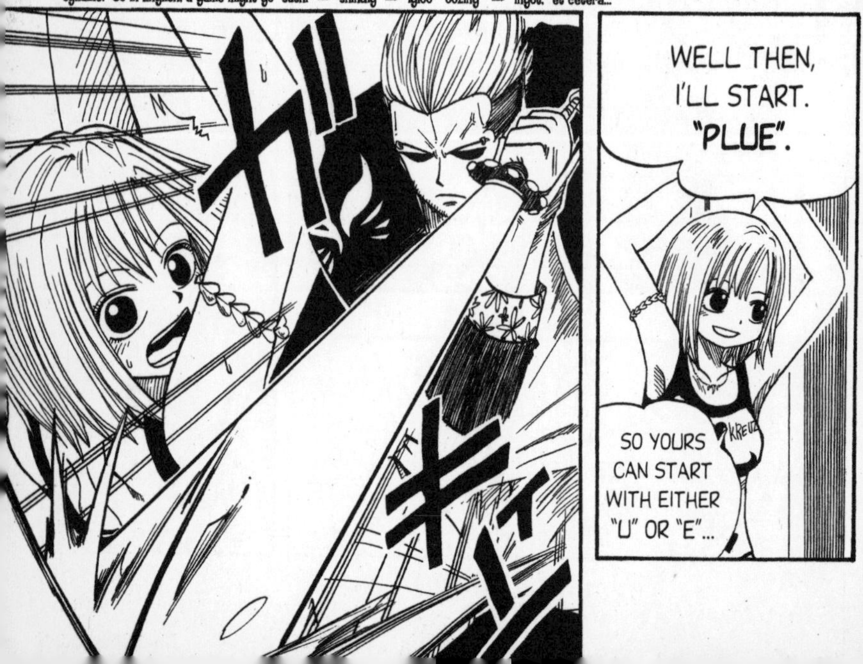
WELL THEN, I'LL START. "PLUE".
SO YOURS CAN START WITH EITHER "U" OR "E"...

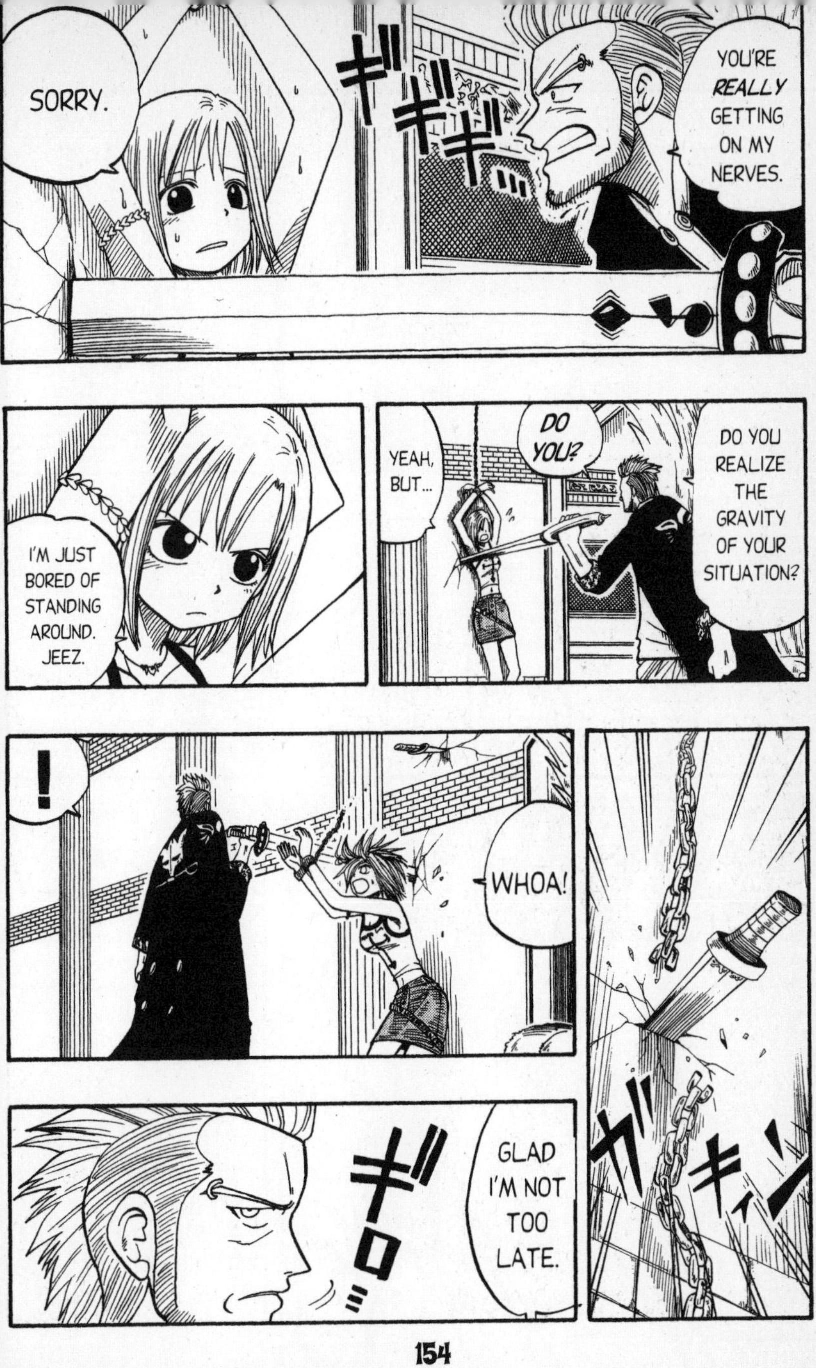
YOU'RE *REALLY* GETTING ON MY NERVES.
ギギギ
SORRY.
DO YOU REALIZE THE GRAVITY OF YOUR SITUATION?
DO YOU?
YEAH, BUT...
I'M JUST BORED OF STANDING AROUND. JEEZ.
ガキィン
WHOA!
!
GLAD I'M NOT TOO LATE.
ギロ

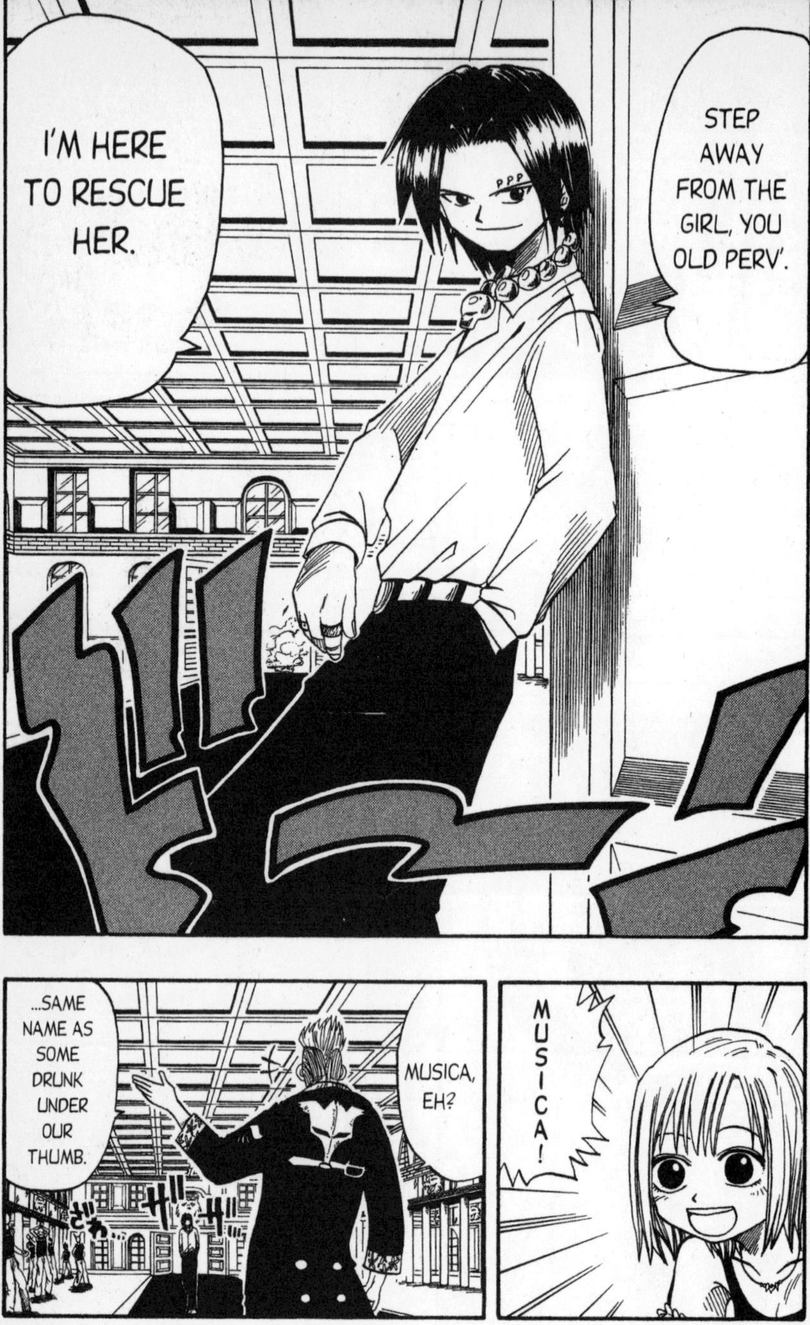
STEP AWAY FROM THE GIRL, YOU OLD PERV'.
I'M HERE TO RESCUE HER.
MUSICA!
MUSICA, EH?
...SAME NAME AS SOME DRUNK UNDER OUR THUMB.

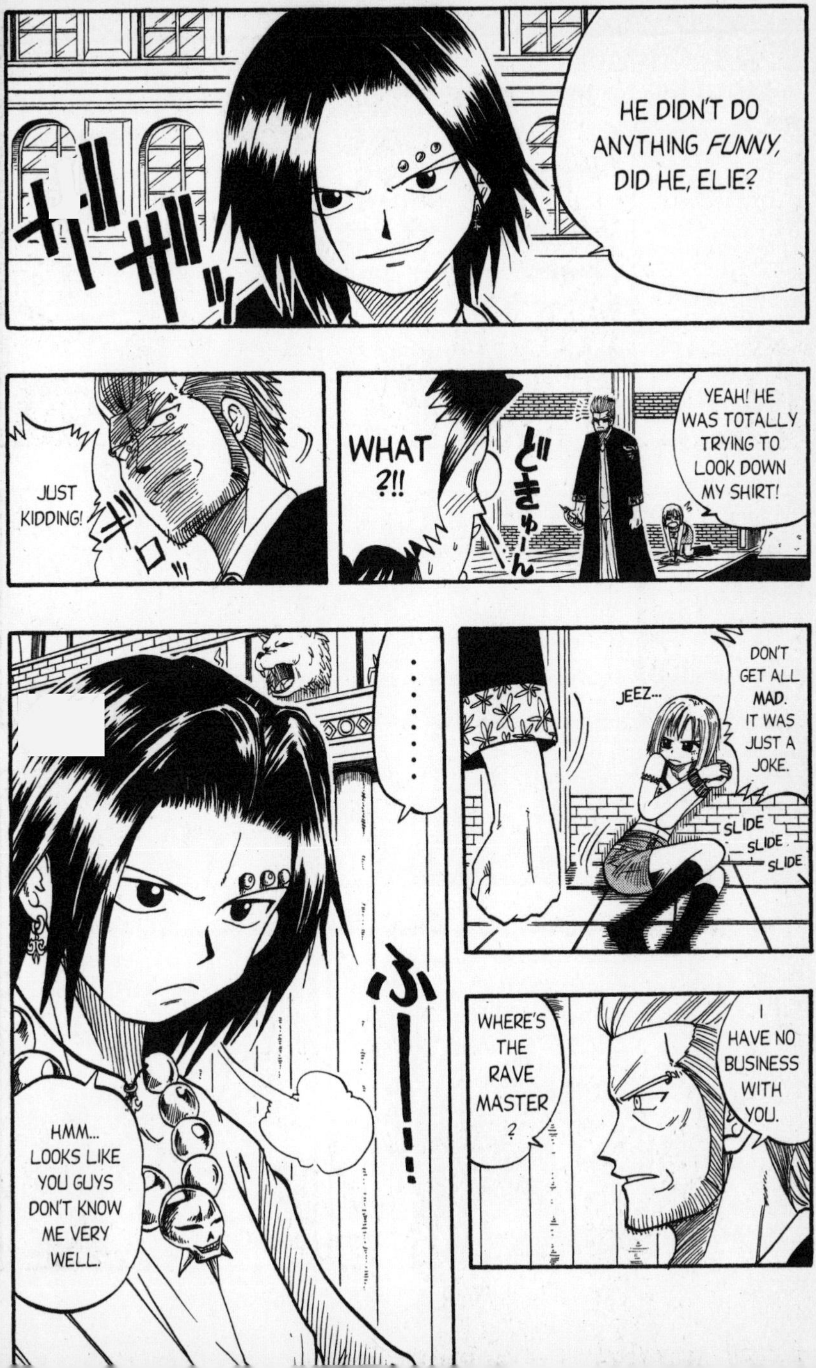
HE DIDN'T DO ANYTHING *FUNNY*, DID HE, ELIE?
YEAH! HE WAS TOTALLY TRYING TO LOOK DOWN MY SHIRT!
WHAT ?!!
JUST KIDDING!
DON'T GET ALL MAD. IT WAS JUST A JOKE.
JEEZ...
SLIDE SLIDE SLIDE
I HAVE NO BUSINESS WITH YOU.
WHERE'S THE RAVE MASTER?
....
HMM... LOOKS LIKE YOU GUYS DON'T KNOW ME VERY WELL.

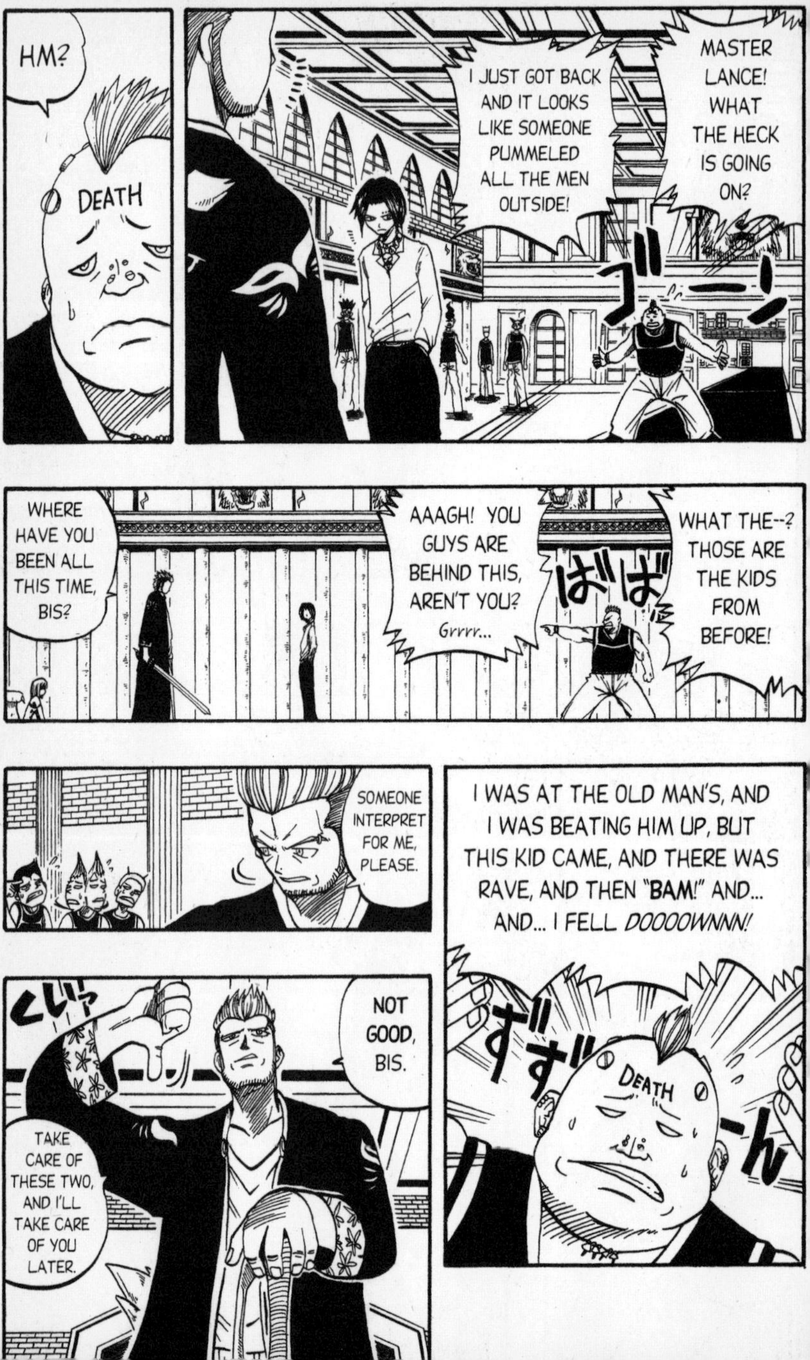
MASTER LANCE! WHAT THE HECK IS GOING ON?
I JUST GOT BACK AND IT LOOKS LIKE SOMEONE PUMMELED ALL THE MEN OUTSIDE!
HM?
DEATH
WHAT THE--? THOSE ARE THE KIDS FROM BEFORE!
ばば
AAAGH! YOU GUYS ARE BEHIND THIS, AREN'T YOU?
Grrrr...
WHERE HAVE YOU BEEN ALL THIS TIME, BIS?
I WAS AT THE OLD MAN'S, AND I WAS BEATING HIM UP, BUT THIS KID CAME, AND THERE WAS RAVE, AND THEN "BAM!" AND... AND... I FELL DOOOOWNNN!
DEATH
SOMEONE INTERPRET FOR ME, PLEASE.
NOT GOOD, BIS.
TAKE CARE OF THESE TWO, AND I'LL TAKE CARE OF YOU LATER.

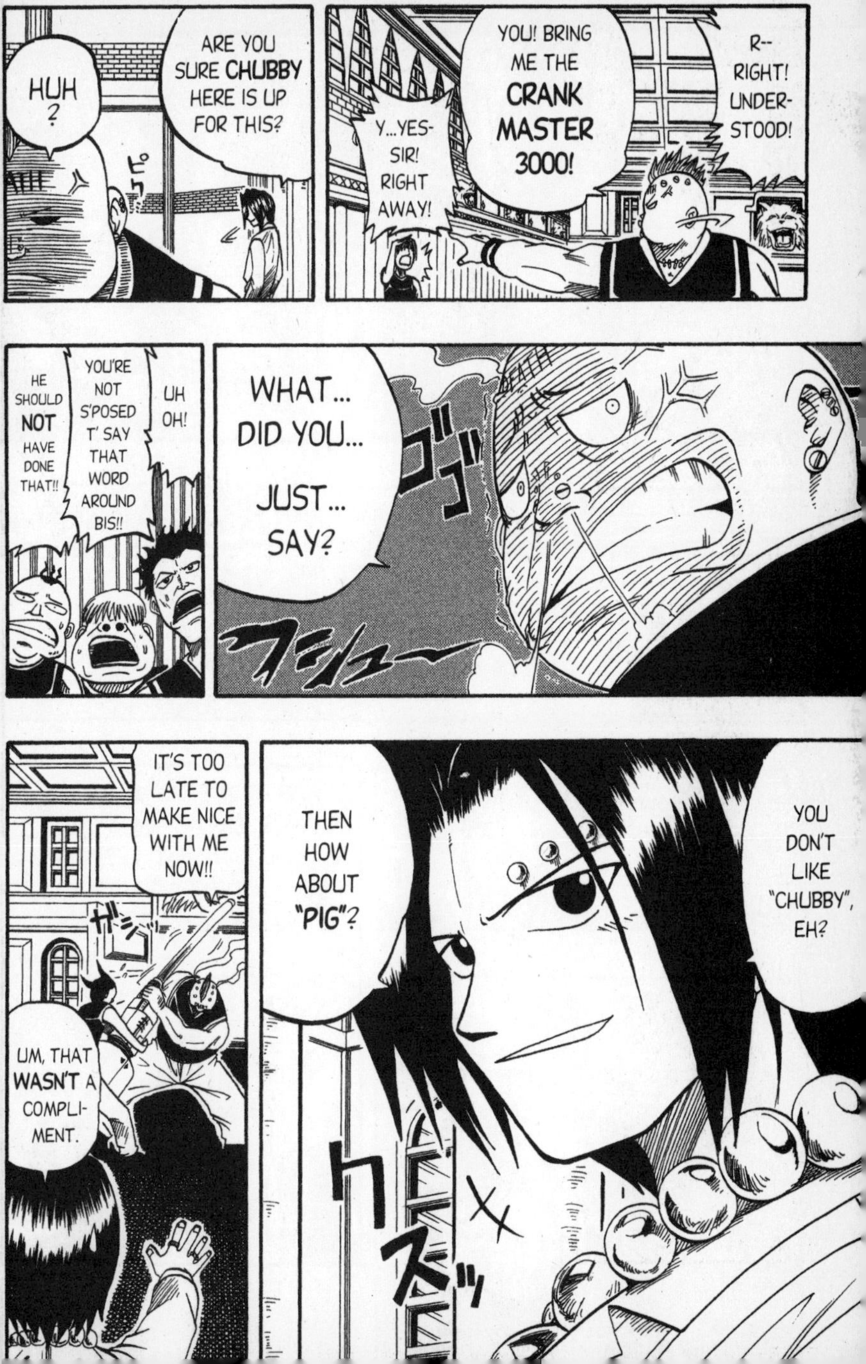
YOU! BRING ME THE CRANK MASTER 3000!
R-- RIGHT! UNDER-STOOD!
Y...YES-SIR! RIGHT AWAY!
ARE YOU SURE CHUBBY HERE IS UP FOR THIS?
HUH?
WHAT... DID YOU... JUST... SAY?
UH OH!
YOU'RE NOT S'POSED T' SAY THAT WORD AROUND BIS!!
HE SHOULD NOT HAVE DONE THAT!!
YOU DON'T LIKE "CHUBBY", EH?
THEN HOW ABOUT "PIG"?
IT'S TOO LATE TO MAKE NICE WITH ME NOW!!
UM, THAT WASN'T A COMPLIMENT.

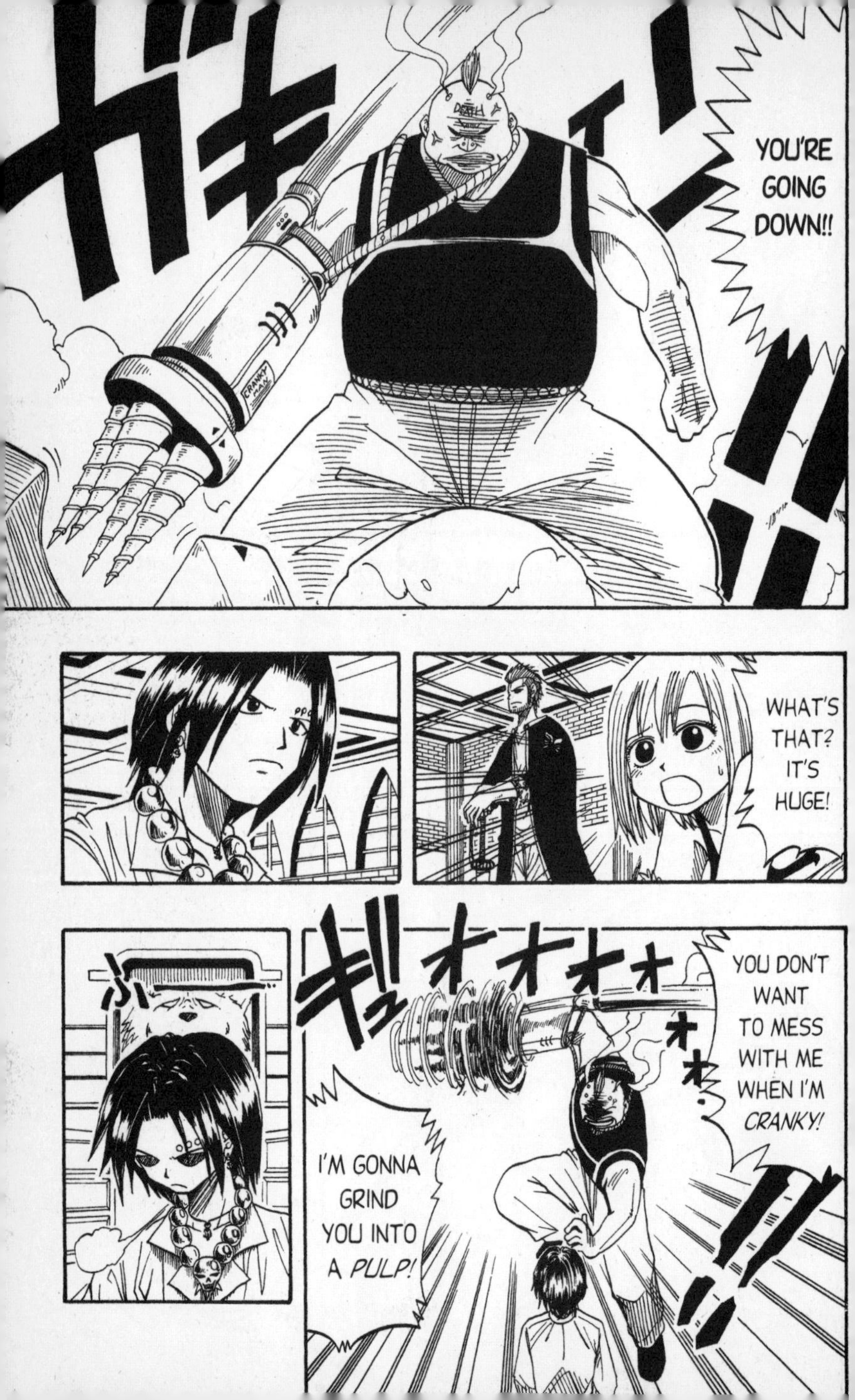
YOU'RE GOING DOWN!!
WHAT'S THAT? IT'S HUGE!
YOU DON'T WANT TO MESS WITH ME WHEN I'M *CRANKY!*
I'M GONNA GRIND YOU INTO A *PULP!*

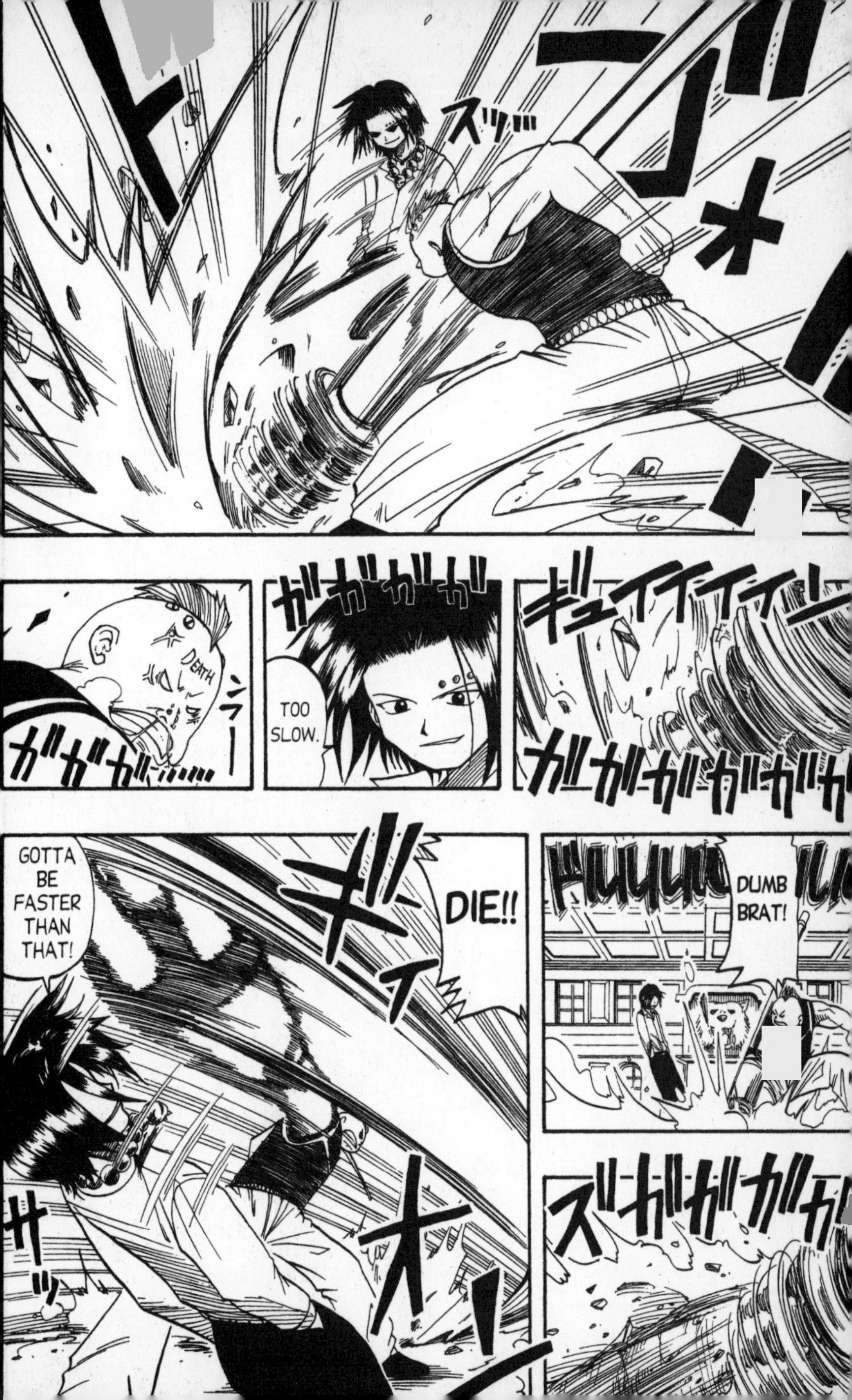
TOO SLOW.
DEATH
DUMB BRAT!
DIE!!
GOTTA BE FASTER THAN THAT!

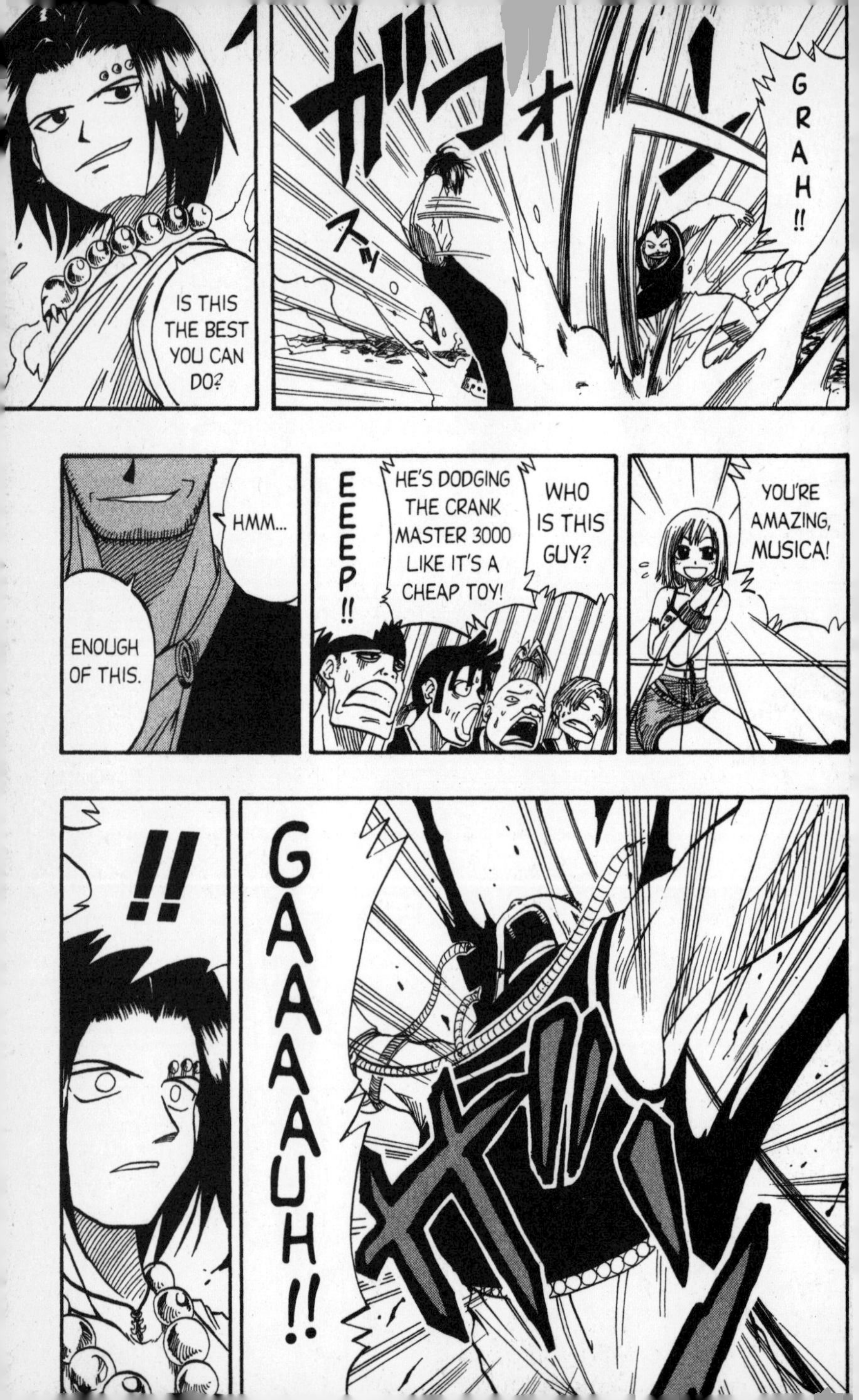
GRAH!!
IS THIS THE BEST YOU CAN DO?
YOU'RE AMAZING, MUSICA!
WHO IS THIS GUY?
HE'S DODGING THE CRANK MASTER 3000 LIKE IT'S A CHEAP TOY!
EEEP!!
HMM...
ENOUGH OF THIS.
GAAAAUH!!
!!

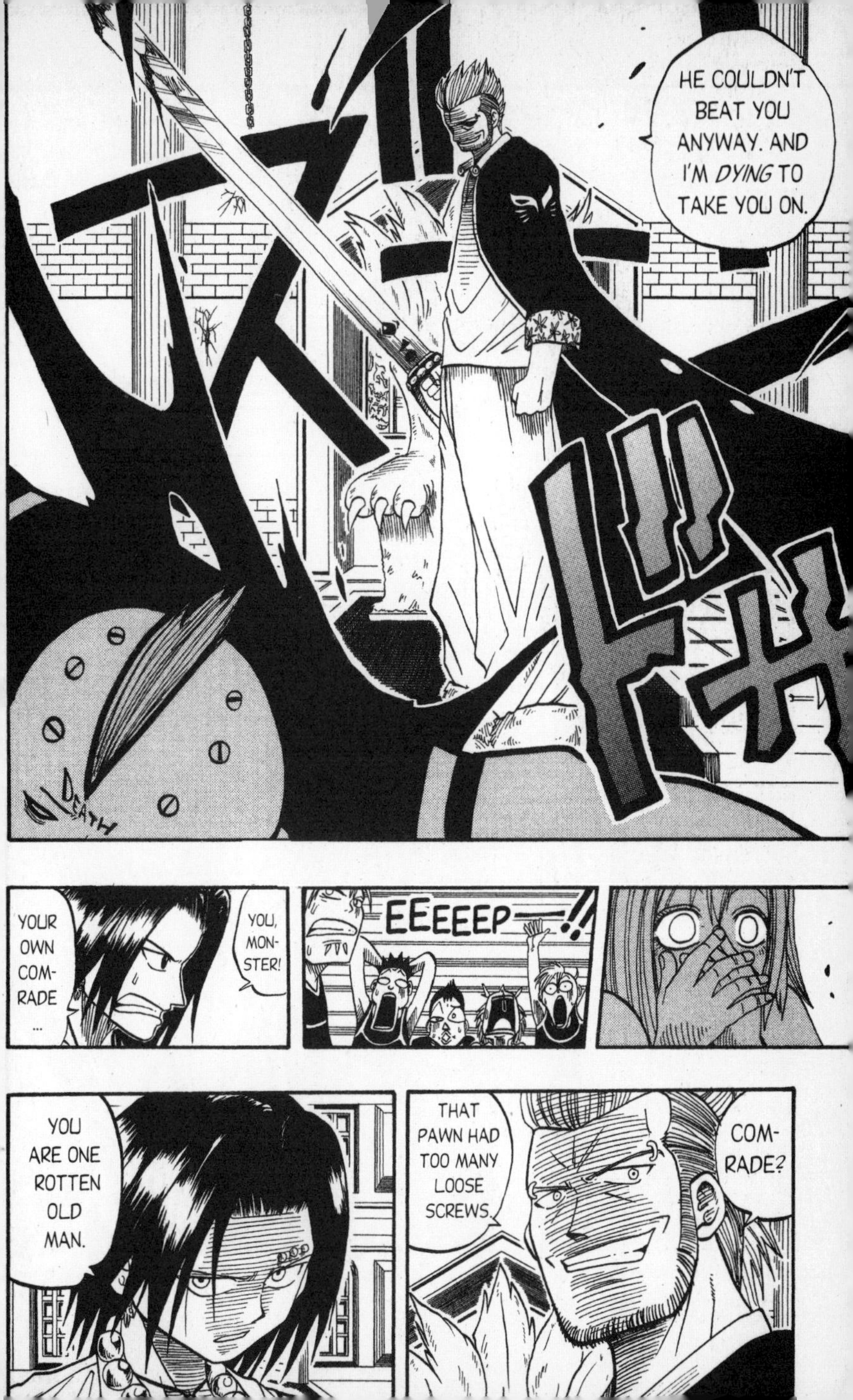
HE COULDN'T BEAT YOU ANYWAY. AND I'M *DYING* TO TAKE YOU ON.
DEATH
EEEEEP—!!
YOU, MONSTER!
YOUR OWN COMRADE ...
COM-RADE?
THAT PAWN HAD TOO MANY LOOSE SCREWS.
YOU ARE ONE ROTTEN OLD MAN.

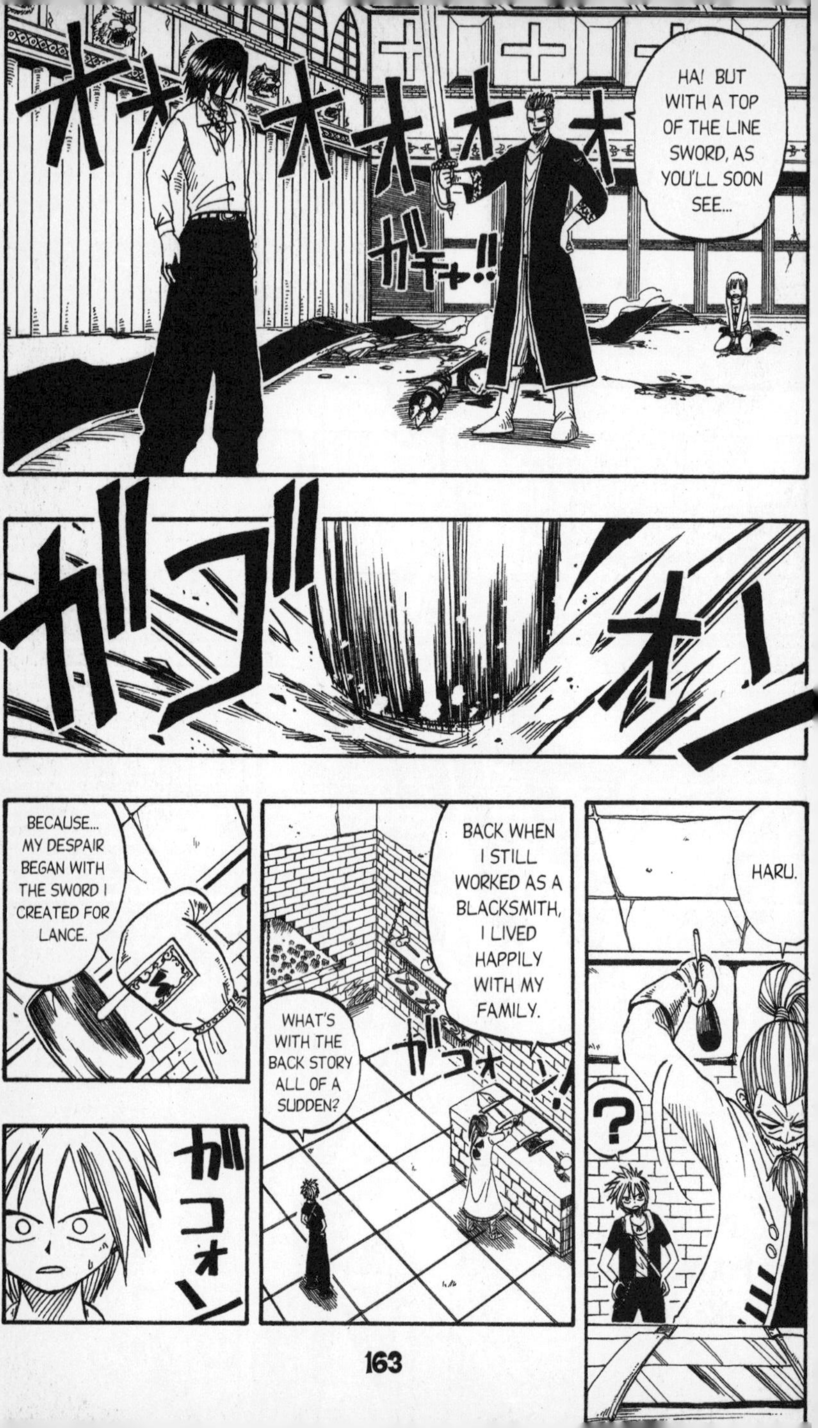

HA! BUT WITH A TOP OF THE LINE SWORD, AS YOU'LL SOON SEE...
ガチャ!!
ガゴォーン
HARU.
?
BACK WHEN I STILL WORKED AS A BLACKSMITH, I LIVED HAPPILY WITH MY FAMILY.
ガコォン!!
WHAT'S WITH THE BACK STORY ALL OF A SUDDEN?
BECAUSE... MY DESPAIR BEGAN WITH THE SWORD I CREATED FOR LANCE.
ガコォン

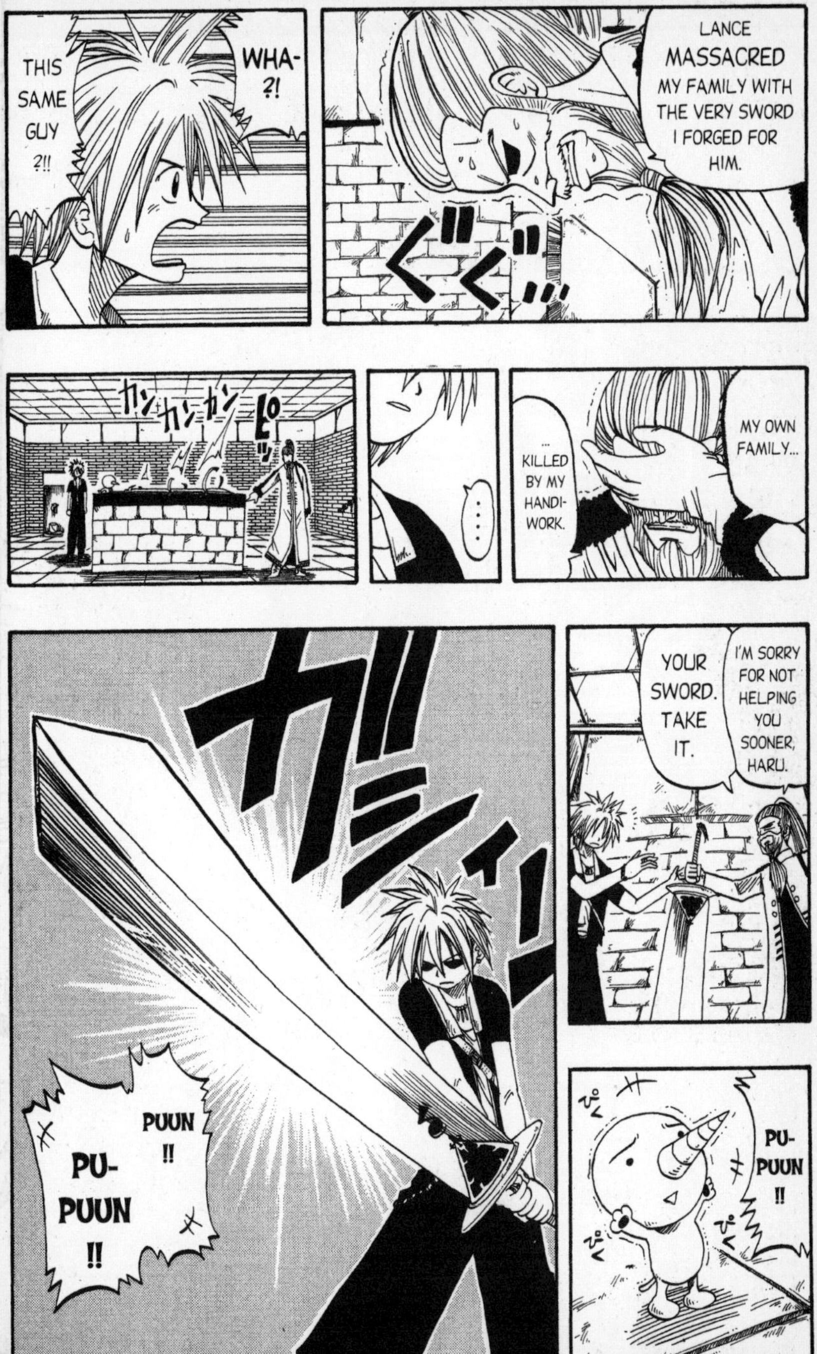
LANCE MASSACRED MY FAMILY WITH THE VERY SWORD I FORGED FOR HIM.
WHA- ?!
THIS SAME GUY ?!!
MY OWN FAMILY...
... KILLED BY MY HANDIWORK.
....
I'M SORRY FOR NOT HELPING YOU SOONER, HARU.
YOUR SWORD. TAKE IT.
PU-PUUN !!
PUUN !!
PU-PUUN !!

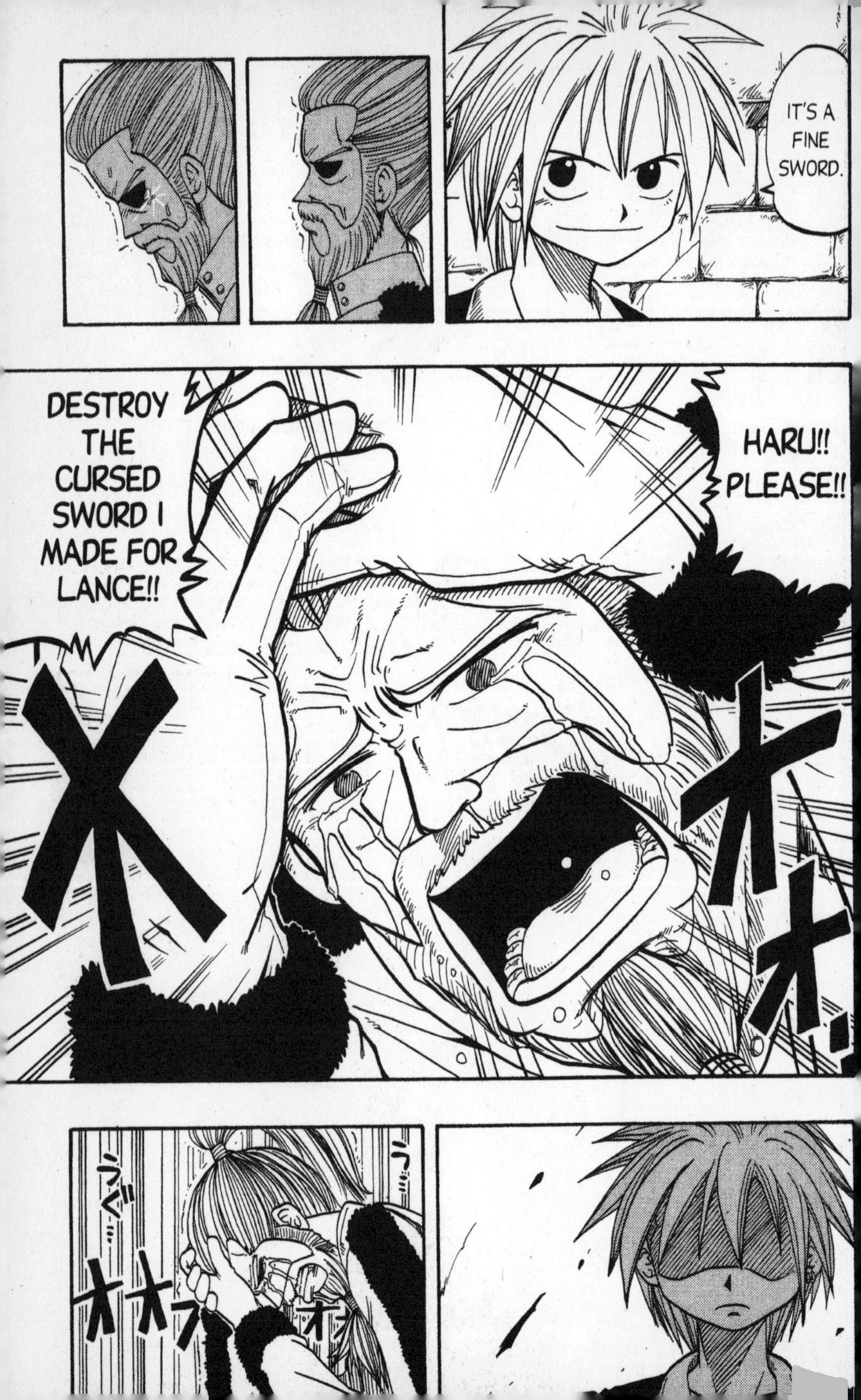
IT'S A FINE SWORD.
HARU!! PLEASE!!
DESTROY THE CURSED SWORD I MADE FOR LANCE!!

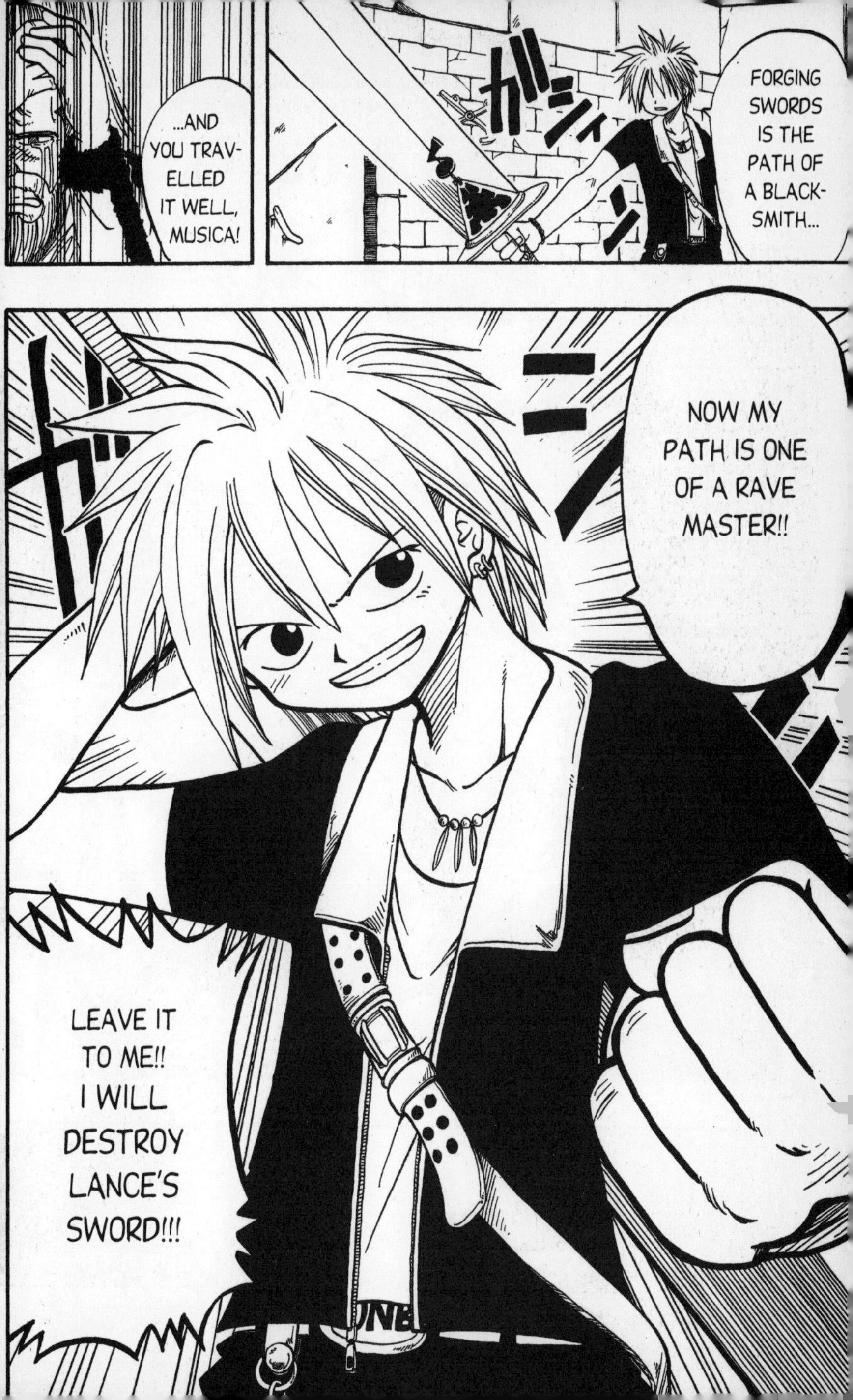

FORGING SWORDS IS THE PATH OF A BLACK-SMITH...
...AND YOU TRAV-ELLED IT WELL, MUSICA!
NOW MY PATH IS ONE OF A RAVE MASTER!!
LEAVE IT TO ME!! I WILL DESTROY LANCE'S SWORD!!!

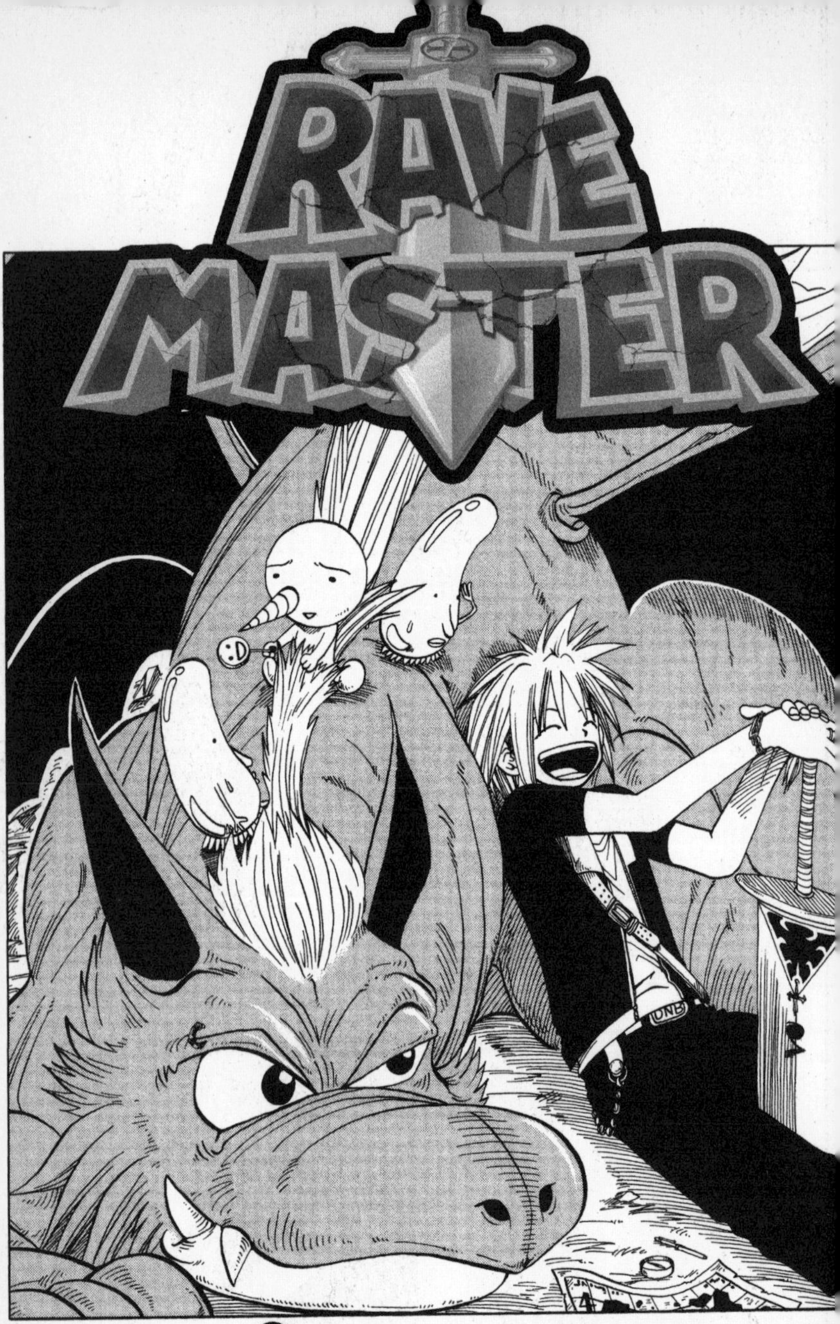
RAVE
MASTER

RAVE 13 THE BRIDGE OF PROMISES

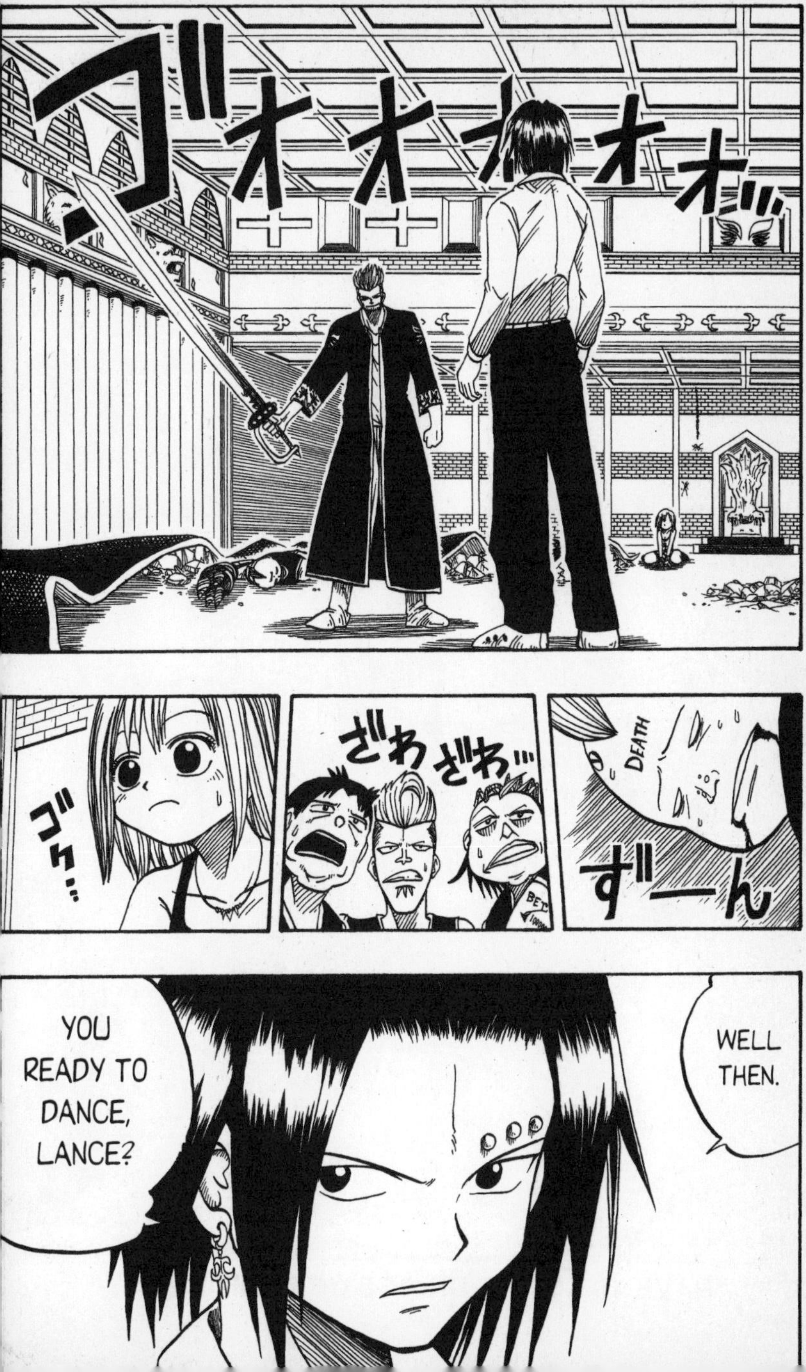

ゴオオオオオ
DEATH
ずーん
ざわざわ
ゴク…
WELL THEN.
YOU READY TO DANCE, LANCE?

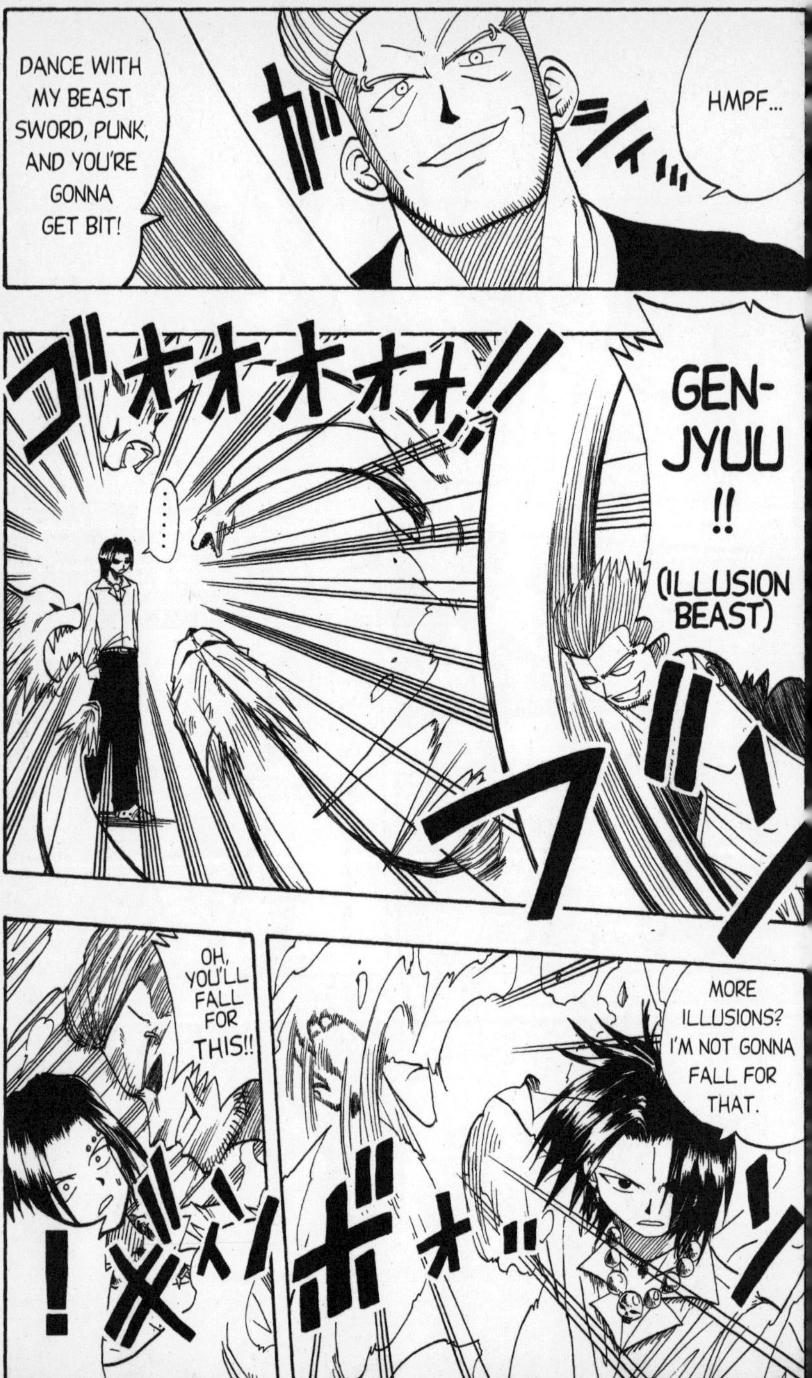
HMPF...
DANCE WITH MY BEAST SWORD, PUNK, AND YOU'RE GONNA GET BIT!
GEN-JYUU!! (ILLUSION BEAST)
......
MORE ILLUSIONS? I'M NOT GONNA FALL FOR THAT.
OH, YOU'LL FALL FOR THIS!!
!

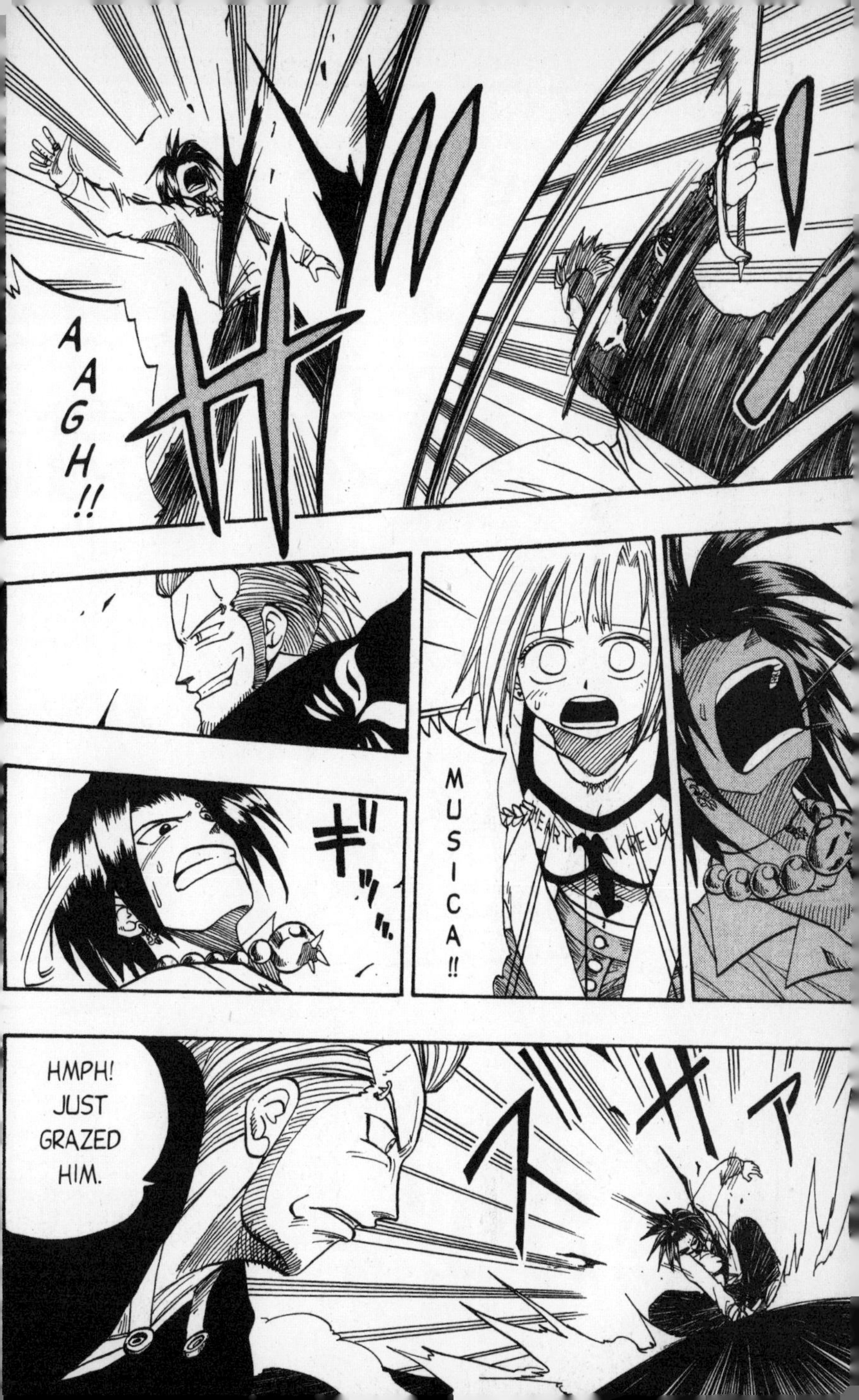
AAGH!!
MUSICA!!
HEART KREUZ
HMPH! JUST GRAZED HIM.

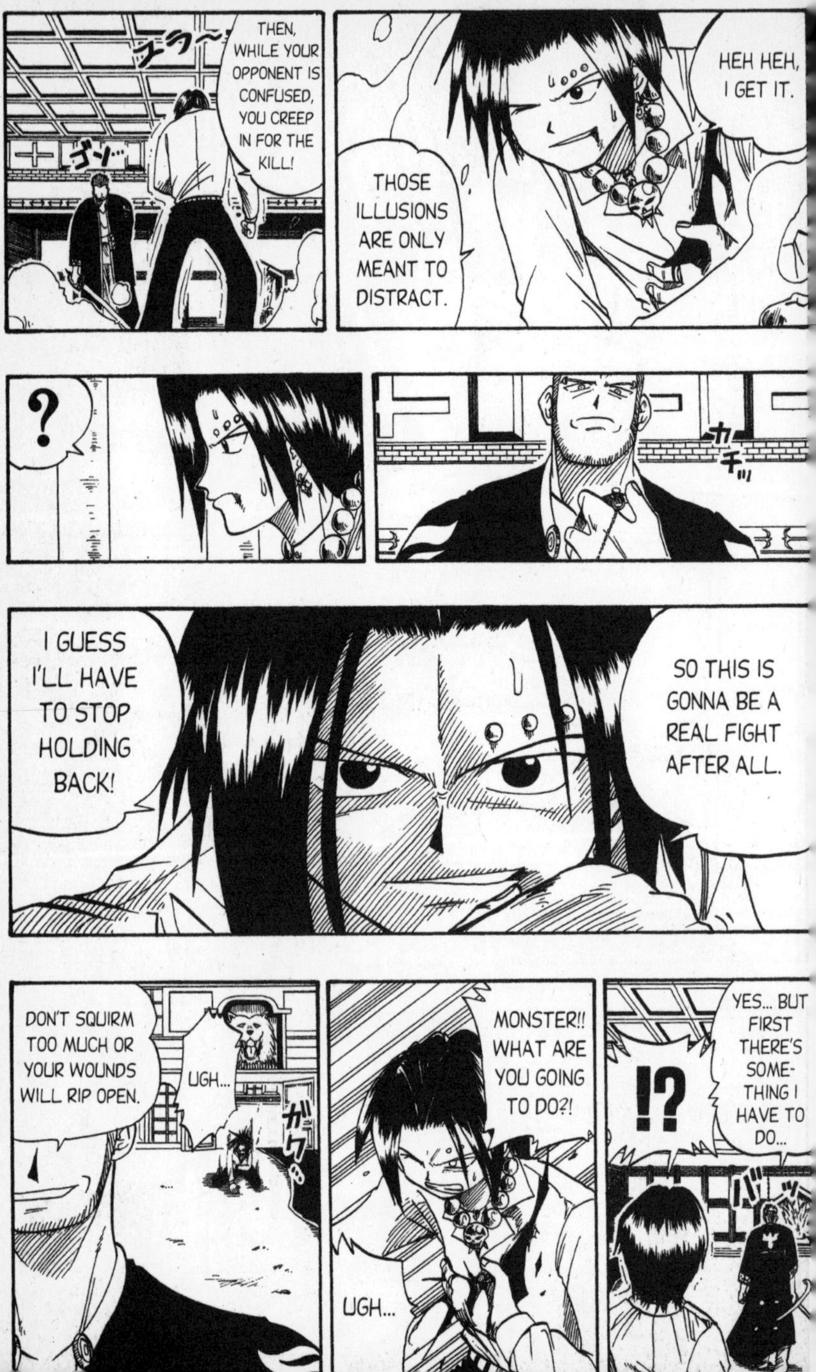
HEH HEH, I GET IT.
THOSE ILLUSIONS ARE ONLY MEANT TO DISTRACT.
THEN, WHILE YOUR OPPONENT IS CONFUSED, YOU CREEP IN FOR THE KILL!
?
SO THIS IS GONNA BE A REAL FIGHT AFTER ALL.
I GUESS I'LL HAVE TO STOP HOLDING BACK!
YES... BUT FIRST THERE'S SOME-THING I HAVE TO DO...
!?
MONSTER!! WHAT ARE YOU GOING TO DO?!
UGH...
DON'T SQUIRM TOO MUCH OR YOUR WOUNDS WILL RIP OPEN.
UGH...

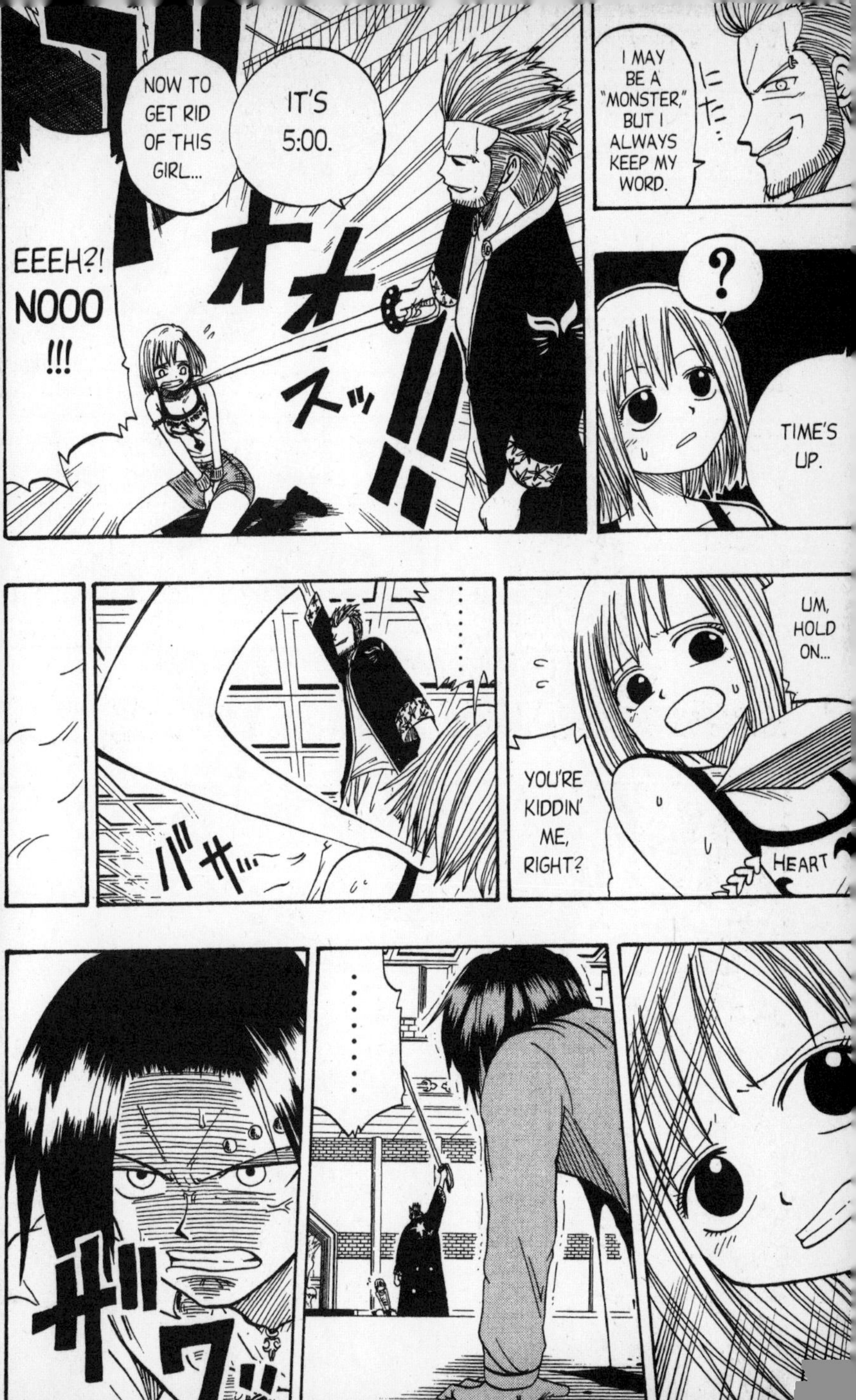
I MAY BE A "MONSTER," BUT I ALWAYS KEEP MY WORD.
?
TIME'S UP.
IT'S 5:00.
NOW TO GET RID OF THIS GIRL...
EEEH?! NOOO !!!
UM, HOLD ON...
YOU'RE KIDDIN' ME, RIGHT?
HEART
......
......

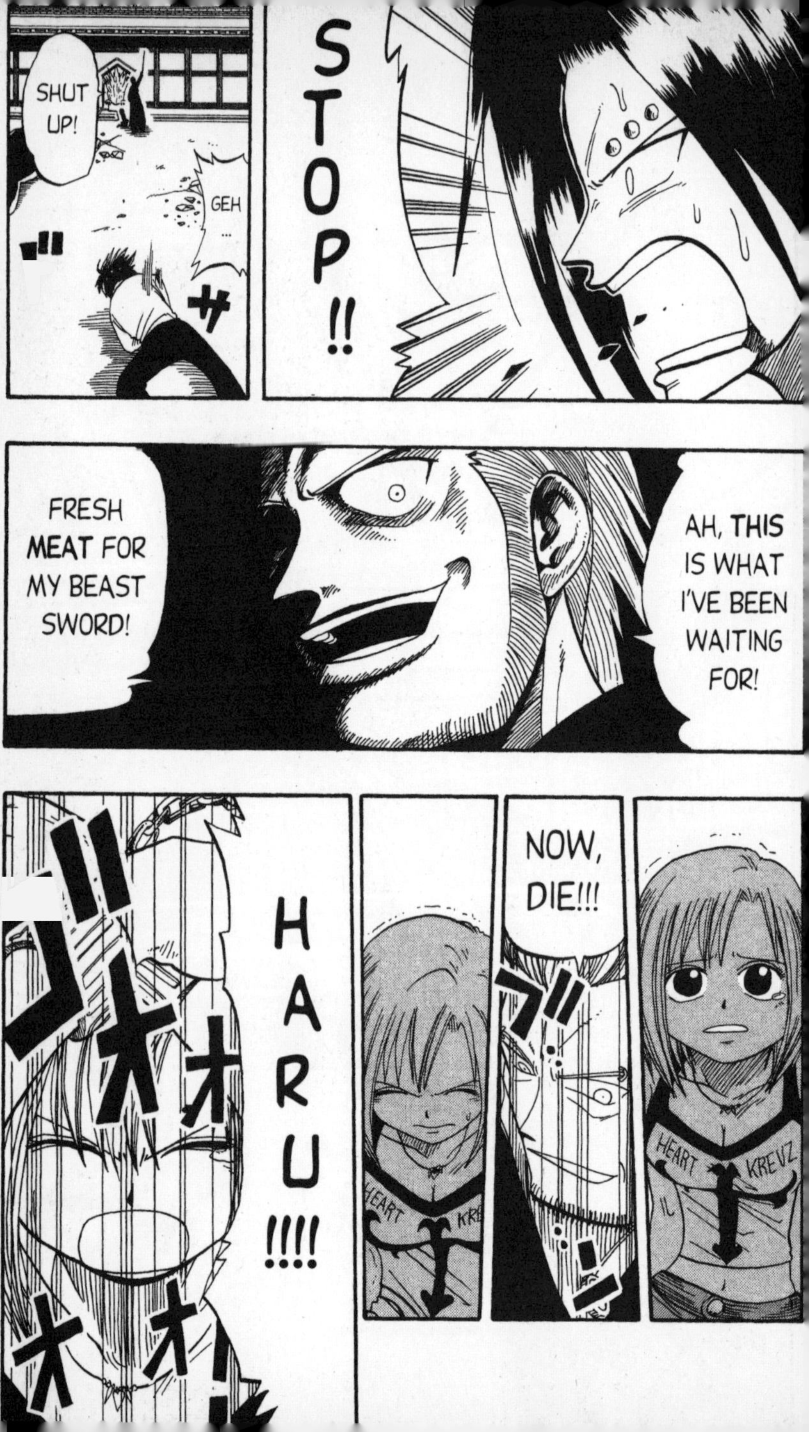
STOP!!
SHUT UP!
GEH ...
AH, THIS IS WHAT I'VE BEEN WAITING FOR!
FRESH MEAT FOR MY BEAST SWORD!
NOW, DIE!!!
HARU!!!!

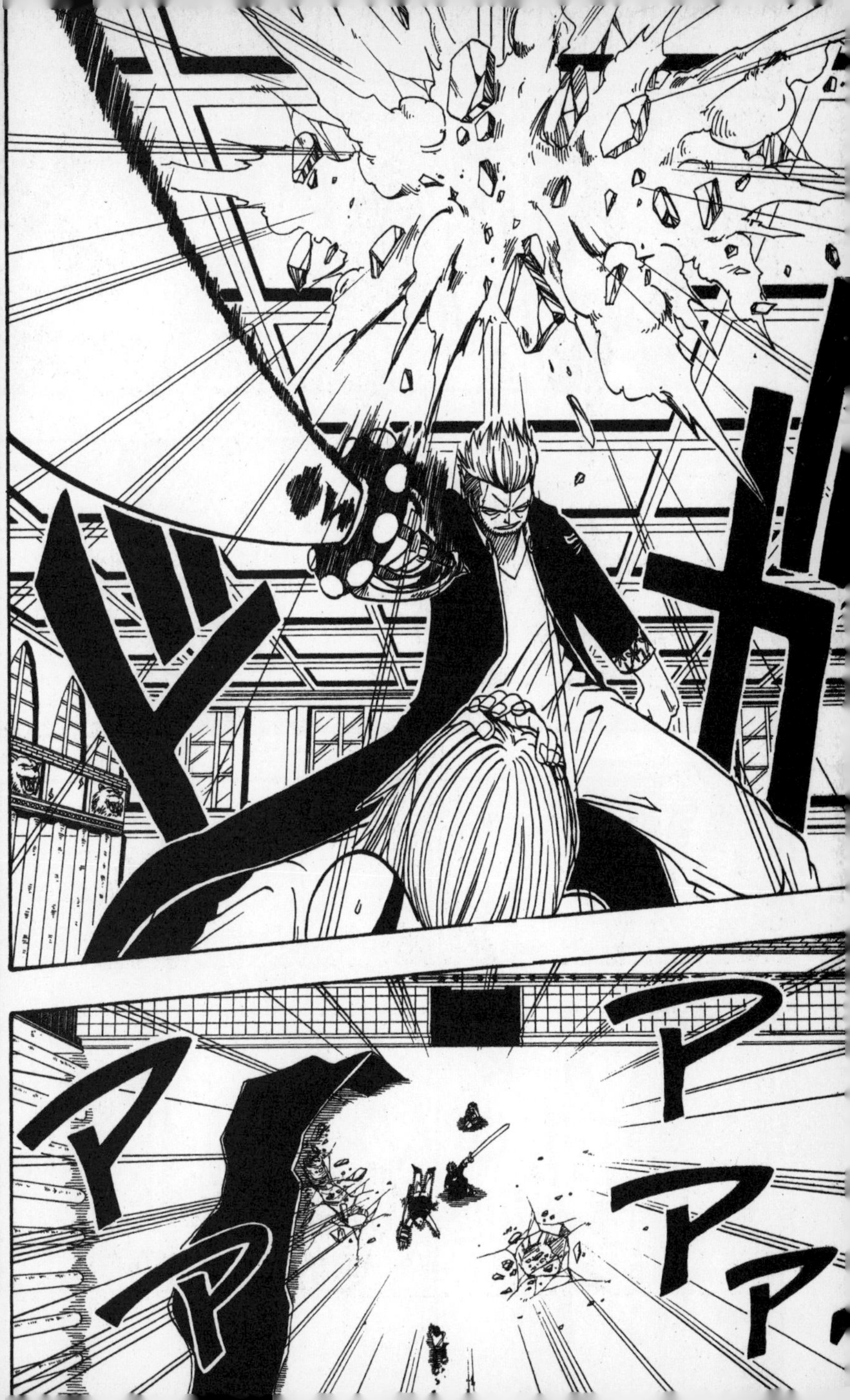
ドガ
アアア・
アア

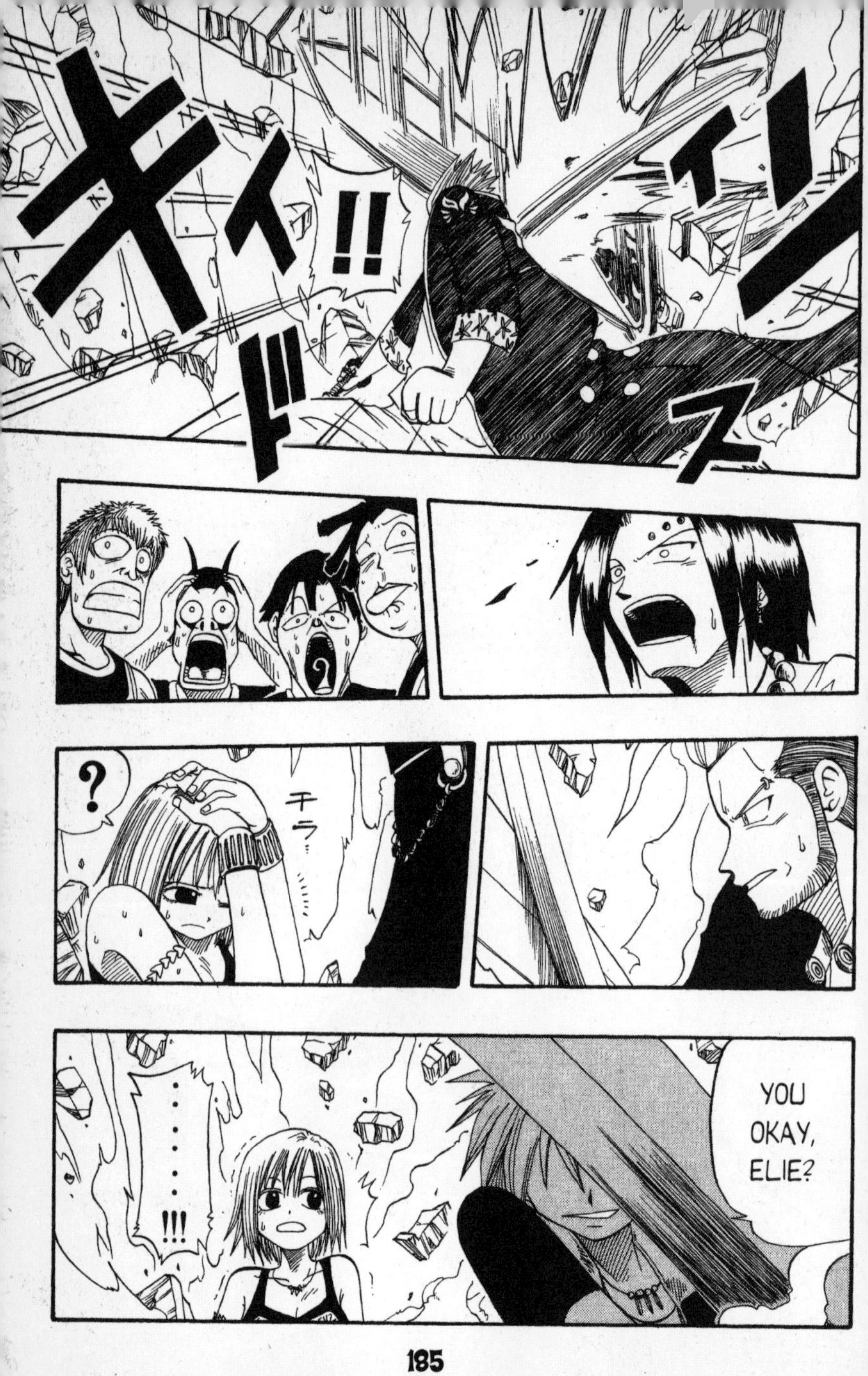
?
チラ…
YOU OKAY, ELIE?
……!!!

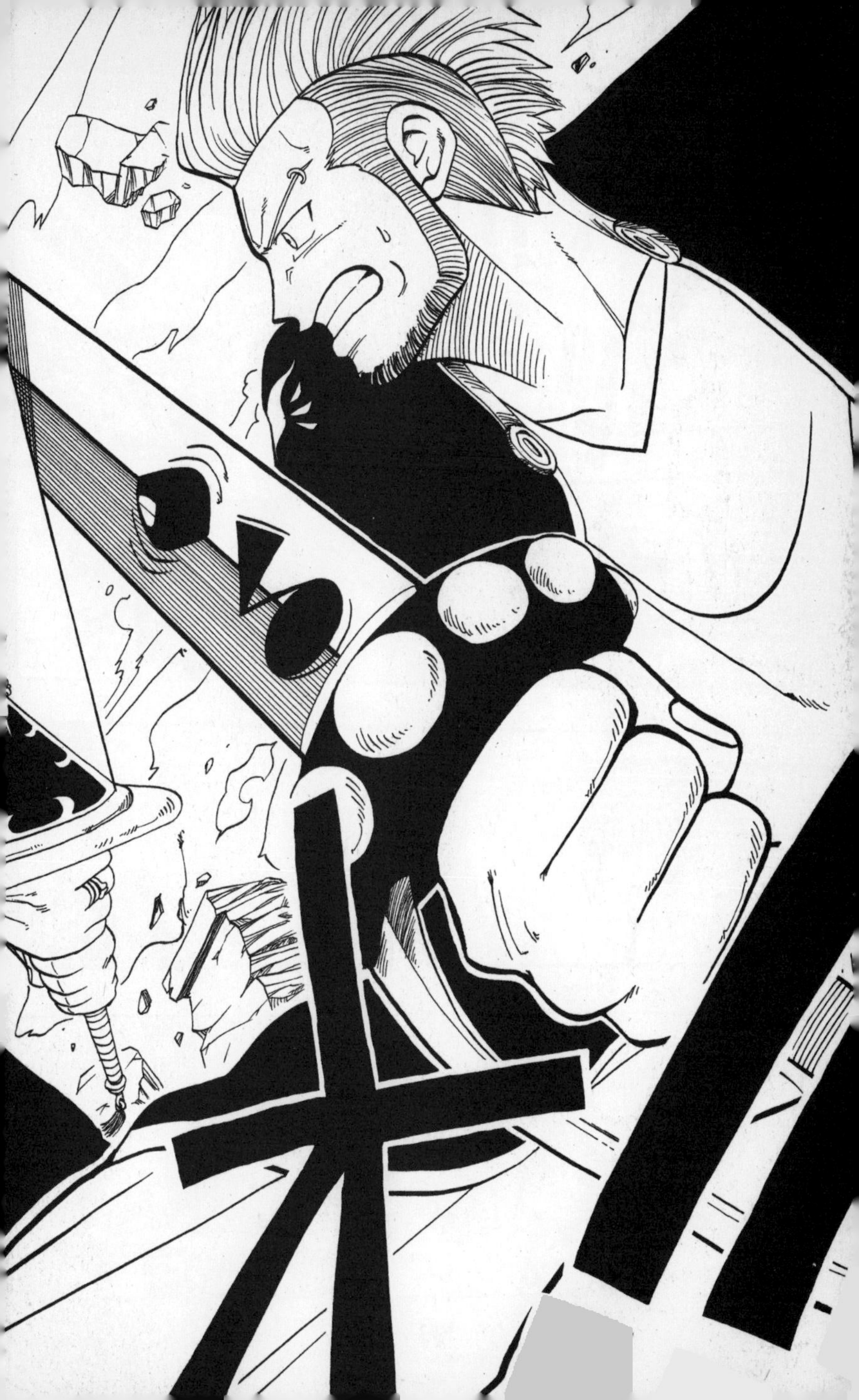

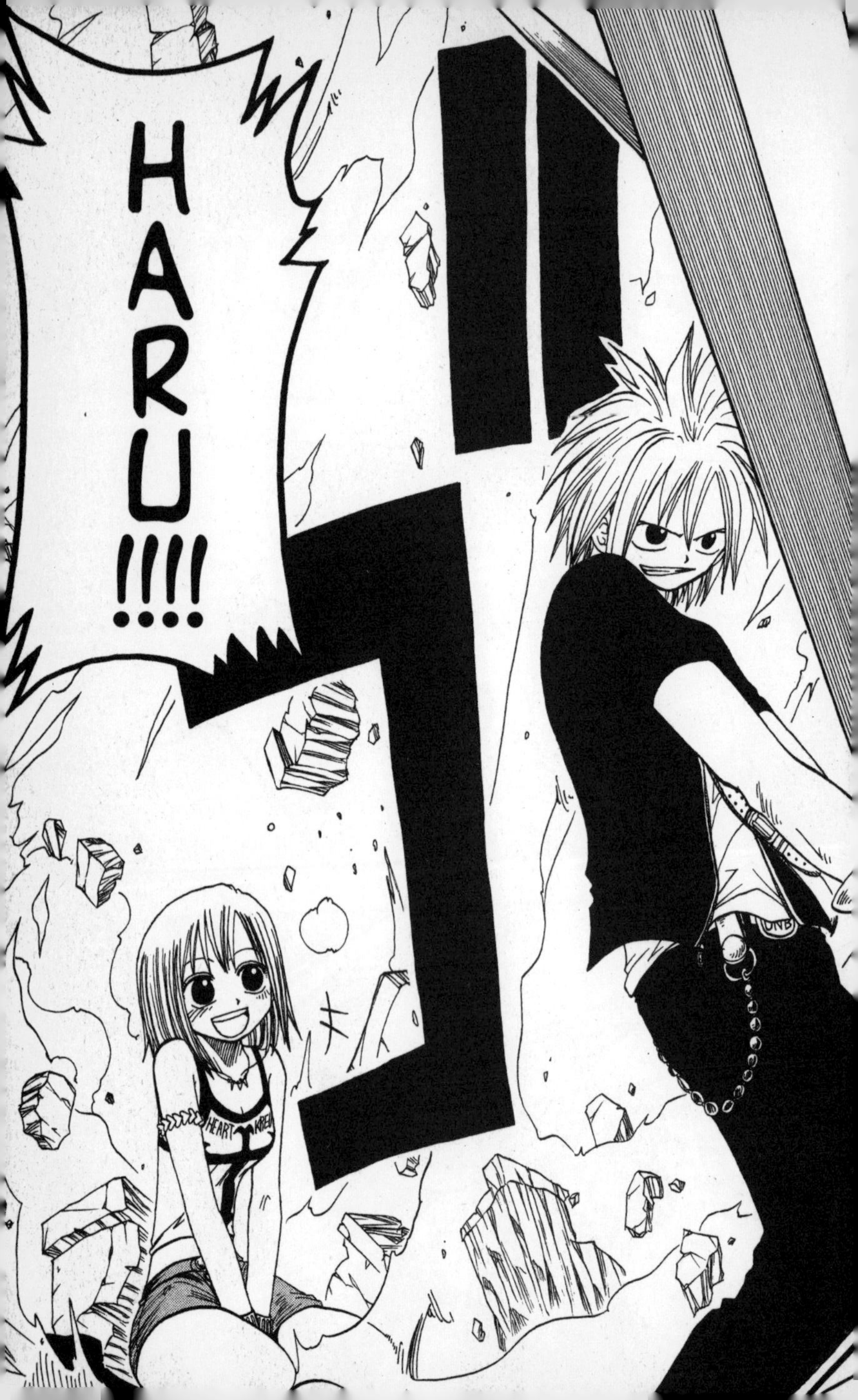
HARU!!!!

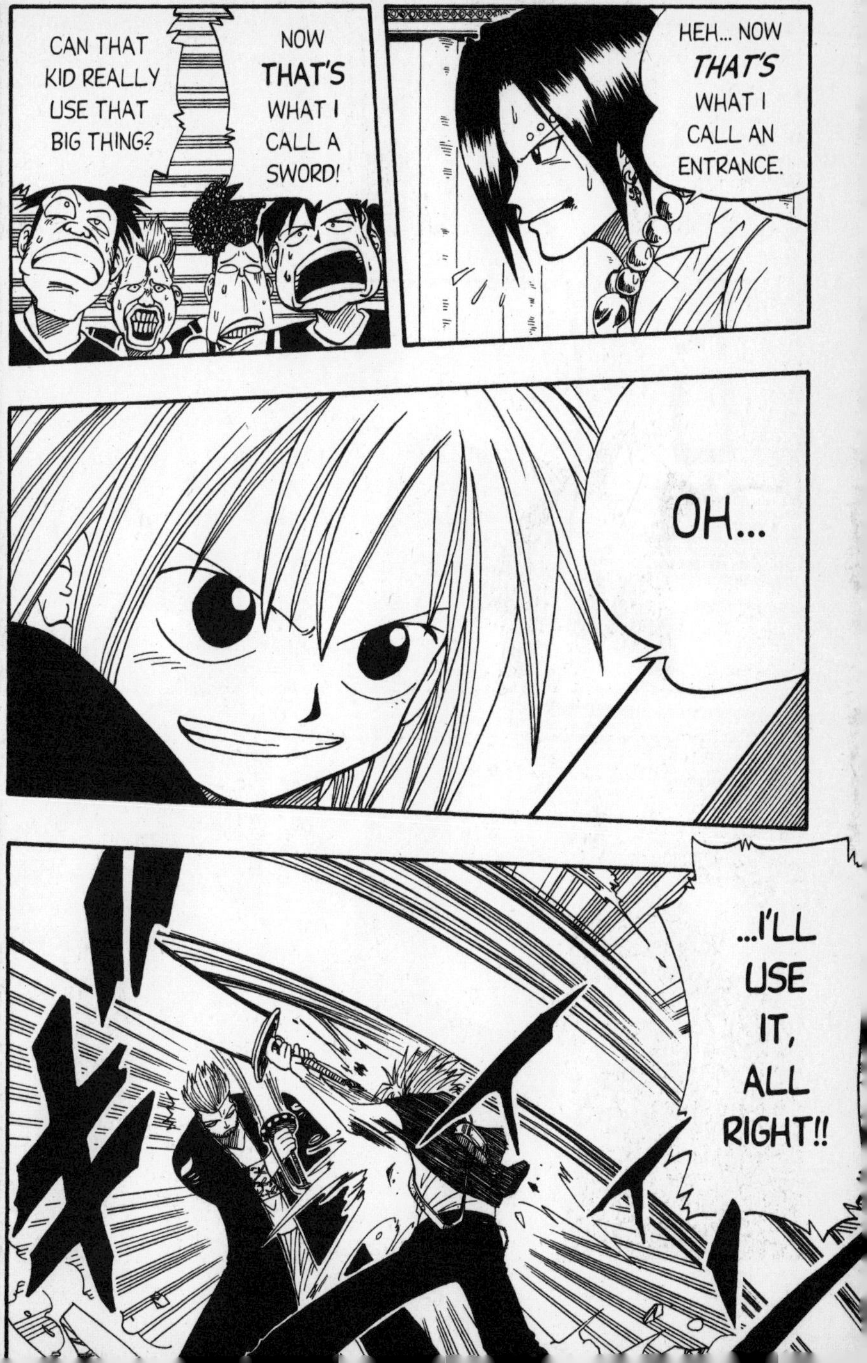
HEH... NOW THAT'S WHAT I CALL AN ENTRANCE.
NOW THAT'S WHAT I CALL A SWORD!
CAN THAT KID REALLY USE THAT BIG THING?
OH...
...I'LL USE IT, ALL RIGHT!!

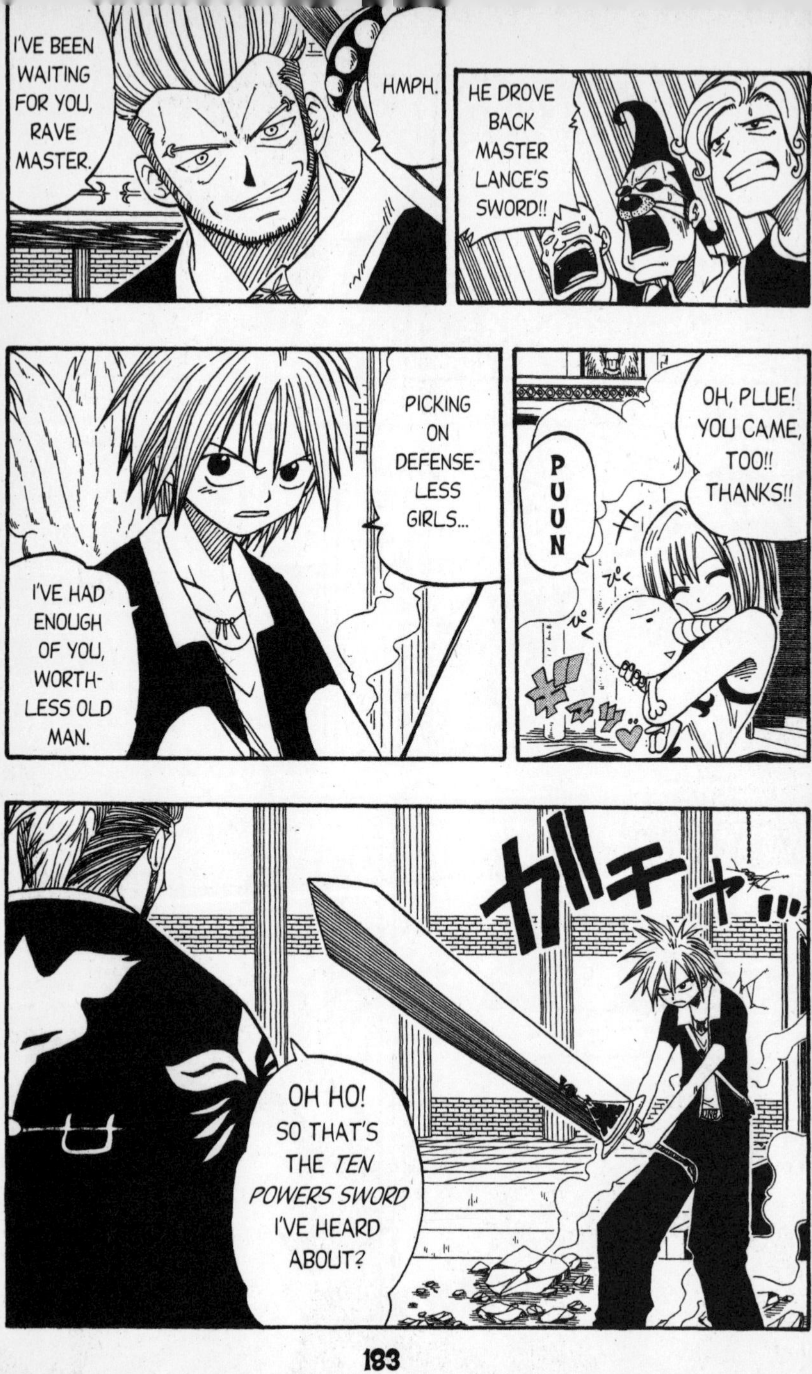
HE DROVE BACK MASTER LANCE'S SWORD!!
HMPH.
I'VE BEEN WAITING FOR YOU, RAVE MASTER.
OH, PLUE! YOU CAME, TOO!! THANKS!!
PUUN
ぴく
ぴく
ギュッ
PICKING ON DEFENSE-LESS GIRLS...
I'VE HAD ENOUGH OF YOU, WORTH-LESS OLD MAN.
ガチャ!!
OH HO! SO THAT'S THE *TEN POWERS SWORD* I'VE HEARD ABOUT?

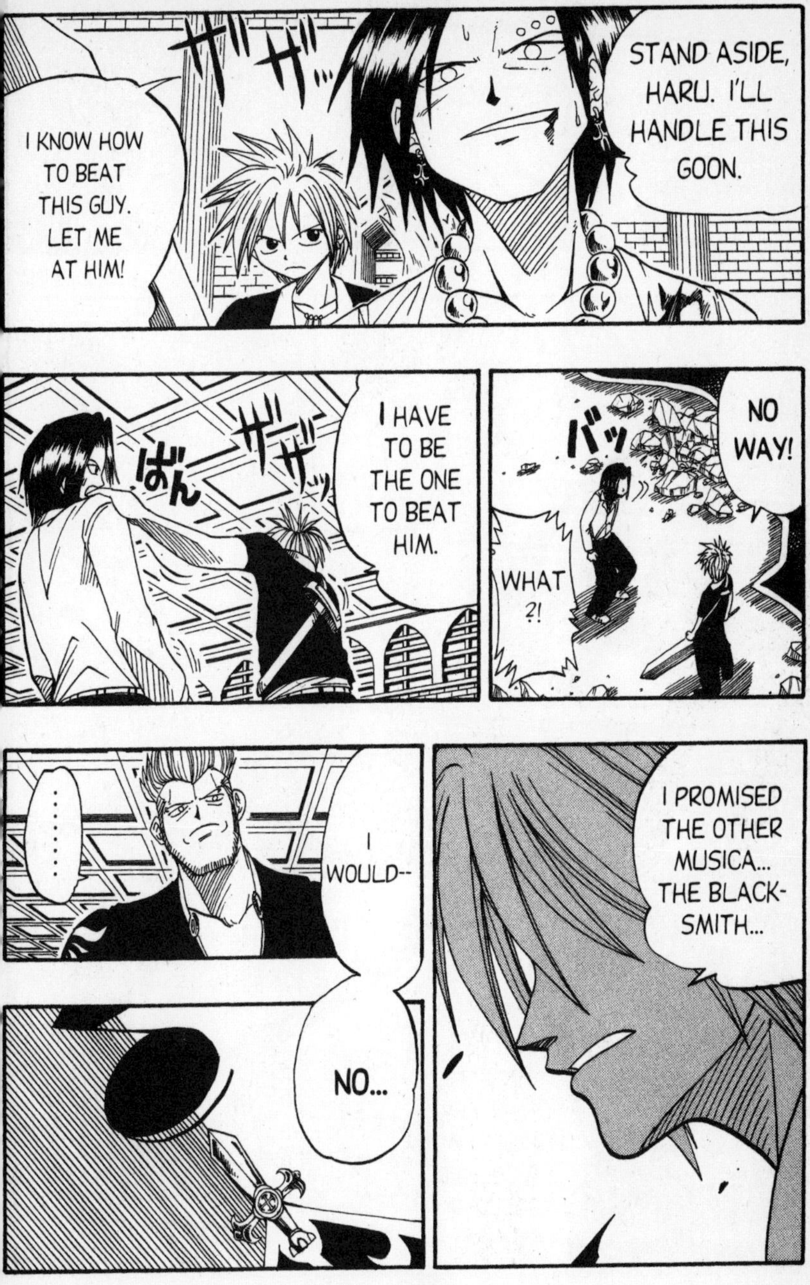
ザザッ
STAND ASIDE, HARU. I'LL HANDLE THIS GOON.
I KNOW HOW TO BEAT THIS GUY. LET ME AT HIM!
バッ
NO WAY!
WHAT?!
I HAVE TO BE THE ONE TO BEAT HIM.
ザザッ
ばん
I PROMISED THE OTHER MUSICA... THE BLACK-SMITH...
I WOULD--
......
NO...

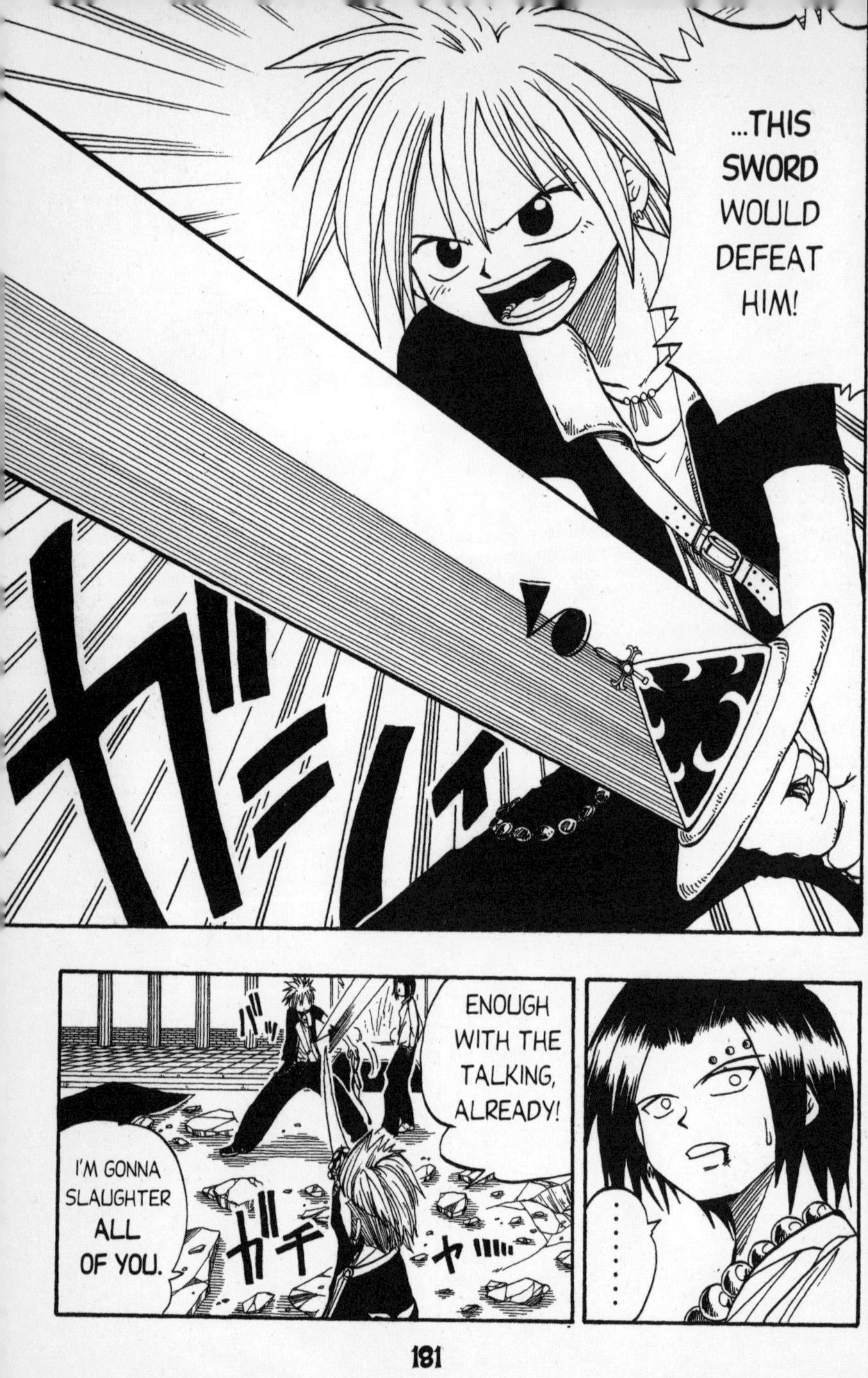
...THIS SWORD WOULD DEFEAT HIM!
......
ENOUGH WITH THE TALKING, ALREADY!
I'M GONNA SLAUGHTER ALL OF YOU.
ガチャ!!!!

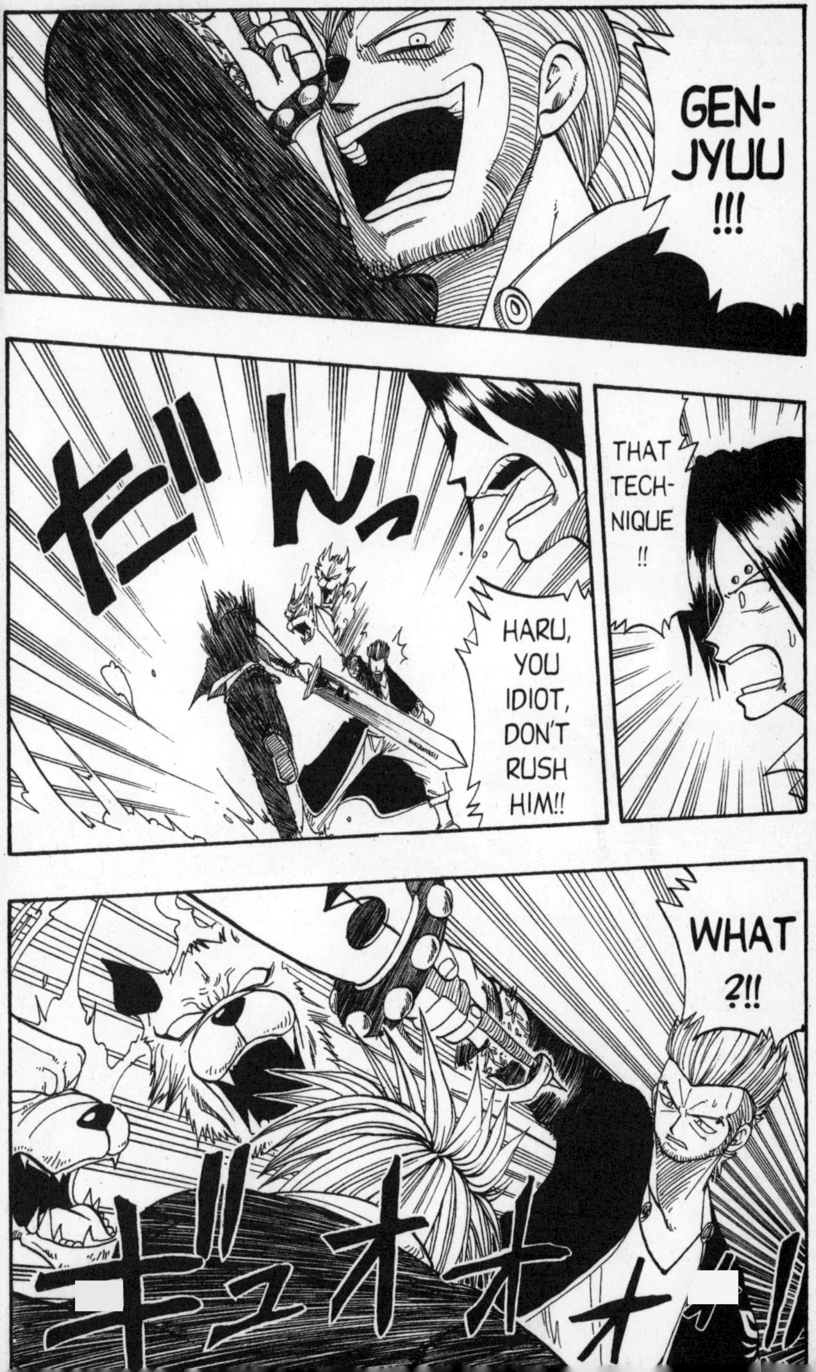
GEN-JYUU!!!
THAT TECHNIQUE!!
だん
HARU, YOU IDIOT, DON'T RUSH HIM!!
WHAT?!!

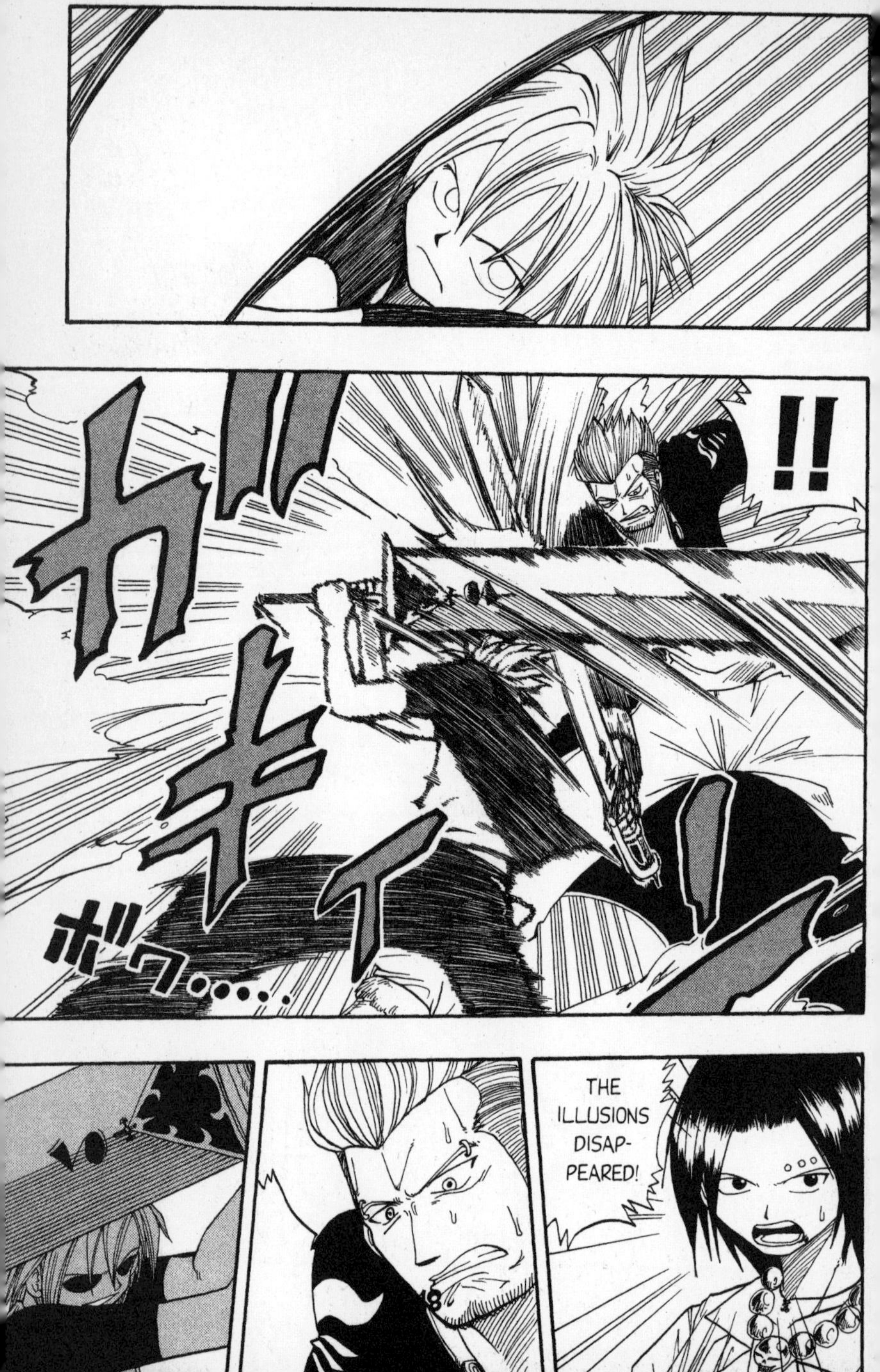

!!
ガキイ
ボワ.....
THE ILLUSIONS DISAP- PEARED!

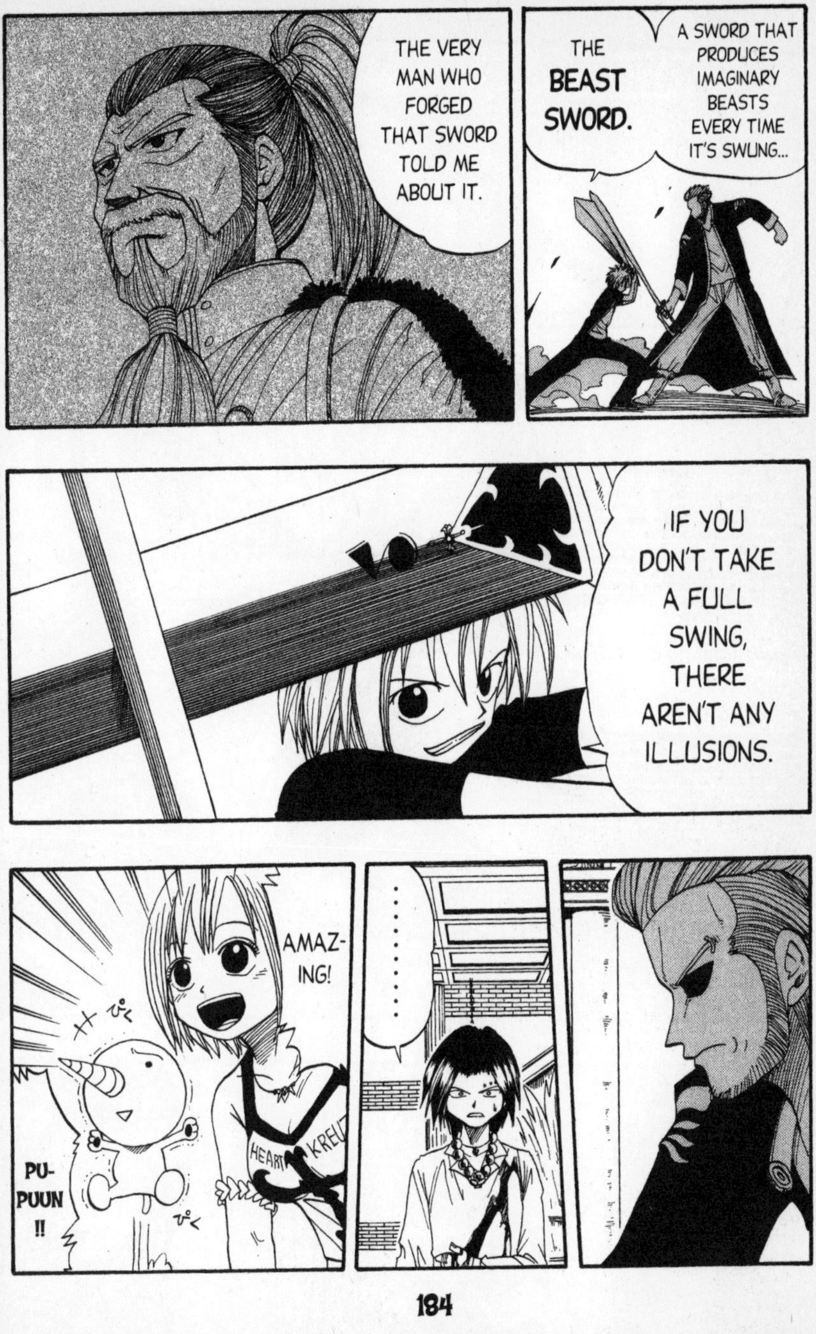
A SWORD THAT PRODUCES IMAGINARY BEASTS EVERY TIME IT'S SWUNG...
THE BEAST SWORD.
THE VERY MAN WHO FORGED THAT SWORD TOLD ME ABOUT IT.
IF YOU DON'T TAKE A FULL SWING, THERE AREN'T ANY ILLUSIONS.
......
AMAZ-ING!
ぴく
PU-PUUN!!
ぴく
HEART
KREU

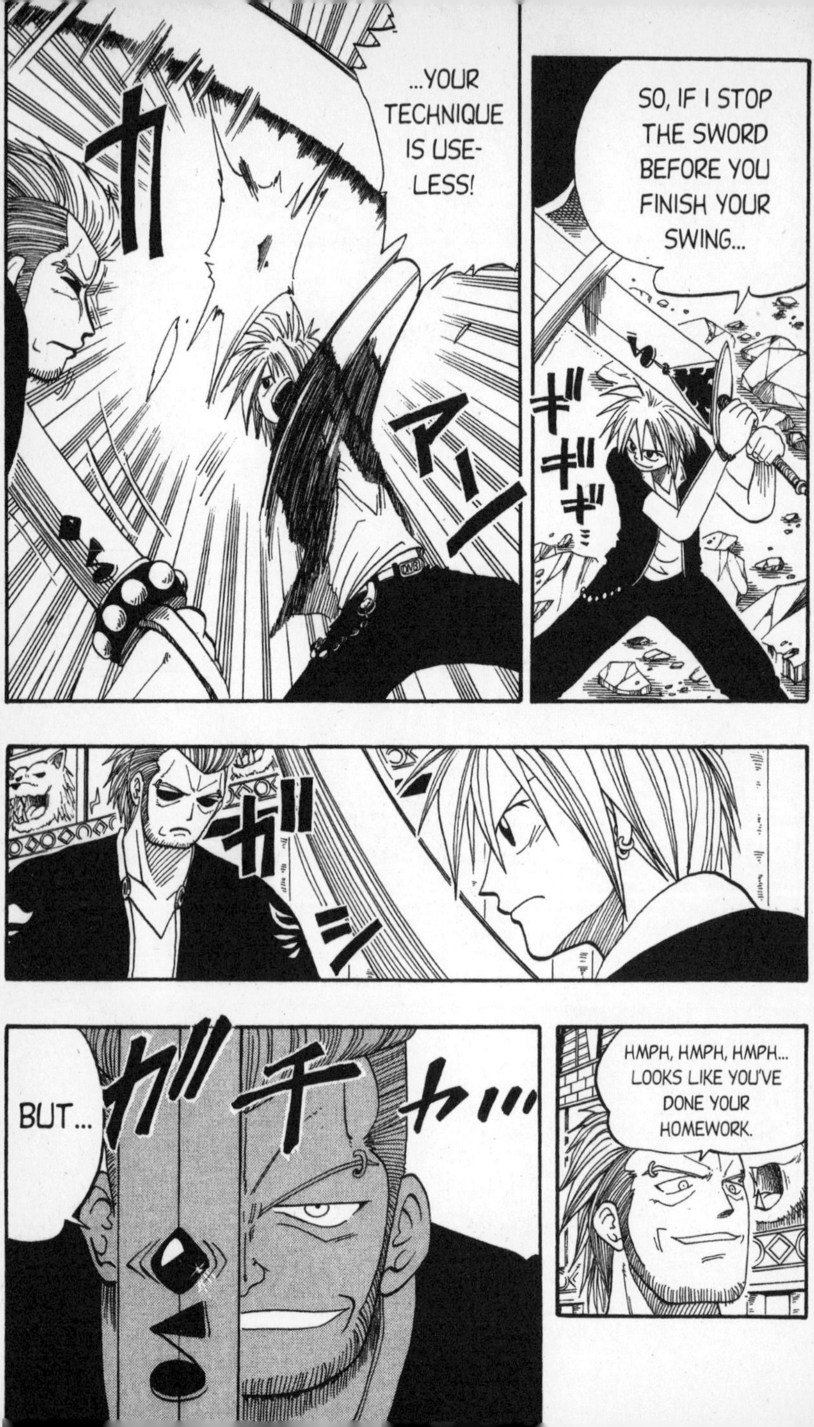
SO, IF I STOP THE SWORD BEFORE YOU FINISH YOUR SWING...
ギギギ
...YOUR TECHNIQUE IS USE-LESS!
HMPH, HMPH, HMPH... LOOKS LIKE YOU'VE DONE YOUR HOMEWORK.
BUT...
ガチャッ

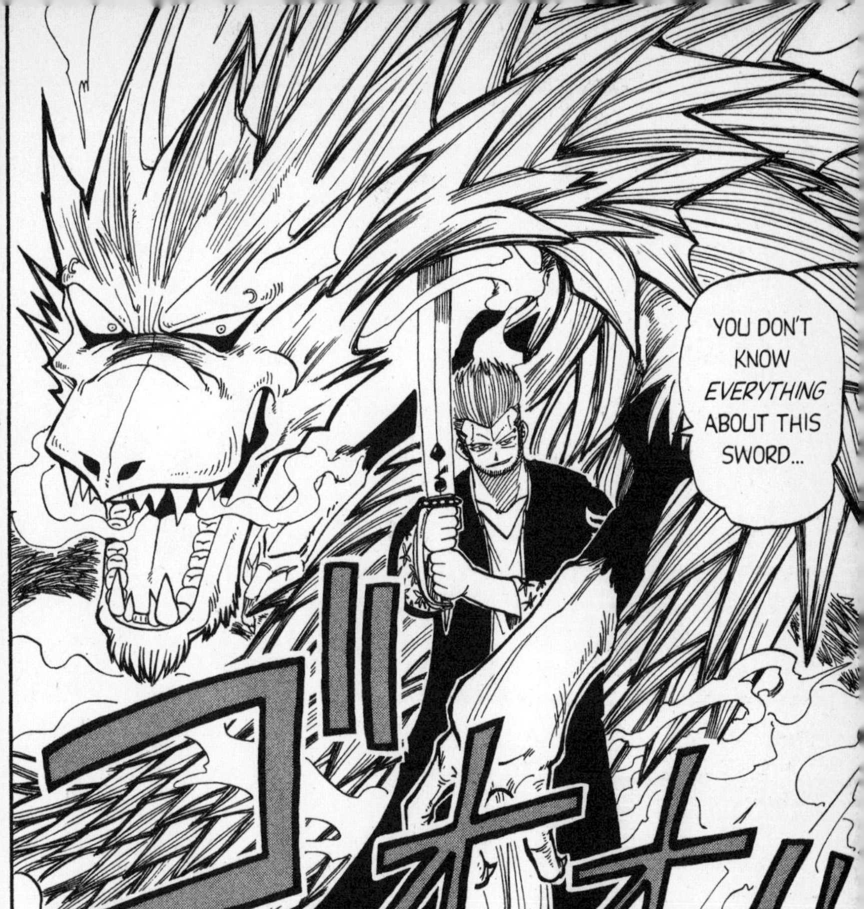
YOU DON'T KNOW *EVERYTHING* ABOUT THIS SWORD...
ゴオオ

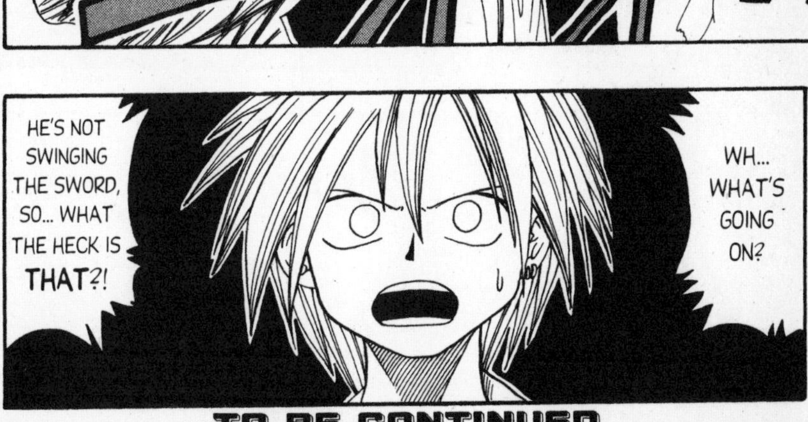
WH... WHAT'S GOING ON?
HE'S NOT SWINGING THE SWORD, SO... WHAT THE HECK IS **THAT**?!

...TO BE CONTINUED

"Afterwords"

PSHAH! IT'S MASHIMA. AS I WRITE THIS, I DON'T KNOW IF IT'S MORNING, AFTERNOON OR NIGHT WHERE YOU ARE, OR IF YOU'RE SLEEPING, OR WHAT! SO I CAME UP WITH A NEW GREETING-- "PSHAH!!" YOU CAN USE THIS GREETING ANY TIME OF DAY OR NIGHT, SO IT'S VERY CONVENIENT. PSHAH! ALL RIGHT, I'LL STOP BEING WEIRD NOW.

SO RAVE IS ALREADY IN ITS SECOND VOLUME. ALL RIGHT!! WITH TWO VOLUMES THEY CAN BE LINED UP ONE, TWO IN A BOOKSTORE!! THAT MAKES ME SO HAPPY! ABOUT 400 PAGES IN TWO GRAPHIC NOVELS, HOW COOL...

BUT THERE'S STILL MORE TO COME!! MY GOAL IS MORE THAN 10 VOLUMES!! AND THEN, THE KODANSHA COMIC AWARD!! I WONDER IF I SET MY SIGHTS TOO HIGH... NO! I'LL DO IT. I'LL GIVE IT A TRY! PSHAH! (NOW I'M BEING STUBBORN.)

SETTING MY HOPES ASIDE, LET'S CHANGE THE TOPIC TO THE STORIES IN THIS VOLUME OF RAVE. THERE MAY NOT BE ANY IMPRESSIVE STORIES, BUT THE MOST DIFFICULT PART OF CHAPTERS 5-13 WAS DRAWING ALL THE MOBS IN THE STREETS AND STADIUMS. IT WAS HARD, BUT ALSO A LOT OF FUN. (LAUGH)

SPEAKING OF FUN, IT WAS FUN TO THINK UP ALL THE CLOTHES THAT HARU AND THE OTHERS WEAR IN THE CHAPTER TITLE PAGES. THE BELT HARU WEARS ON THE TITLE PAGE FOR CHAPTER SIX IS THE FICTIONAL BRAND NAME "OWNER LOVELY". IF YOU WRITE THAT IN JAPANESE LETTERS, IT WOULD BE "ON-NA-RA-BU-RI"... "ONARABURI"... WHICH SOUNDS LIKE "HONORABLY"!! HOW CHEESY! THIS TIME, THINGS GOT STRANGE LIKE THAT!

SEE YOU AGAIN IN VOLUME THREE!! I'M TIRED, SO I'M GOING TO BED. PSH-- GOOD NIGHT.

RAVE0077

LEVIN MINDS THE HOUSE

#2 Mom and Dad

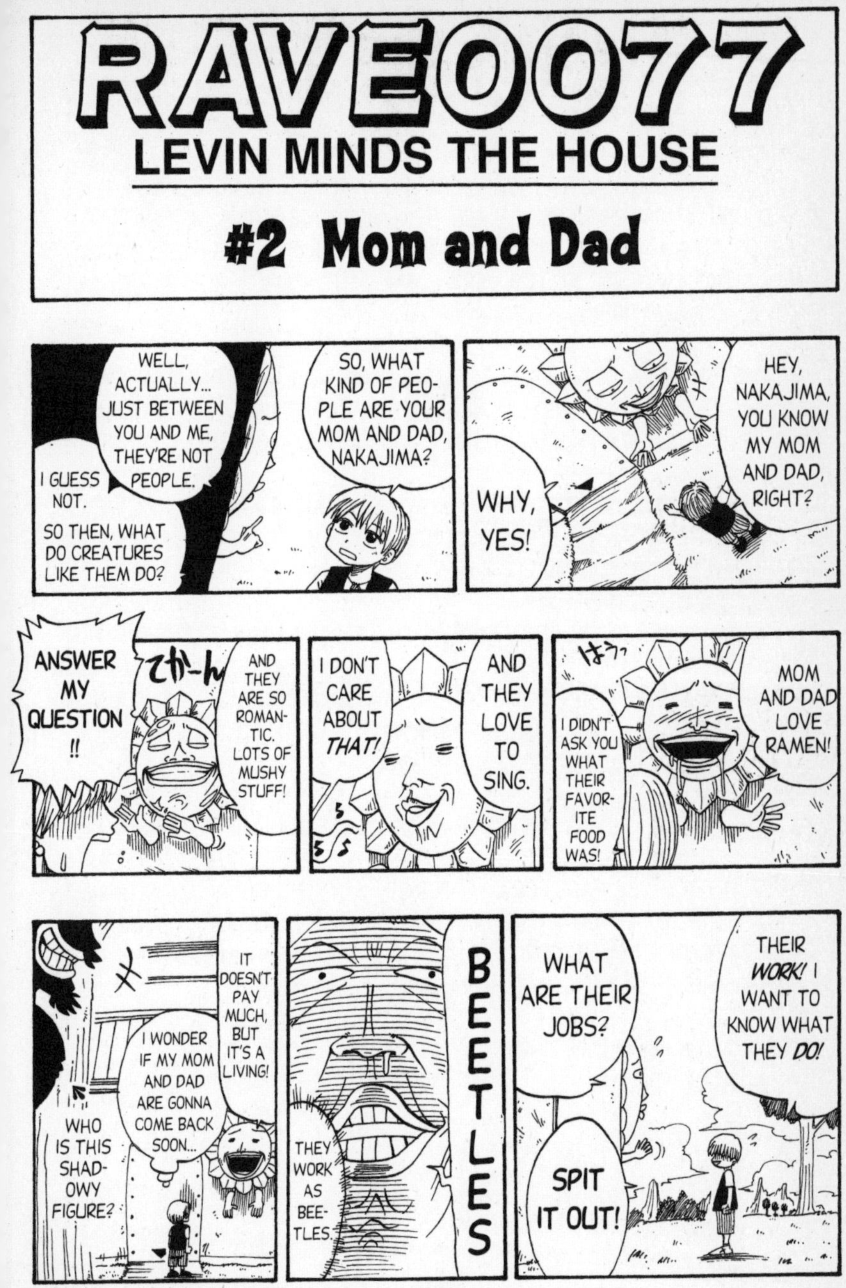
HEY, NAKAJIMA, YOU KNOW MY MOM AND DAD, RIGHT?
WHY, YES!
SO, WHAT KIND OF PEO-PLE ARE YOUR MOM AND DAD, NAKAJIMA?
WELL, ACTUALLY... JUST BETWEEN YOU AND ME, THEY'RE NOT PEOPLE.
I GUESS NOT.
SO THEN, WHAT DO CREATURES LIKE THEM DO?
はうっ
MOM AND DAD LOVE RAMEN!
I DIDN'T ASK YOU WHAT THEIR FAVOR-ITE FOOD WAS!
AND THEY LOVE TO SING.
I DON'T CARE ABOUT *THAT!*
AND THEY ARE SO ROMAN-TIC. LOTS OF MUSHY STUFF!
てかーん
ANSWER MY QUESTION !!
THEIR *WORK!* I WANT TO KNOW WHAT THEY *DO!*
WHAT ARE THEIR JOBS?
SPIT IT OUT!
BEETLES
THEY WORK AS BEE-TLES.
IT DOESN'T PAY MUCH, BUT IT'S A LIVING!
I WONDER IF MY MOM AND DAD ARE GONNA COME BACK SOON...
WHO IS THIS SHAD-OWY FIGURE?

Continued in Vol. 3?

Hiro Mashima and His Staff

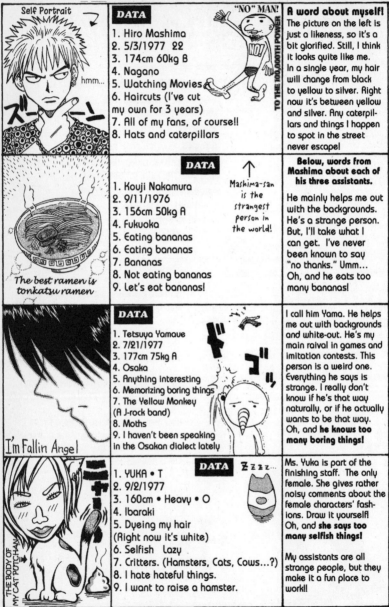

Self Portrait
hmm...
ズーン

DATA

"NO" MAN!
NO!
TO THE 100,000TH POWER

1. Hiro Mashima
2. 5/3/1977 22
3. 174cm 60kg B
4. Nagano
5. Watching Movies
6. Haircuts (I've cut my own for 3 years)
7. All of my fans, of course!!
8. Hats and caterpillars

A word about myself!
The picture on the left is just a likeness, so it's a bit glorified. Still, I think it looks quite like me. In a single year, my hair will change from black to yellow to silver. Right now it's between yellow and silver. Any caterpillars and things I happen to spot in the street never escape!

The best ramen is tonkatsu ramen

DATA

1. Kouji Nakamura
2. 9/11/1976
3. 156cm 50kg A
4. Fukuoka
5. Eating bananas
6. Eating bananas
7. Bananas
8. Not eating bananas
9. Let's eat bananas!

↑ Mashima-san is the strangest person in the world!

Below, words from Mashima about each of his three assistants.

He mainly helps me out with the backgrounds. He's a strange person. But, I'll take what I can get. I've never been known to say "no thanks." Umm... Oh, and he eats too many bananas!

I'm Fallin Angel

DATA

ドゴッ

1. Tetsuya Yamaue
2. 7/21/1977
3. 177cm 75kg A
4. Osaka
5. Anything interesting
6. Memorizing boring things
7. The Yellow Monkey (A J-rock band)
8. Moths
9. I haven't been speaking in the Osakan dialect lately

I call him Yama. He helps me out with backgrounds and white-out. He's my main raival in games and imitation contests. This person is a weird one. Everything he says is strange. I really don't know if he's that way naturally, or if he actually wants to be that way. Oh, and **he knows too many boring things!**

THE BODY OF MY CAT PUTCHAN

DATA

Zzzz...

1. YUKA • T
2. 9/2/1977
3. 160cm • Heavy • O
4. Ibaraki
5. Dyeing my hair (Right now it's white)
6. Selfish Lazy
7. Critters. (Hamsters, Cats, Cows...?)
8. I hate hateful things.
9. I want to raise a hamster.

Ms. Yuka is part of the finishing staff. The only female. She gives rather noisy comments about the female characters' fashions. Draw it yourself! Oh, and **she says too many selfish things!**

My assistants are all strange people, but they make it a fun place to work!!

How to read the data: 1) Name; 2) Birthday/Age; 3) Height/Weight/Blood Type 4) Birthplace; 5) Hobbies; 6) Special Abilities; 7) Likes; 8) Hates; 9) Message

THE GIRL WITHOUT MEMORY: ELIE

WEAPON: TONFA BLASTERS

BIRTHDAY/AGE: UNKNOWN / UNKNOWN (ABOUT 16)

HEIGHT/WEIGHT/BLOODTYPE: 160CM / 45KG / UNKNOWN (PROBABLY O)

BIRTHPLACE: UNKNOWN

HOBBIES: PLAYING WITH PLUE, SHOPPING

SPECIAL SKILLS: GAMBLING (SHE HAS THE LUCK OF THE GODS)

LIKES: HEART KREUZ, LOVE BELIEVER (BRAND NAME CLOTHES)

HATES: THUNDER

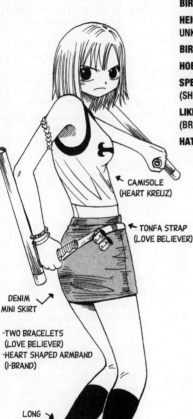

CAMISOLE (HEART KREUZ)

TONFA STRAP (LOVE BELIEVER)

DENIM MINI SKIRT

-TWO BRACELETS (LOVE BELIEVER)
-HEART SHAPED ARMBAND (I-BRAND)

LONG BOOTS

She turned out to be a rather crazy character. But, well, she's fun to draw, because there aren't many rules or limits with her.

I really wanted to do something with memory loss. I know, not the newest material, but I love mystery.

So I created Elie having lost her memory already. I'm so sorry, Elie!!

How does everyone like trying to figure out the "joke"? (laugh) By the way, I've already decided on the "punchline." Elie is actually...

THIS IS THE HEART KREUZ LOGO, APPROPRIATE BECAUSE IT INCORPORATES A "HEART" AND A "CROSS" LIKE THE BRAND NAME. ELIE LIKES THE CLOTHES BECAUSE THEY ARE LIKE WHAT A 10 YEAR OLD GIRL MIGHT WEAR.

THE LEGENDARY BLACKSMITH: MUSICA

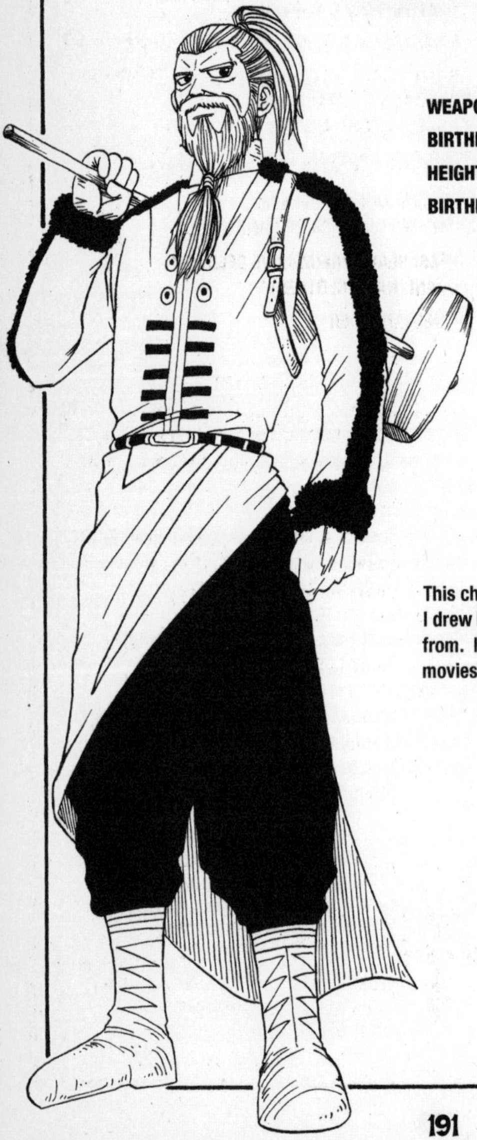

WEAPON: IRON HAMMER

BIRTHDAY/AGE: OCT. 4, 9998 / 70

HEIGHT/WEIGHT/BLOODTYPE: 171CM / 62KG / B

BIRTHPLACE: PUNK STREET

HOBBIES: DRINKING

SPECIAL SKILLS: GREATEST BLACKSMITH IN THE WORLD

LIKES: GUYS WHO CAN DRINK

HATES: LANCE

This character was a problem at first because I drew him without much background to work from. I've only seen a few blacksmith shops in movies, so I just drew him as I pleased.

"MUSICA" IS THE ITALIAN WORD FOR "MUSIC", SO ← THIS IS HIS LOGO!

PRESIDENT OF THE DOGTRACK: GEORCO

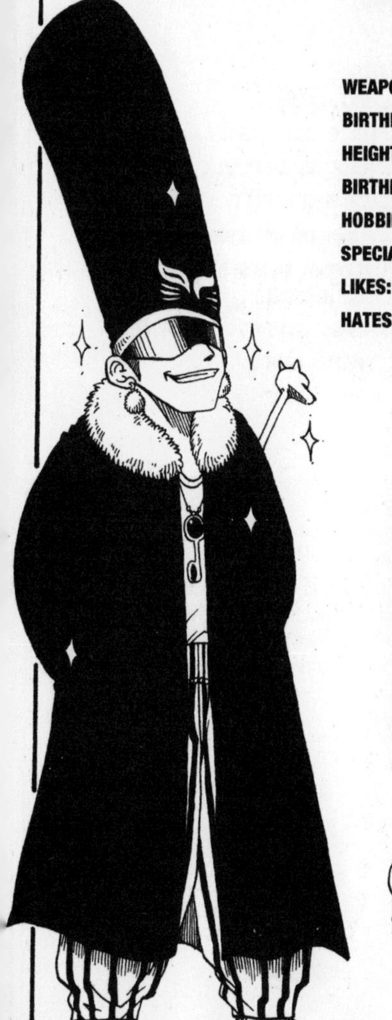

WEAPON: CANE & DARK BRING (SMOKE BAY)

BIRTHDAY/AGE: MARCH 14, 0026 / 40

HEIGHT/WEIGHT/BLOODTYPE: 142CM / 40KG / O

BIRTHPLACE: HIP HOP TOWN

HOBBIES: PICKING ON HIS SUBORDINATES

SPECIAL SKILLS: GUZZLING MILK

LIKES: BLING BLING

HATES: MESSY CUSTOMERS

He's really easygoing at heart, but as president he surrounds himself with all that glitters. However, in the grand scheme of Demon Card, Georco is still an underling. (Within the Demon Card organization, raw strength is more important than money or status.)

It would seem like the power to turn into smoke IS quite strong, but actually, that's not the case! Georco can't fight on a windy day, and doesn't have any battle experience; he's just a regular guy who happens to have a Dark Bring. That's why he never did get that promotion in Demon Card... even though he's already President.

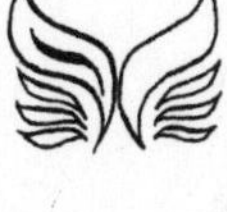

← THIS IS THE DEMON CARD LOGO! YOU CAN CHANGE IT INTO THE LETTERS "DC".

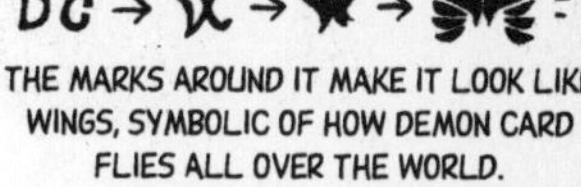
DC →

THE MARKS AROUND IT MAKE IT LOOK LIKE WINGS, SYMBOLIC OF HOW DEMON CARD FLIES ALL OVER THE WORLD.

COMMANDER OF THE DEMON CARD ARMY 17TH UNIT:
LANCE, THE "BEAST SWORD"

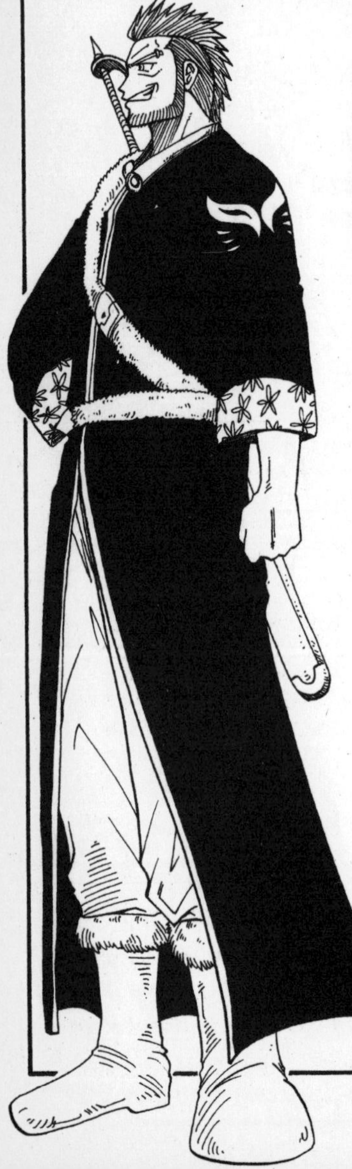

WEAPON: SWORD (DEMON SWORD) & DARK BRING (REAL MOMENT)

BIRTHDAY/AGE: FEB 6, 0028 / 38

HEIGHT/WEIGHT/BLOODTYPE: 218CM / 97KG / A

BIRTHPLACE: BLUES CITY

HOBBIES: KILLING PEOPLE

SPECIAL SKILLS: HE'S UNLICENSED, BUT HAS THE SKILLS TO BE A VETERINARIAN

LIKES: STRAWBERRIES

HATES: STUPID PEOPLE AND SLACKERS

Umm... He turned out to be a scoundrel (of course). In the 8th chapter, I suddenly wanted to name a character "Lance," and at that time, I thought I'd make him a really bizarre gag character. But then the story headed in a heavier direction, so I decided on having him appear as this evil guy.

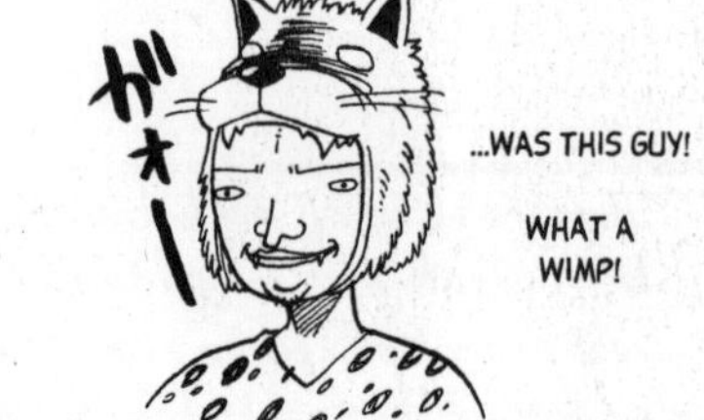
THE ORIGINAL LANCE...
ガォー
...WAS THIS GUY!
WHAT A WIMP!

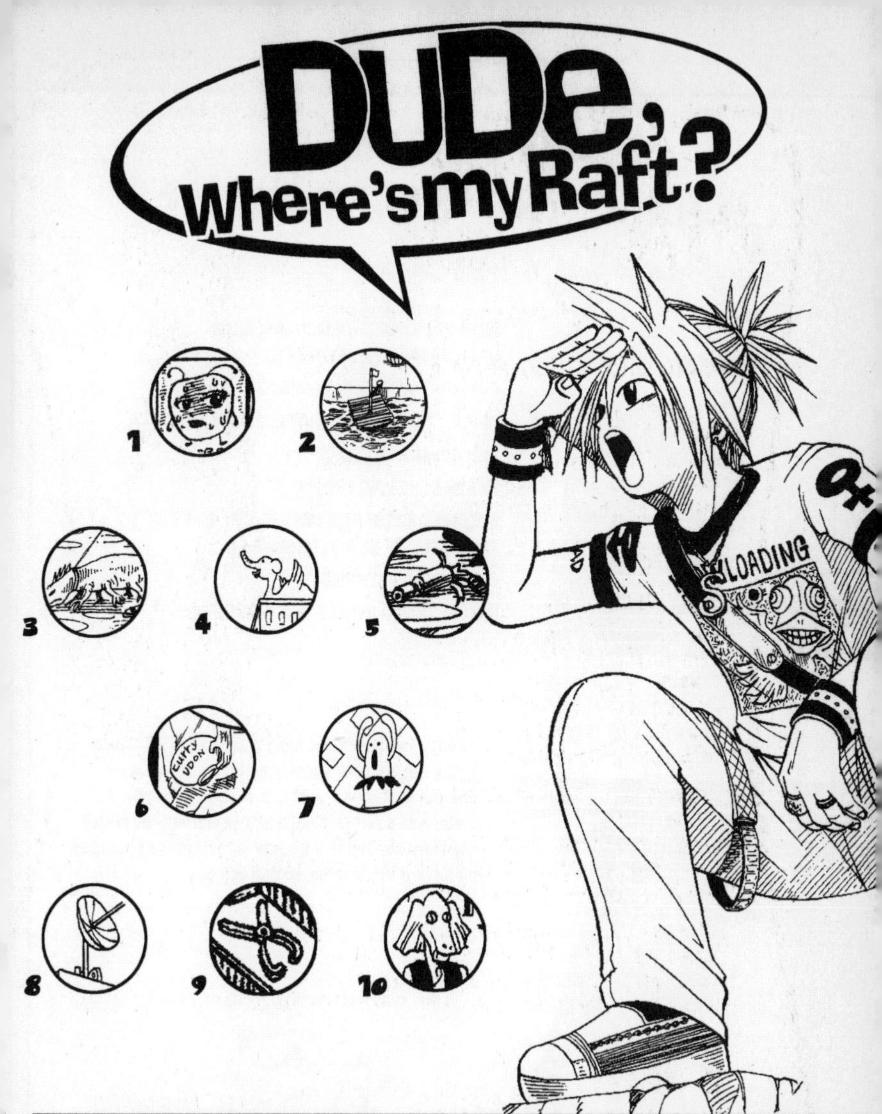
DUDE, Where's my Raft?
1
2
3
4
5
6
7
8
9
10
Curry UDON
LOADING

Aw, snap! In all my battles in Hip Hop Town and Punk Street, I lost the raft that I used to get here, not to mention all this totally sweet swag I picked up along the way. Since I'm a little busy right now getting my butt kicked by Lance, maybe you could help me out. Take a good look at these pics, then see if you can't find the originals scattered throughout the book. If you get stuck, check out the RAVE MASTER web page at www.tokyopop.com for the answers.

RAVE MASTER

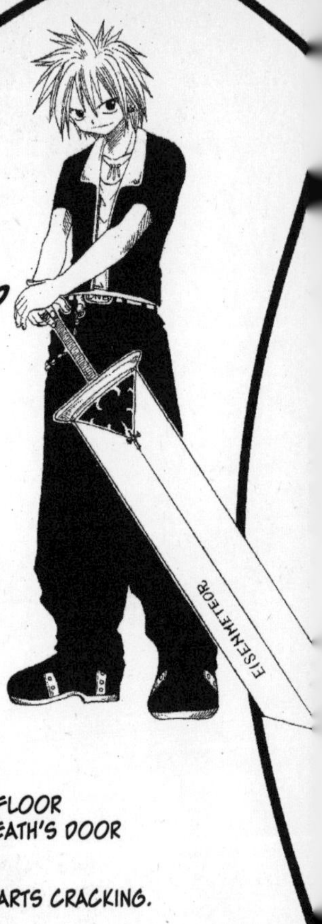
EISENMETEOR

Volume 3 Preview:

PRESSURE OF THE BEAST SWORD

PRESSURE, PUSHING DOWN ON HIM
LANCE IS PRESSING WITH HIS SWORD
UNDER PRESSURE FROM THE BEAST SWORD
THAT WOULD SPLIT HARU IN TWO
MAKES PEOPLE SEE THINGS

BA BA BA BAH! BA BA BA BA BAH!

HE'LL BE OKAY!
IT'S THE TERROR INDUCED
BY THE DARK BRING'S CLOUT
HIS FRIENDS ON THE SIDELINES SCREAM
"HARU, WATCH OUT!"
PRAY THAT SOMEONE WILL STOP LANCE
MAKES PEOPLE SEE THINGS,
PEOPLE SEE THINGS

DOH DOH DOH BA BA BA BA BAH
OKAY
FLAILING AROUND, HARU'S KNOCKED TO THE FLOOR
WHO WILL COME SAVE HIM? THE KID'S AT DEATH'S DOOR
PEOPLE SEE THINGS, PEOPLE SEE THINGS

THE MADMAN LAUGHS WHILE THE BUILDING STARTS CRACKING.
CAN'T WE FIND SOMEONE TO STOP LANCE?
WHY CAN'T SOMEONE SAVE HARU FROM LANCE?
WHY CAN'T SOMEONE SAVE HARU, SAVE HARU, SAVE HARU FROM LANCE?

CAUSE HARU IS JUST AN OLD-FASHIONED KID
AND HARU DARES TO CARE
FOR THE PEOPLE AT GARAGE ISLAND
AND HE DARES US TO STAND AGAINST
THOSE VILLAINS AT DEMON CARD
THIS IS THEIR LAST CARD
THIS IS HIS QUEST
THE RAVE MASTER
THE RAVE MASTER
MASTER

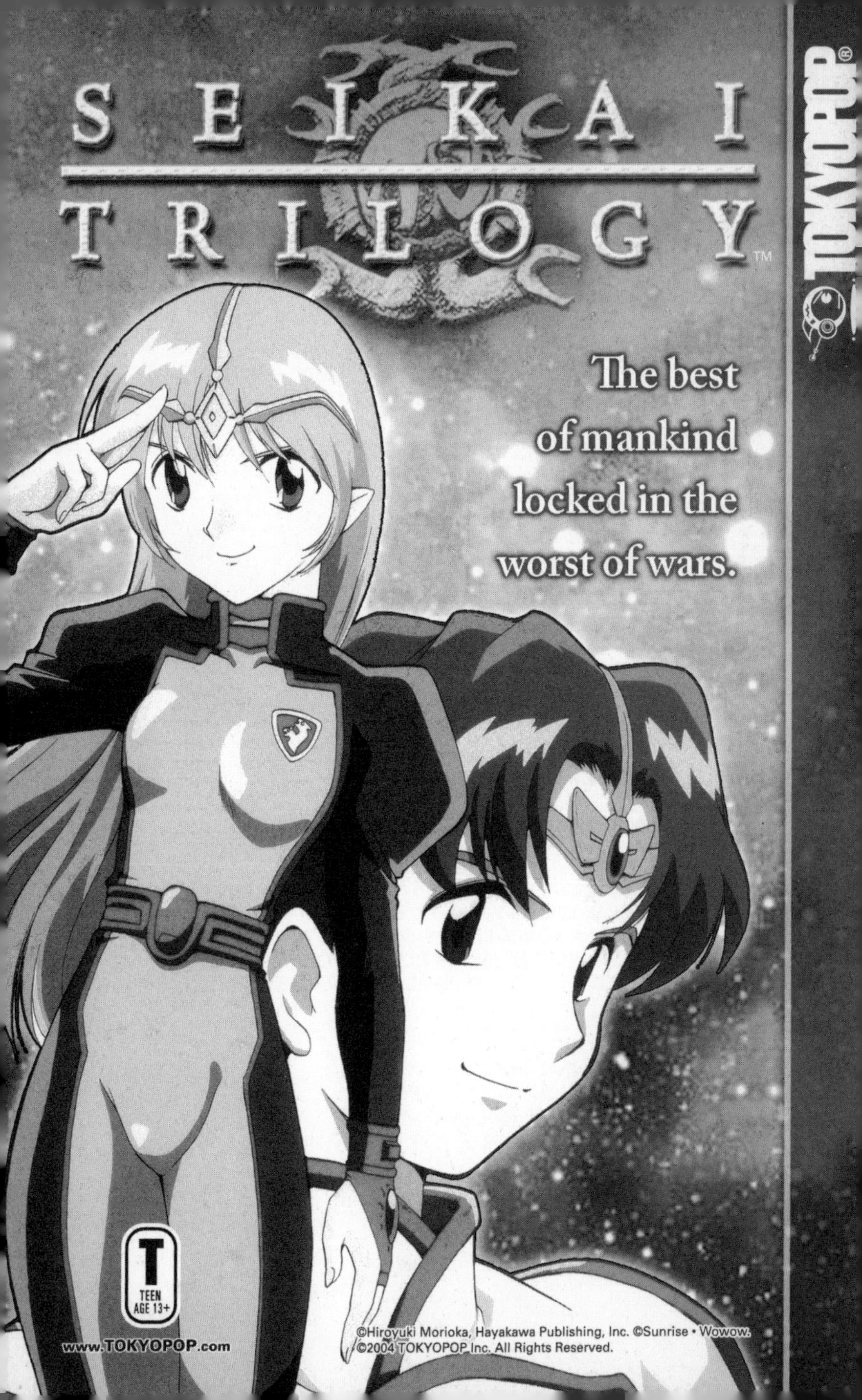
SEIKAI TRILOGY™
TOKYOPOP®
The best of mankind locked in the worst of wars.
T TEEN AGE 13+
www.TOKYOPOP.com
©Hiroyuki Morioka, Hayakawa Publishing, Inc. ©Sunrise • Wowow.
©2004 TOKYOPOP Inc. All Rights Reserved.

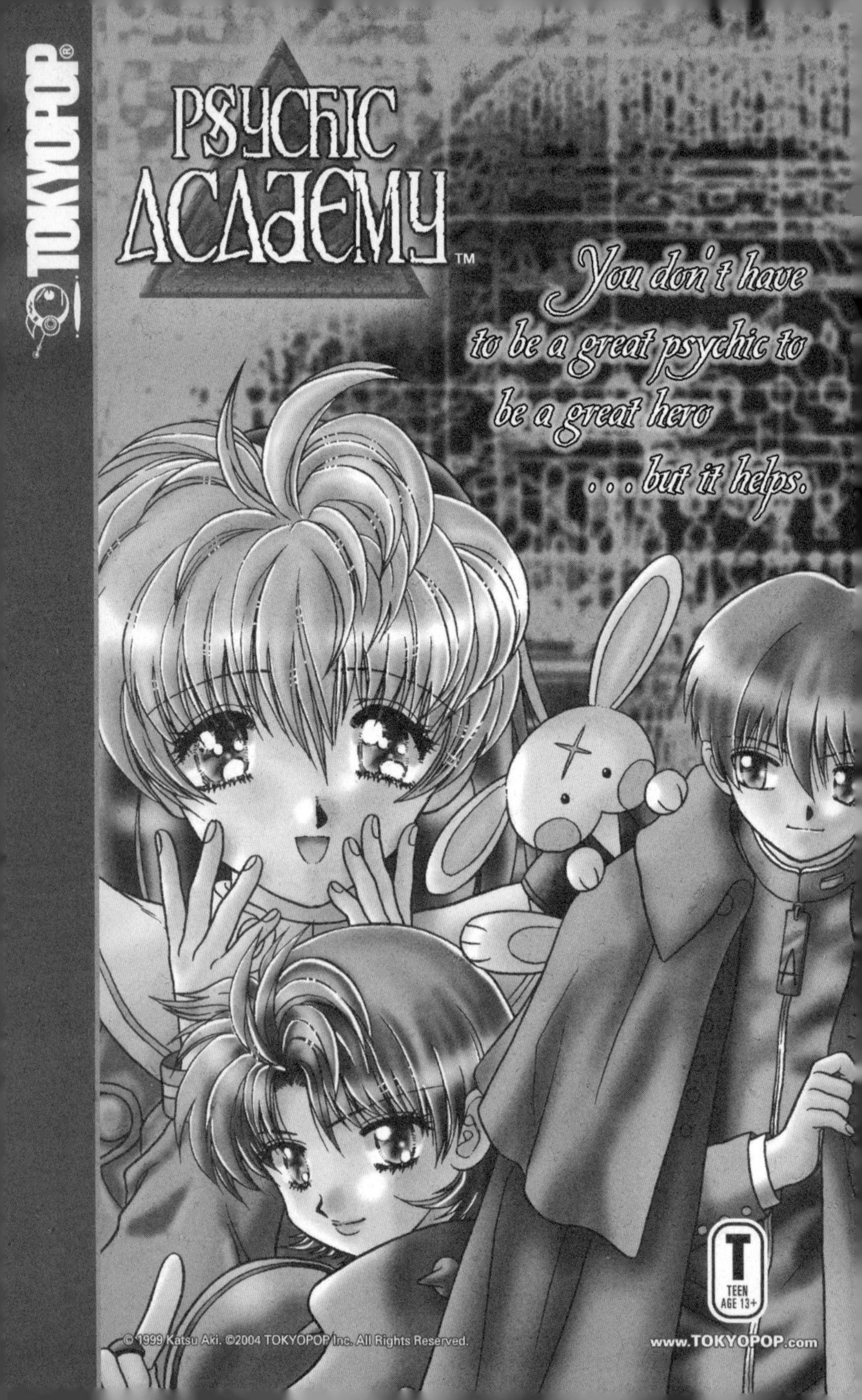
TOKYOPOP®
PSYCHIC ACADEMY™
You don't have to be a great psychic to be a great hero . . . but it helps.
T TEEN AGE 13+
© 1999 Katsu Aki. ©2004 TOKYOPOP Inc. All Rights Reserved.
www.TOKYOPOP.com

ALSO AVAILABLE FROM TOKYOPOP®

For more information visit www.TOKYOPOP.com

03.30.04Y

ALSO AVAILABLE FROM TOKYOPOP®

MANGA

03.30.04Y

STOP!

This is the back of the book.
You wouldn't want to spoil a great ending!

This book is printed "manga-style," in the authentic Japanese right-to-left format. Since none of the artwork has been flipped or altered, readers get to experience the story just as the creator intended. You've been asking for it, so TOKYOPOP® delivered: authentic, hot-off-the-press, and far more fun!

DIRECTIONS

If this is your first time reading manga-style, here's a quick guide to help you understand how it works.

It's easy... just start in the top right panel and follow the numbers. Have fun, and look for more 100% authentic manga from TOKYOPOP®!

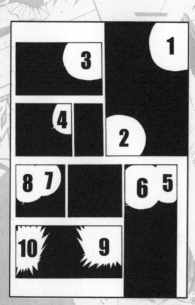

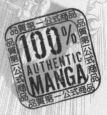